SUPERGIRL

COSMIC ADVENTURES IN THE 8TH GRADE

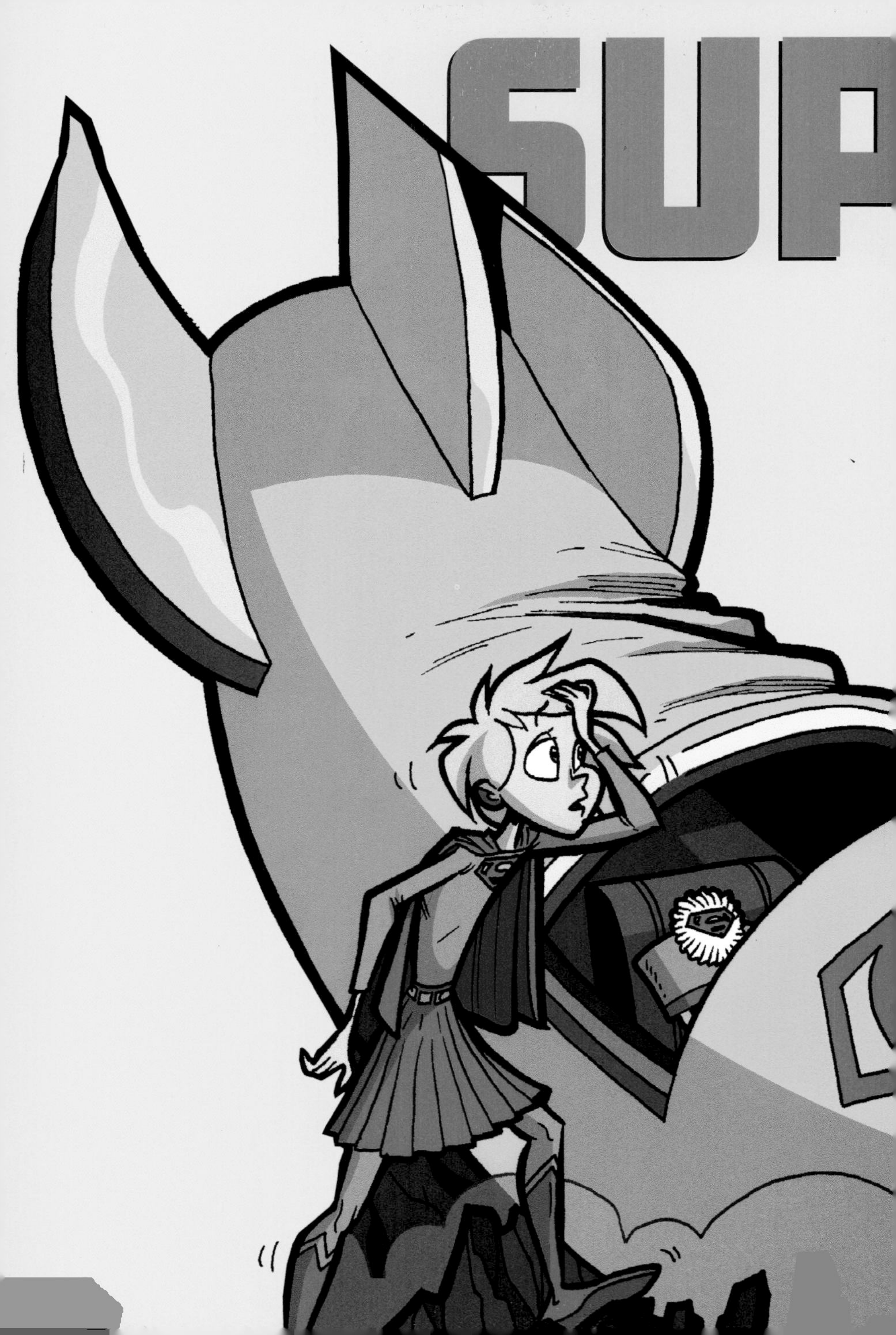
SUP

ERGIRL

COSMIC ADVENTURES IN THE 8TH GRADE

LANDRY Q. WALKER writer

ERIC JONES artist

JOEY MASON colorist

PAT BROSSEAU
TRAVIS LANHAM
SAL CIPRIANO letterers

ERIC JONES collection cover artist

Supergirl based on characters created by Jerry Siegel and Joe Shuster
Superman created by Jerry Siegel and Joe Shuster
By special arrangement with the Jerry Siegel family

JANN JONES
ELISABETH V. GEHRLEIN
Editors - Original Series
ADAM SHLAGMAN
Associate Editor - Original Series
SIMONE MARTORE
Assistant Editor - Original Series
JEB WOODARD
Group Editor - Collected Editions
ROBIN WILDMAN
Editor - Collected Edition
STEVE COOK
Design Director - Books
AMIE BROCKWAY-METCALF
Publication Design
KATE DURRÉ
Publication Production

BOB HARRAS
Senior VP - Editor-in-Chief, DC Comics

JIM LEE
Publisher & Chief Creative Officer
BOBBIE CHASE
VP - Global Publishing Initiatives & Digital Strategy
DON FALLETTI
VP - Manufacturing Operations & Workflow Management
LAWRENCE GANEM
VP - Talent Services
ALISON GILL
Senior VP - Manufacturing & Operations
HANK KANALZ
Senior VP - Publishing Strategy & Support Services
DAN MIRON
VP - Publishing Operations
NICK J. NAPOLITANO
VP - Manufacturing Administration & Design
NANCY SPEARS
VP - Sales
JONAH WEILAND
VP - Marketing & Creative Services
MICHELE R. WELLS
VP & Executive Editor, Young Reader

SUPERGIRL: COSMIC ADVENTURES IN THE 8TH GRADE

Published by DC Comics. Compilation and all new material Copyright © 2020 DC Comics. All Rights Reserved. Originally published in single magazine form in *Supergirl: Cosmic Adventures in the 8th Grade* 1-6. Copyright © 2009 DC Comics. All Rights Reserved. All characters, their distinctive likenesses, and related elements featured in this publication are trademarks of DC Comics. The stories, characters, and incidents featured in this publication are entirely fictional. DC Comics does not read or accept unsolicited submissions of ideas, stories, or artwork. DC - a WarnerMedia Company.

DC Comics, 2900 West Alameda Ave., Burbank, CA 91505
Printed by LSC Communications, Crawfordsville, IN. 7/24/20. First Printing.
ISBN: 978-1-77950-670-2
Library of Congress Cataloging-in-Publication Data is available.

PEFC Certified
This product is from
sustainably managed
forests and controlled
sources
PEFC/29-31-337   www.pefc.org

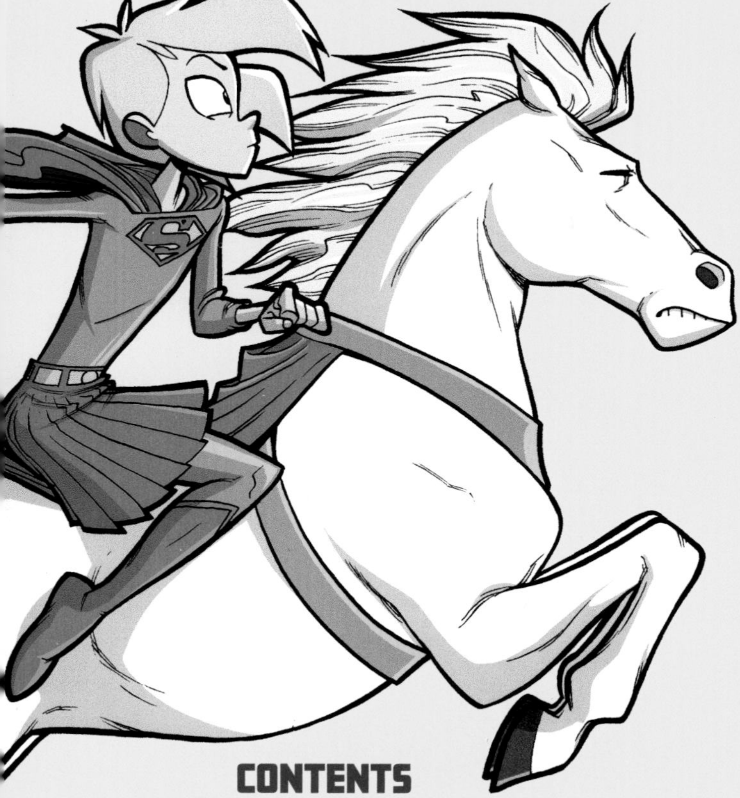

CONTENTS

COSMIC ADVENTURES IN THE 8TH GRADE

SUPERGIRL

SUPERGIRL

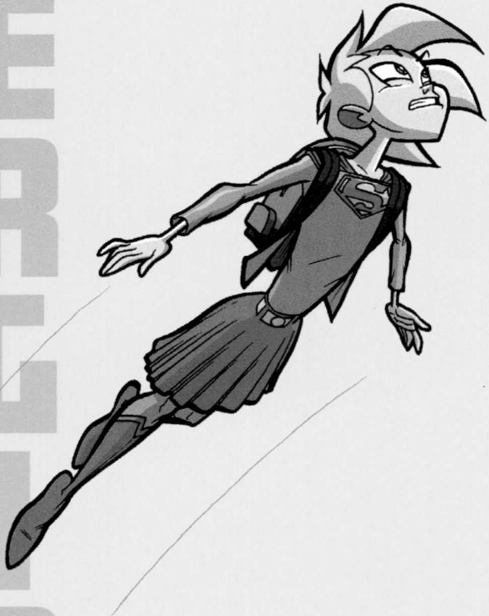

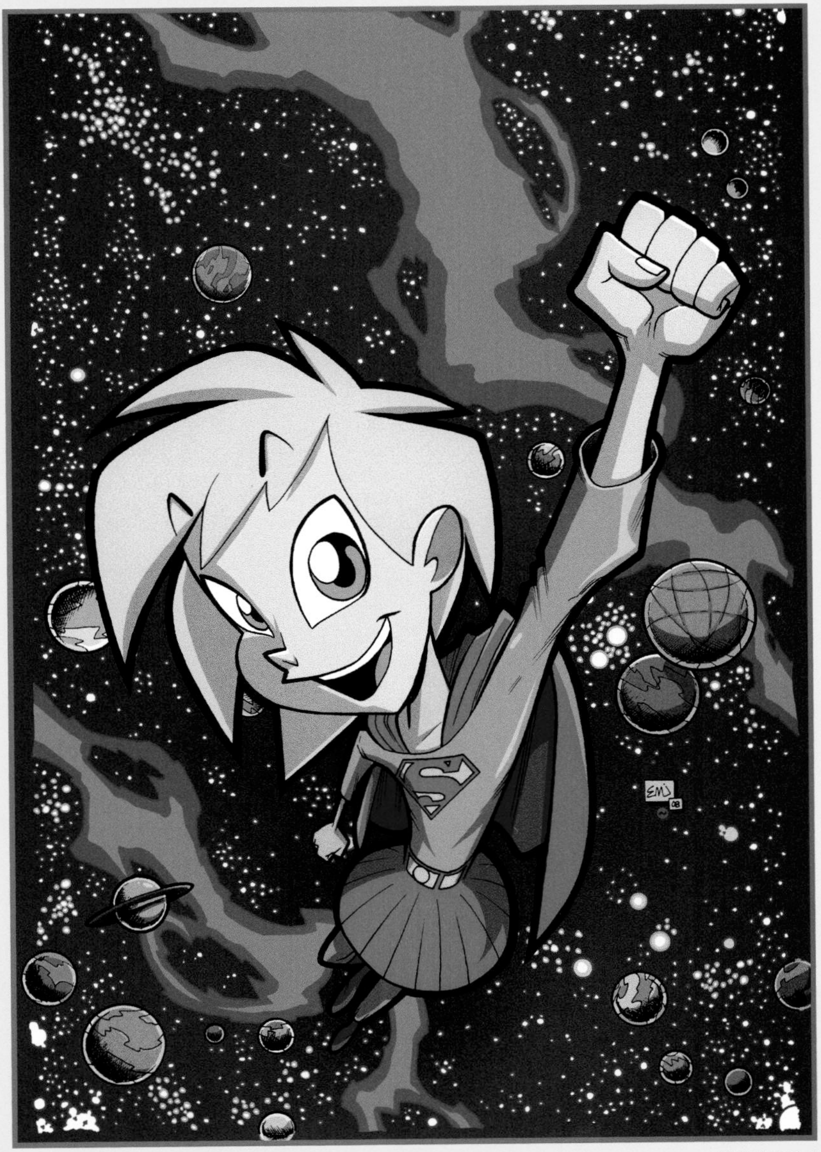

CHAPTER 1

SUPERGIRL

COSMIC ADVENTURES IN THE 8TH GRADE

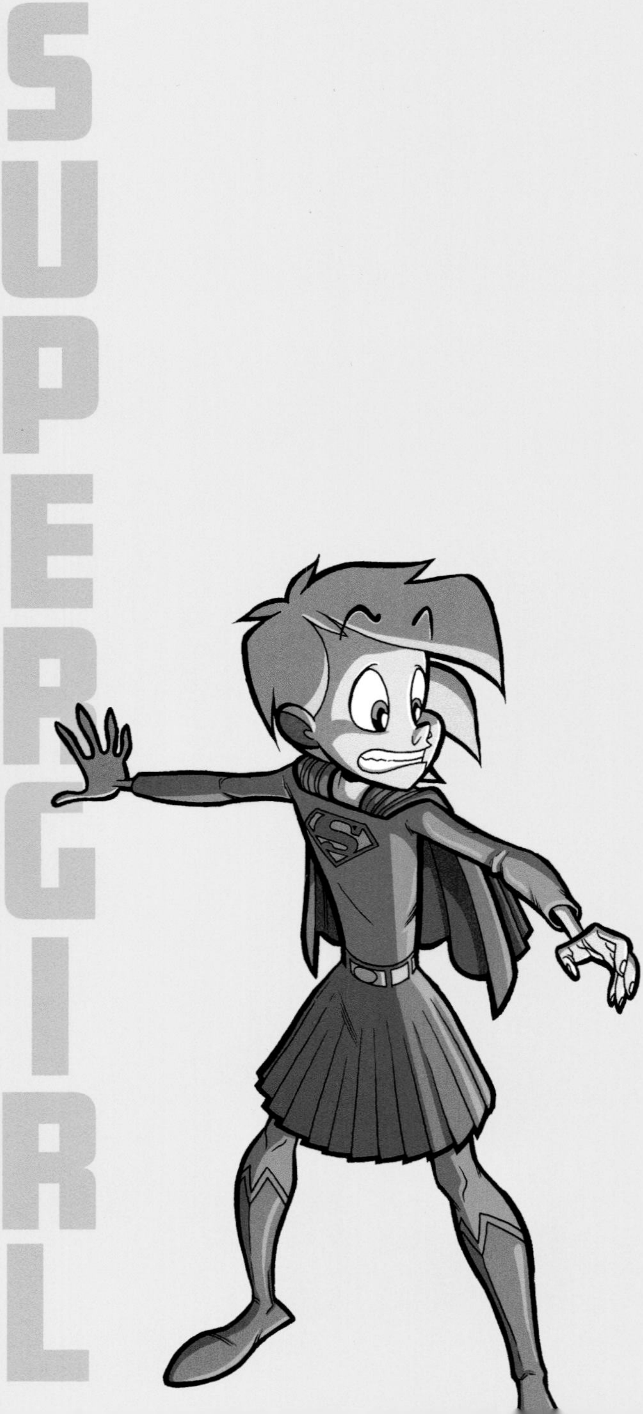
SUPERGIRL

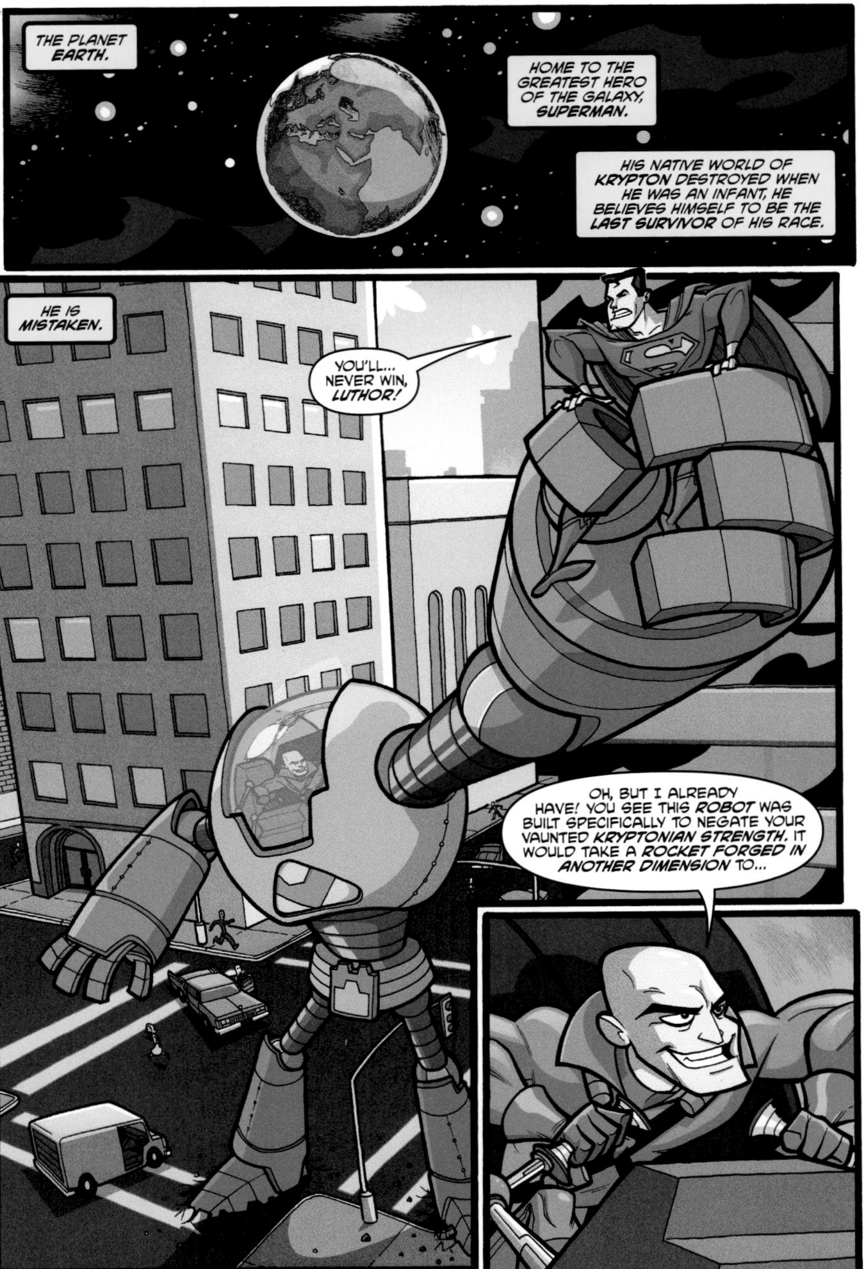
THE PLANET EARTH.
HOME TO THE GREATEST HERO OF THE GALAXY, SUPERMAN.
HIS NATIVE WORLD OF KRYPTON DESTROYED WHEN HE WAS AN INFANT, HE BELIEVES HIMSELF TO BE THE LAST SURVIVOR OF HIS RACE.
HE IS MISTAKEN.
YOU'LL... NEVER WIN, LUTHOR!
OH, BUT I ALREADY HAVE! YOU SEE THIS ROBOT WAS BUILT SPECIFICALLY TO NEGATE YOUR VAUNTED KRYPTONIAN STRENGTH. IT WOULD TAKE A ROCKET FORGED IN ANOTHER DIMENSION TO...

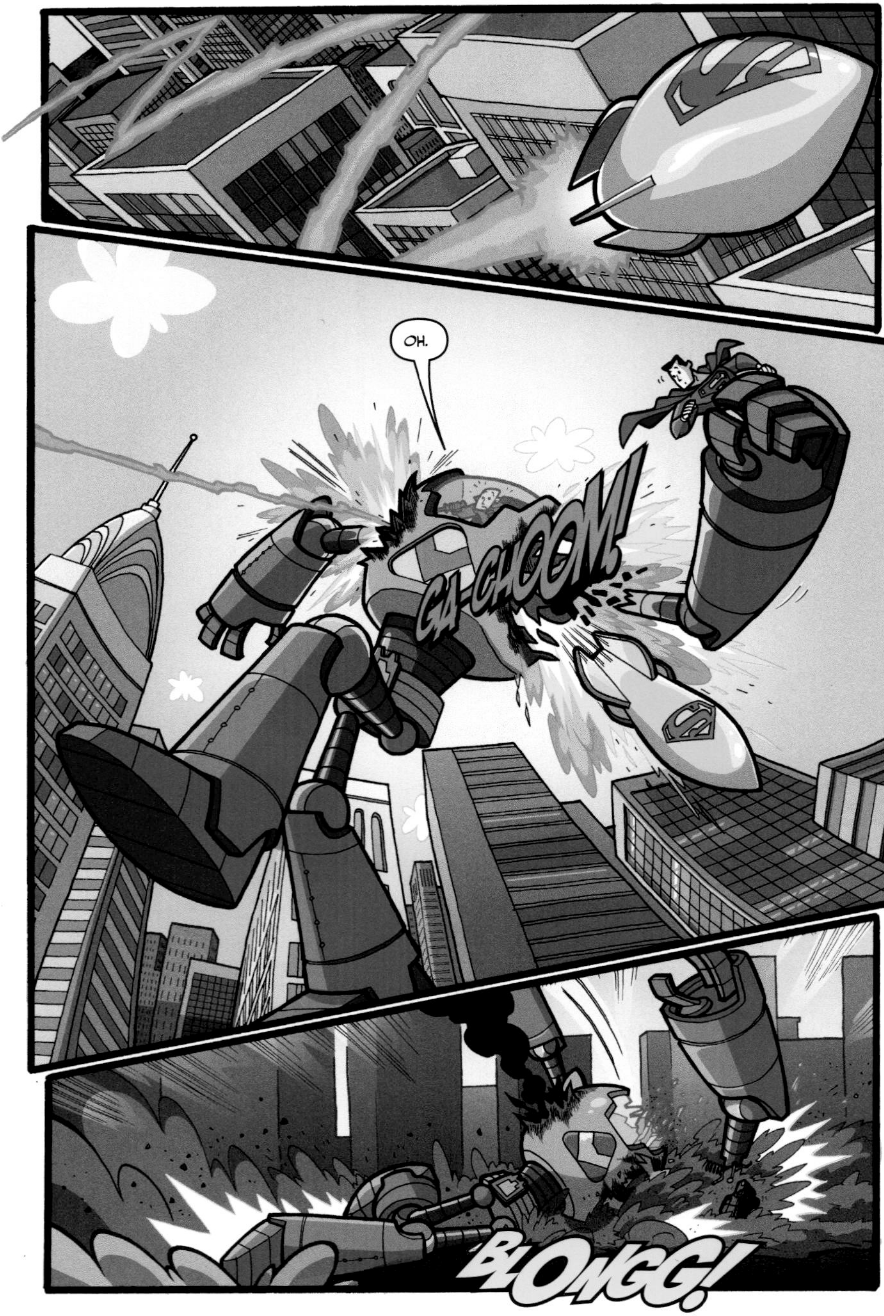
OH.
GA-CHOOM!
BLONGG!

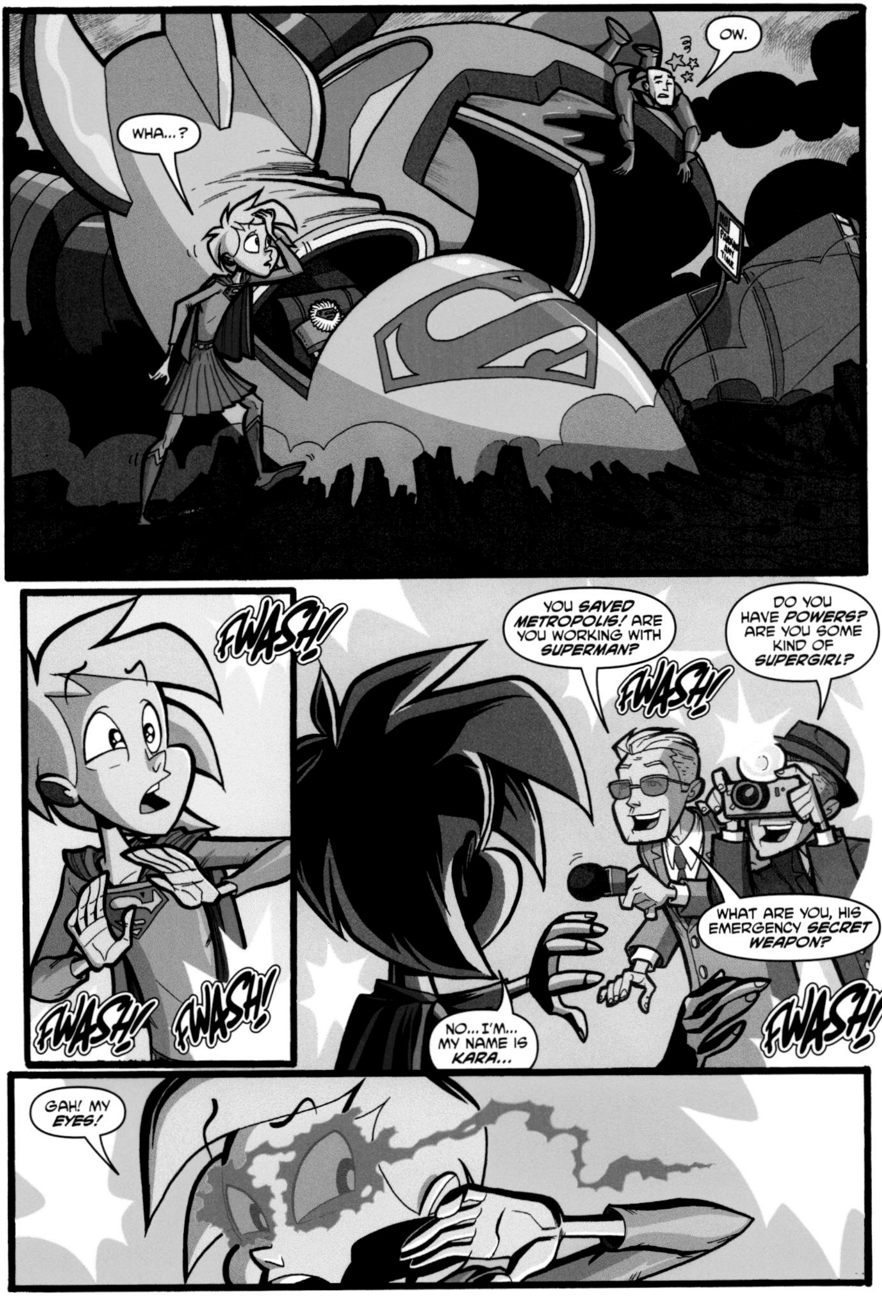
WHA...?
OW.
NO PARKING ANY TIME
FWASH!
YOU SAVED METROPOLIS! ARE YOU WORKING WITH SUPERMAN?
FWASH!
DO YOU HAVE POWERS? ARE YOU SOME KIND OF SUPERGIRL?
WHAT ARE YOU, HIS EMERGENCY SECRET WEAPON?
FWASH!
FWASH!
FWASH!
NO... I'M... MY NAME IS KARA...
GAH! MY EYES!

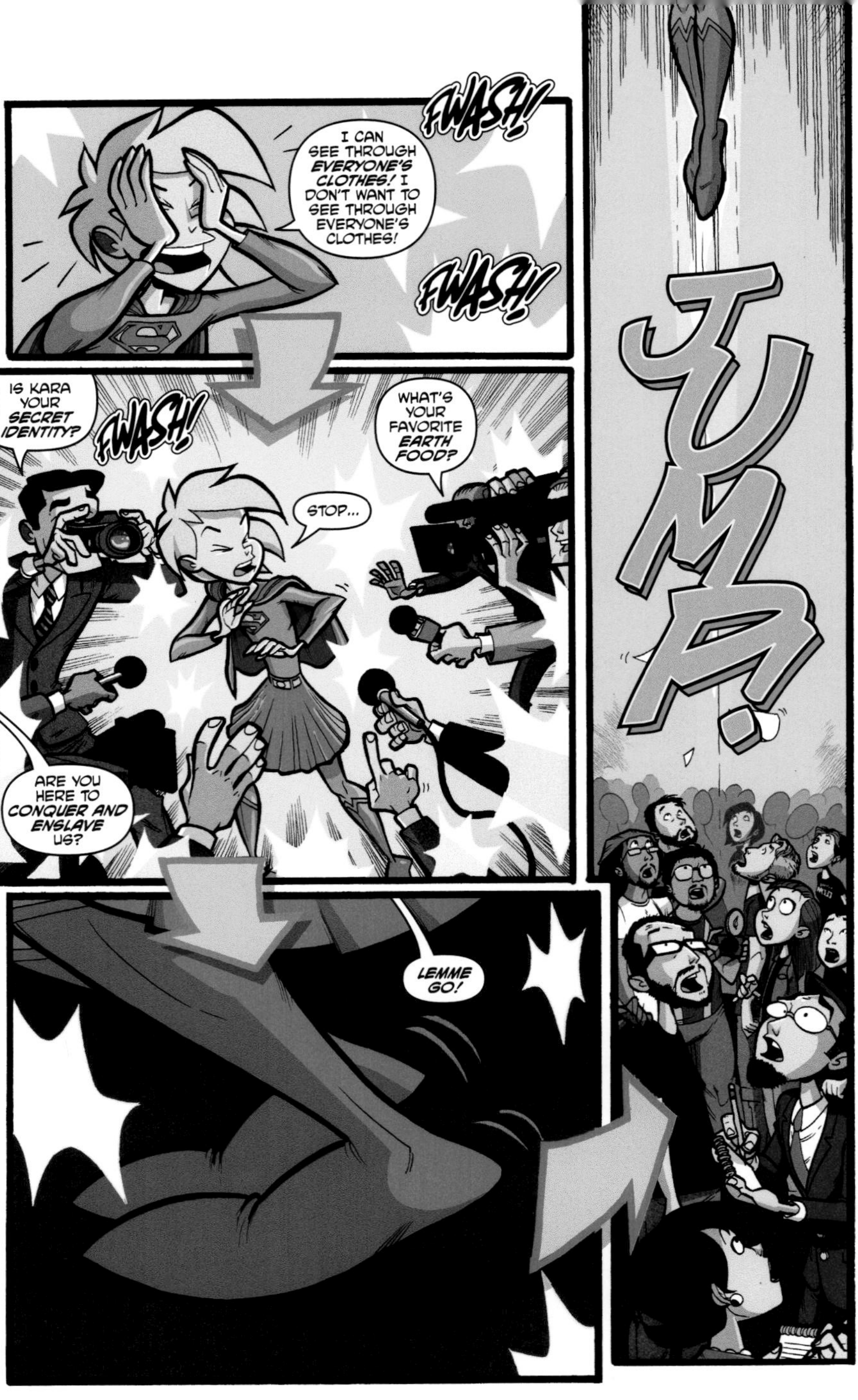
FWASH!
I CAN SEE THROUGH EVERYONE'S CLOTHES! I DON'T WANT TO SEE THROUGH EVERYONE'S CLOTHES!
FWASH!
IS KARA YOUR SECRET IDENTITY?
FWASH!
WHAT'S YOUR FAVORITE EARTH FOOD?
STOP...
ARE YOU HERE TO CONQUER AND ENSLAVE US?
LEMME GO!
JUMP!

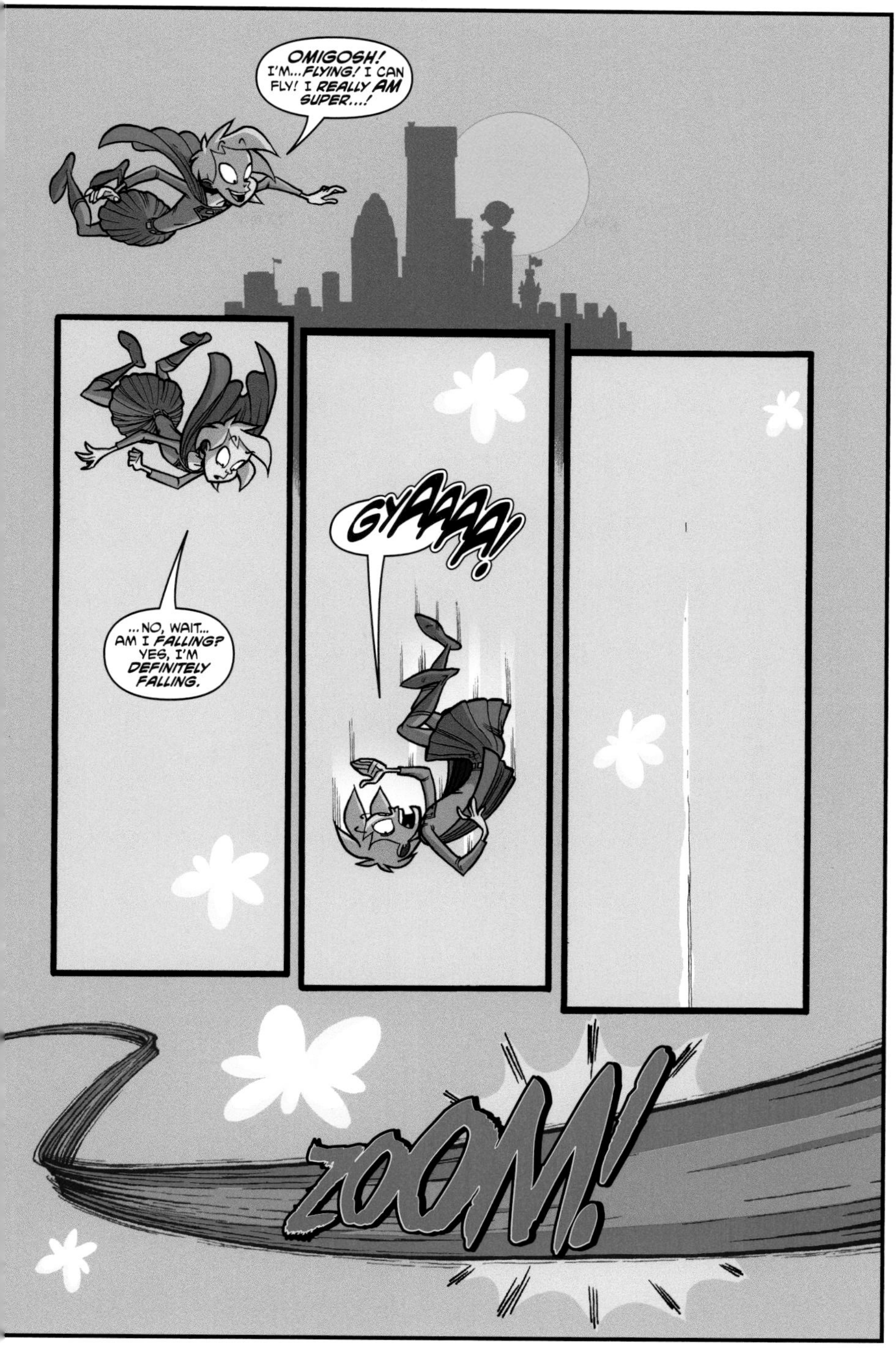
OMIGOSH! I'M...FLYING! I CAN FLY! I REALLY AM SUPER...!
...NO, WAIT... AM I FALLING? YES, I'M DEFINITELY FALLING.
GYAAAA!
ZOOM!

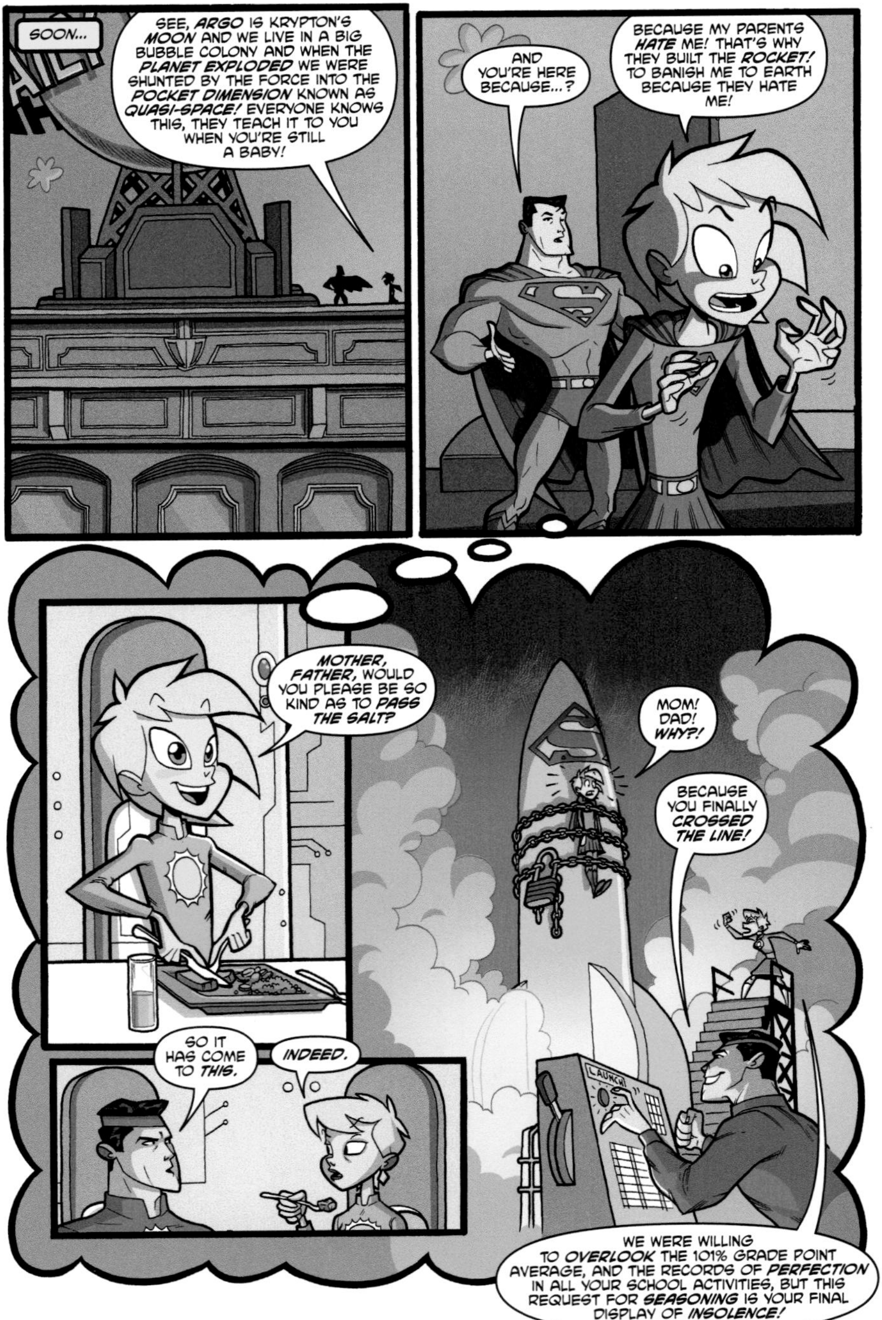
SOON...
SEE, ARGO IS KRYPTON'S MOON AND WE LIVE IN A BIG BUBBLE COLONY AND WHEN THE PLANET EXPLODED WE WERE SHUNTED BY THE FORCE INTO THE POCKET DIMENSION KNOWN AS QUASI-SPACE! EVERYONE KNOWS THIS, THEY TEACH IT TO YOU WHEN YOU'RE STILL A BABY!
AND YOU'RE HERE BECAUSE...?
BECAUSE MY PARENTS HATE ME! THAT'S WHY THEY BUILT THE ROCKET! TO BANISH ME TO EARTH BECAUSE THEY HATE ME!
MOTHER, FATHER, WOULD YOU PLEASE BE SO KIND AS TO PASS THE SALT?
SO IT HAS COME TO THIS.
INDEED.
MOM! DAD! WHY?!
BECAUSE YOU FINALLY CROSSED THE LINE!
LAUNCH
WE WERE WILLING TO OVERLOOK THE 101% GRADE POINT AVERAGE, AND THE RECORDS OF PERFECTION IN ALL YOUR SCHOOL ACTIVITIES, BUT THIS REQUEST FOR SEASONING IS YOUR FINAL DISPLAY OF INSOLENCE!

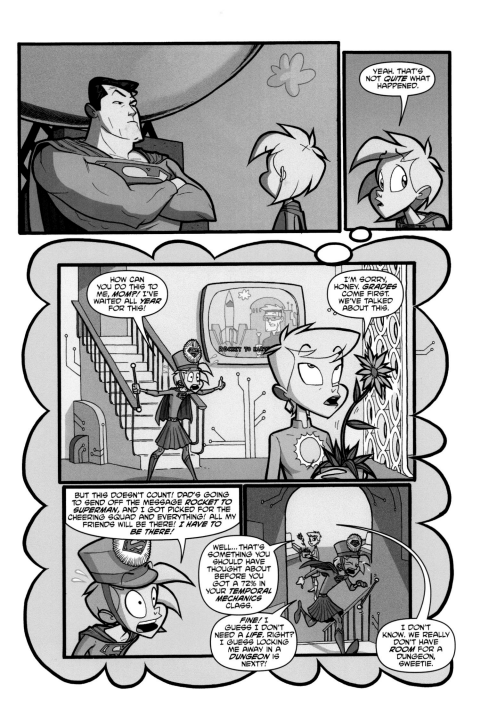

YEAH. THAT'S NOT *QUITE* WHAT HAPPENED.

HOW CAN YOU DO THIS TO ME, *MOM?!* I'VE WAITED ALL *YEAR* FOR THIS!

I'M SORRY, HONEY. *GRADES* COME FIRST. WE'VE TALKED ABOUT THIS.

ROCKET TO EART

BUT THIS DOESN'T COUNT! DAD'S GOING TO SEND OFF THE MESSAGE *ROCKET TO SUPERMAN*, AND I GOT PICKED FOR THE CHEERING SQUAD AND EVERYTHING! ALL MY FRIENDS WILL BE THERE! *I HAVE TO BE THERE!*

WELL...THAT'S SOMETHING YOU SHOULD HAVE THOUGHT ABOUT BEFORE YOU GOT A 72% IN YOUR *TEMPORAL MECHANICS* CLASS.

FINE! I GUESS I DON'T NEED A *LIFE*, RIGHT? I GUESS LOCKING ME AWAY IN A *DUNGEON* IS NEXT?!

I DON'T KNOW. WE REALLY DON'T HAVE *ROOM* FOR A DUNGEON, SWEETIE.

15

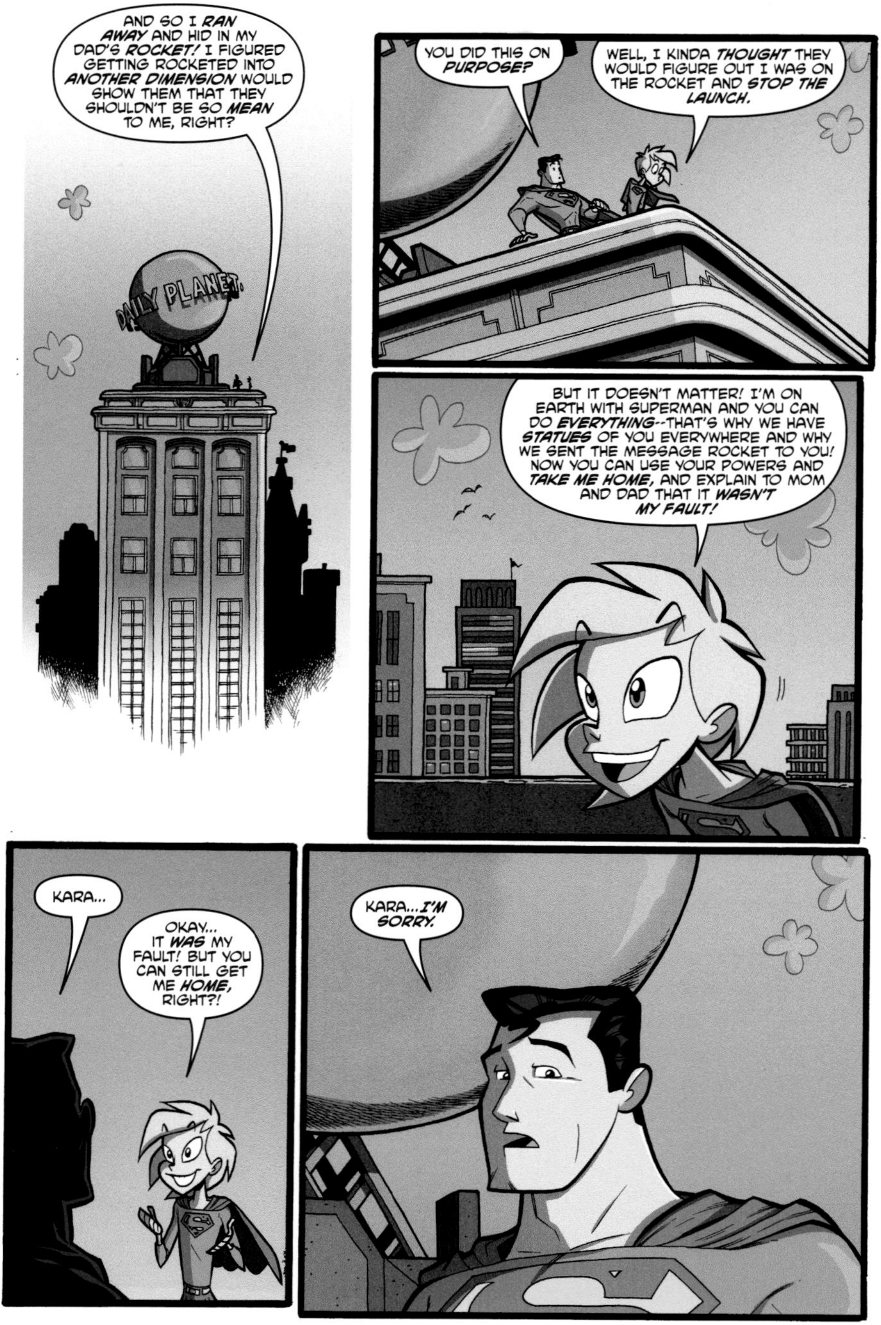

AND SO I RAN AWAY AND HID IN MY DAD'S ROCKET! I FIGURED GETTING ROCKETED INTO ANOTHER DIMENSION WOULD SHOW THEM THAT THEY SHOULDN'T BE SO MEAN TO ME, RIGHT?
DAILY PLANET
YOU DID THIS ON PURPOSE?
WELL, I KINDA THOUGHT THEY WOULD FIGURE OUT I WAS ON THE ROCKET AND STOP THE LAUNCH.
BUT IT DOESN'T MATTER! I'M ON EARTH WITH SUPERMAN AND YOU CAN DO EVERYTHING--THAT'S WHY WE HAVE STATUES OF YOU EVERYWHERE AND WHY WE SENT THE MESSAGE ROCKET TO YOU! NOW YOU CAN USE YOUR POWERS AND TAKE ME HOME, AND EXPLAIN TO MOM AND DAD THAT IT WASN'T MY FAULT!
KARA...
OKAY... IT WAS MY FAULT! BUT YOU CAN STILL GET ME HOME, RIGHT?!
KARA...I'M SORRY.

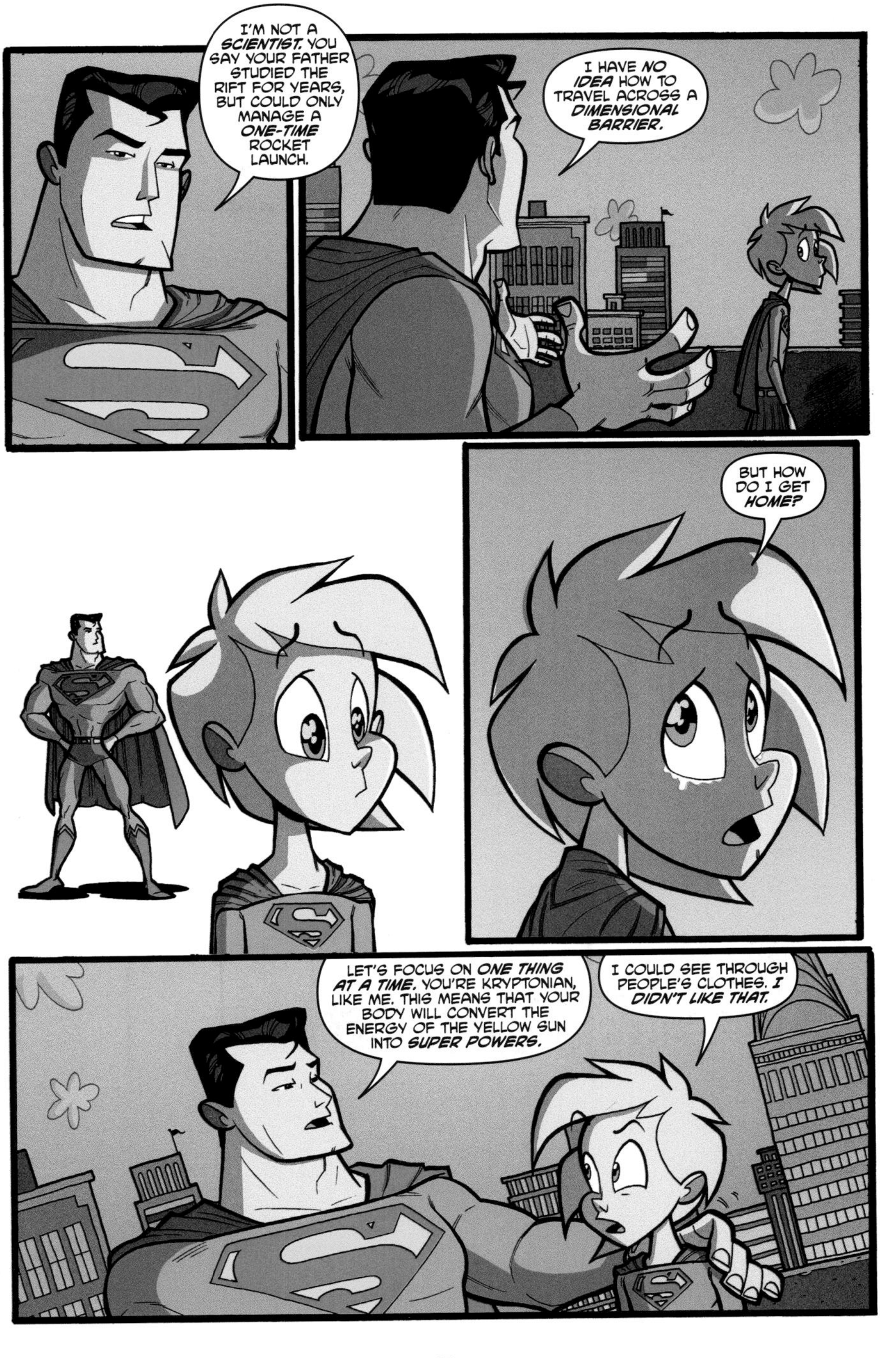
I'M NOT A SCIENTIST. YOU SAY YOUR FATHER STUDIED THE RIFT FOR YEARS, BUT COULD ONLY MANAGE A ONE-TIME ROCKET LAUNCH.
I HAVE NO IDEA HOW TO TRAVEL ACROSS A DIMENSIONAL BARRIER.
BUT HOW DO I GET HOME?
LET'S FOCUS ON ONE THING AT A TIME. YOU'RE KRYPTONIAN, LIKE ME. THIS MEANS THAT YOUR BODY WILL CONVERT THE ENERGY OF THE YELLOW SUN INTO SUPER POWERS.
I COULD SEE THROUGH PEOPLE'S CLOTHES. I DIDN'T LIKE THAT.

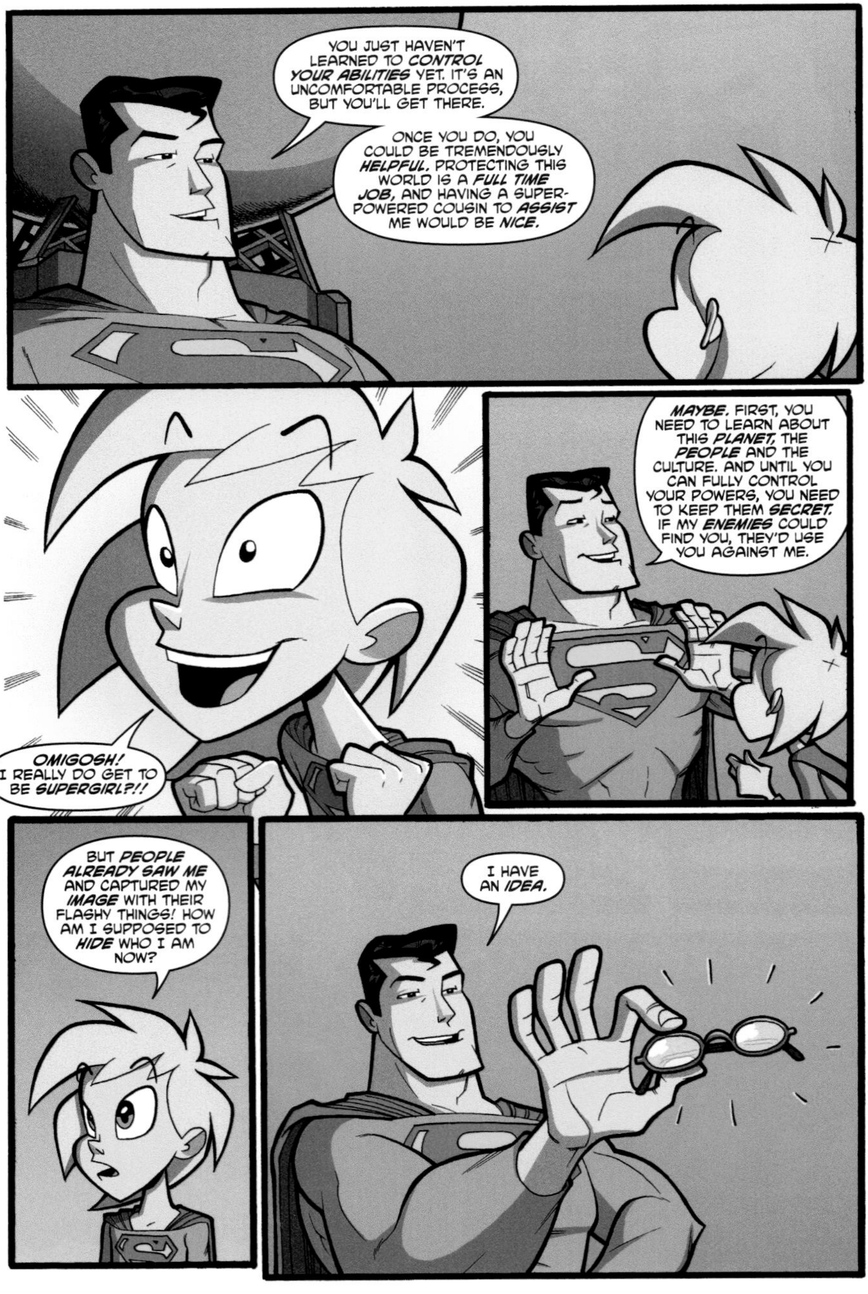
YOU JUST HAVEN'T LEARNED TO CONTROL YOUR ABILITIES YET. IT'S AN UNCOMFORTABLE PROCESS, BUT YOU'LL GET THERE.
ONCE YOU DO, YOU COULD BE TREMENDOUSLY HELPFUL. PROTECTING THIS WORLD IS A FULL TIME JOB, AND HAVING A SUPER-POWERED COUSIN TO ASSIST ME WOULD BE NICE.
OMIGOSH! I REALLY DO GET TO BE SUPERGIRL?!!
MAYBE. FIRST, YOU NEED TO LEARN ABOUT THIS PLANET, THE PEOPLE AND THE CULTURE. AND UNTIL YOU CAN FULLY CONTROL YOUR POWERS, YOU NEED TO KEEP THEM SECRET. IF MY ENEMIES COULD FIND YOU, THEY'D USE YOU AGAINST ME.
BUT PEOPLE ALREADY SAW ME AND CAPTURED MY IMAGE WITH THEIR FLASHY THINGS! HOW AM I SUPPOSED TO HIDE WHO I AM NOW?
I HAVE AN IDEA.

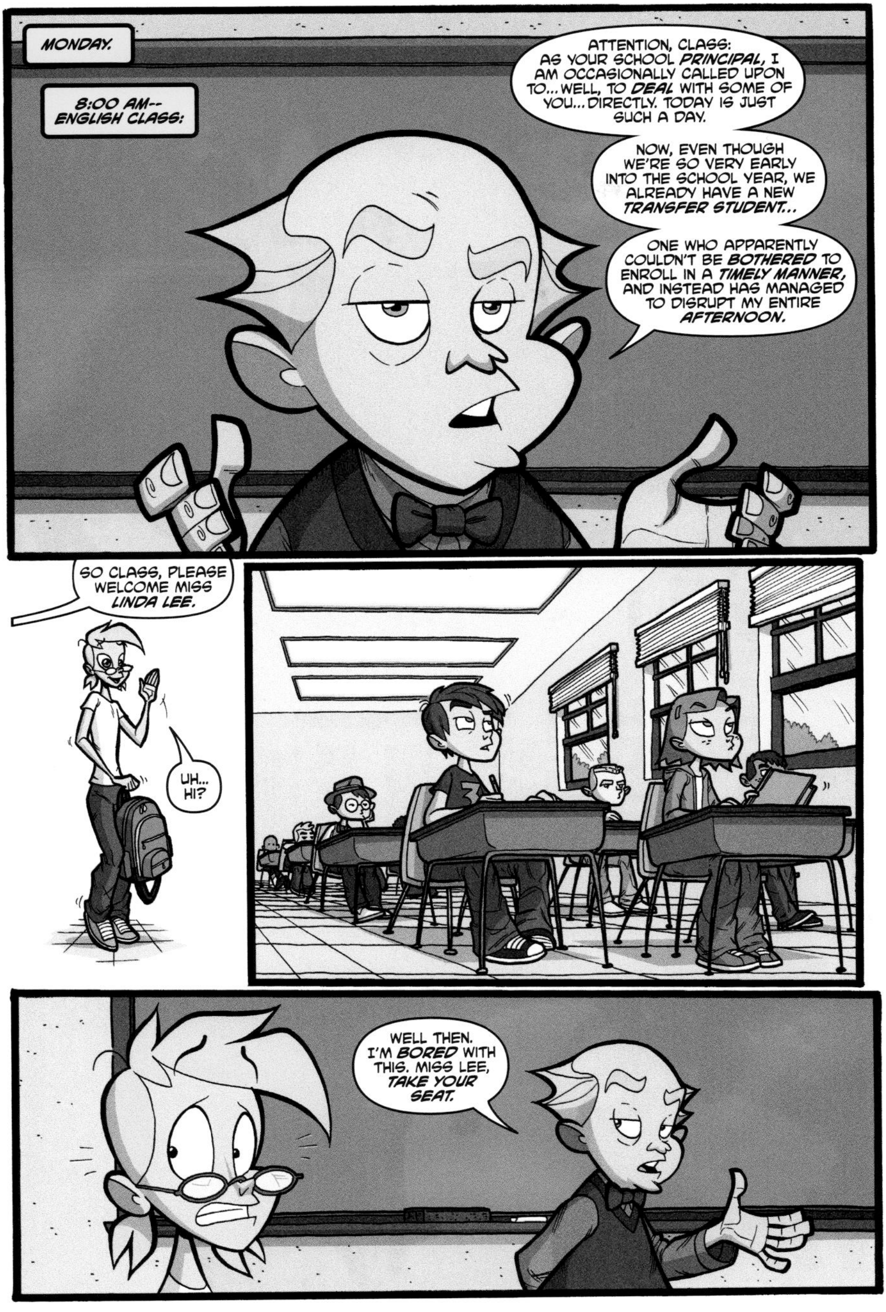
MONDAY.
8:00 AM-- ENGLISH CLASS:
ATTENTION, CLASS: AS YOUR SCHOOL PRINCIPAL, I AM OCCASIONALLY CALLED UPON TO...WELL, TO DEAL WITH SOME OF YOU...DIRECTLY. TODAY IS JUST SUCH A DAY.
NOW, EVEN THOUGH WE'RE SO VERY EARLY INTO THE SCHOOL YEAR, WE ALREADY HAVE A NEW TRANSFER STUDENT...
ONE WHO APPARENTLY COULDN'T BE BOTHERED TO ENROLL IN A TIMELY MANNER, AND INSTEAD HAS MANAGED TO DISRUPT MY ENTIRE AFTERNOON.
SO CLASS, PLEASE WELCOME MISS LINDA LEE.
UH... HI?
WELL THEN. I'M BORED WITH THIS. MISS LEE, TAKE YOUR SEAT.

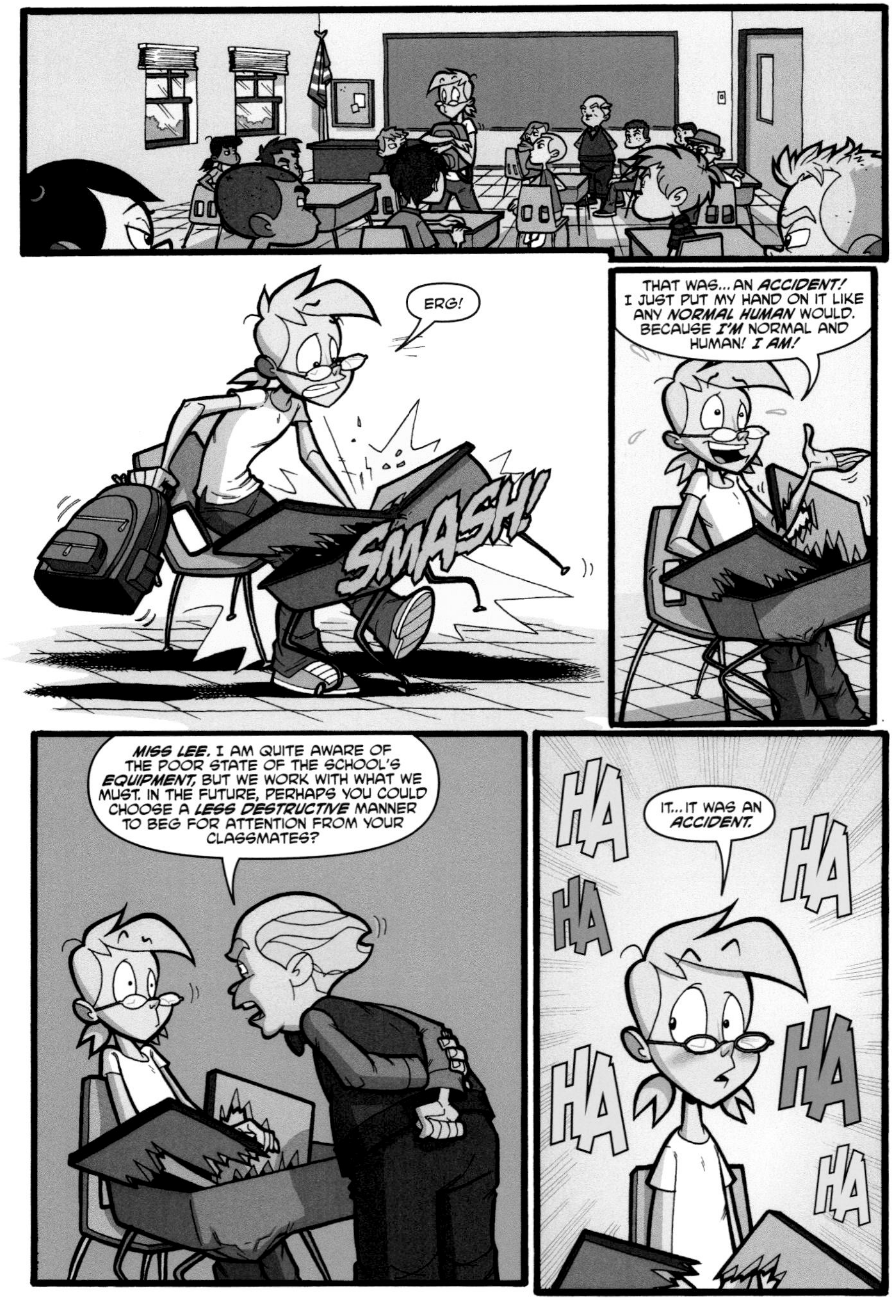
ERG!
SMASH!
THAT WAS... AN ACCIDENT! I JUST PUT MY HAND ON IT LIKE ANY NORMAL HUMAN WOULD. BECAUSE I'M NORMAL AND HUMAN! I AM!
MISS LEE. I AM QUITE AWARE OF THE POOR STATE OF THE SCHOOL'S EQUIPMENT, BUT WE WORK WITH WHAT WE MUST. IN THE FUTURE, PERHAPS YOU COULD CHOOSE A LESS DESTRUCTIVE MANNER TO BEG FOR ATTENTION FROM YOUR CLASSMATES?
HA HA HA
IT... IT WAS AN ACCIDENT.
HA HA HA HA

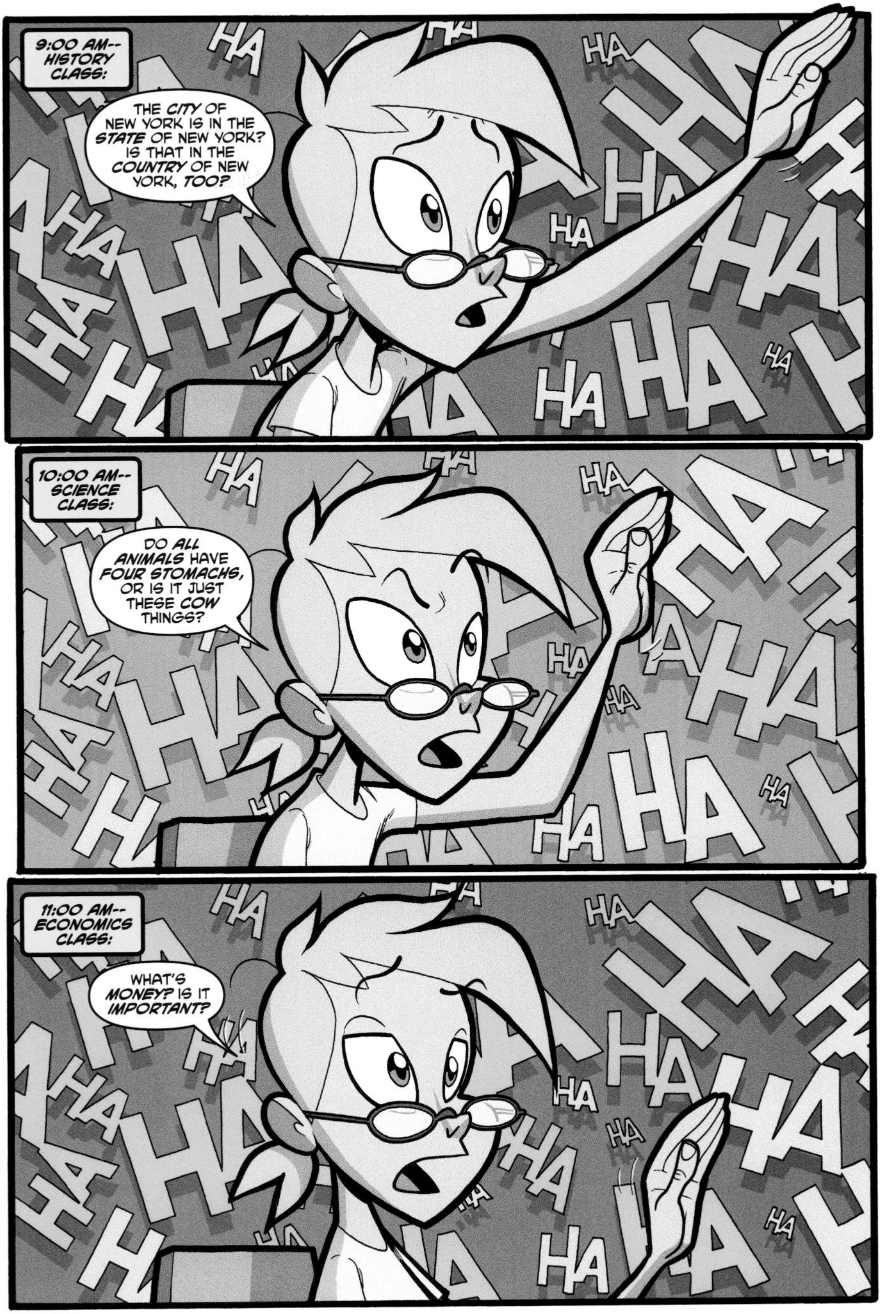
9:00 AM--
HISTORY CLASS:
THE CITY OF NEW YORK IS IN THE STATE OF NEW YORK? IS THAT IN THE COUNTRY OF NEW YORK, TOO?
HA HA HA HA HA HA HA HA HA HA
10:00 AM--
SCIENCE CLASS:
DO ALL ANIMALS HAVE FOUR STOMACHS, OR IS IT JUST THESE COW THINGS?
HA HA HA HA HA HA HA HA HA HA
11:00 AM--
ECONOMICS CLASS:
WHAT'S MONEY? IS IT IMPORTANT?
HA HA HA HA HA HA HA HA HA HA

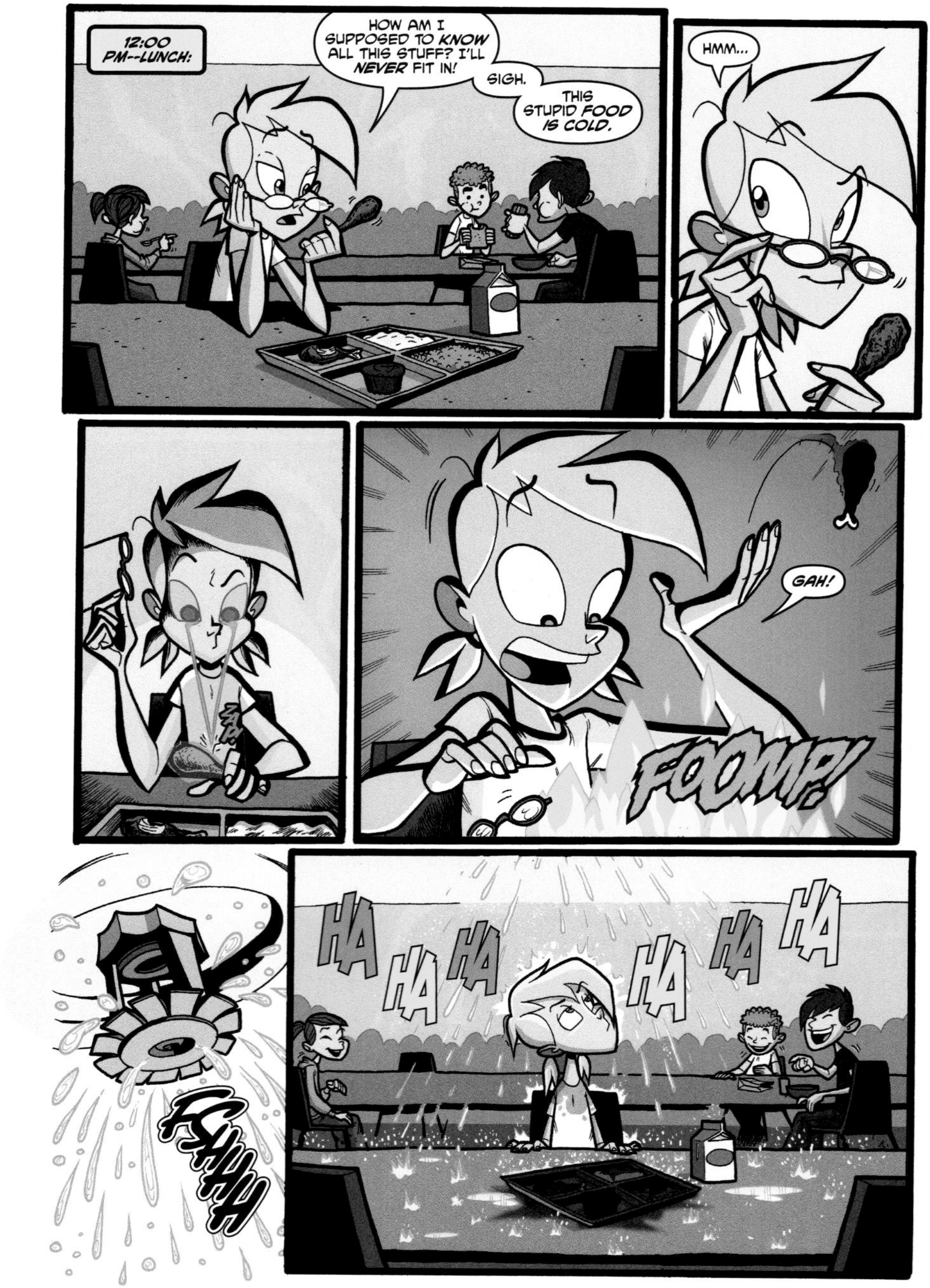
12:00 PM--LUNCH:
HOW AM I SUPPOSED TO KNOW ALL THIS STUFF? I'LL NEVER FIT IN!
SIGH.
THIS STUPID FOOD IS COLD.
HMM...
ZAP!
GAH!
FOOMP!
FSHHHH
HA HA HA HA HA HA HA

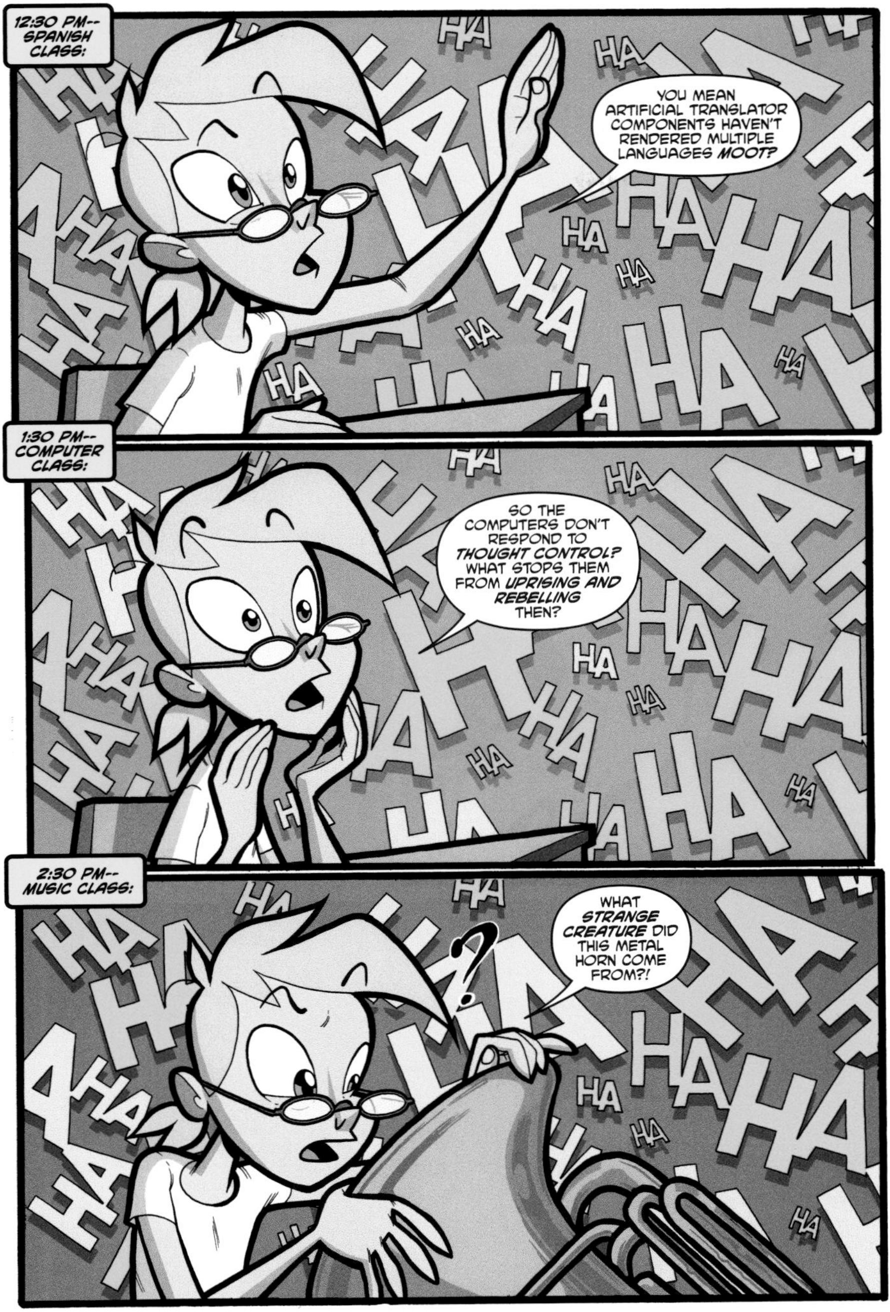
12:30 PM-- SPANISH CLASS:
YOU MEAN ARTIFICIAL TRANSLATOR COMPONENTS HAVEN'T RENDERED MULTIPLE LANGUAGES *MOOT?*
1:30 PM-- COMPUTER CLASS:
SO THE COMPUTERS DON'T RESPOND TO *THOUGHT CONTROL?* WHAT STOPS THEM FROM *UPRISING AND REBELLING* THEN?
2:30 PM-- MUSIC CLASS:
WHAT *STRANGE CREATURE* DID THIS METAL HORN COME FROM?!

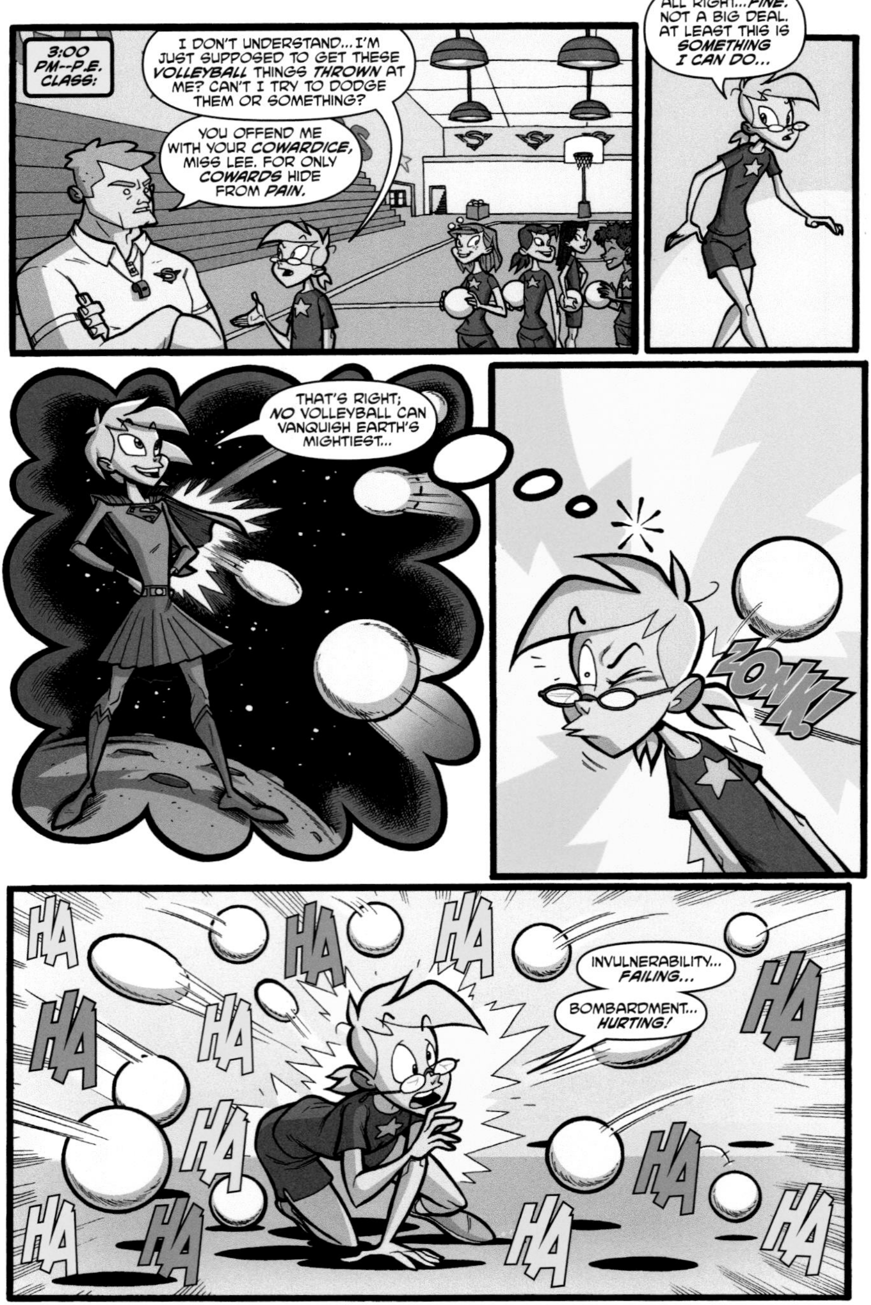
3:00 PM--P.E. CLASS:
I DON'T UNDERSTAND... I'M JUST SUPPOSED TO GET THESE VOLLEYBALL THINGS THROWN AT ME? CAN'T I TRY TO DODGE THEM OR SOMETHING?
YOU OFFEND ME WITH YOUR COWARDICE, MISS LEE. FOR ONLY COWARDS HIDE FROM PAIN.
ALL RIGHT... FINE. NOT A BIG DEAL. AT LEAST THIS IS SOMETHING I CAN DO...
THAT'S RIGHT; NO VOLLEYBALL CAN VANQUISH EARTH'S MIGHTIEST...
ZONK!
HA HA HA HA HA HA HA HA HA HA HA HA HA
INVULNERABILITY... FAILING...
BOMBARDMENT... HURTING!

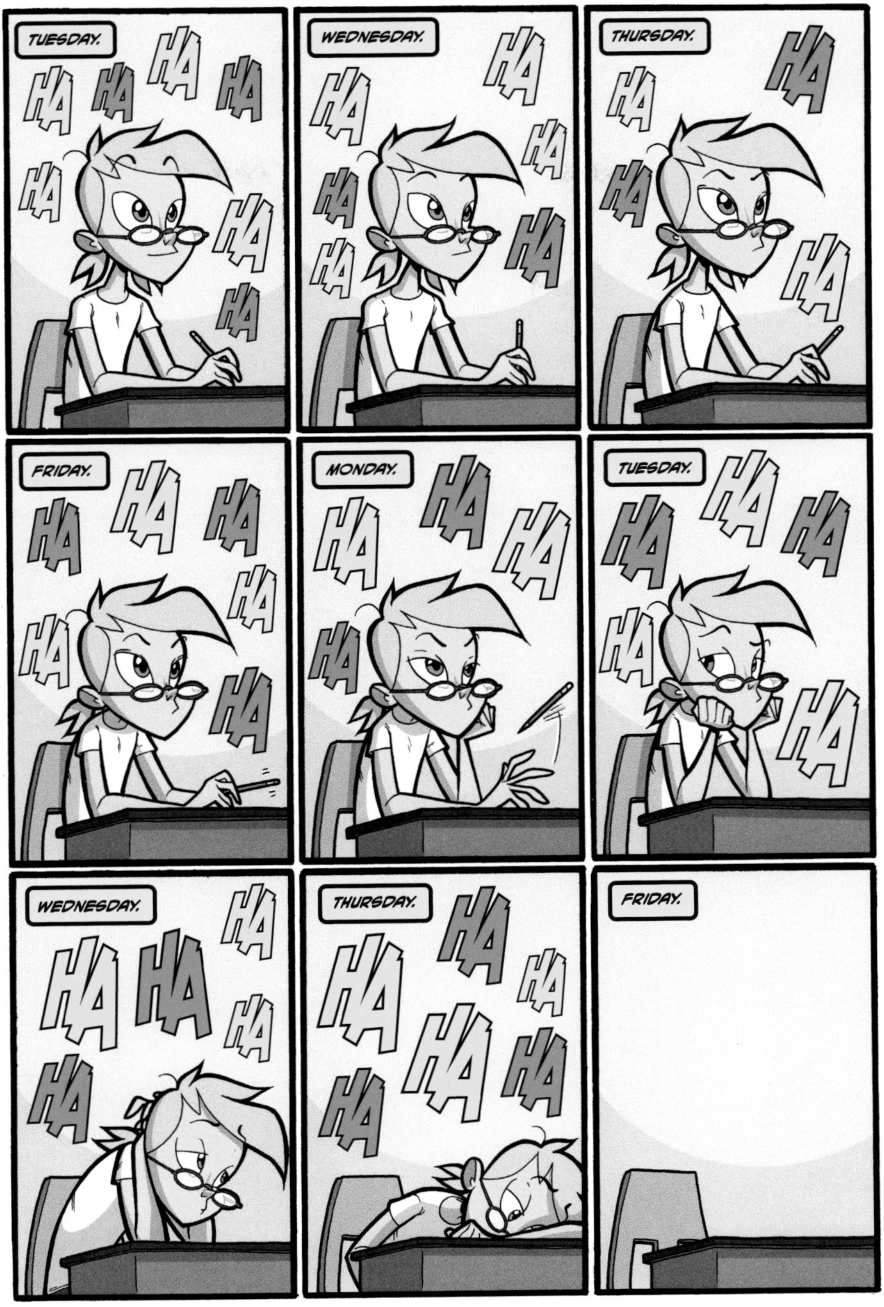
TUESDAY.
HA HA HA HA HA HA HA
WEDNESDAY.
HA HA HA HA HA HA
THURSDAY.
HA HA HA HA
FRIDAY.
HA HA HA HA HA HA
MONDAY.
HA HA HA HA
TUESDAY.
HA HA HA HA HA
WEDNESDAY.
HA HA HA HA HA
THURSDAY.
HA HA HA HA HA HA
FRIDAY.

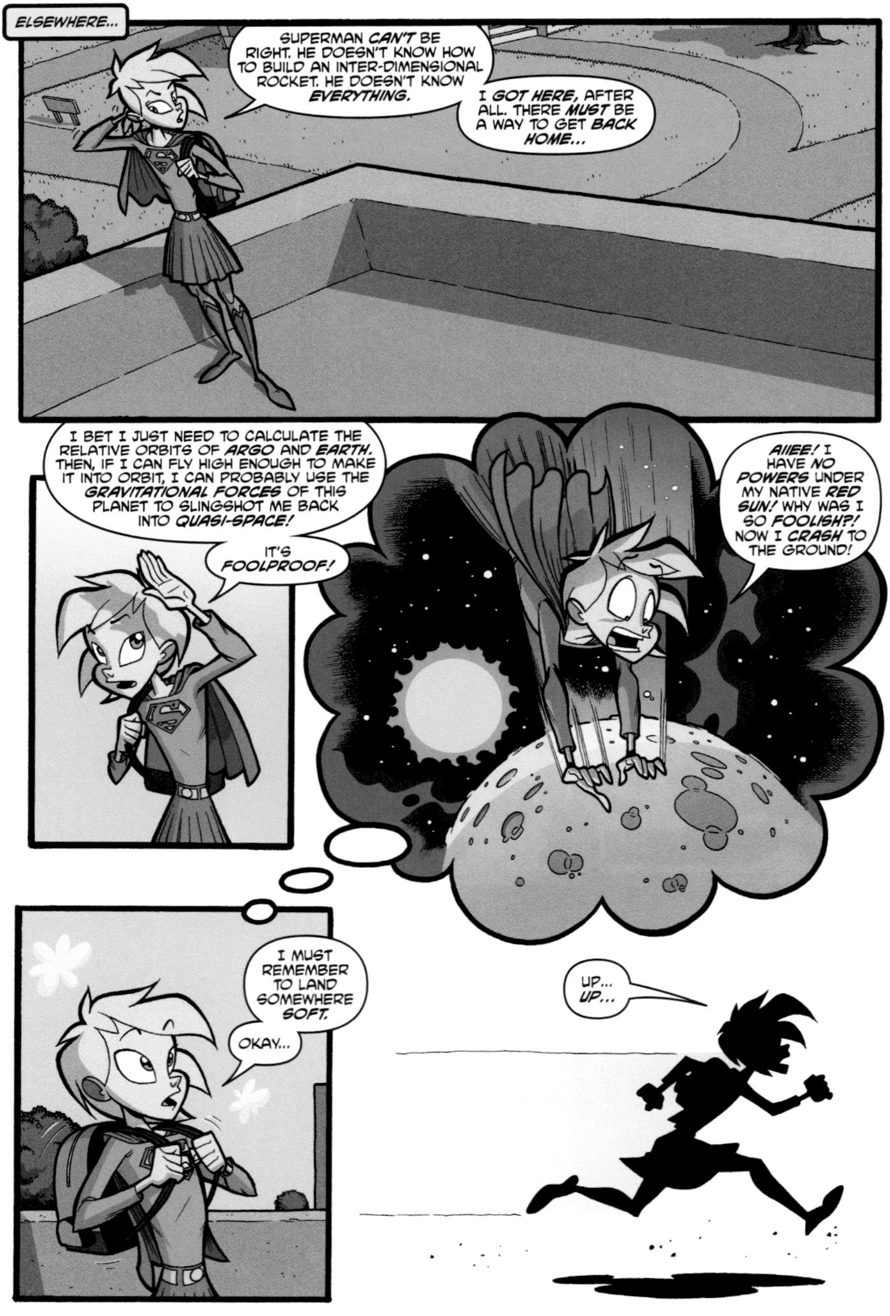
ELSEWHERE...
SUPERMAN CAN'T BE RIGHT. HE DOESN'T KNOW HOW TO BUILD AN INTER-DIMENSIONAL ROCKET. HE DOESN'T KNOW EVERYTHING.
I GOT HERE, AFTER ALL. THERE MUST BE A WAY TO GET BACK HOME...
I BET I JUST NEED TO CALCULATE THE RELATIVE ORBITS OF ARGO AND EARTH. THEN, IF I CAN FLY HIGH ENOUGH TO MAKE IT INTO ORBIT, I CAN PROBABLY USE THE GRAVITATIONAL FORCES OF THIS PLANET TO SLINGSHOT ME BACK INTO QUASI-SPACE!
IT'S FOOLPROOF!
AIIEE! I HAVE NO POWERS UNDER MY NATIVE RED SUN! WHY WAS I SO FOOLISH?! NOW I CRASH TO THE GROUND!
I MUST REMEMBER TO LAND SOMEWHERE SOFT.
OKAY...
UP... UP...

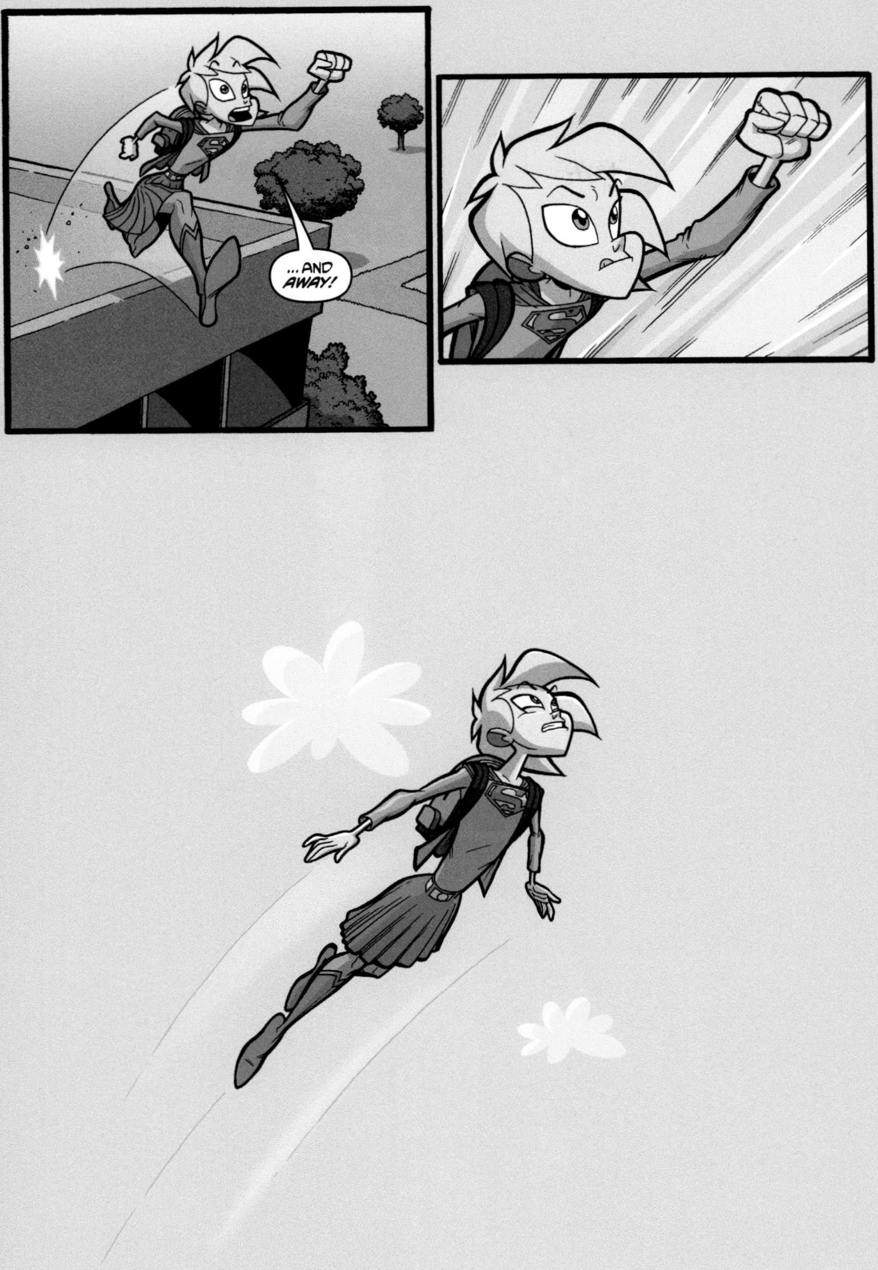
...AND AWAY!

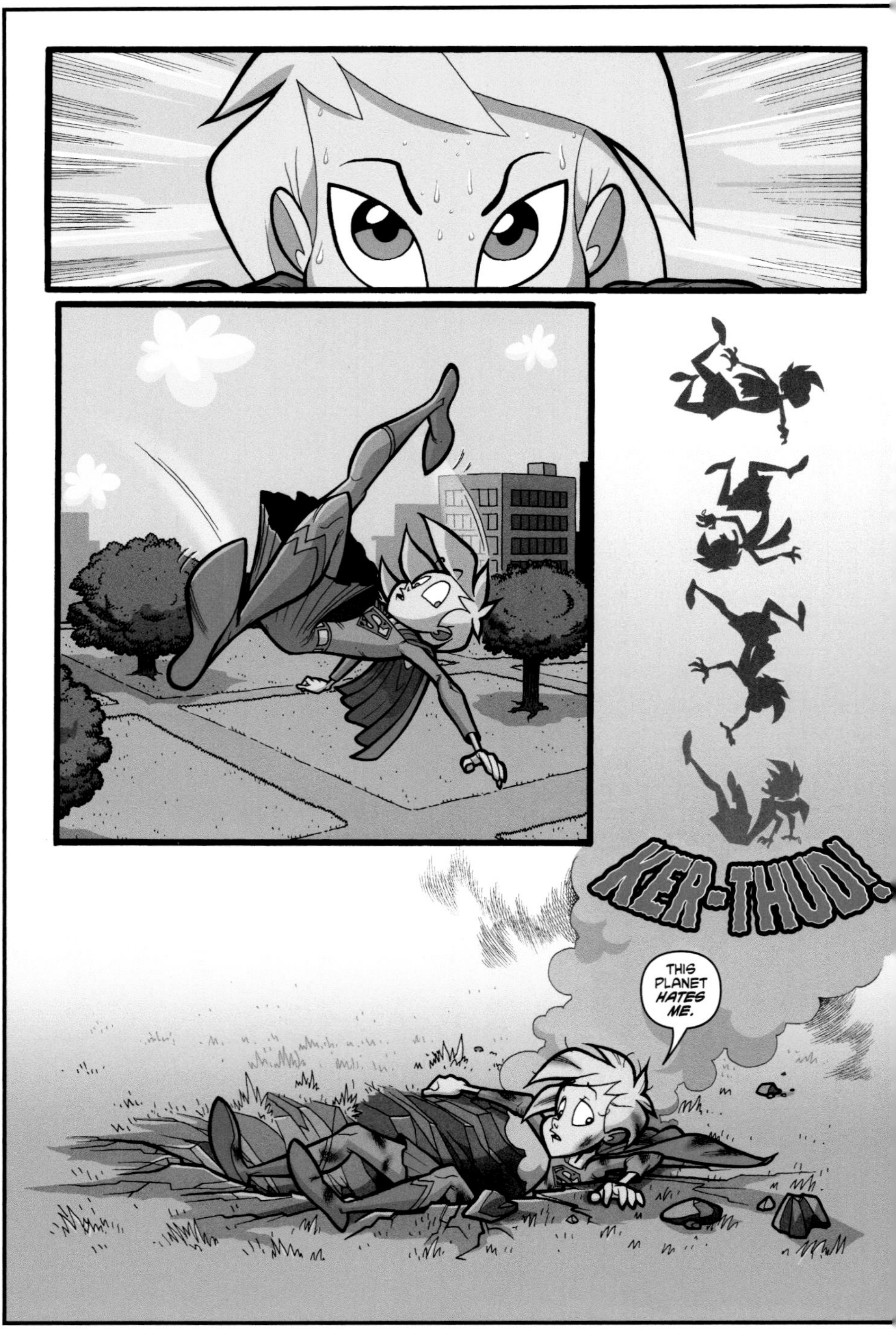
KER-THUD!
THIS PLANET HATES ME.

AND SO...

HOW AM I SUPPOSED TO BECOME A *SUPERHERO?* I DON'T UNDERSTAND THIS WORLD AT ALL! MY POWERS ARE ALL *WEIRD,* AND *NOBODY* ANYWHERE *LIKES* ME!

WHA..? *SUPERMAN?*

You are not alone. -S

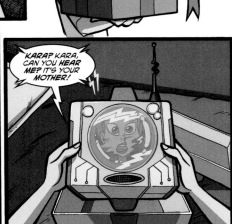

HEY... THIS WAS PART OF THE *ROCKET...* BUT THIS STUFF ONLY WORKS IN QUASI--

ZZZZZRK!!

KARA? KARA, CAN YOU *HEAR* ME? IT'S YOUR *MOTHER!*

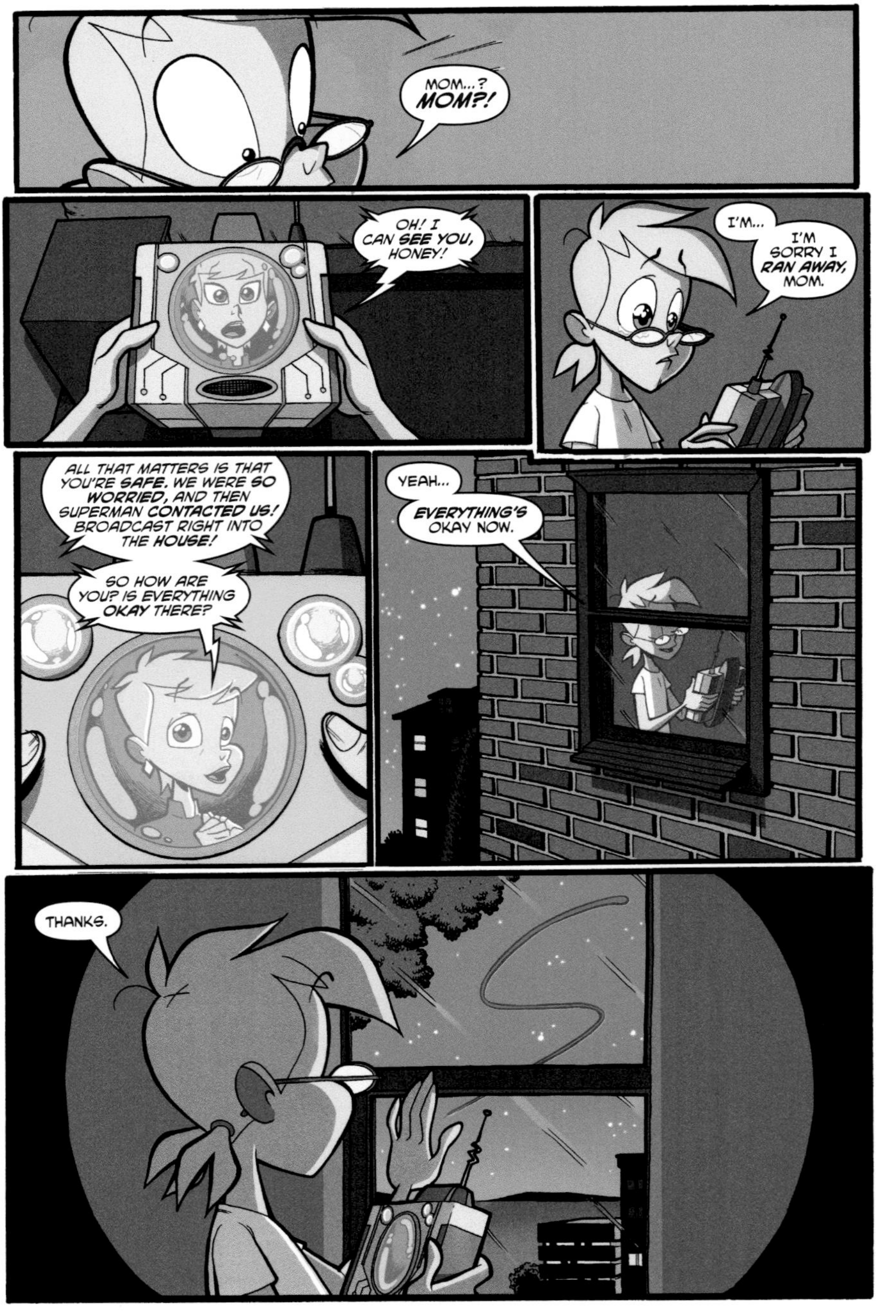

MOM...? MOM?!
OH! I CAN SEE YOU, HONEY!
I'M...
I'M SORRY I RAN AWAY, MOM.
ALL THAT MATTERS IS THAT YOU'RE SAFE. WE WERE SO WORRIED, AND THEN SUPERMAN CONTACTED US! BROADCAST RIGHT INTO THE HOUSE!
SO HOW ARE YOU? IS EVERYTHING OKAY THERE?
YEAH...
EVERYTHING'S OKAY NOW.
THANKS.

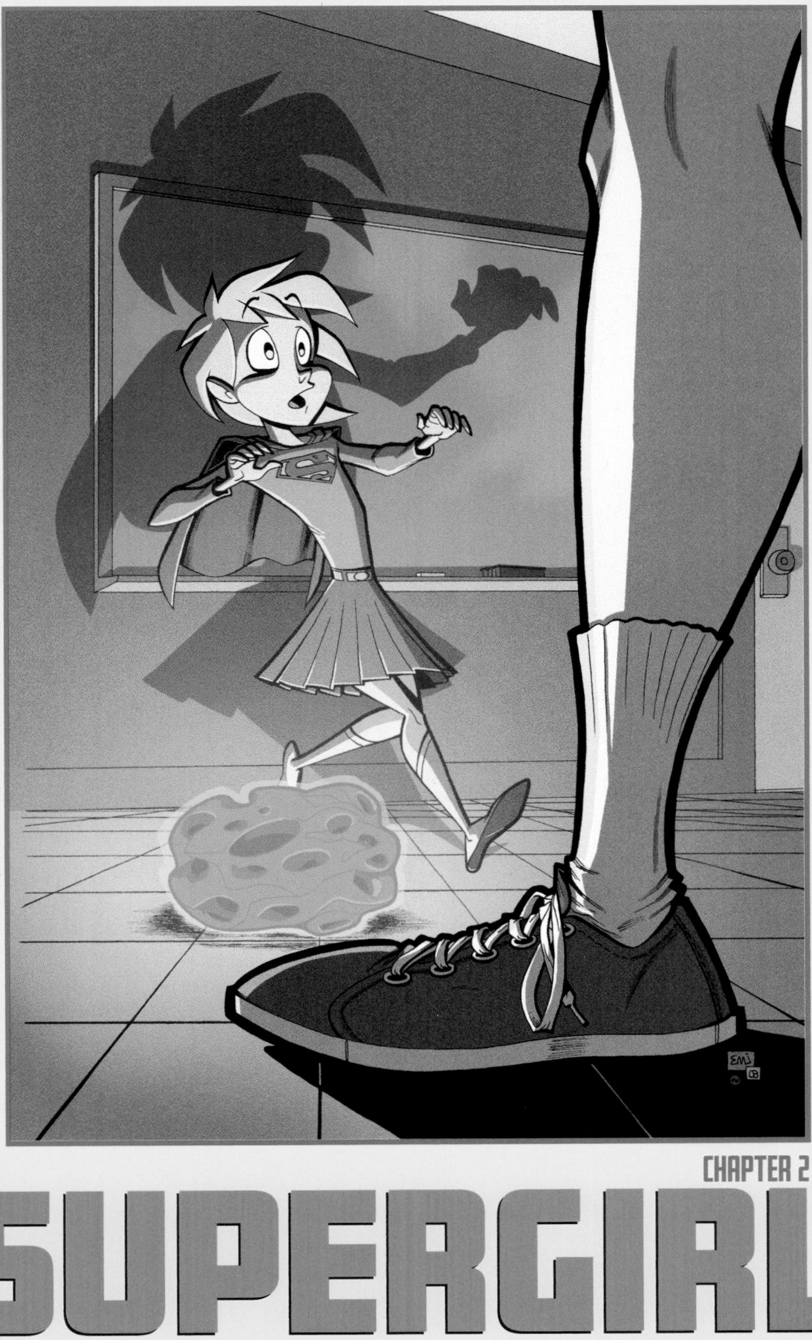

CHAPTER 2

SUPERGIRL

COSMIC ADVENTURES IN THE 8TH GRADE

SUPERGIRL

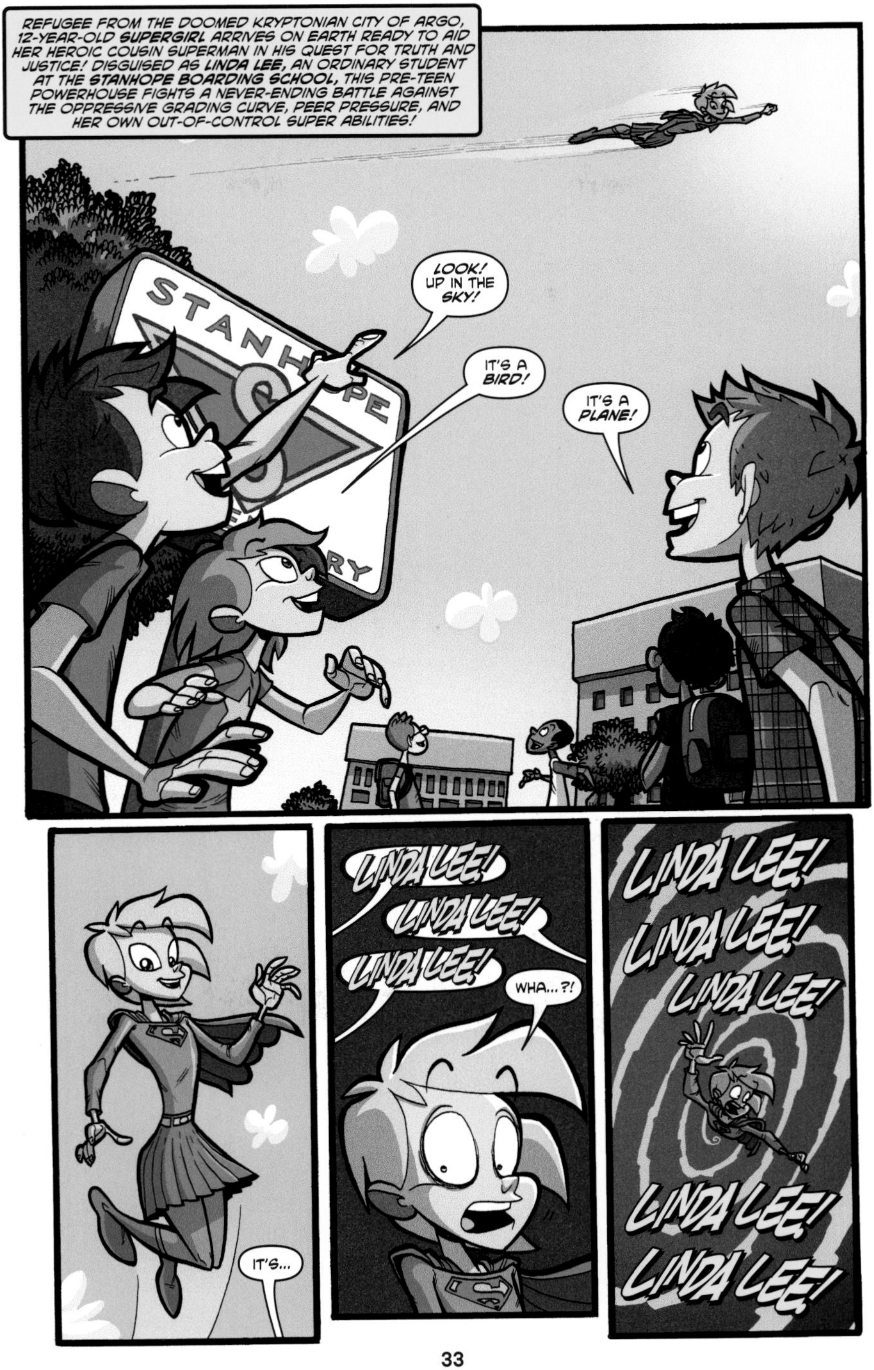

REFUGEE FROM THE DOOMED KRYPTONIAN CITY OF ARGO, 12-YEAR-OLD SUPERGIRL ARRIVES ON EARTH READY TO AID HER HEROIC COUSIN SUPERMAN IN HIS QUEST FOR TRUTH AND JUSTICE! DISGUISED AS LINDA LEE, AN ORDINARY STUDENT AT THE STANHOPE BOARDING SCHOOL, THIS PRE-TEEN POWERHOUSE FIGHTS A NEVER-ENDING BATTLE AGAINST THE OPPRESSIVE GRADING CURVE, PEER PRESSURE, AND HER OWN OUT-OF-CONTROL SUPER ABILITIES!
STANHOPE
LOOK! UP IN THE SKY!
IT'S A BIRD!
IT'S A PLANE!
IT'S...
LINDA LEE!
LINDA LEE!
LINDA LEE!
WHA...?!
LINDA LEE!
LINDA LEE!
LINDA LEE!
LINDA LEE!
LINDA LEE!

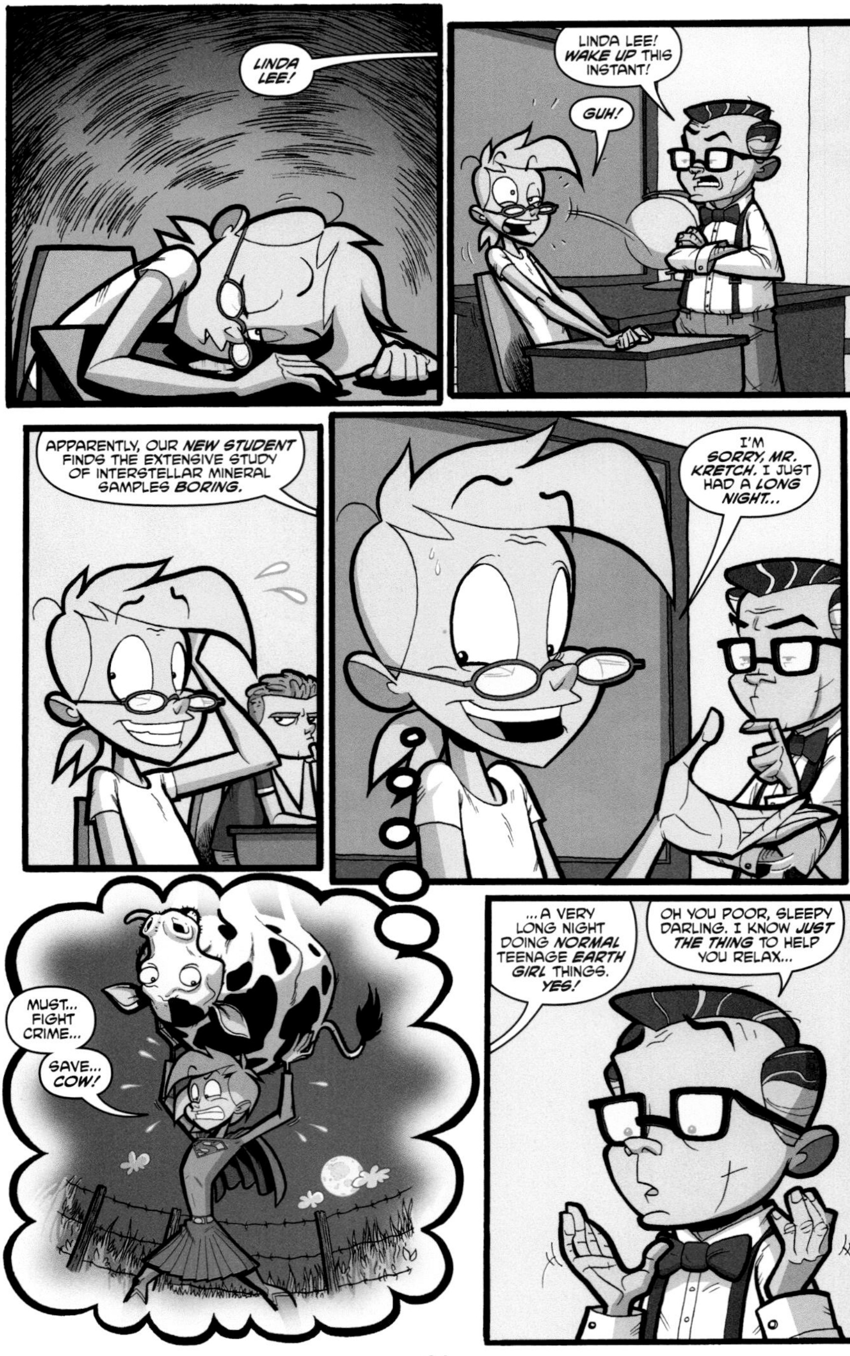
LINDA LEE!
LINDA LEE! WAKE UP THIS INSTANT!
GUH!
APPARENTLY, OUR NEW STUDENT FINDS THE EXTENSIVE STUDY OF INTERSTELLAR MINERAL SAMPLES BORING.
I'M SORRY, MR. KRETCH. I JUST HAD A LONG NIGHT...
MUST... FIGHT CRIME...
SAVE... COW!
...A VERY LONG NIGHT DOING NORMAL TEENAGE EARTH GIRL THINGS. YES!
OH YOU POOR, SLEEPY DARLING. I KNOW JUST THE THING TO HELP YOU RELAX...

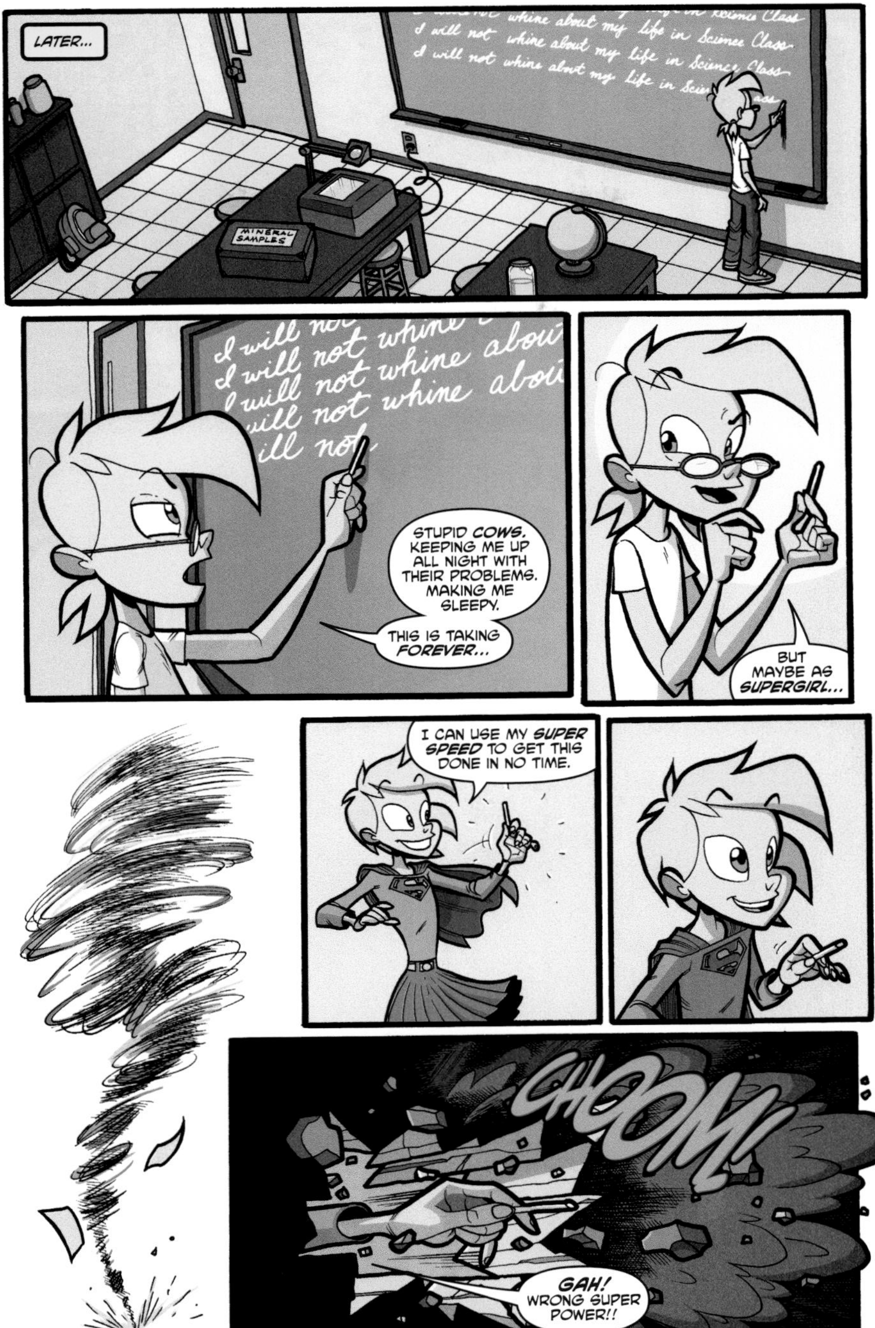
LATER...
I will not whine about my life in Science Class
I will not whine about my life in Science Class
I will not whine about my life in Science Class
STUPID COWS. KEEPING ME UP ALL NIGHT WITH THEIR PROBLEMS. MAKING ME SLEEPY.
THIS IS TAKING FOREVER...
BUT MAYBE AS SUPERGIRL...
I CAN USE MY SUPER SPEED TO GET THIS DONE IN NO TIME.
CHOOOM!
GAH! WRONG SUPER POWER!!

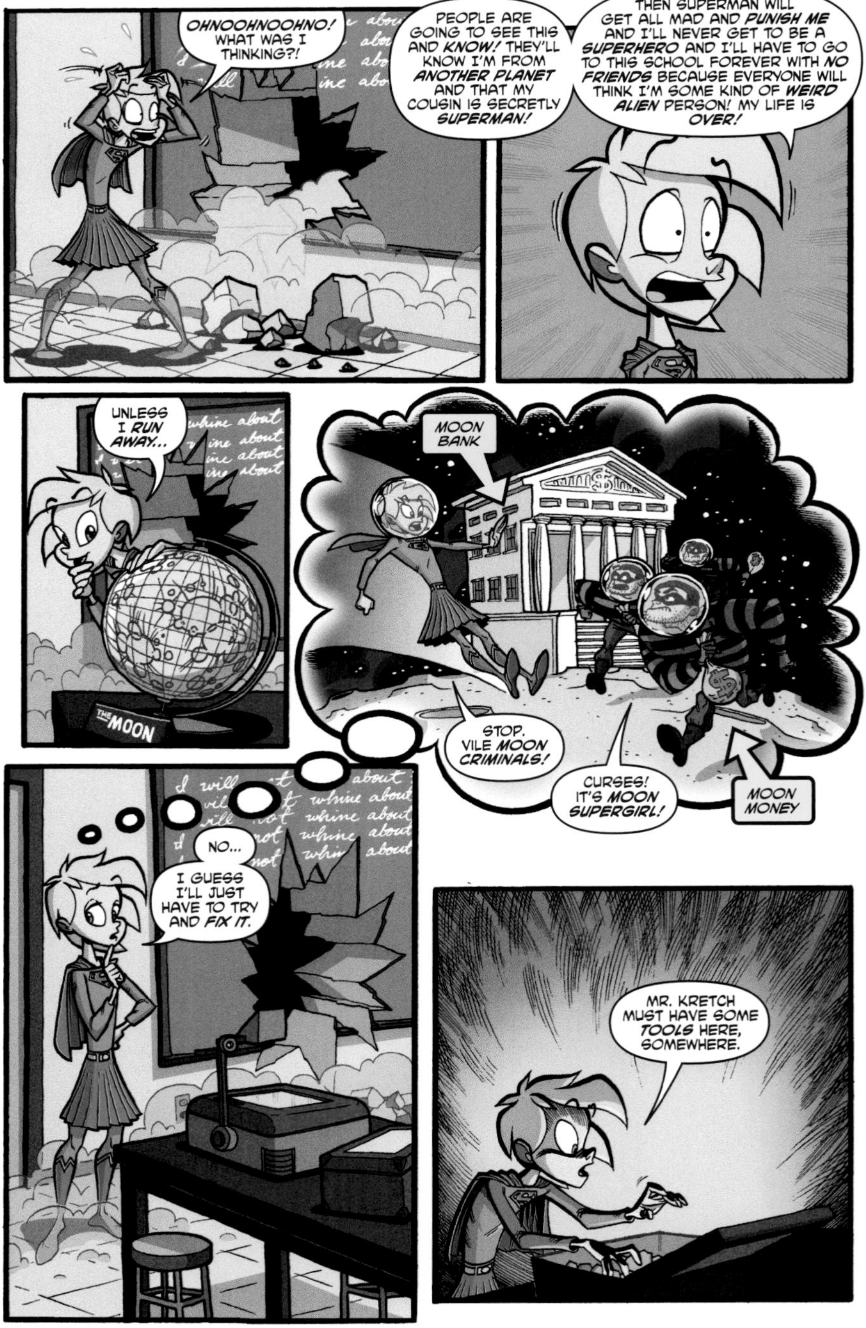
OHNOOHNOOHNO! WHAT WAS I THINKING?!
PEOPLE ARE GOING TO SEE THIS AND KNOW! THEY'LL KNOW I'M FROM ANOTHER PLANET AND THAT MY COUSIN IS SECRETLY SUPERMAN!
THEN SUPERMAN WILL GET ALL MAD AND PUNISH ME AND I'LL NEVER GET TO BE A SUPERHERO AND I'LL HAVE TO GO TO THIS SCHOOL FOREVER WITH NO FRIENDS BECAUSE EVERYONE WILL THINK I'M SOME KIND OF WEIRD ALIEN PERSON! MY LIFE IS OVER!
UNLESS I RUN AWAY...
THE MOON
MOON BANK
STOP. VILE MOON CRIMINALS!
CURSES! IT'S MOON SUPERGIRL!
MOON MONEY
NO...
I GUESS I'LL JUST HAVE TO TRY AND FIX IT.
MR. KRETCH MUST HAVE SOME TOOLS HERE, SOMEWHERE.

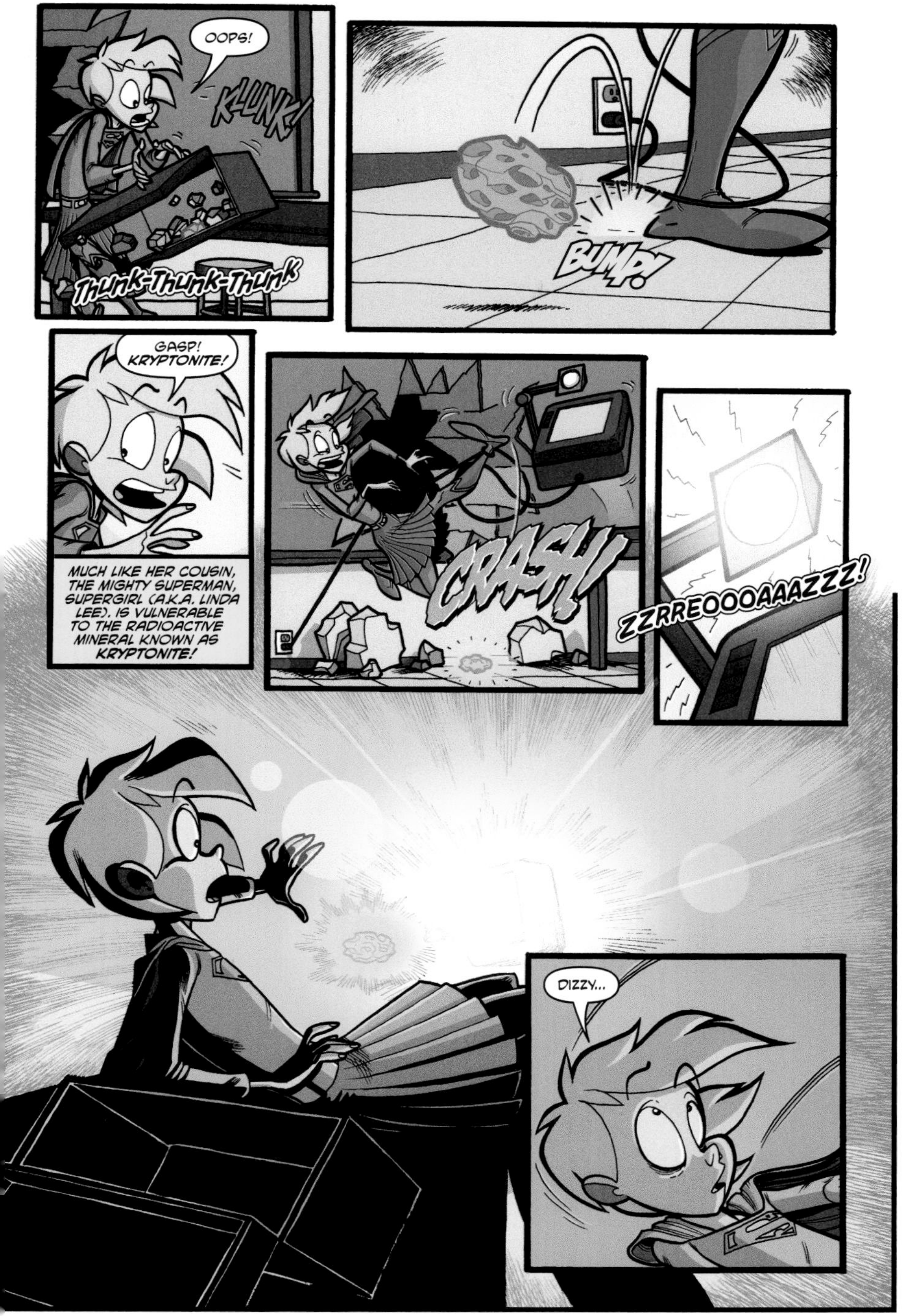
OOPS!
KLUNK!
THUNK-THUNK-THUNK
BUMP!
GASP! KRYPTONITE!
MUCH LIKE HER COUSIN, THE MIGHTY SUPERMAN, SUPERGIRL (A.K.A. LINDA LEE), IS VULNERABLE TO THE RADIOACTIVE MINERAL KNOWN AS KRYPTONITE!
CRASH!
ZZRREOOOAAAZZZ!
DIZZY...

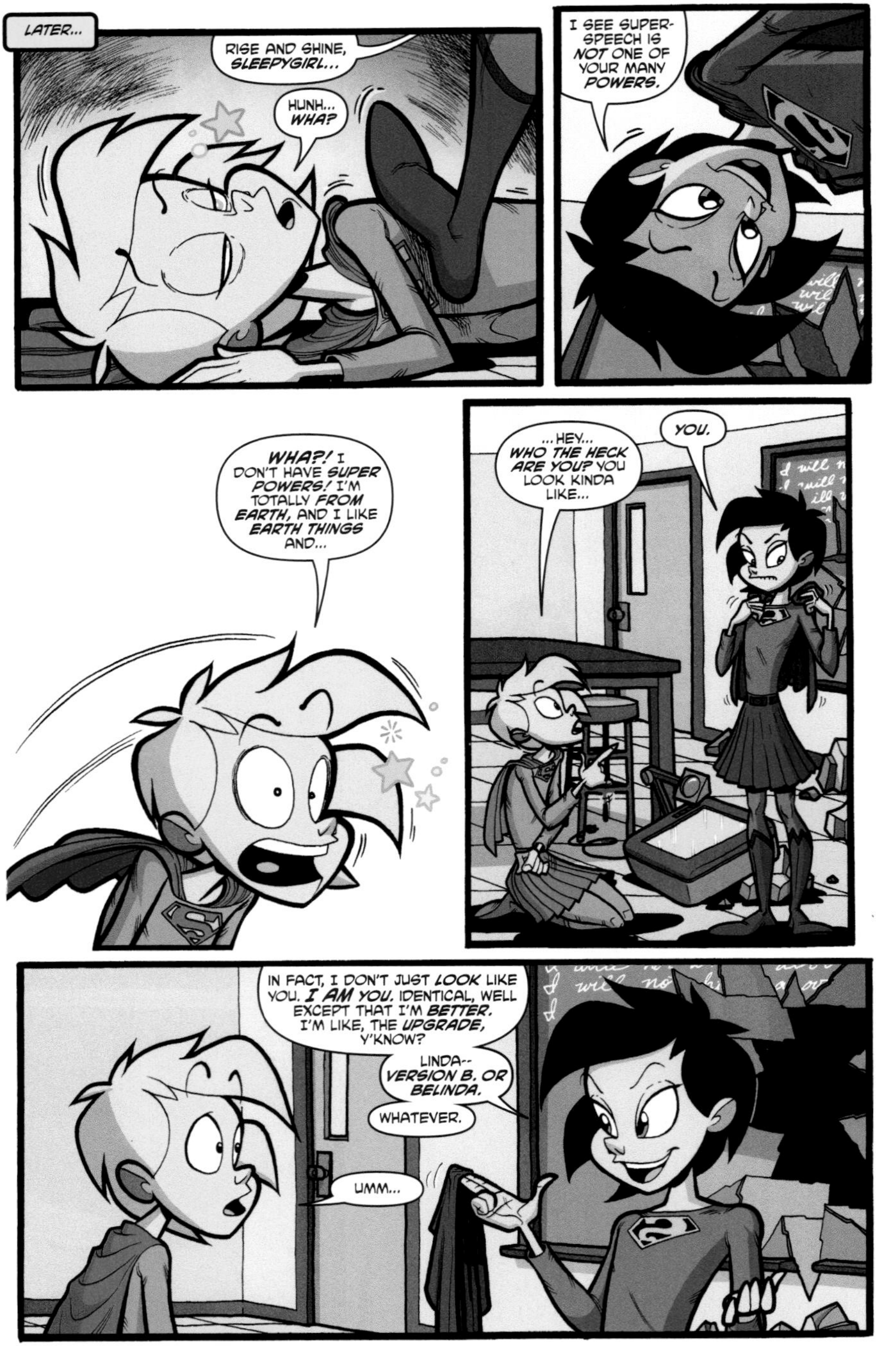
LATER...
RISE AND SHINE, SLEEPYGIRL...
HUNH... WHA?
I SEE SUPER-SPEECH IS NOT ONE OF YOUR MANY POWERS.
WHA?! I DON'T HAVE SUPER POWERS! I'M TOTALLY FROM EARTH, AND I LIKE EARTH THINGS AND...
...HEY... WHO THE HECK ARE YOU? YOU LOOK KINDA LIKE...
YOU.
IN FACT, I DON'T JUST LOOK LIKE YOU. I AM YOU. IDENTICAL, WELL EXCEPT THAT I'M BETTER. I'M LIKE, THE UPGRADE, Y'KNOW?
LINDA-- VERSION B. OR BELINDA.
WHATEVER.
UMM...

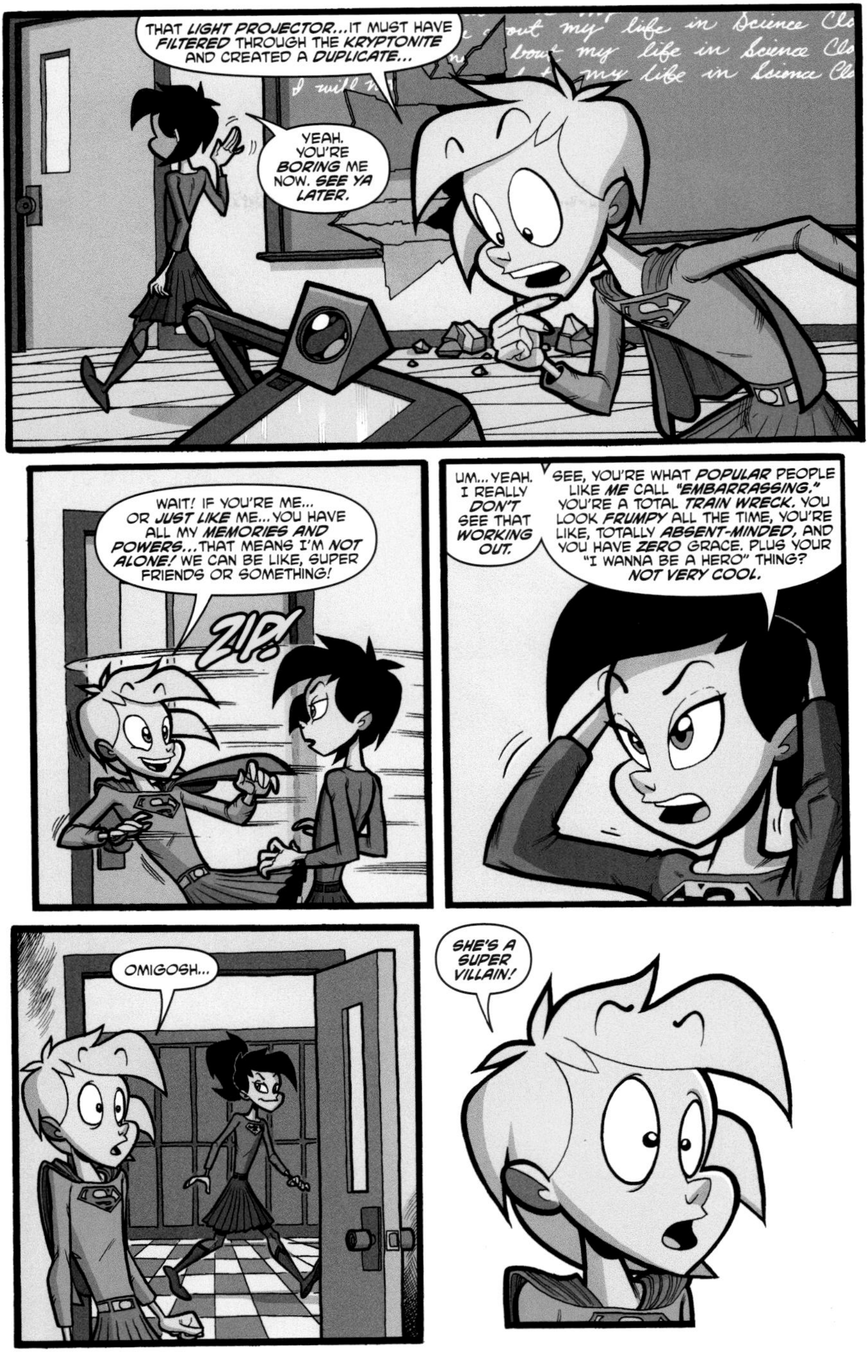
THAT LIGHT PROJECTOR...IT MUST HAVE FILTERED THROUGH THE KRYPTONITE AND CREATED A DUPLICATE...
YEAH. YOU'RE BORING ME NOW. SEE YA LATER.
WAIT! IF YOU'RE ME... OR JUST LIKE ME...YOU HAVE ALL MY MEMORIES AND POWERS...THAT MEANS I'M NOT ALONE! WE CAN BE LIKE, SUPER FRIENDS OR SOMETHING!
ZIP!
UM...YEAH. I REALLY DON'T SEE THAT WORKING OUT.
SEE, YOU'RE WHAT POPULAR PEOPLE LIKE ME CALL "EMBARRASSING." YOU'RE A TOTAL TRAIN WRECK. YOU LOOK FRUMPY ALL THE TIME, YOU'RE LIKE, TOTALLY ABSENT-MINDED, AND YOU HAVE ZERO GRACE. PLUS YOUR "I WANNA BE A HERO" THING? NOT VERY COOL.
OMIGOSH...
SHE'S A SUPER VILLAIN!

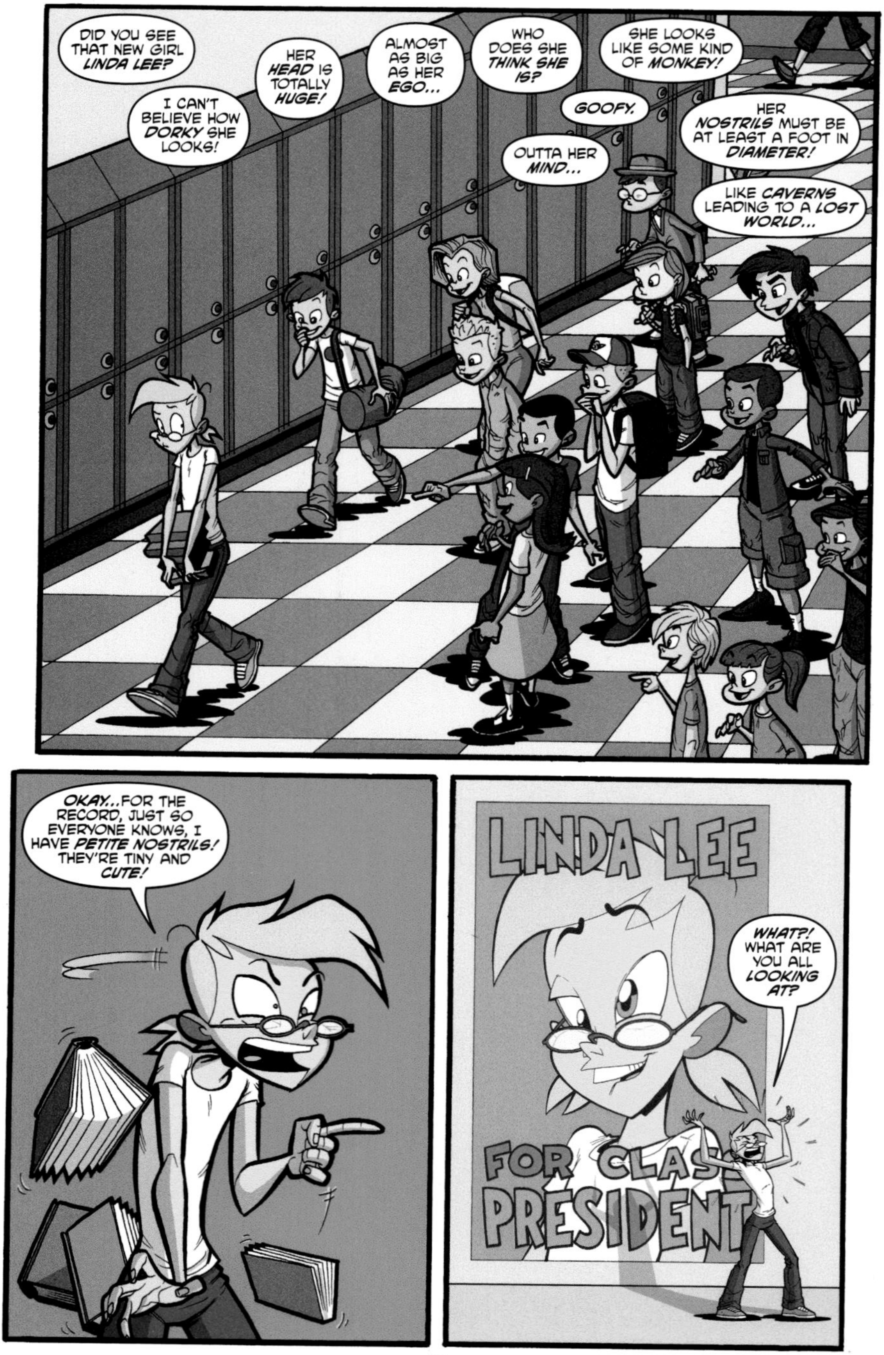
DID YOU SEE THAT NEW GIRL *LINDA LEE?*
I CAN'T BELIEVE HOW *DORKY* SHE LOOKS!
HER *HEAD* IS TOTALLY *HUGE!*
ALMOST AS BIG AS HER *EGO...*
WHO DOES SHE *THINK SHE IS?*
GOOFY.
OUTTA HER *MIND...*
SHE LOOKS LIKE SOME KIND OF *MONKEY!*
HER *NOSTRILS* MUST BE AT LEAST A FOOT IN *DIAMETER!*
LIKE *CAVERNS* LEADING TO A *LOST WORLD...*
OKAY... FOR THE RECORD, JUST SO EVERYONE KNOWS, I HAVE *PETITE NOSTRILS!* THEY'RE TINY AND *CUTE!*
LINDA LEE
FOR CLAS
PRESIDENT
WHAT?! WHAT ARE YOU ALL *LOOKING AT?*

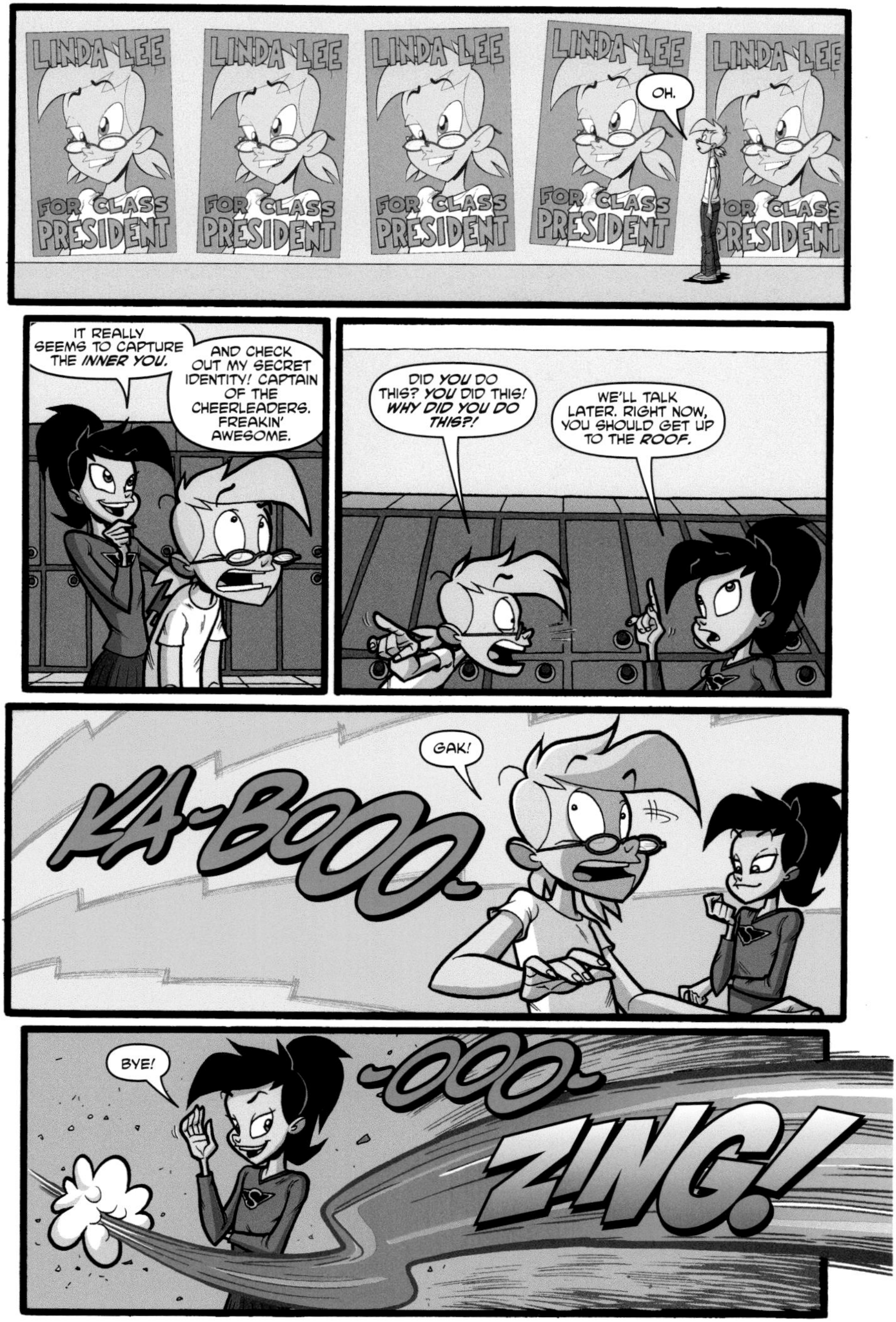
LINDA LEE FOR CLASS PRESIDENT
OH.
IT REALLY SEEMS TO CAPTURE THE *INNER YOU.*
AND CHECK OUT MY SECRET IDENTITY! CAPTAIN OF THE CHEERLEADERS. FREAKIN' AWESOME.
DID *YOU* DO THIS? *YOU* DID THIS! *WHY DID YOU DO THIS?!*
WE'LL TALK LATER. RIGHT NOW, YOU SHOULD GET UP TO THE *ROOF.*
KA-BOOO-
GAK!
BYE!
-OOO-
ZING!

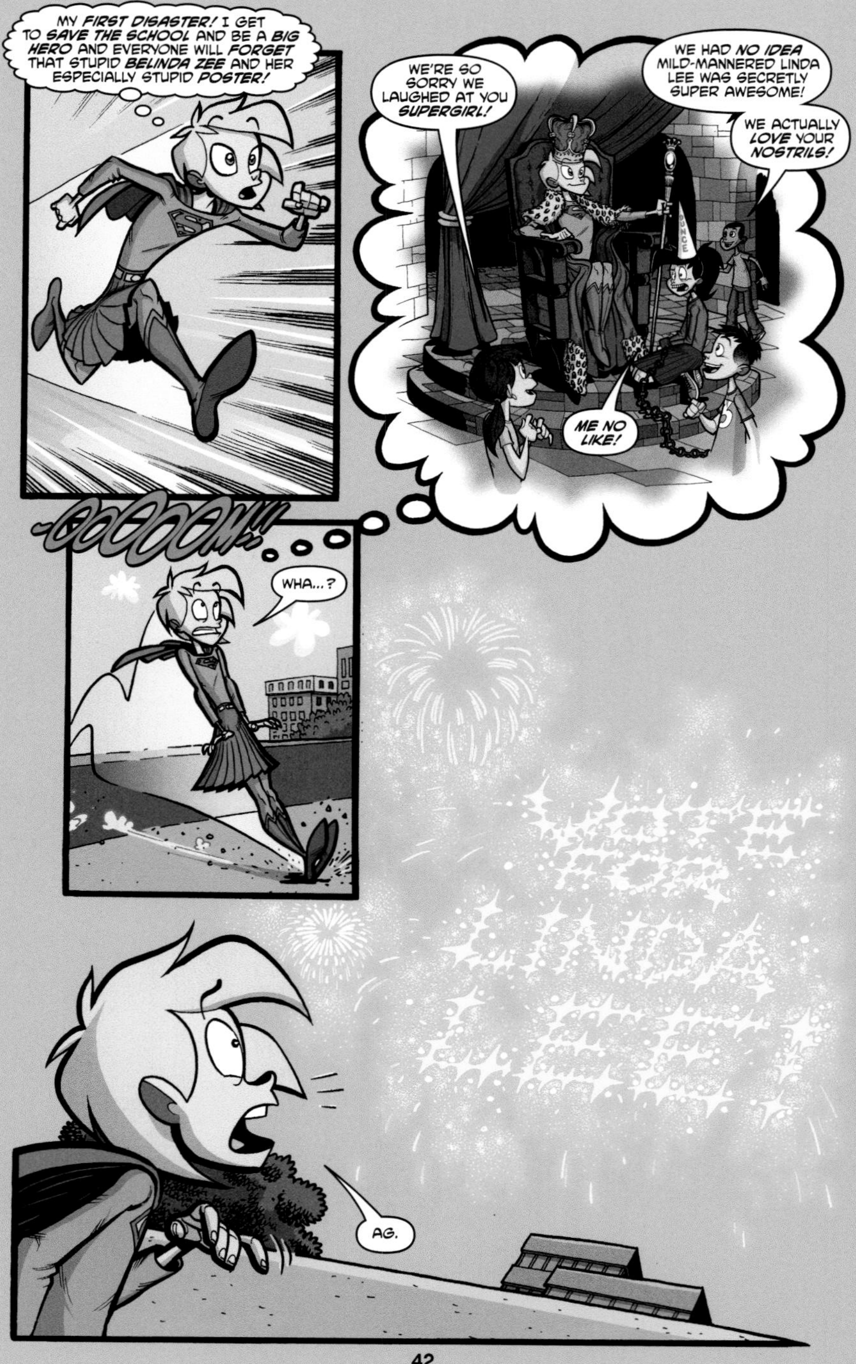

MY FIRST DISASTER! I GET TO SAVE THE SCHOOL AND BE A BIG HERO AND EVERYONE WILL FORGET THAT STUPID BELINDA ZEE AND HER ESPECIALLY STUPID POSTER!
WE'RE SO SORRY WE LAUGHED AT YOU SUPERGIRL!
WE HAD NO IDEA MILD-MANNERED LINDA LEE WAS SECRETLY SUPER AWESOME!
WE ACTUALLY LOVE YOUR NOSTRILS!
DUNCE
ME NO LIKE!
-OOOOOOM!!
WHA...?
AG.

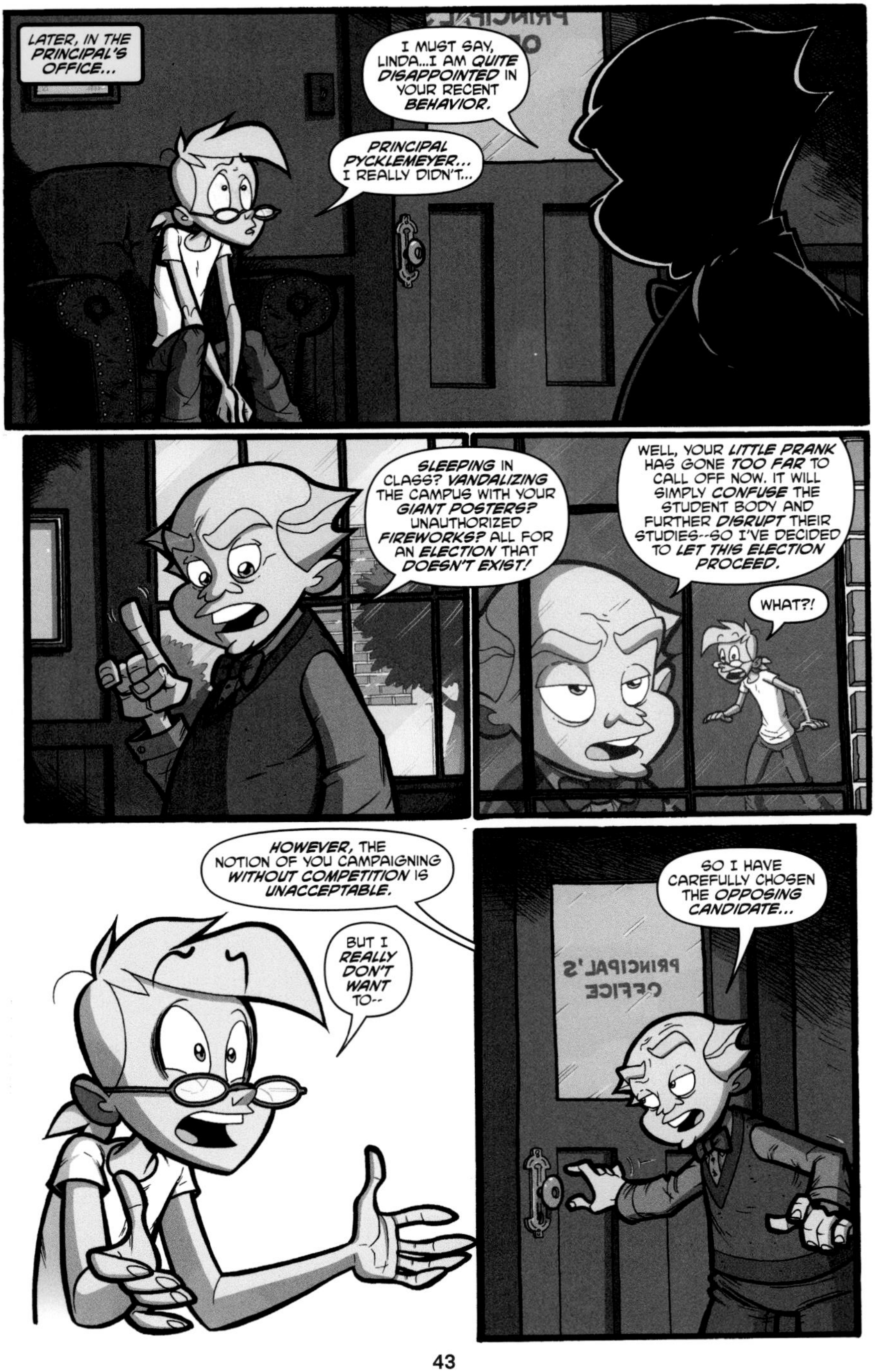

LATER, IN THE PRINCIPAL'S OFFICE...
I MUST SAY, LINDA...I AM QUITE DISAPPOINTED IN YOUR RECENT BEHAVIOR.
PRINCIPAL PYCKLEMEYER... I REALLY DIDN'T...
SLEEPING IN CLASS? VANDALIZING THE CAMPUS WITH YOUR GIANT POSTERS? UNAUTHORIZED FIREWORKS? ALL FOR AN ELECTION THAT DOESN'T EXIST!
WELL, YOUR LITTLE PRANK HAS GONE TOO FAR TO CALL OFF NOW. IT WILL SIMPLY CONFUSE THE STUDENT BODY AND FURTHER DISRUPT THEIR STUDIES--SO I'VE DECIDED TO LET THIS ELECTION PROCEED.
WHAT?!
HOWEVER, THE NOTION OF YOU CAMPAIGNING WITHOUT COMPETITION IS UNACCEPTABLE.
BUT I REALLY DON'T WANT TO--
SO I HAVE CAREFULLY CHOSEN THE OPPOSING CANDIDATE...

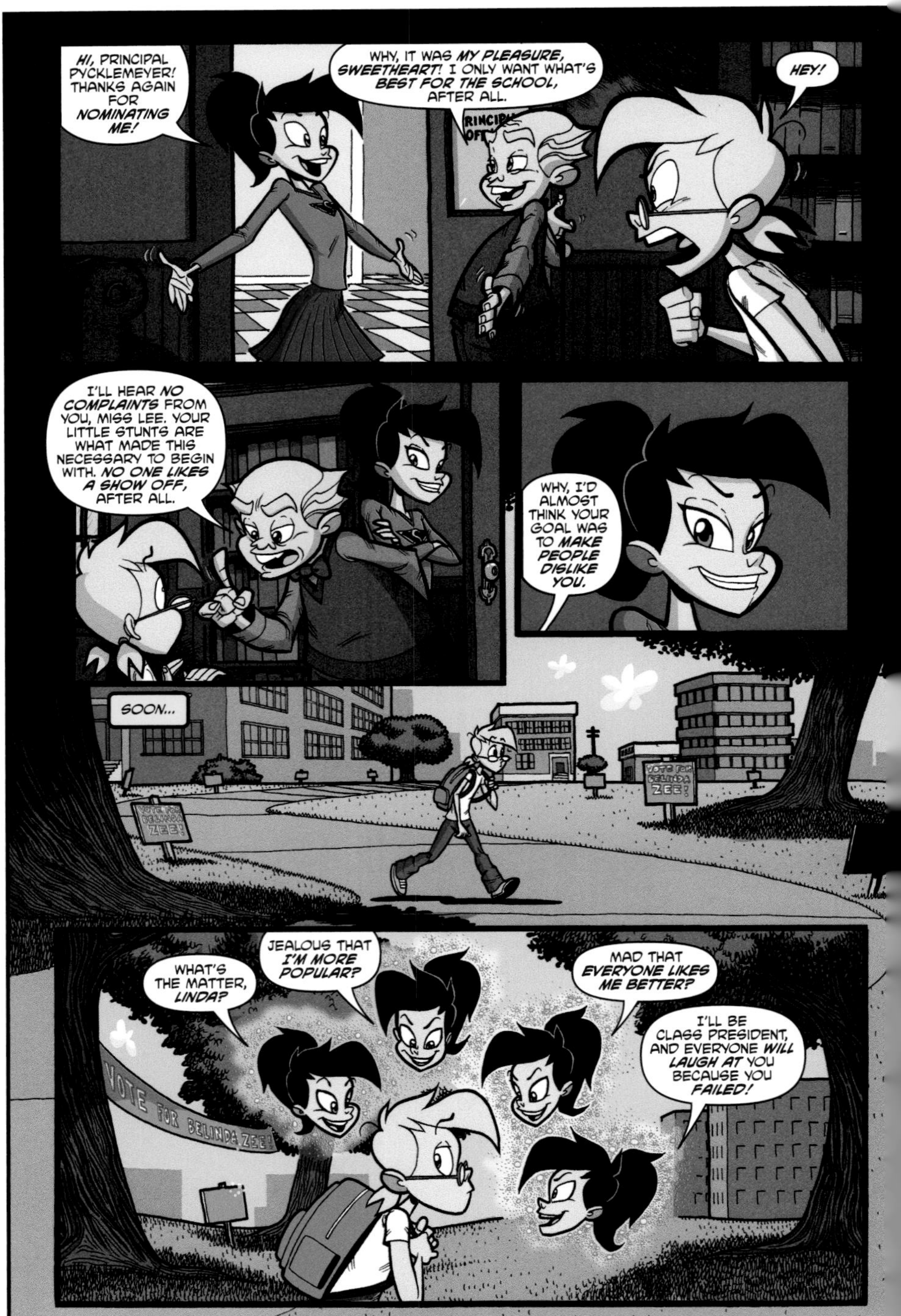
HI, PRINCIPAL PYCKLEMEYER! THANKS AGAIN FOR NOMINATING ME!
WHY, IT WAS MY PLEASURE, SWEETHEART! I ONLY WANT WHAT'S BEST FOR THE SCHOOL, AFTER ALL.
HEY!
I'LL HEAR NO COMPLAINTS FROM YOU, MISS LEE. YOUR LITTLE STUNTS ARE WHAT MADE THIS NECESSARY TO BEGIN WITH. NO ONE LIKES A SHOW OFF, AFTER ALL.
WHY, I'D ALMOST THINK YOUR GOAL WAS TO MAKE PEOPLE DISLIKE YOU.
SOON...
VOTE FOR BELINDA ZEE!
VOTE FOR BELINDA ZEE!
WHAT'S THE MATTER, LINDA?
JEALOUS THAT I'M MORE POPULAR?
MAD THAT EVERYONE LIKES ME BETTER?
I'LL BE CLASS PRESIDENT, AND EVERYONE WILL LAUGH AT YOU BECAUSE YOU FAILED!
VOTE FOR BELINDA ZEE!

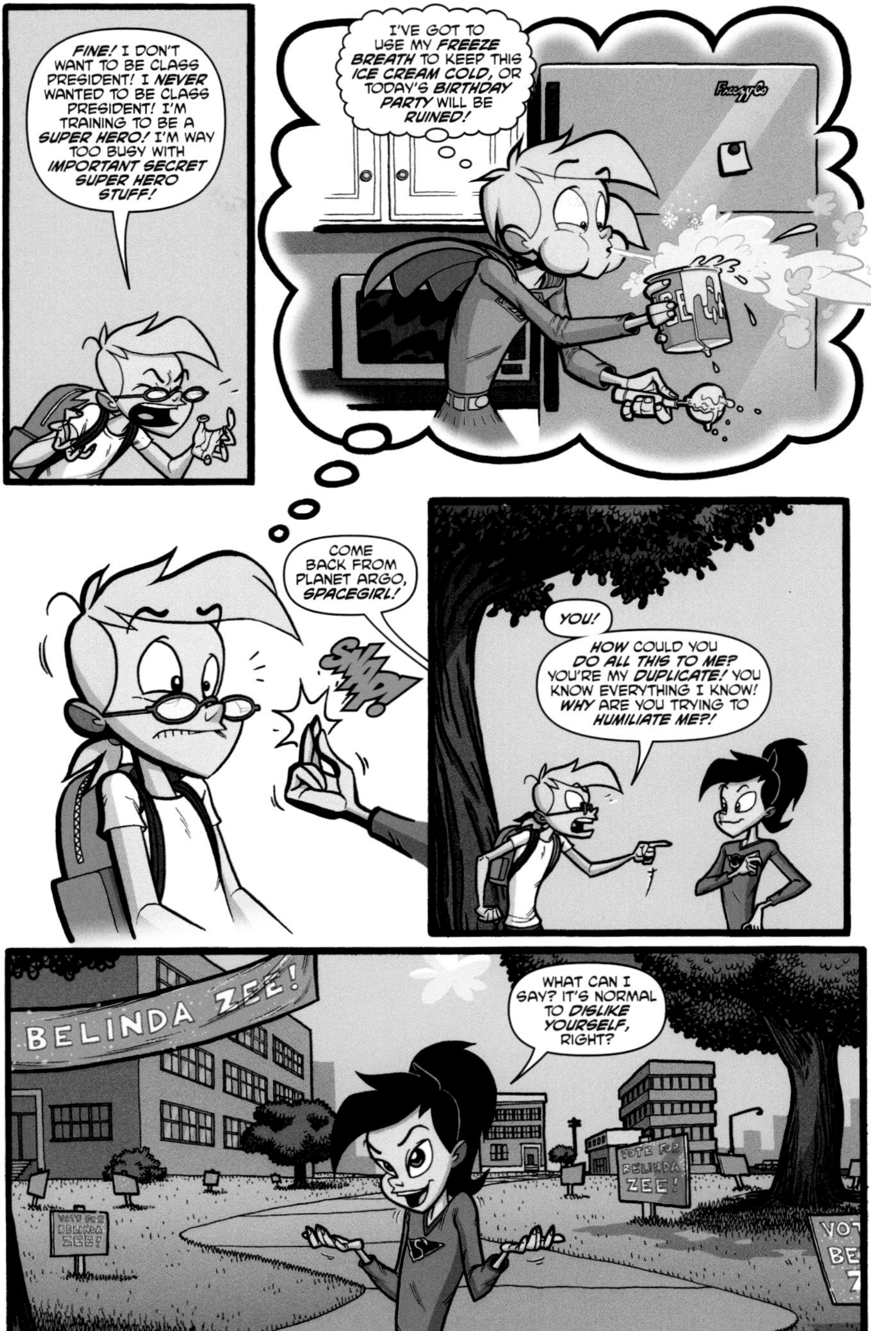
FINE! I DON'T WANT TO BE CLASS PRESIDENT! I NEVER WANTED TO BE CLASS PRESIDENT! I'M TRAINING TO BE A SUPER HERO! I'M WAY TOO BUSY WITH IMPORTANT SECRET SUPER HERO STUFF!
I'VE GOT TO USE MY FREEZE BREATH TO KEEP THIS ICE CREAM COLD, OR TODAY'S BIRTHDAY PARTY WILL BE RUINED!
COME BACK FROM PLANET ARGO, SPACEGIRL!
SNAP!
YOU!
HOW COULD YOU DO ALL THIS TO ME? YOU'RE MY DUPLICATE! YOU KNOW EVERYTHING I KNOW! WHY ARE YOU TRYING TO HUMILIATE ME?!
BELINDA ZEE!
WHAT CAN I SAY? IT'S NORMAL TO DISLIKE YOURSELF, RIGHT?
VOTE FOR BELINDA ZEE!
VOTE FOR BELINDA ZEE!

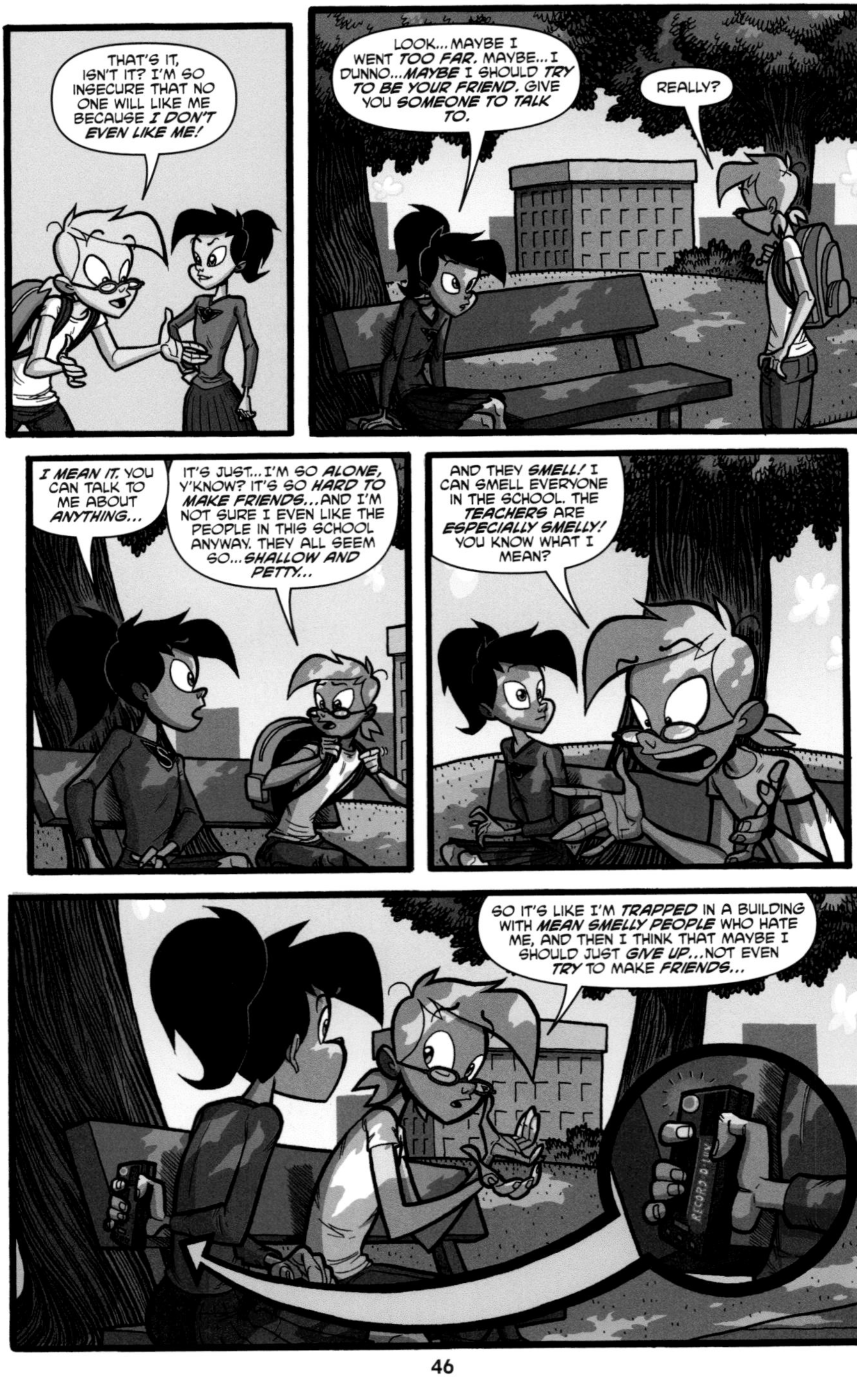
THAT'S IT, ISN'T IT? I'M SO INSECURE THAT NO ONE WILL LIKE ME BECAUSE *I DON'T EVEN LIKE ME!*
LOOK... MAYBE I WENT *TOO FAR.* MAYBE... I DUNNO... *MAYBE* I SHOULD *TRY TO BE YOUR FRIEND.* GIVE YOU *SOMEONE TO TALK TO.*
REALLY?
I MEAN IT. YOU CAN TALK TO ME ABOUT *ANYTHING...*
IT'S JUST... I'M SO *ALONE,* Y'KNOW? IT'S SO *HARD TO MAKE FRIENDS...* AND I'M NOT SURE I EVEN LIKE THE PEOPLE IN THIS SCHOOL ANYWAY. THEY ALL SEEM SO... *SHALLOW AND PETTY...*
AND THEY *SMELL!* I CAN SMELL EVERYONE IN THE SCHOOL. THE *TEACHERS* ARE *ESPECIALLY SMELLY!* YOU KNOW WHAT I MEAN?
SO IT'S LIKE I'M *TRAPPED* IN A BUILDING WITH *MEAN SMELLY PEOPLE* WHO HATE ME, AND THEN I THINK THAT MAYBE I SHOULD JUST *GIVE UP...* NOT EVEN *TRY* TO MAKE *FRIENDS...*

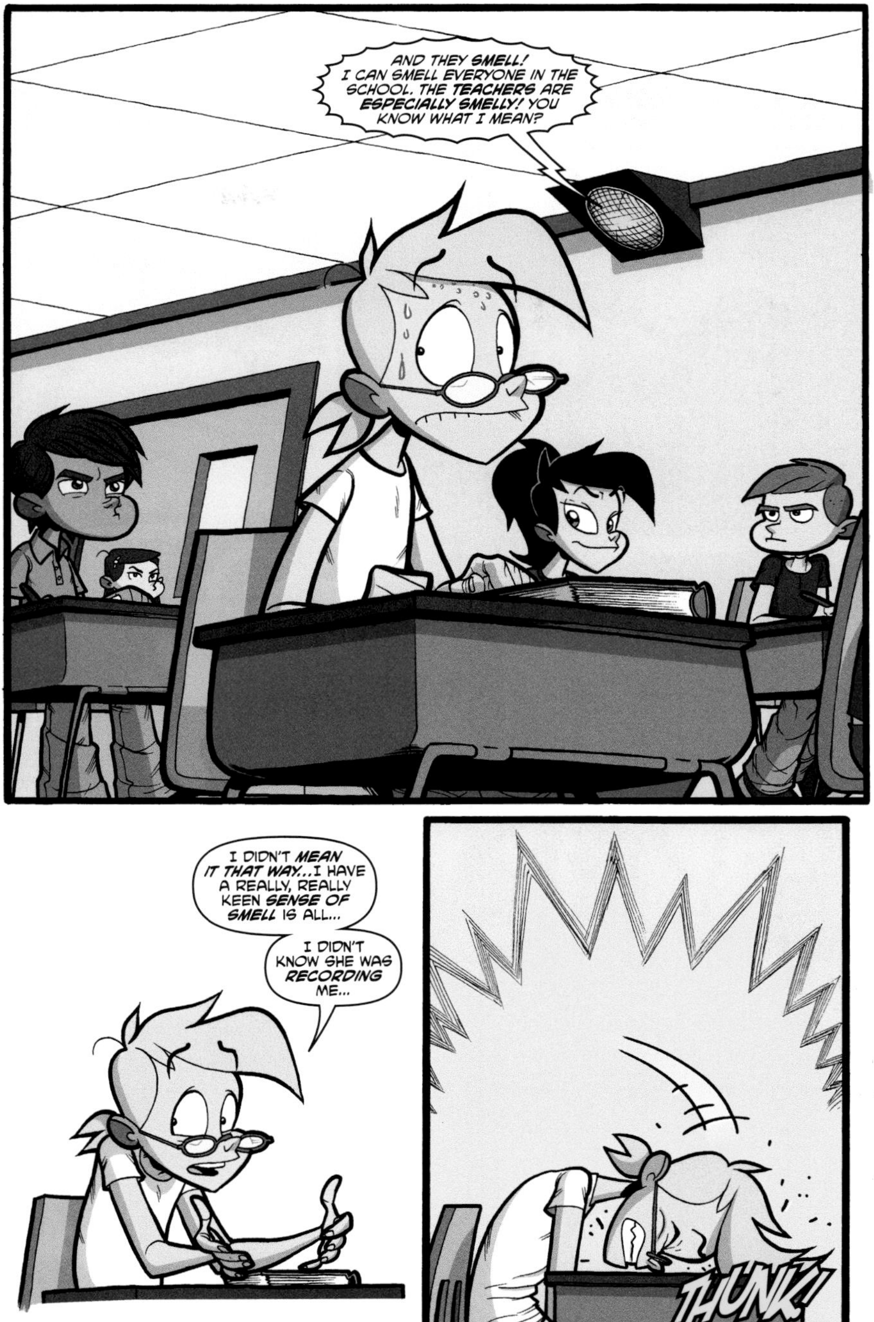
AND THEY SMELL! I CAN SMELL EVERYONE IN THE SCHOOL. THE TEACHERS ARE ESPECIALLY SMELLY! YOU KNOW WHAT I MEAN?
I DIDN'T MEAN IT THAT WAY...I HAVE A REALLY, REALLY KEEN SENSE OF SMELL IS ALL...
I DIDN'T KNOW SHE WAS RECORDING ME...
THUNK!

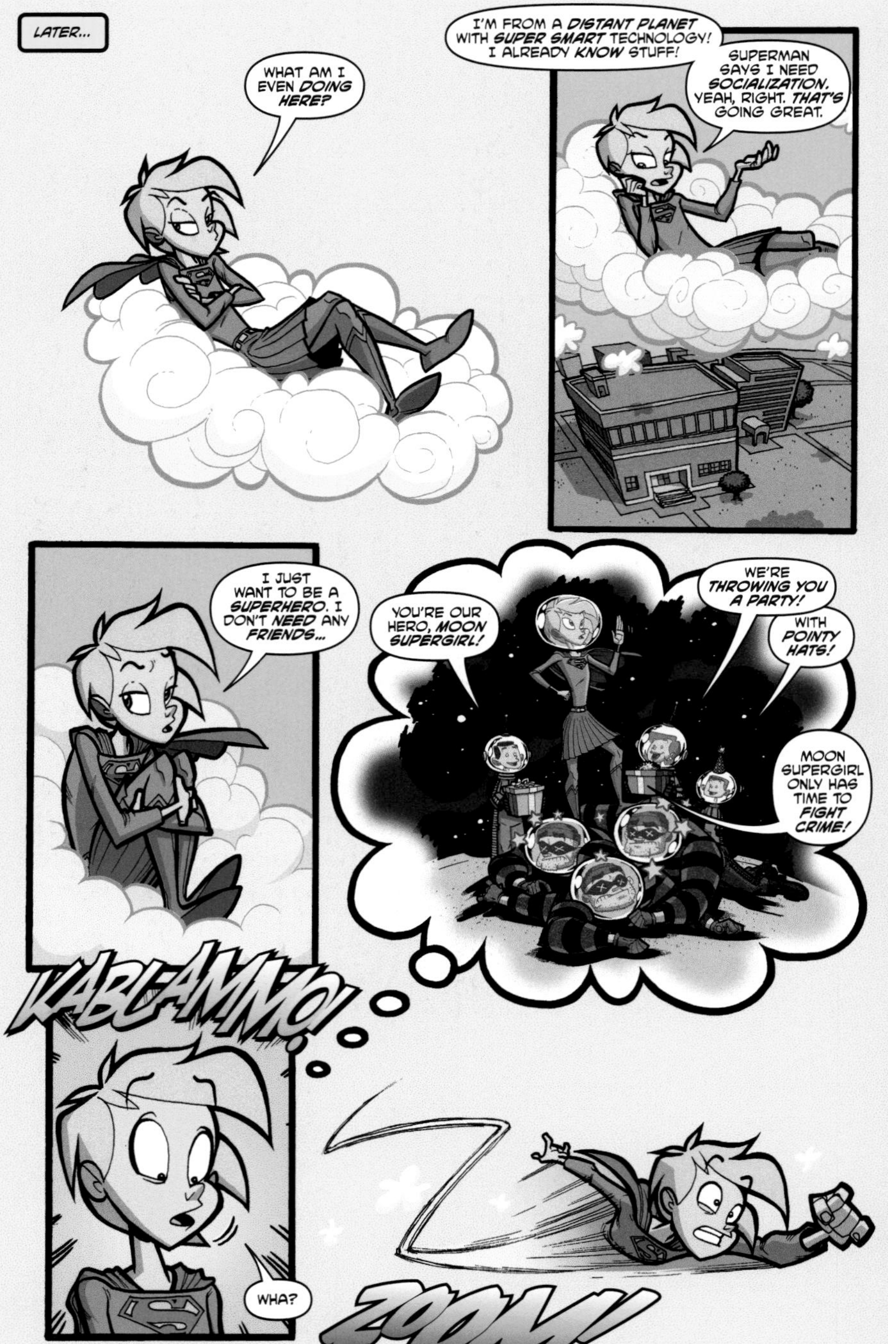
LATER...
WHAT AM I EVEN DOING HERE?
I'M FROM A DISTANT PLANET WITH SUPER SMART TECHNOLOGY! I ALREADY KNOW STUFF!
SUPERMAN SAYS I NEED SOCIALIZATION. YEAH, RIGHT. THAT'S GOING GREAT.
I JUST WANT TO BE A SUPERHERO. I DON'T NEED ANY FRIENDS...
YOU'RE OUR HERO, MOON SUPERGIRL!
WE'RE THROWING YOU A PARTY!
WITH POINTY HATS!
MOON SUPERGIRL ONLY HAS TIME TO FIGHT CRIME!
KABLAMMO!
WHA?
ZOOM!

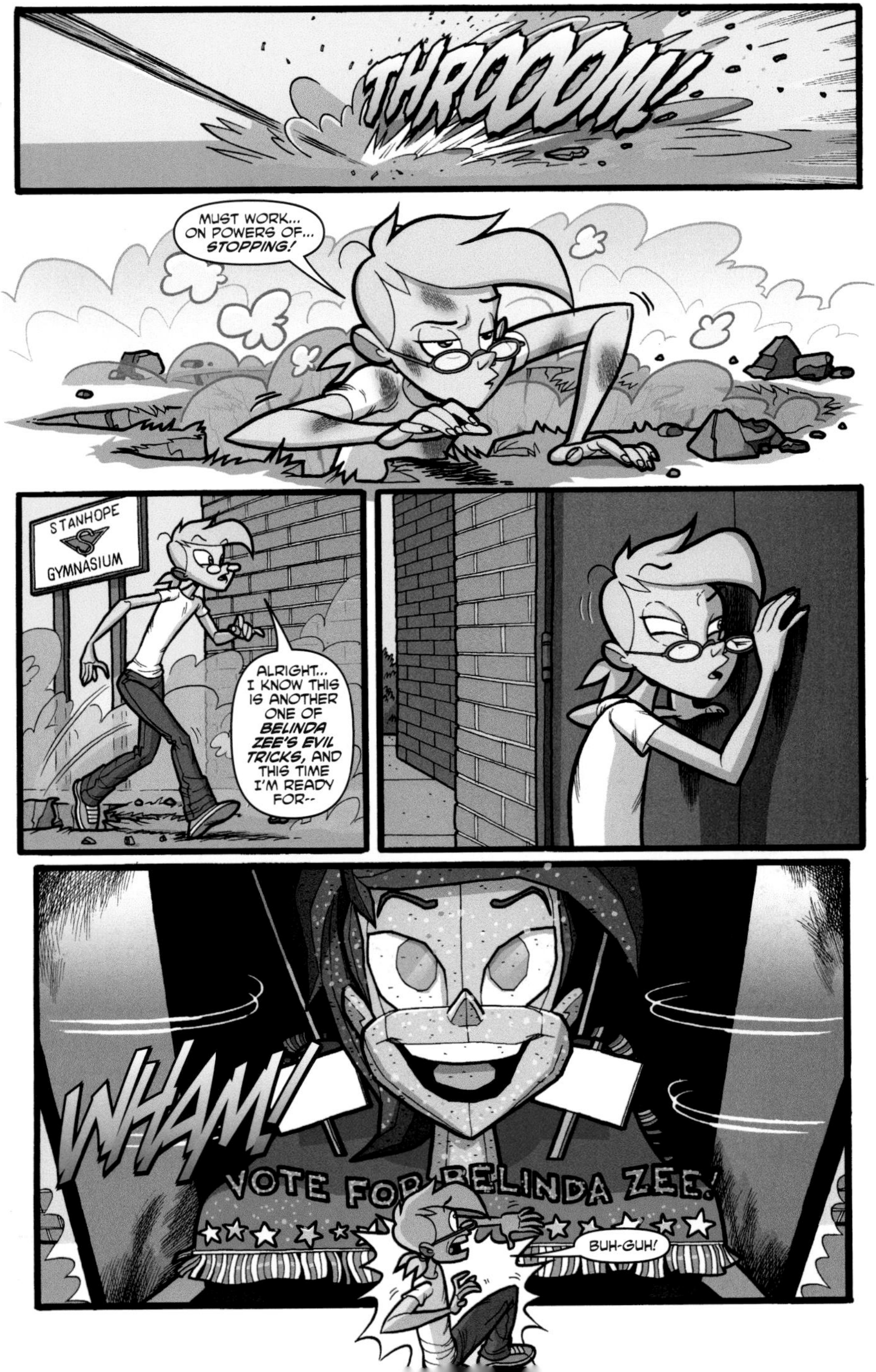
THROOOOM!
MUST WORK... ON POWERS OF... STOPPING!
STANHOPE GYMNASIUM
ALRIGHT... I KNOW THIS IS ANOTHER ONE OF BELINDA ZEE'S EVIL TRICKS, AND THIS TIME I'M READY FOR--
WHAM!
VOTE FOR BELINDA ZEE!
BUH-GUH!

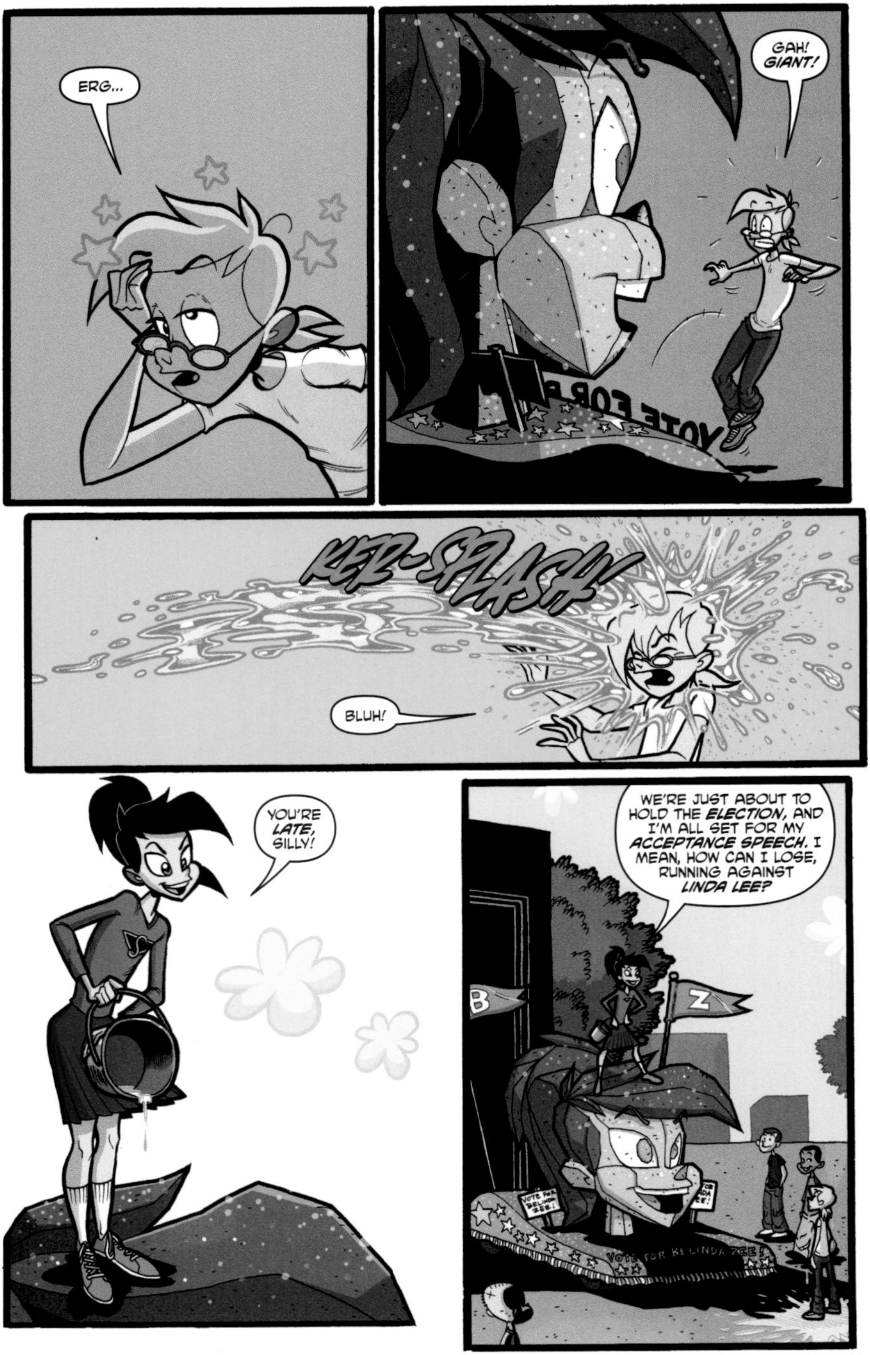
ERG...
GAH! GIANT!
KER-SPLASH!
BLUH!
YOU'RE LATE, SILLY!
WE'RE JUST ABOUT TO HOLD THE ELECTION, AND I'M ALL SET FOR MY ACCEPTANCE SPEECH. I MEAN, HOW CAN I LOSE, RUNNING AGAINST LINDA LEE?
B
Z
VOTE FOR BELINDA ZEE!

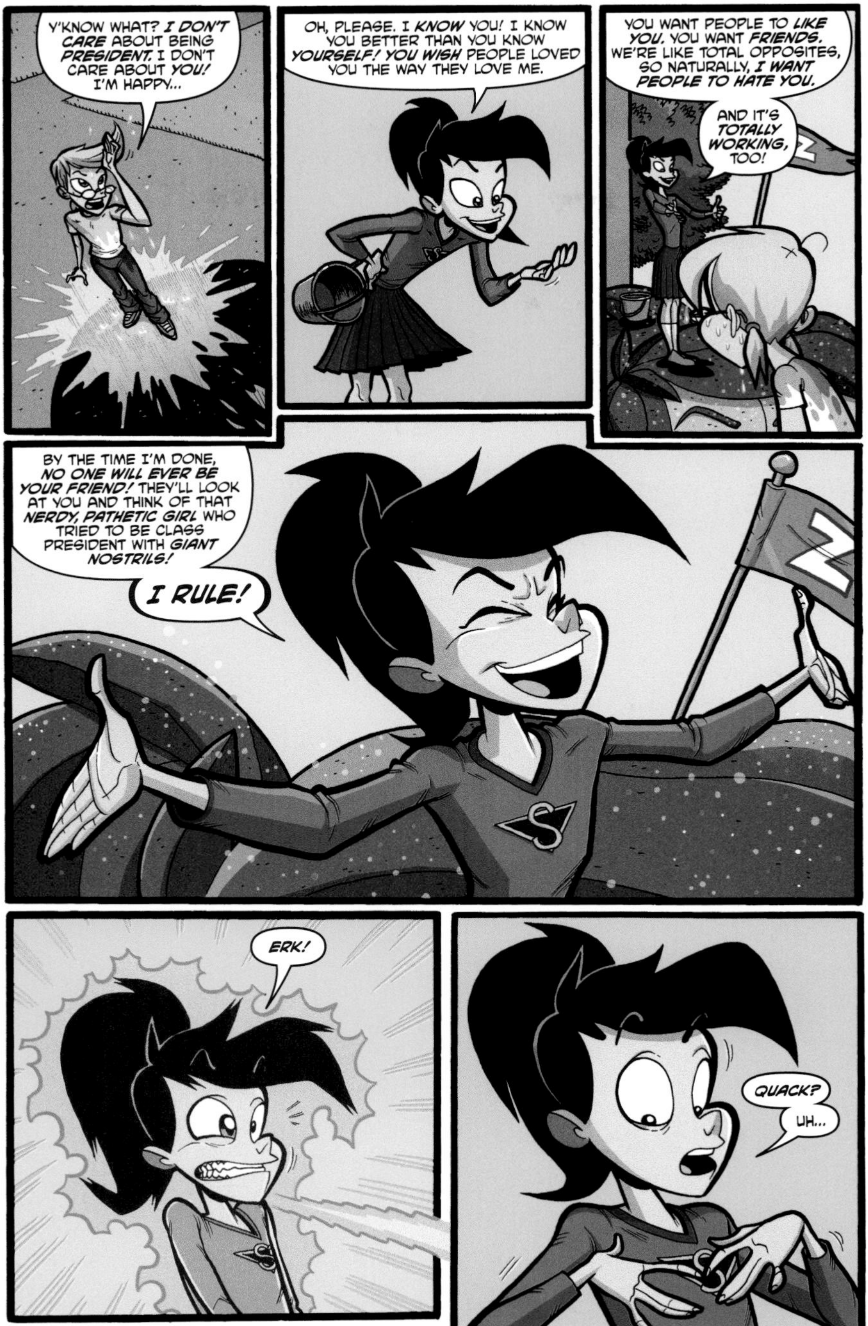
Y'KNOW WHAT? I DON'T CARE ABOUT BEING PRESIDENT. I DON'T CARE ABOUT YOU! I'M HAPPY...
OH, PLEASE. I KNOW YOU! I KNOW YOU BETTER THAN YOU KNOW YOURSELF! YOU WISH PEOPLE LOVED YOU THE WAY THEY LOVE ME.
YOU WANT PEOPLE TO LIKE YOU. YOU WANT FRIENDS. WE'RE LIKE TOTAL OPPOSITES, SO NATURALLY, I WANT PEOPLE TO HATE YOU.
AND IT'S TOTALLY WORKING, TOO!
BY THE TIME I'M DONE, NO ONE WILL EVER BE YOUR FRIEND! THEY'LL LOOK AT YOU AND THINK OF THAT NERDY, PATHETIC GIRL WHO TRIED TO BE CLASS PRESIDENT WITH GIANT NOSTRILS!
I RULE!
ERK!
QUACK?
UH...

QUACK! QUACK! QUACK!

QUACK!

QUACK!

QUACK!

'E FOR
ELINDA
ZEE?

BELINDA
ZEE #1!

VOTE FOR BELINDA ZEE!

OKAY. THE PLANET EARTH *OFFICIALLY SCARES ME.*

THAT'S A *WEIRD THING TO SAY.*

UH...IT'S AN EXPRESSION FROM...*KANSAS.* MY VERY *NORMAL* HOMETOWN.

AH.

DO YOU KNOW WHY EVERYONE THINKS THEY'RE *DUCKS?*

YEAH...UH. THAT WAS SORTA *MY FAULT.* I BUILT THIS *MIND CONTROL HELMET THING* BUT IT DOESN'T WORK RIGHT. IT MAKES PEOPLE *THINK THEY'RE DUCKS.*

I'M LENA. *LENA THORUL.*

I'M LINDA. *LINDA LEE.*

YEAH, I KNOW. WE'RE IN *SCIENCE* TOGETHER. AND I SAW THE *GIANT SCARY POSTER* OF YOU IN THE HALL.

THAT'S KINDA WHY I BUILT THE *MIND-CONTROL-ACCIDENTAL-DUCK MACHINE.*

EVERYONE WAS BEING *REALLY MEAN TO YOU,* ESPECIALLY THAT *CHEERLEADER* GIRL. AND *WE'RE BOTH NEW* HERE, AND I THOUGHT MAYBE WE *SHOULD BE FRIENDS,* AND IF YOU WERE GOING TO BE MY FRIEND, I DIDN'T WANT PEOPLE BEING MEAN TO YOU.

OH.

SO I BUILT THIS. I'M A LITTLE BIT OF A *SCIENCE TECH NERD.*

SO DO YOU WANNA BE *FRIENDS?*

UM... *YEAH,* YEAH, I DO.

WILL THEY ALL *STOP BEING DUCKS?*

I THINK SO. *MAYBE.*

LATER...

This has been the craziest week.

I'm not really popular. It's hard to fit in to this culture. No one really liked me much at first.

I made my first super enemy. An evil doppelganger of me. She's a cheerleader, and really popular, and a jerk.

But now I have a new best friend. She's kinda nerdy (in a good way) and she likes helping people like me, and we even managed to get into the same dorm room.

Send

From: LINDA LEE
To: SUPERMAN
Subject: The usual ramblings...

This has been the craziest week. I'm really popular. It's hard to fit in to this liked me much ... enemy. An evil She's a cheerle d a je

For the first time, I feel like I'll be okay on this planet. Anyway, I hope you visit soon.

Love, Linda.

KLICK

This has been the craziest week. I'm not really popular. It's hard to fit in to this culture. No one really liked me much at first. I made my first super enemy. An evil doppelganger of me. She's a cheerleader, and really popular, and a jerk.

I finally feel settled in.

The school is kinda weird. Science class is too easy, and the teachers are dumb.

But I have a best friend now. You'd like her. She's not at all like the regular people of Metropolis.

53

I wish I could come visit you in prison. But I know we have to watch out for that stupid Superman until the time is right. I can't tell you how much I hate him for making my big brother out to be a criminal.

Anyway, you take care and thanks again for sending me here to the Stanhope Boarding School. I miss you.

Love, Lena.

Send:

From: LENA THORUL

To: LEX LUTHOR

Subject: re:Revenge!!!!

I wish I could come visit prison. But I know we have watch out for that stupid Superman until the time is r I can't tell you how much I h him for making my big bro to be a criminal.

Anyway, you take care and again for sending me here Stanhope Boarding School. I miss you.

Love, Lena.

KLIK

NIGHT, LENA.

NIGHT, LINDA.

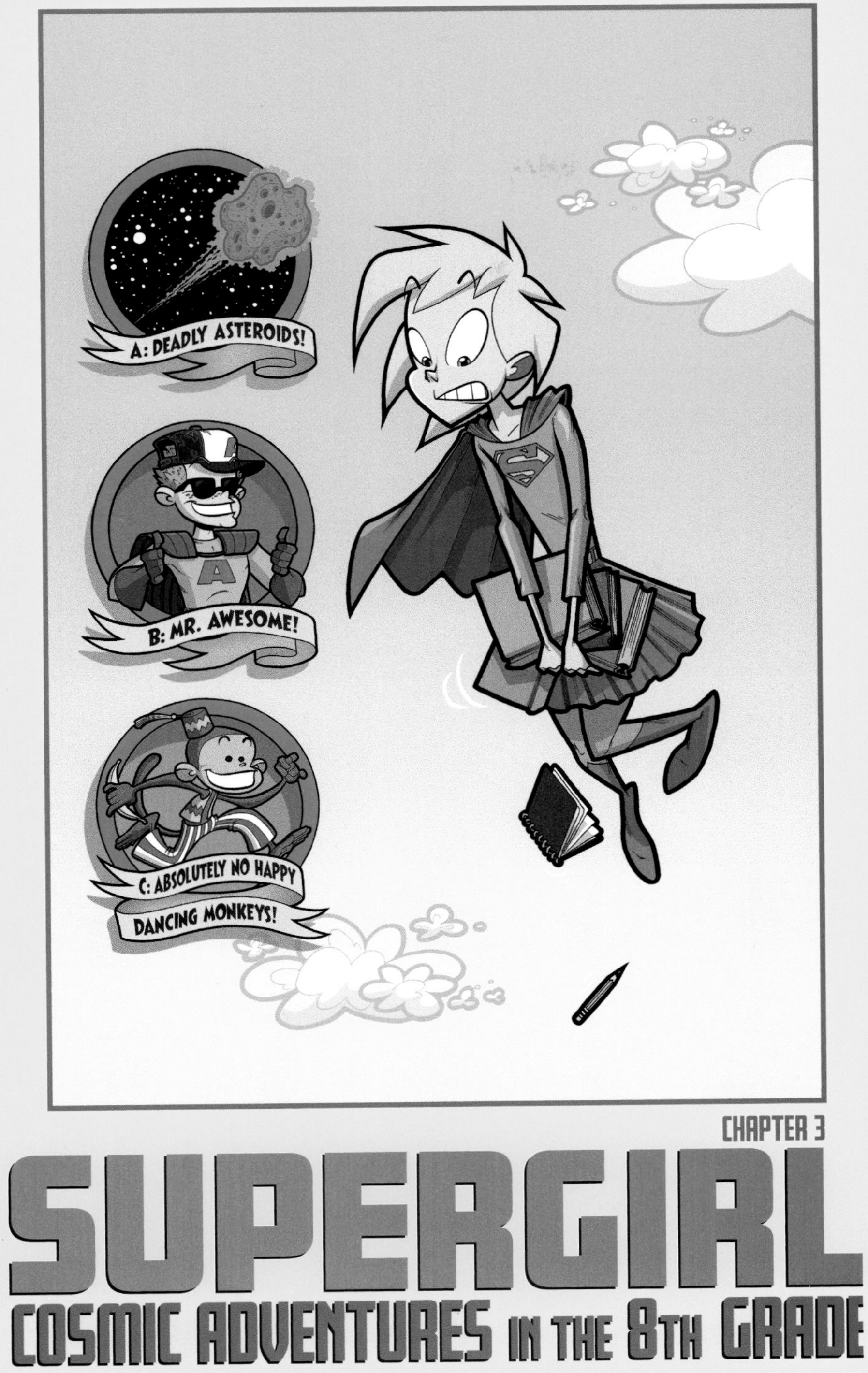
A: DEADLY ASTEROIDS!
B: MR. AWESOME!
C: ABSOLUTELY NO HAPPY
DANCING MONKEYS!

CHAPTER 3

SUPERGIRL
COSMIC ADVENTURES IN THE 8TH GRADE

SUPERGIRL

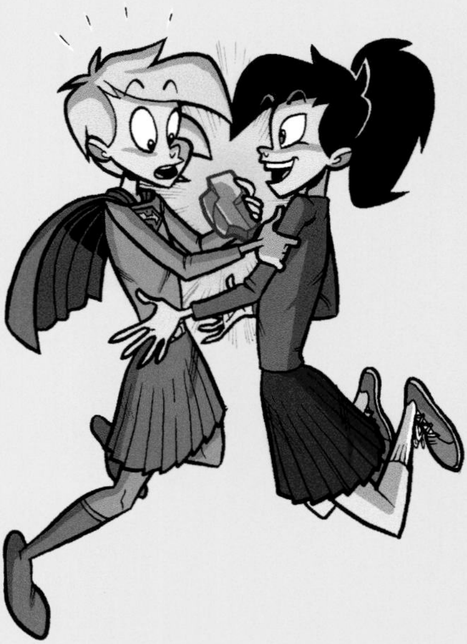

PART 1: LOOK! UP IN THE SKY!

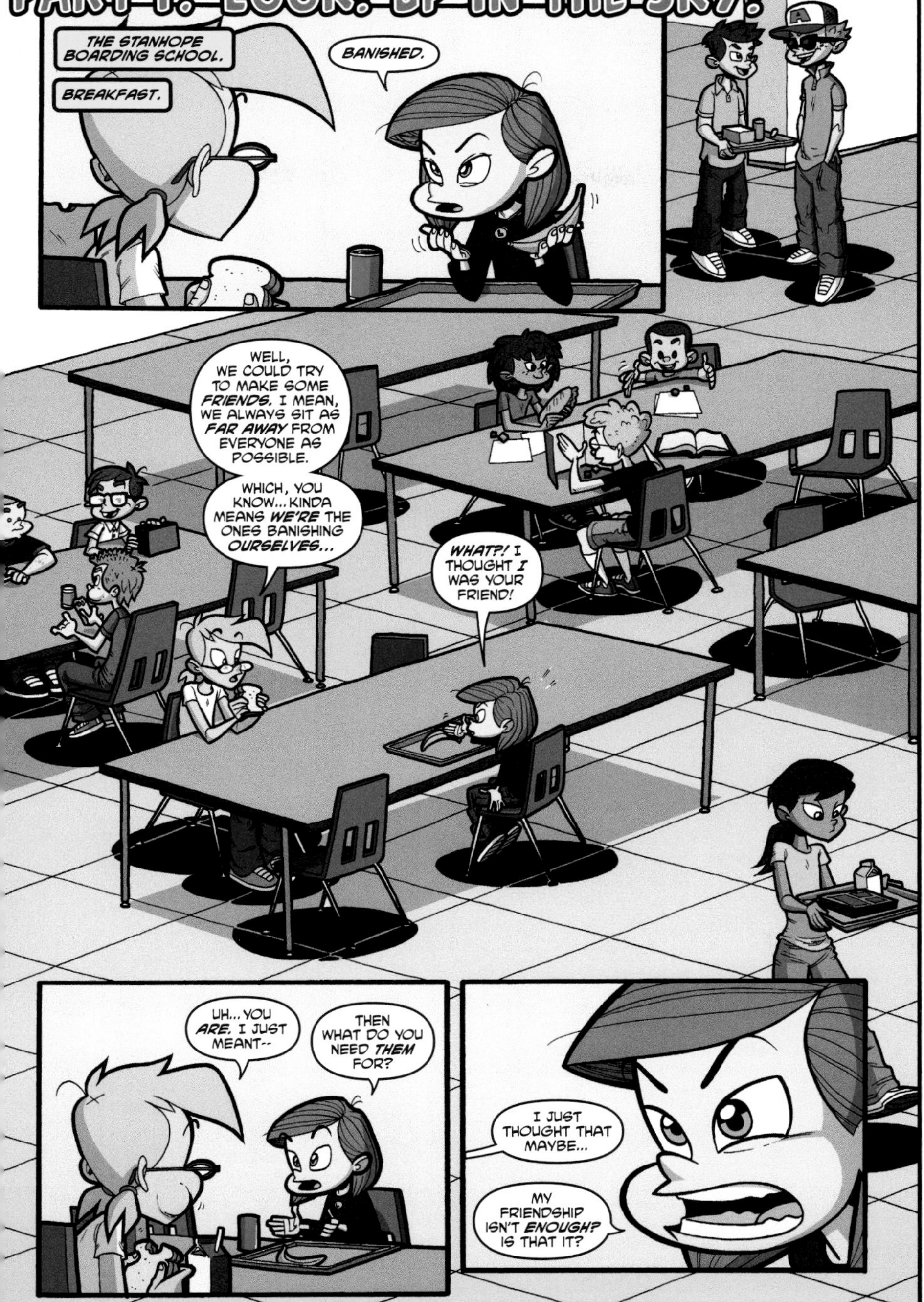
THE STANHOPE BOARDING SCHOOL.
BREAKFAST.
BANISHED.
WELL, WE COULD TRY TO MAKE SOME FRIENDS. I MEAN, WE ALWAYS SIT AS FAR AWAY FROM EVERYONE AS POSSIBLE.
WHICH, YOU KNOW... KINDA MEANS WE'RE THE ONES BANISHING OURSELVES...
WHAT?! I THOUGHT I WAS YOUR FRIEND!
UH... YOU ARE. I JUST MEANT--
THEN WHAT DO YOU NEED THEM FOR?
I JUST THOUGHT THAT MAYBE...
MY FRIENDSHIP ISN'T ENOUGH? IS THAT IT?

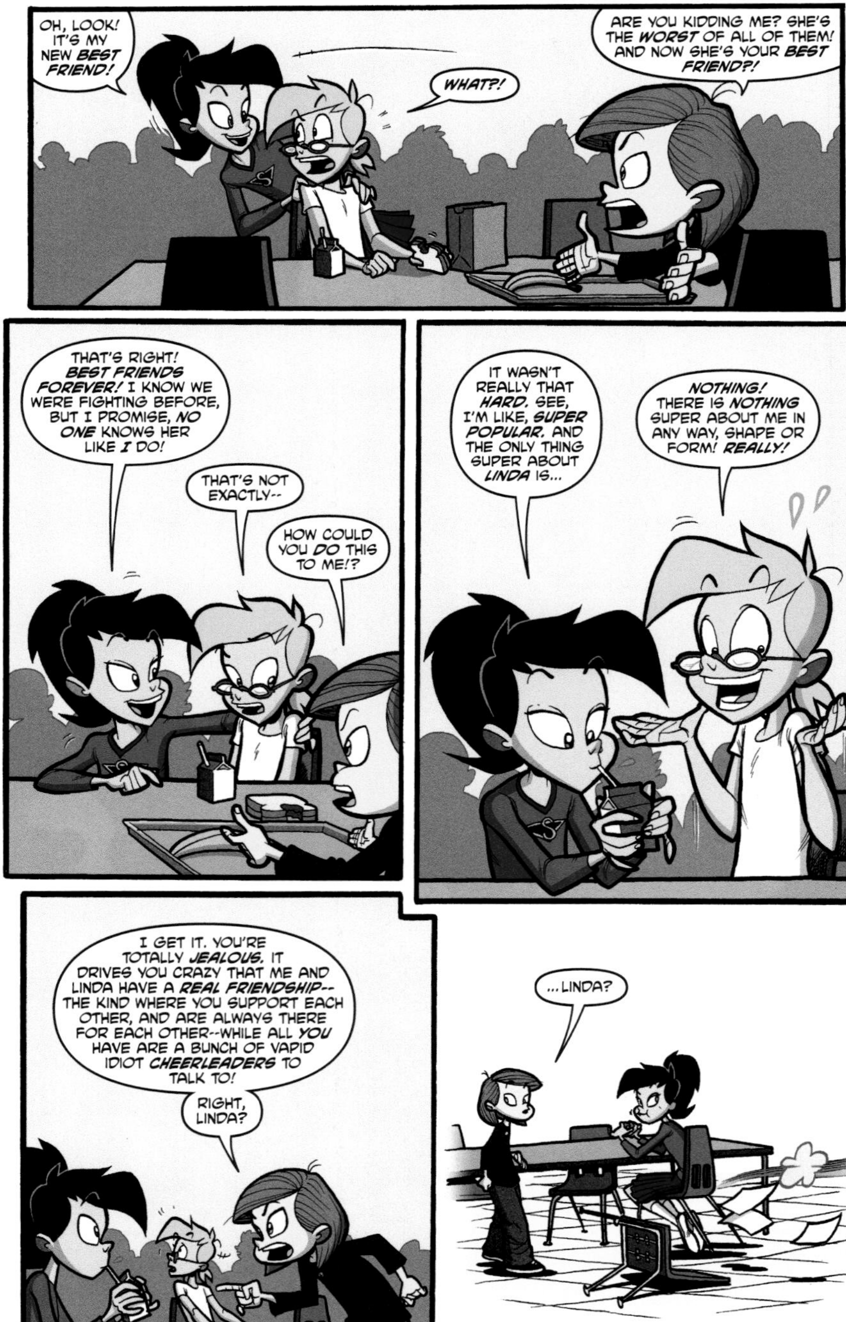
OH, LOOK! IT'S MY NEW *BEST FRIEND!*
WHAT?!
ARE YOU KIDDING ME? SHE'S THE *WORST* OF ALL OF THEM! AND NOW SHE'S YOUR *BEST FRIEND?!*
THAT'S RIGHT! *BEST FRIENDS FOREVER!* I KNOW WE WERE FIGHTING BEFORE, BUT I PROMISE, *NO ONE* KNOWS HER LIKE *I* DO!
THAT'S NOT EXACTLY--
HOW COULD YOU *DO* THIS TO ME!?
IT WASN'T REALLY THAT *HARD.* SEE, I'M LIKE, *SUPER POPULAR.* AND THE ONLY THING SUPER ABOUT *LINDA* IS...
NOTHING! THERE IS *NOTHING* SUPER ABOUT ME IN ANY WAY, SHAPE OR FORM! *REALLY!*
I GET IT. YOU'RE TOTALLY *JEALOUS.* IT DRIVES YOU CRAZY THAT ME AND LINDA HAVE A *REAL FRIENDSHIP*-- THE KIND WHERE YOU SUPPORT EACH OTHER, AND ARE ALWAYS THERE FOR EACH OTHER--WHILE ALL *YOU* HAVE ARE A BUNCH OF VAPID IDIOT *CHEERLEADERS* TO TALK TO!
RIGHT, LINDA?
...LINDA?

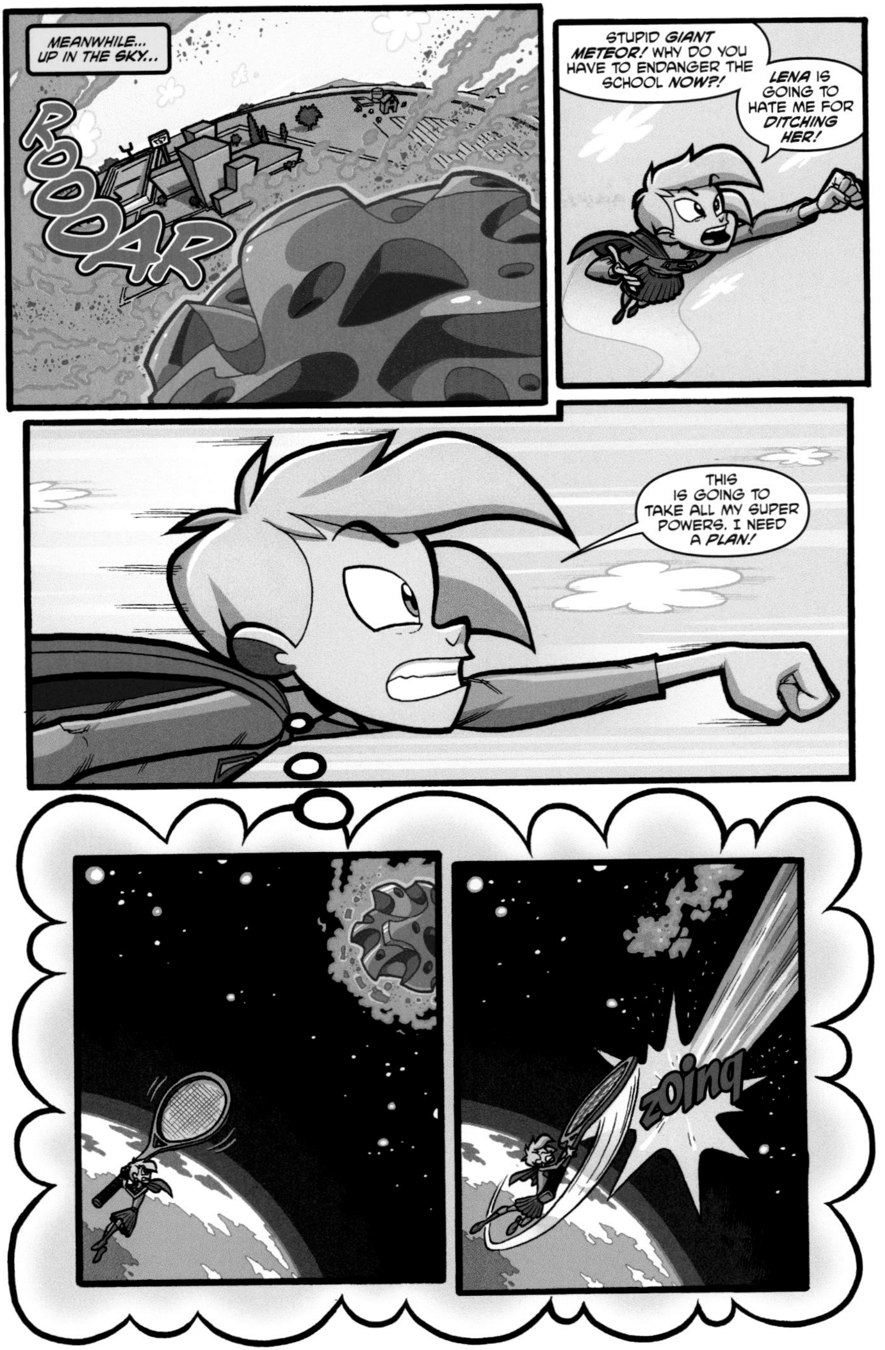
MEANWHILE... UP IN THE SKY...
ROOOAR
STUPID GIANT METEOR! WHY DO YOU HAVE TO ENDANGER THE SCHOOL NOW?!
LENA IS GOING TO HATE ME FOR DITCHING HER!
THIS IS GOING TO TAKE ALL MY SUPER POWERS. I NEED A PLAN!
zoing

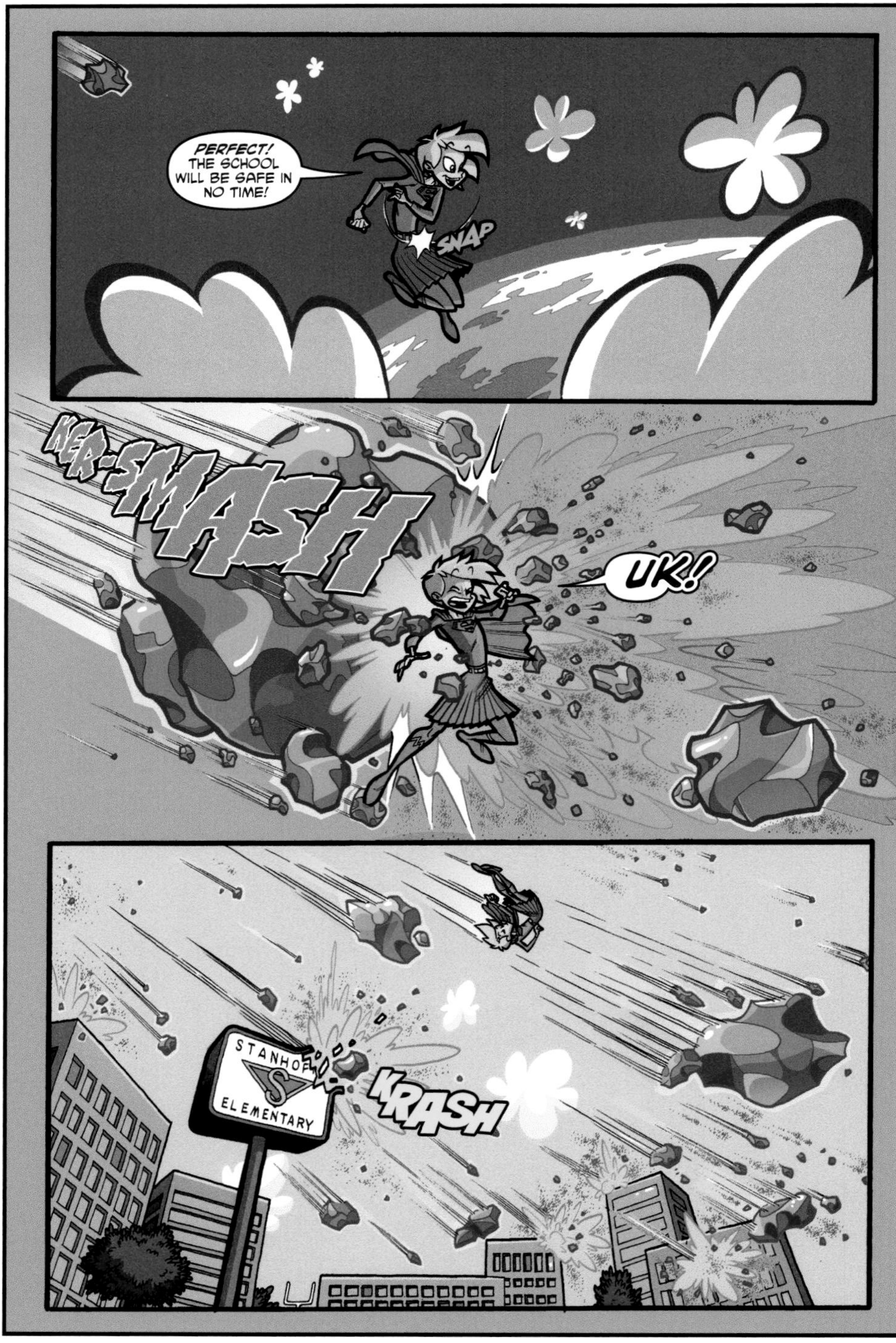
PERFECT! THE SCHOOL WILL BE SAFE IN NO TIME!
SNAP
KER-SMASH
UK!
STANHOP
S
ELEMENTARY
KRASH

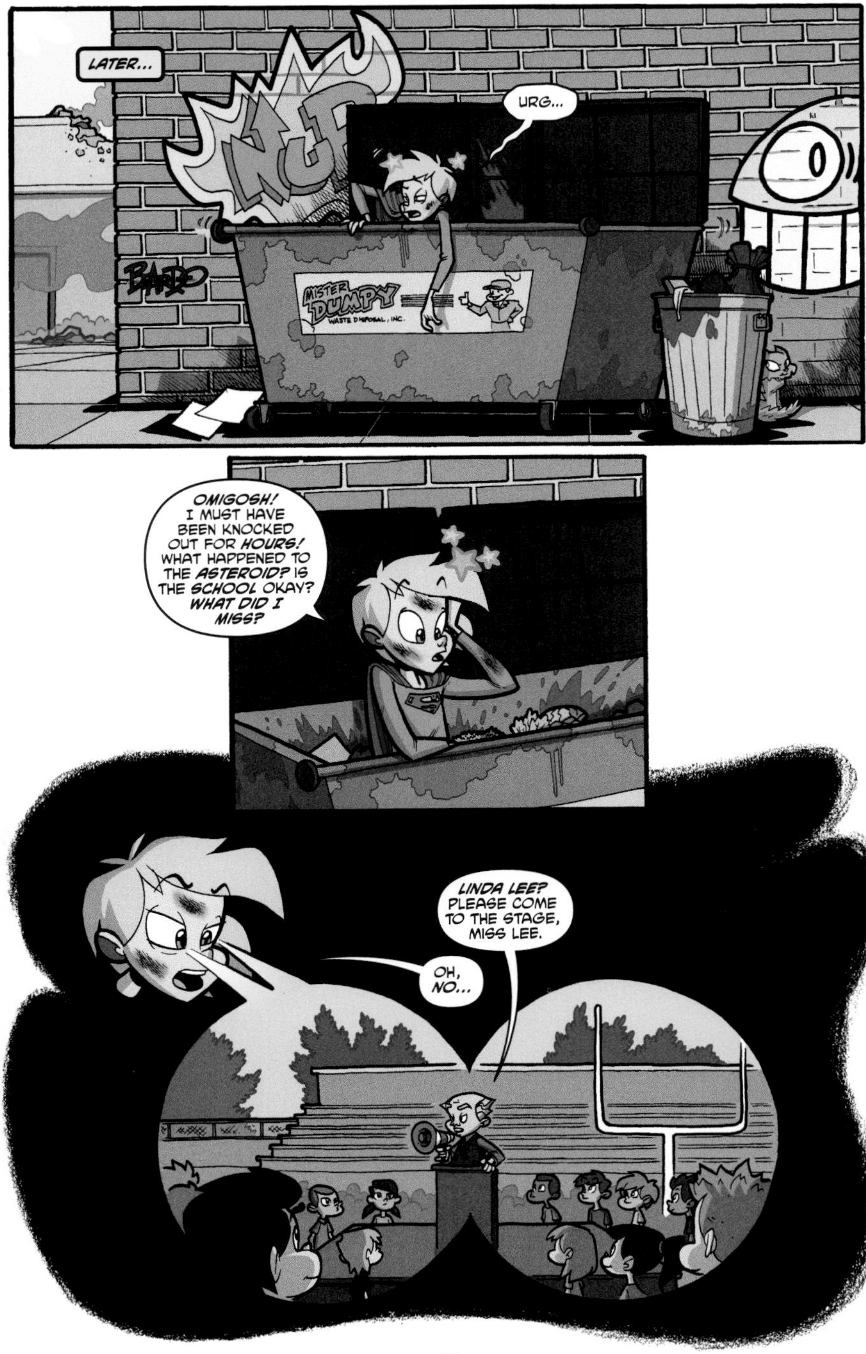
LATER...
NUF
URG...
MISTER DUMPY WASTE DISPOSAL, INC.
BARDO
OMIGOSH! I MUST HAVE BEEN KNOCKED OUT FOR HOURS! WHAT HAPPENED TO THE ASTEROID? IS THE SCHOOL OKAY? WHAT DID I MISS?
LINDA LEE? PLEASE COME TO THE STAGE, MISS LEE.
OH, NO...

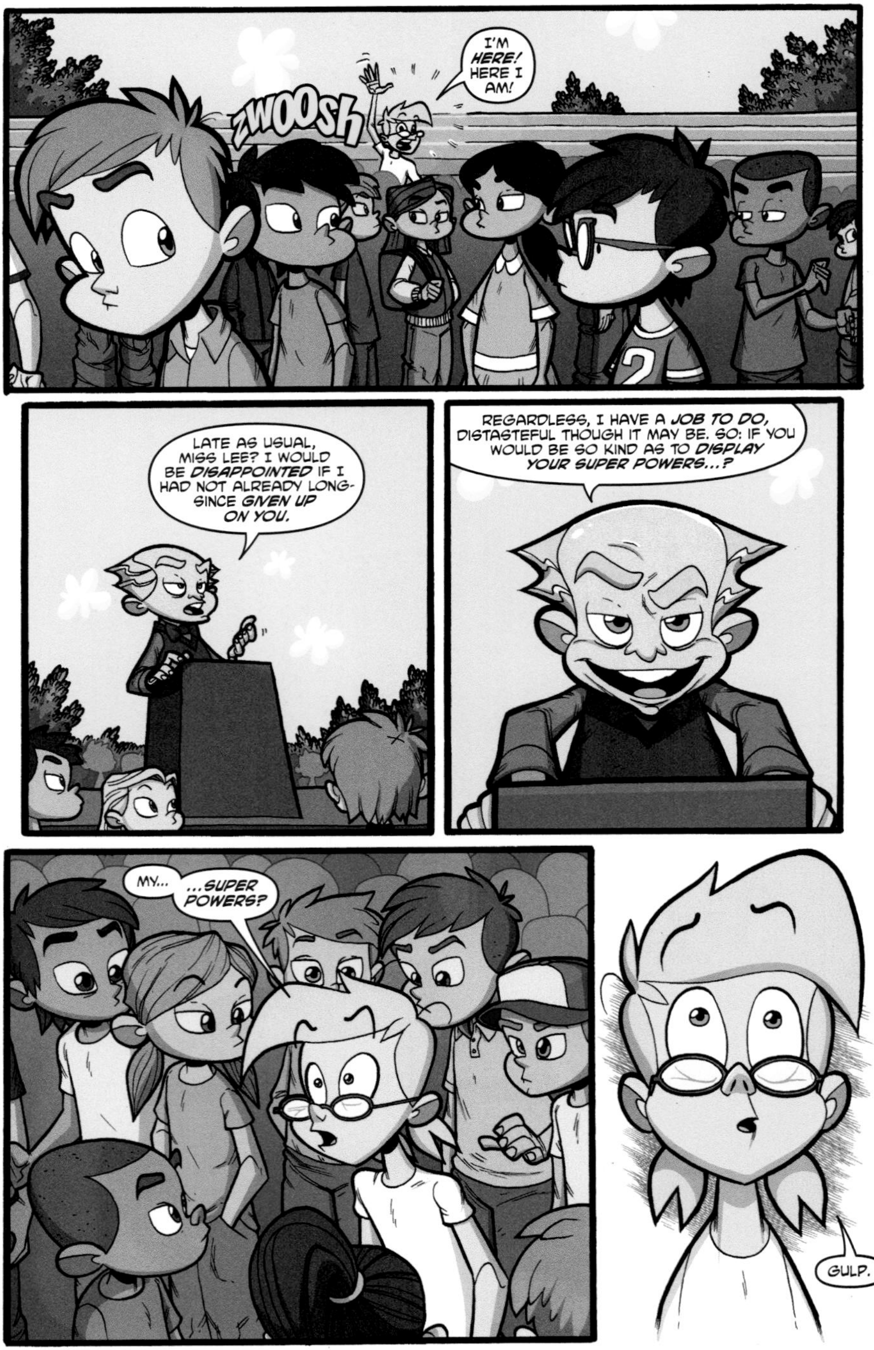

ZWOOSH
I'M HERE! HERE I AM!
LATE AS USUAL, MISS LEE? I WOULD BE DISAPPOINTED IF I HAD NOT ALREADY LONG-SINCE GIVEN UP ON YOU.
REGARDLESS, I HAVE A JOB TO DO, DISTASTEFUL THOUGH IT MAY BE. SO: IF YOU WOULD BE SO KIND AS TO DISPLAY YOUR SUPER POWERS...?
MY...
...SUPER POWERS?
GULP.

PART 2: WITH GREAT POWER...

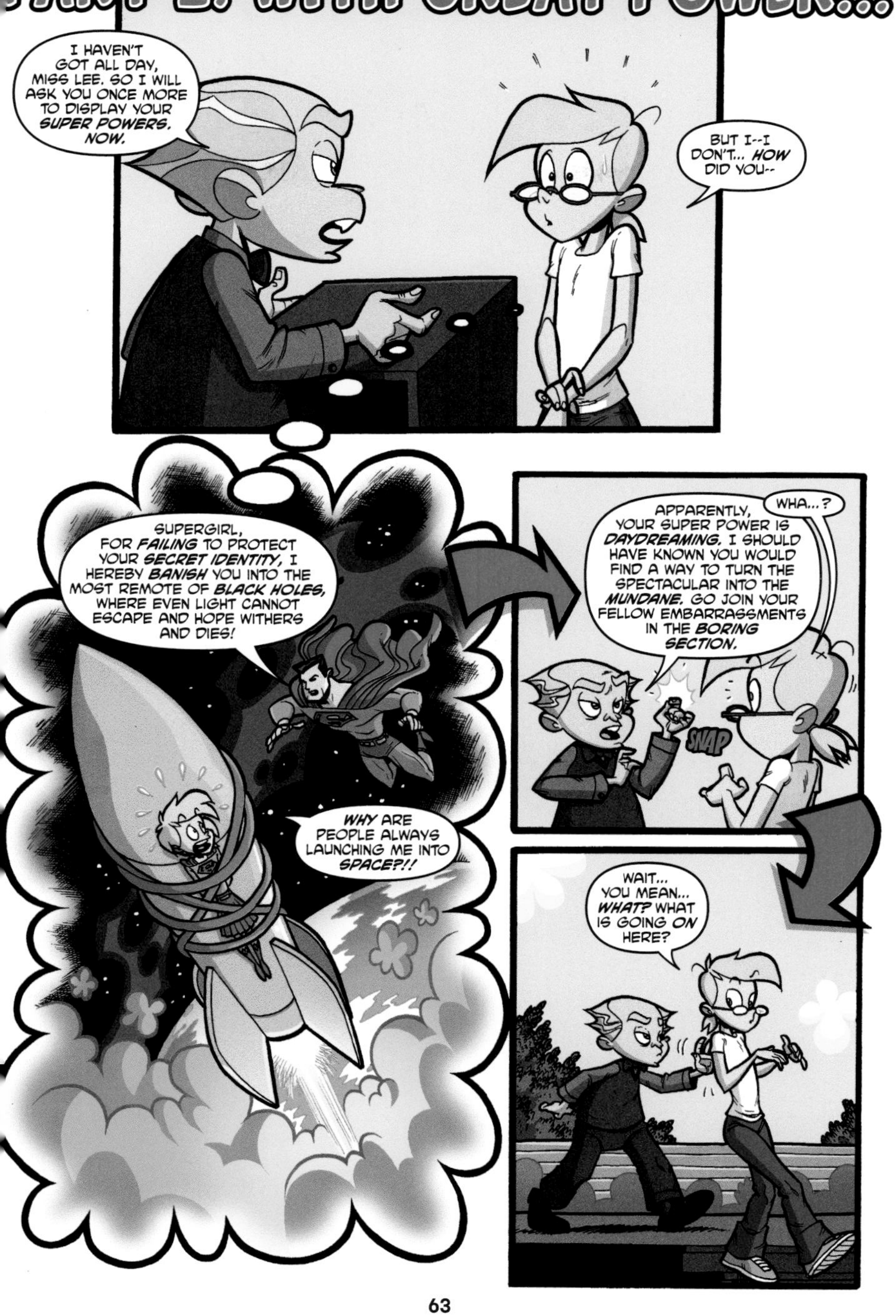
I HAVEN'T GOT ALL DAY, MISS LEE. SO I WILL ASK YOU ONCE MORE TO DISPLAY YOUR SUPER POWERS. NOW.
BUT I--I DON'T... HOW DID YOU--
SUPERGIRL, FOR FAILING TO PROTECT YOUR SECRET IDENTITY, I HEREBY BANISH YOU INTO THE MOST REMOTE OF BLACK HOLES, WHERE EVEN LIGHT CANNOT ESCAPE AND HOPE WITHERS AND DIES!
WHY ARE PEOPLE ALWAYS LAUNCHING ME INTO SPACE?!!
APPARENTLY, YOUR SUPER POWER IS DAYDREAMING. I SHOULD HAVE KNOWN YOU WOULD FIND A WAY TO TURN THE SPECTACULAR INTO THE MUNDANE. GO JOIN YOUR FELLOW EMBARRASSMENTS IN THE BORING SECTION.
WHA...?
SNAP
WAIT... YOU MEAN... WHAT? WHAT IS GOING ON HERE?

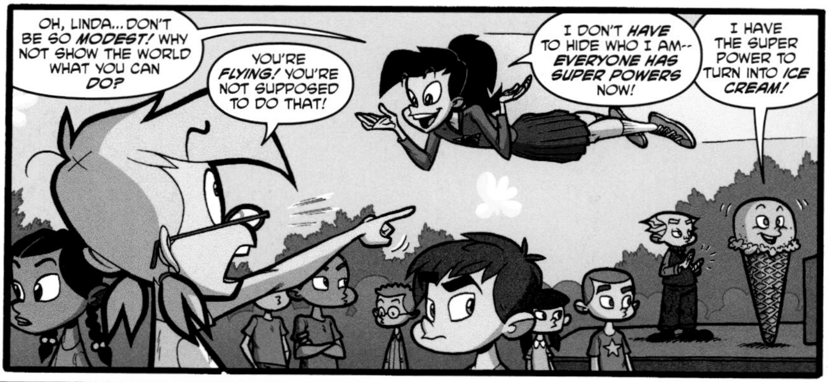
OH, LINDA... DON'T BE SO MODEST! WHY NOT SHOW THE WORLD WHAT YOU CAN DO?
YOU'RE FLYING! YOU'RE NOT SUPPOSED TO DO THAT!
I DON'T HAVE TO HIDE WHO I AM-- EVERYONE HAS SUPER POWERS NOW!
I HAVE THE SUPER POWER TO TURN INTO ICE CREAM!

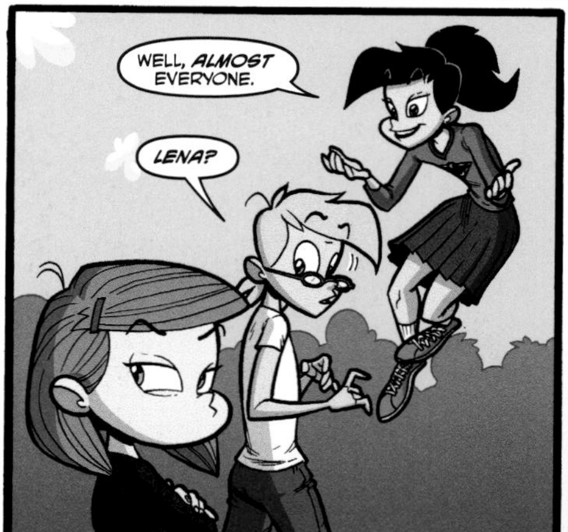
WELL, ALMOST EVERYONE.
LENA?

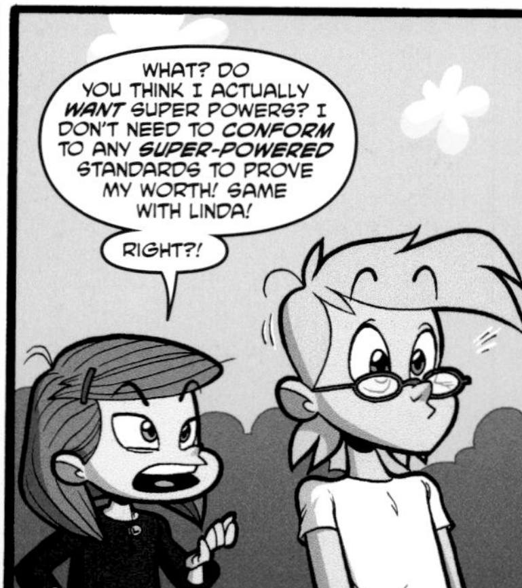
WHAT? DO YOU THINK I ACTUALLY WANT SUPER POWERS? I DON'T NEED TO CONFORM TO ANY SUPER-POWERED STANDARDS TO PROVE MY WORTH! SAME WITH LINDA!
RIGHT?!

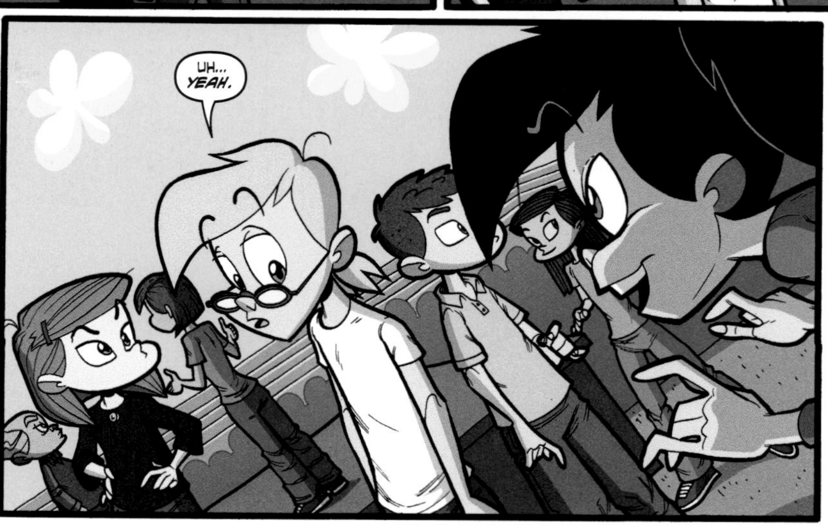
UH... YEAH.

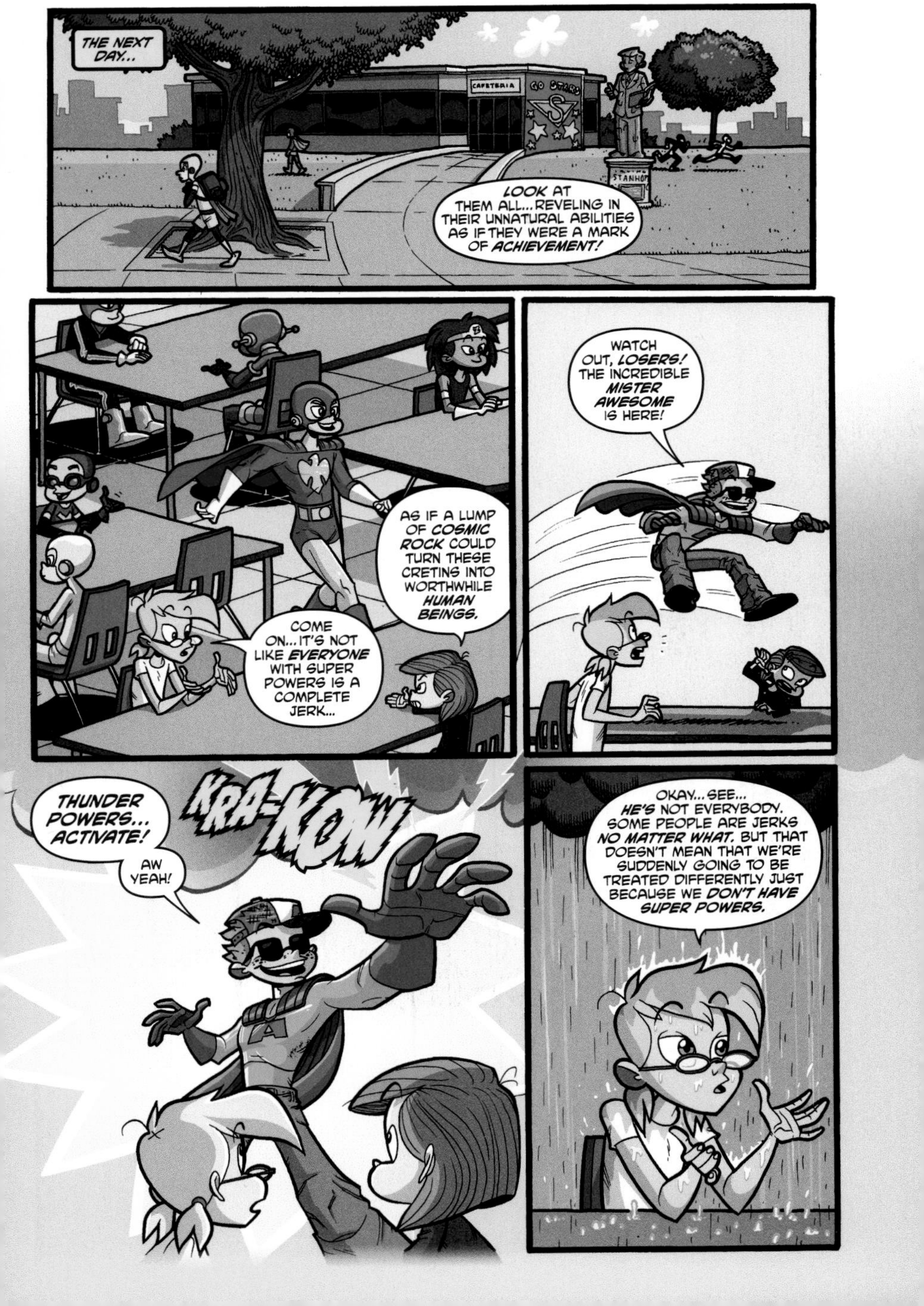

THE NEXT DAY...
CAFETERIA
GO STARS
STANHOP
LOOK AT THEM ALL... REVELING IN THEIR UNNATURAL ABILITIES AS IF THEY WERE A MARK OF ACHIEVEMENT!
AS IF A LUMP OF COSMIC ROCK COULD TURN THESE CRETINS INTO WORTHWHILE HUMAN BEINGS.
COME ON... IT'S NOT LIKE EVERYONE WITH SUPER POWERS IS A COMPLETE JERK...
WATCH OUT, LOSERS! THE INCREDIBLE MISTER AWESOME IS HERE!
THUNDER POWERS... ACTIVATE!
KRA-KOW
AW YEAH!
OKAY... SEE... HE'S NOT EVERYBODY. SOME PEOPLE ARE JERKS NO MATTER WHAT. BUT THAT DOESN'T MEAN THAT WE'RE SUDDENLY GOING TO BE TREATED DIFFERENTLY JUST BECAUSE WE DON'T HAVE SUPER POWERS.

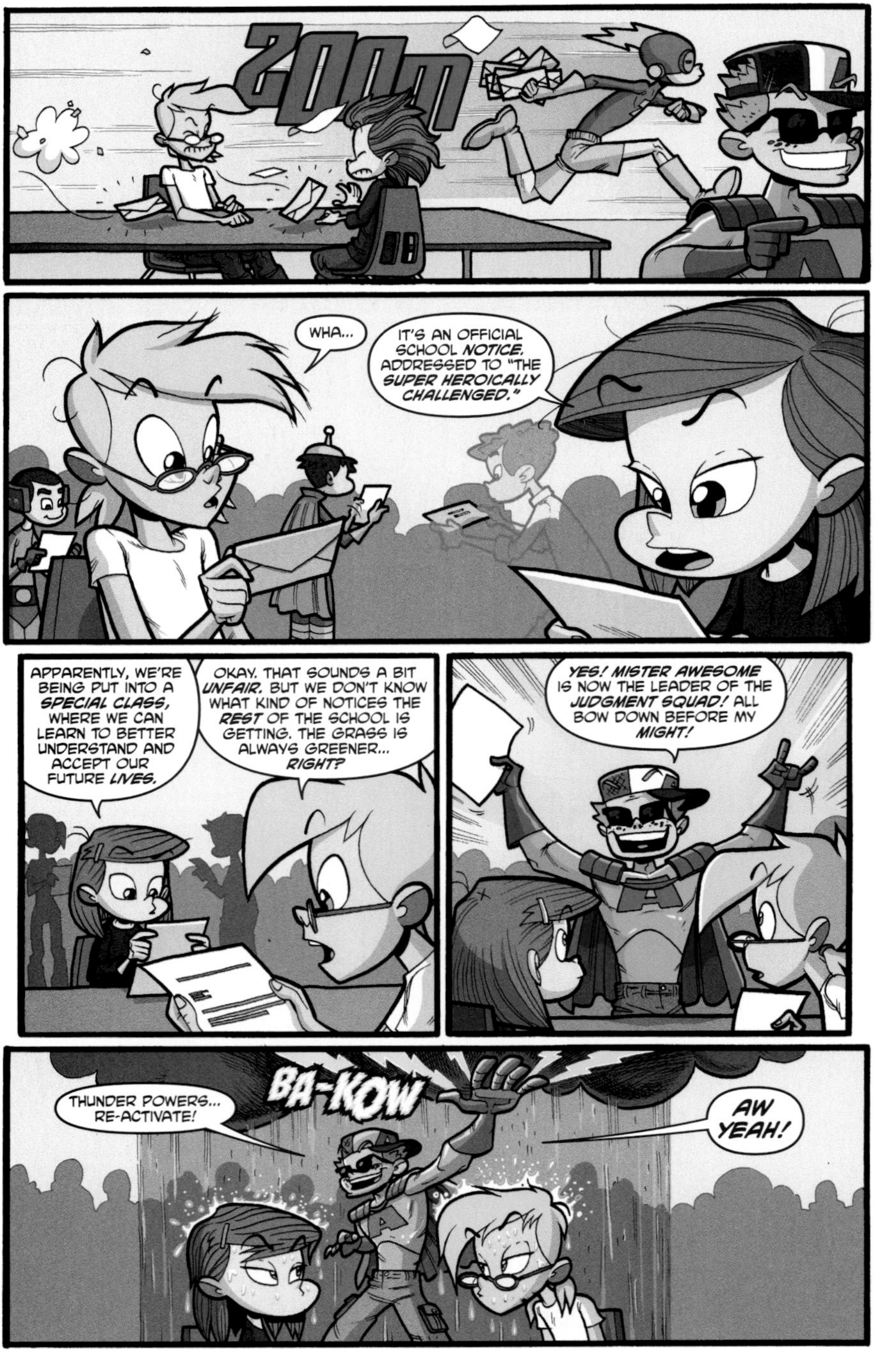
ZOOM
WHA...
IT'S AN OFFICIAL SCHOOL NOTICE. ADDRESSED TO "THE SUPER HEROICALLY CHALLENGED."
APPARENTLY, WE'RE BEING PUT INTO A SPECIAL CLASS, WHERE WE CAN LEARN TO BETTER UNDERSTAND AND ACCEPT OUR FUTURE LIVES.
OKAY. THAT SOUNDS A BIT UNFAIR. BUT WE DON'T KNOW WHAT KIND OF NOTICES THE REST OF THE SCHOOL IS GETTING. THE GRASS IS ALWAYS GREENER... RIGHT?
YES! MISTER AWESOME IS NOW THE LEADER OF THE JUDGMENT SQUAD! ALL BOW DOWN BEFORE MY MIGHT!
BA-KOW
THUNDER POWERS... RE-ACTIVATE!
AW YEAH!

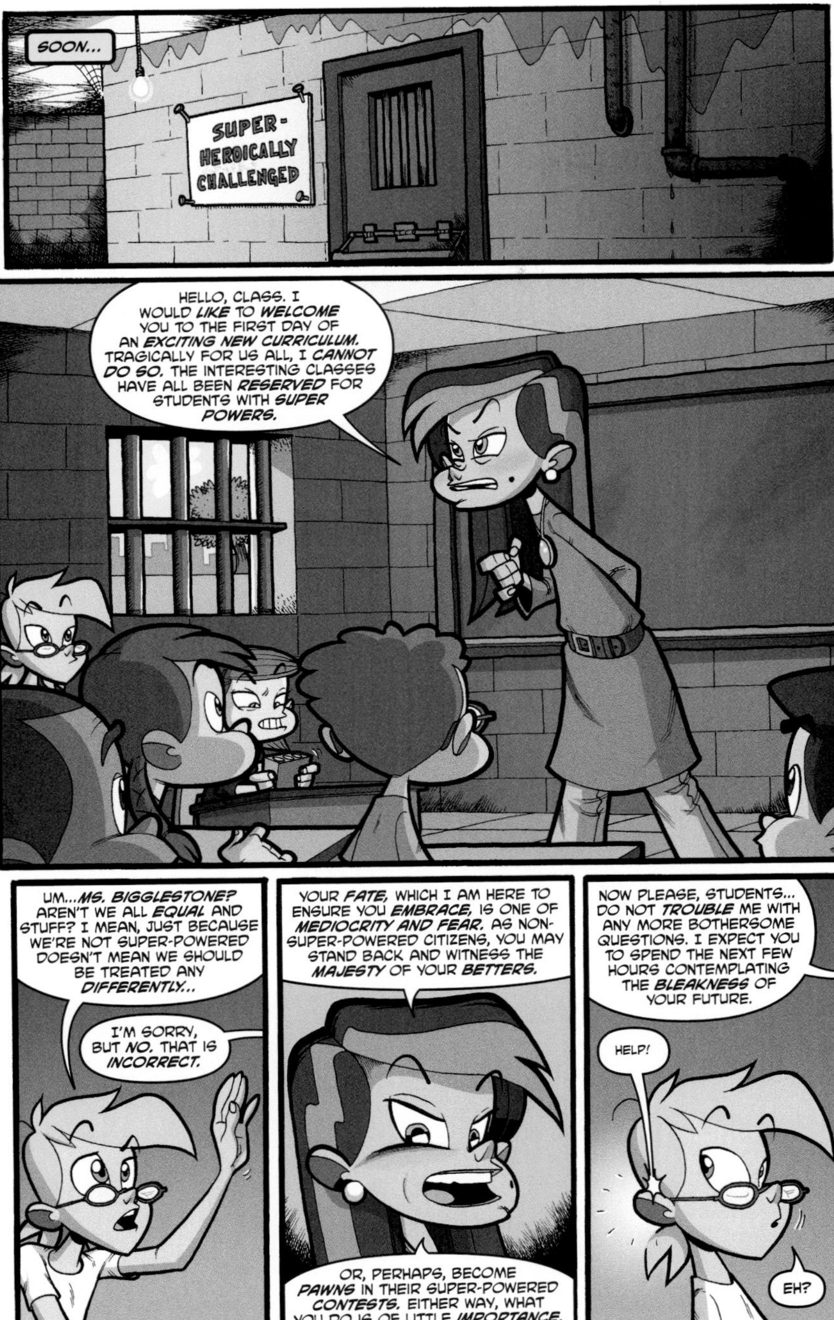
SOON...
SUPER-HEROICALLY CHALLENGED
HELLO, CLASS. I WOULD LIKE TO WELCOME YOU TO THE FIRST DAY OF AN EXCITING NEW CURRICULUM. TRAGICALLY FOR US ALL, I CANNOT DO SO. THE INTERESTING CLASSES HAVE ALL BEEN RESERVED FOR STUDENTS WITH SUPER POWERS.
UM...MS. BIGGLESTONE? AREN'T WE ALL EQUAL AND STUFF? I MEAN, JUST BECAUSE WE'RE NOT SUPER-POWERED DOESN'T MEAN WE SHOULD BE TREATED ANY DIFFERENTLY...
I'M SORRY, BUT NO. THAT IS INCORRECT.
YOUR FATE, WHICH I AM HERE TO ENSURE YOU EMBRACE, IS ONE OF MEDIOCRITY AND FEAR. AS NON-SUPER-POWERED CITIZENS, YOU MAY STAND BACK AND WITNESS THE MAJESTY OF YOUR BETTERS.
OR, PERHAPS, BECOME PAWNS IN THEIR SUPER-POWERED CONTESTS. EITHER WAY, WHAT YOU DO IS OF LITTLE IMPORTANCE.
NOW PLEASE, STUDENTS... DO NOT TROUBLE ME WITH ANY MORE BOTHERSOME QUESTIONS. I EXPECT YOU TO SPEND THE NEXT FEW HOURS CONTEMPLATING THE BLEAKNESS OF YOUR FUTURE.
HELP!
EH?

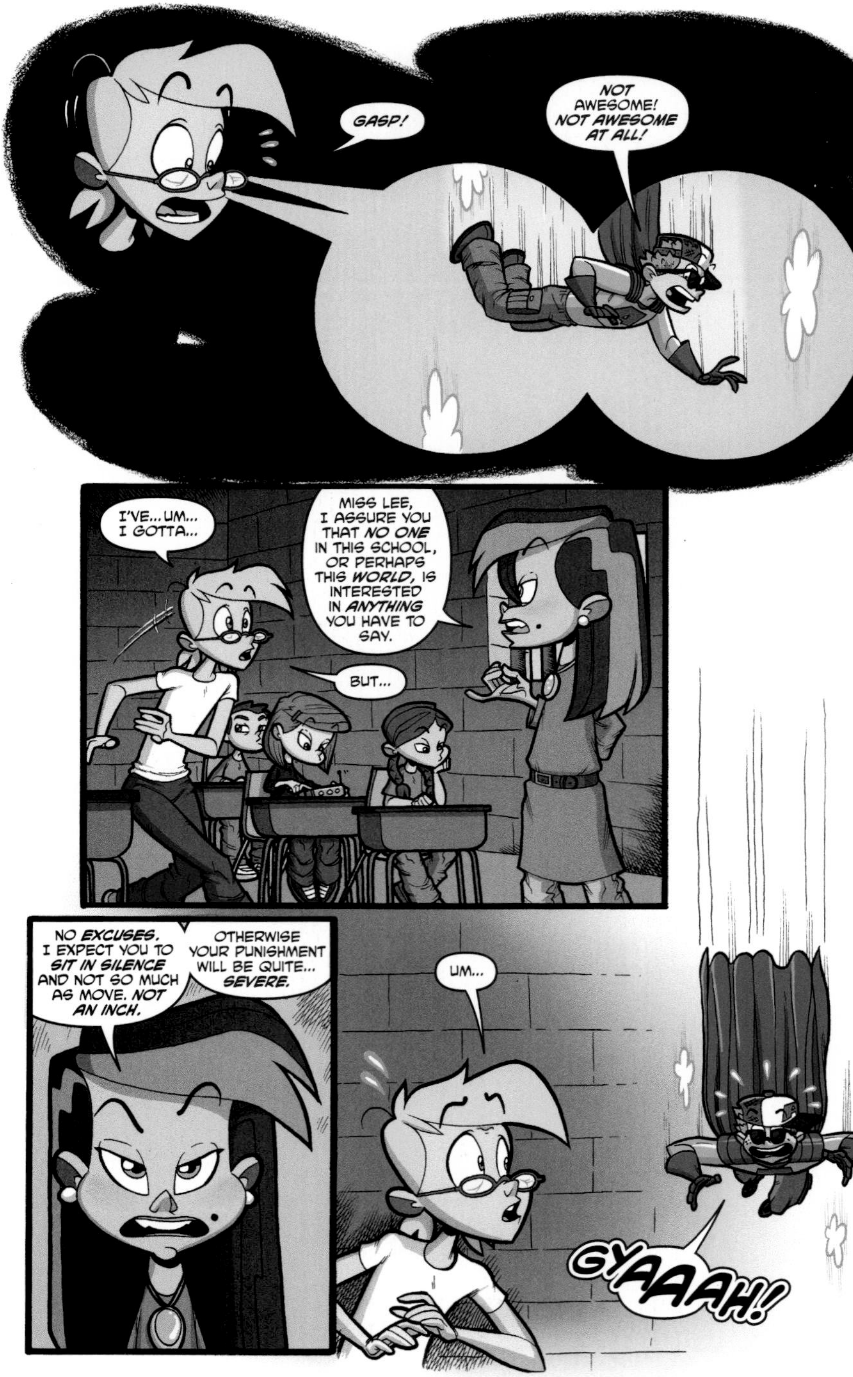
GASP!
NOT AWESOME! NOT AWESOME AT ALL!
I'VE...UM... I GOTTA...
MISS LEE, I ASSURE YOU THAT NO ONE IN THIS SCHOOL, OR PERHAPS THIS WORLD, IS INTERESTED IN ANYTHING YOU HAVE TO SAY.
BUT...
NO EXCUSES. I EXPECT YOU TO SIT IN SILENCE AND NOT SO MUCH AS MOVE. NOT AN INCH.
OTHERWISE YOUR PUNISHMENT WILL BE QUITE... SEVERE.
UM...
GYAAAAH!

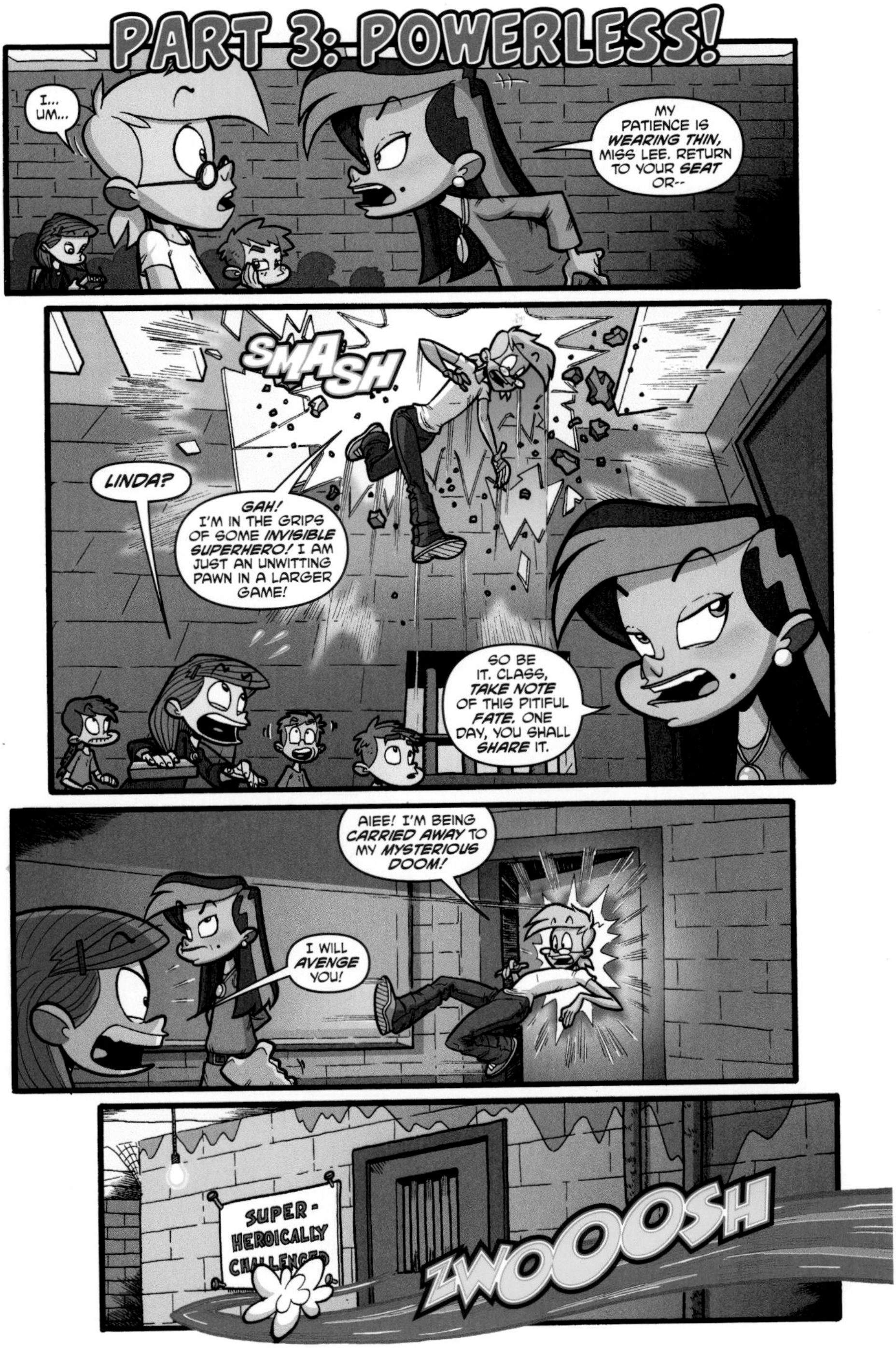
PART 3: POWERLESS!
I... UM...
MY PATIENCE IS WEARING THIN, MISS LEE. RETURN TO YOUR SEAT OR--
SMASH
LINDA?
GAH! I'M IN THE GRIPS OF SOME INVISIBLE SUPERHERO! I AM JUST AN UNWITTING PAWN IN A LARGER GAME!
SO BE IT. CLASS, TAKE NOTE OF THIS PITIFUL FATE. ONE DAY, YOU SHALL SHARE IT.
AIEE! I'M BEING CARRIED AWAY TO MY MYSTERIOUS DOOM!
I WILL AVENGE YOU!
SUPER-HEROICALLY CHALLENGED
ZWOOOOSH

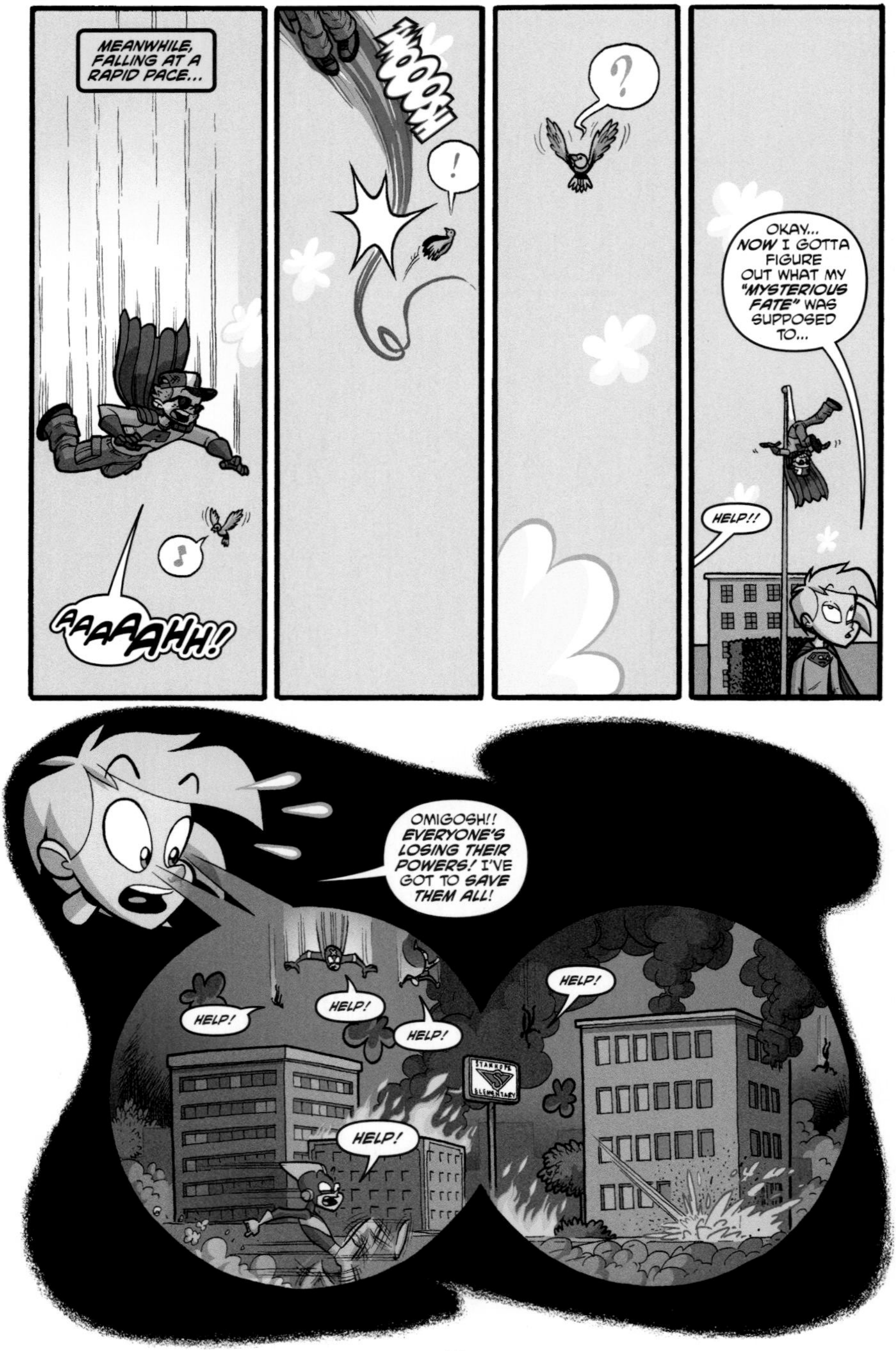
MEANWHILE, FALLING AT A RAPID PACE...
AAAAAHH!
WHOOOOSH
!
?
OKAY... NOW I GOTTA FIGURE OUT WHAT MY "MYSTERIOUS FATE" WAS SUPPOSED TO...
HELP!!
OMIGOSH!! EVERYONE'S LOSING THEIR POWERS! I'VE GOT TO SAVE THEM ALL!
HELP!
HELP!
HELP!
HELP!
HELP!

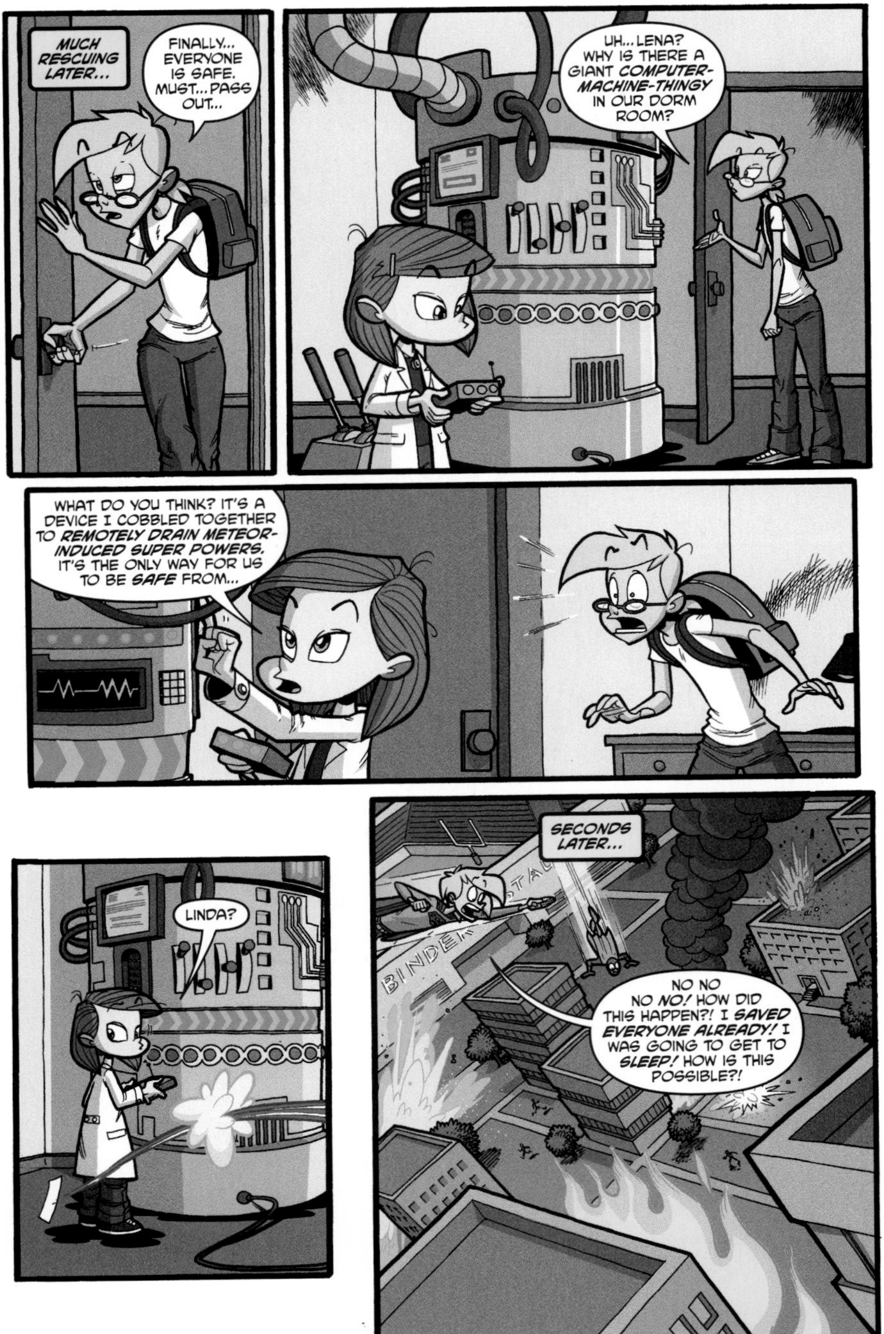
MUCH RESCUING LATER...
FINALLY... EVERYONE IS SAFE. MUST... PASS OUT...
UH... LENA? WHY IS THERE A GIANT COMPUTER-MACHINE-THINGY IN OUR DORM ROOM?
WHAT DO YOU THINK? IT'S A DEVICE I COBBLED TOGETHER TO REMOTELY DRAIN METEOR-INDUCED SUPER POWERS. IT'S THE ONLY WAY FOR US TO BE SAFE FROM...
LINDA?
SECONDS LATER...
NO NO NO NO! HOW DID THIS HAPPEN?! I SAVED EVERYONE ALREADY! I WAS GOING TO GET TO SLEEP! HOW IS THIS POSSIBLE?!

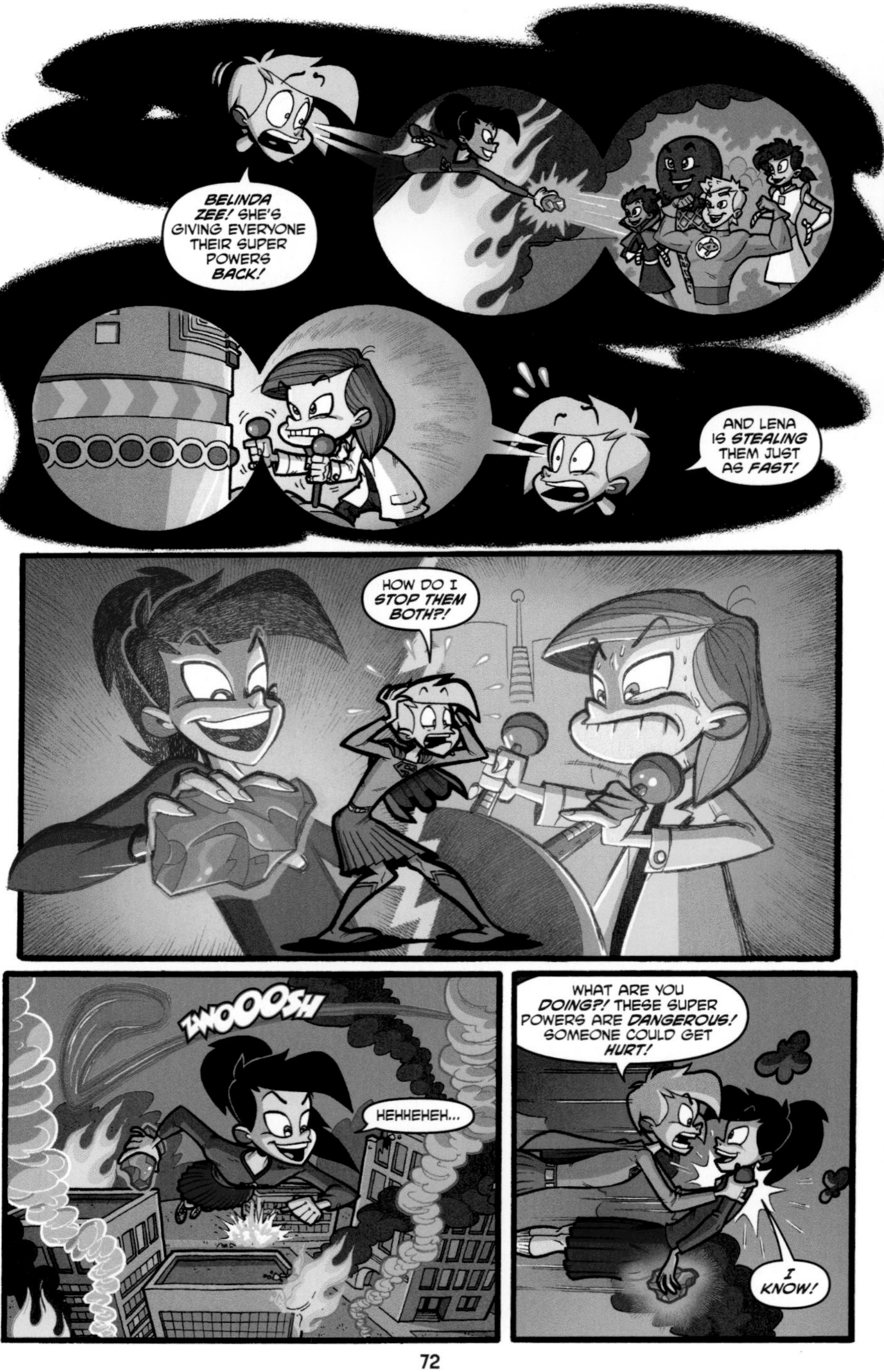
BELINDA ZEE! SHE'S GIVING EVERYONE THEIR SUPER POWERS BACK!
AND LENA IS STEALING THEM JUST AS FAST!
HOW DO I STOP THEM BOTH?!
ZWOOOSH
HEHHEHEH...
WHAT ARE YOU DOING?! THESE SUPER POWERS ARE DANGEROUS! SOMEONE COULD GET HURT!
I KNOW!

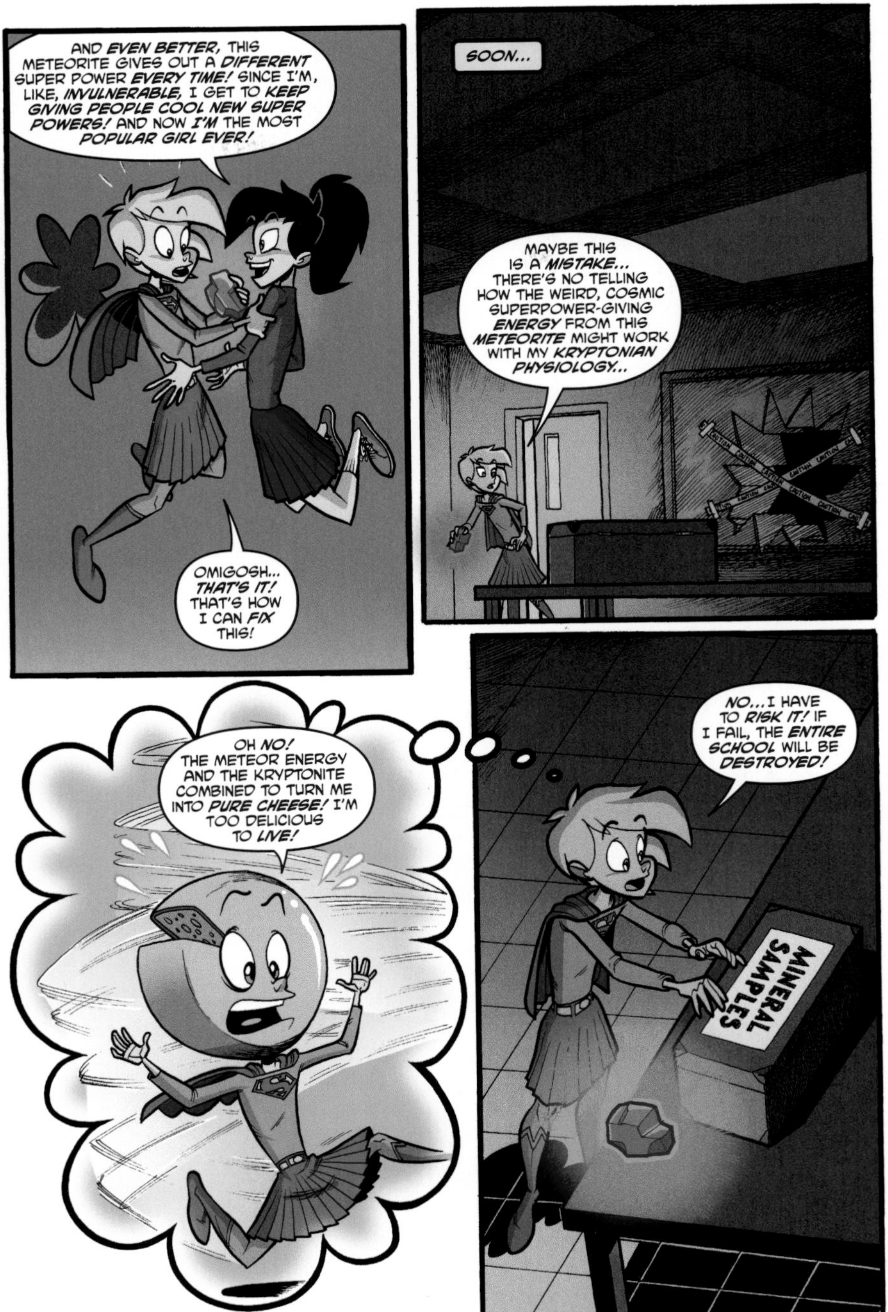
AND EVEN BETTER, THIS METEORITE GIVES OUT A DIFFERENT SUPER POWER EVERY TIME! SINCE I'M, LIKE, INVULNERABLE, I GET TO KEEP GIVING PEOPLE COOL NEW SUPER POWERS! AND NOW I'M THE MOST POPULAR GIRL EVER!
OMIGOSH... THAT'S IT! THAT'S HOW I CAN FIX THIS!
SOON...
MAYBE THIS IS A MISTAKE... THERE'S NO TELLING HOW THE WEIRD, COSMIC SUPERPOWER-GIVING ENERGY FROM THIS METEORITE MIGHT WORK WITH MY KRYPTONIAN PHYSIOLOGY...
OH NO! THE METEOR ENERGY AND THE KRYPTONITE COMBINED TO TURN ME INTO PURE CHEESE! I'M TOO DELICIOUS TO LIVE!
NO...I HAVE TO RISK IT! IF I FAIL, THE ENTIRE SCHOOL WILL BE DESTROYED!
MINERAL SAMPLES

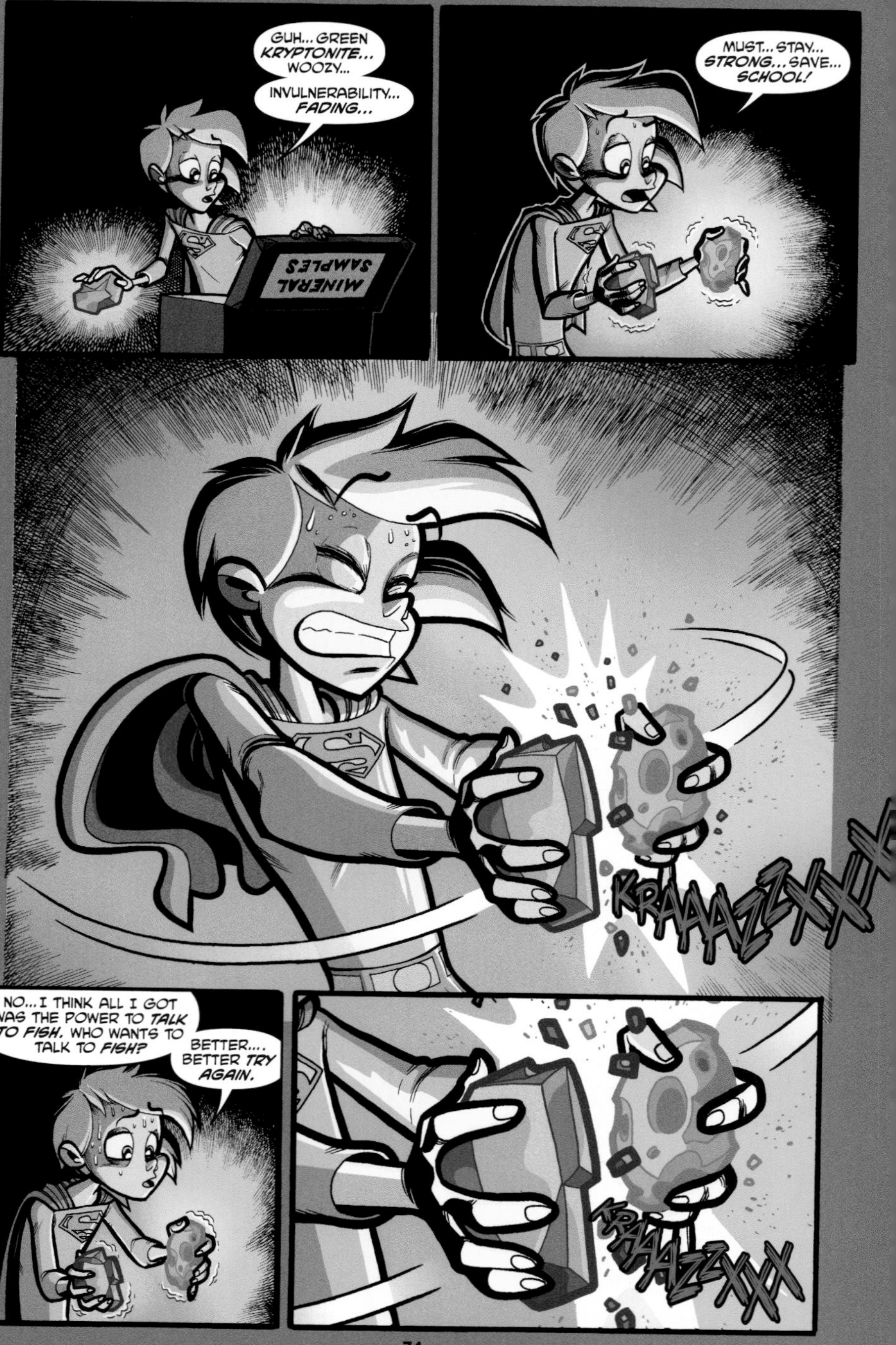
GUH... GREEN KRYPTONITE... WOOZY...
INVULNERABILITY... FADING...
MINERAL SAMPLES
MUST... STAY... STRONG... SAVE... SCHOOL!
KRAAAAZZXXX
NO... I THINK ALL I GOT WAS THE POWER TO TALK TO FISH. WHO WANTS TO TALK TO FISH?
BETTER.... BETTER TRY AGAIN.
KRAAAZZZXXX

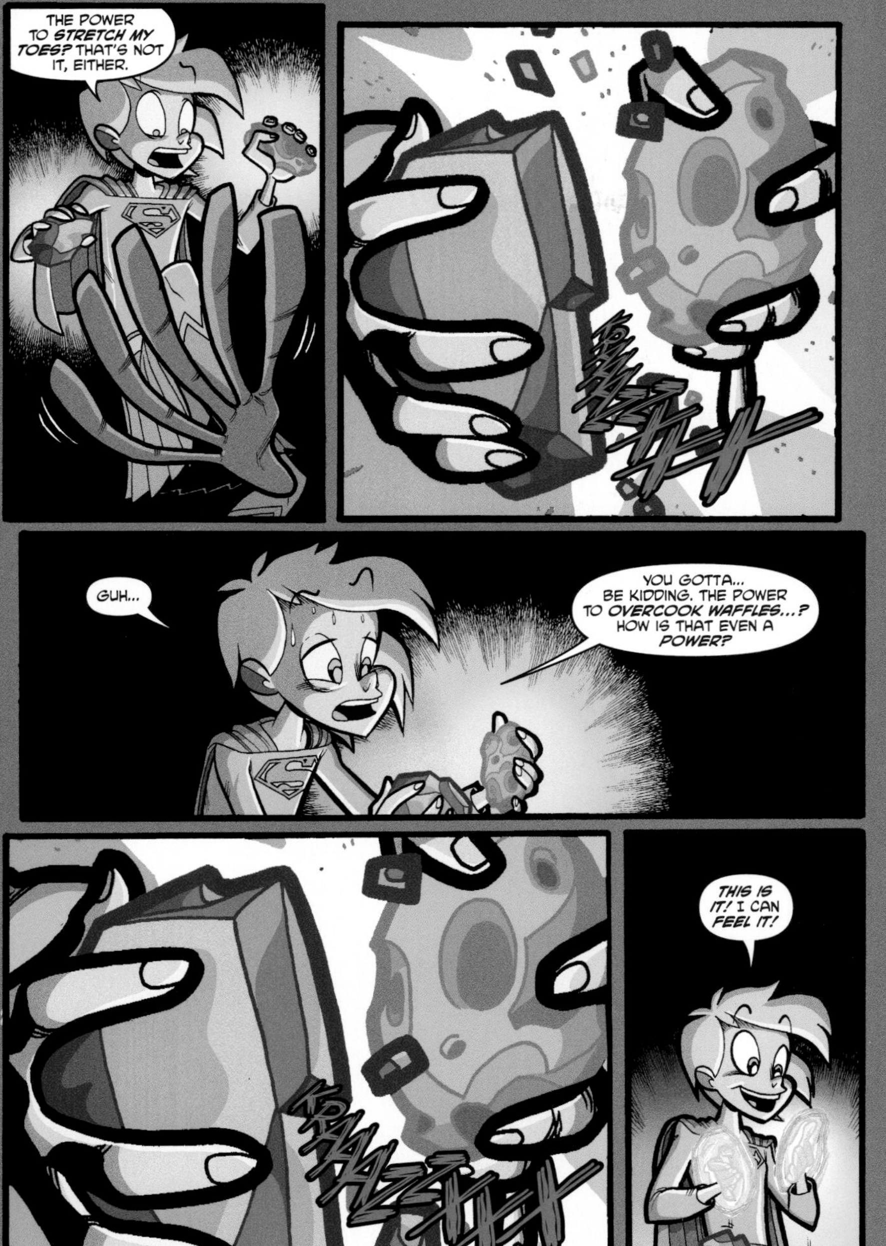
THE POWER TO STRETCH MY TOES? THAT'S NOT IT, EITHER.
GUH...
YOU GOTTA... BE KIDDING. THE POWER TO OVERCOOK WAFFLES...? HOW IS THAT EVEN A POWER?
THIS IS IT! I CAN FEEL IT!

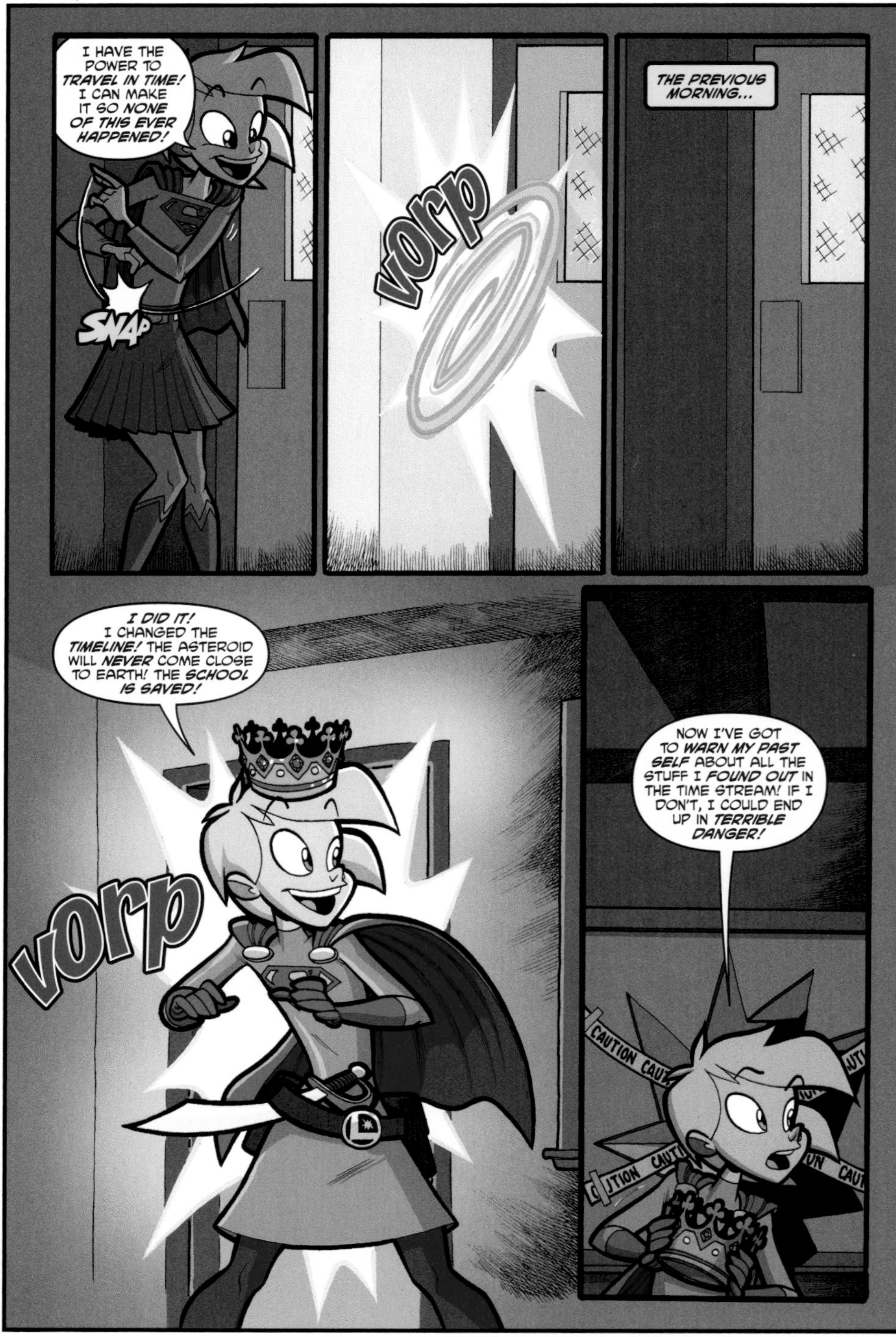
I HAVE THE POWER TO TRAVEL IN TIME! I CAN MAKE IT SO NONE OF THIS EVER HAPPENED!
SNAP
VORP
THE PREVIOUS MORNING...
I DID IT! I CHANGED THE TIMELINE! THE ASTEROID WILL NEVER COME CLOSE TO EARTH! THE SCHOOL IS SAVED!
VORP
NOW I'VE GOT TO WARN MY PAST SELF ABOUT ALL THE STUFF I FOUND OUT IN THE TIME STREAM! IF I DON'T, I COULD END UP IN TERRIBLE DANGER!
CAUTION CAUTI
CAUTION CAUTI

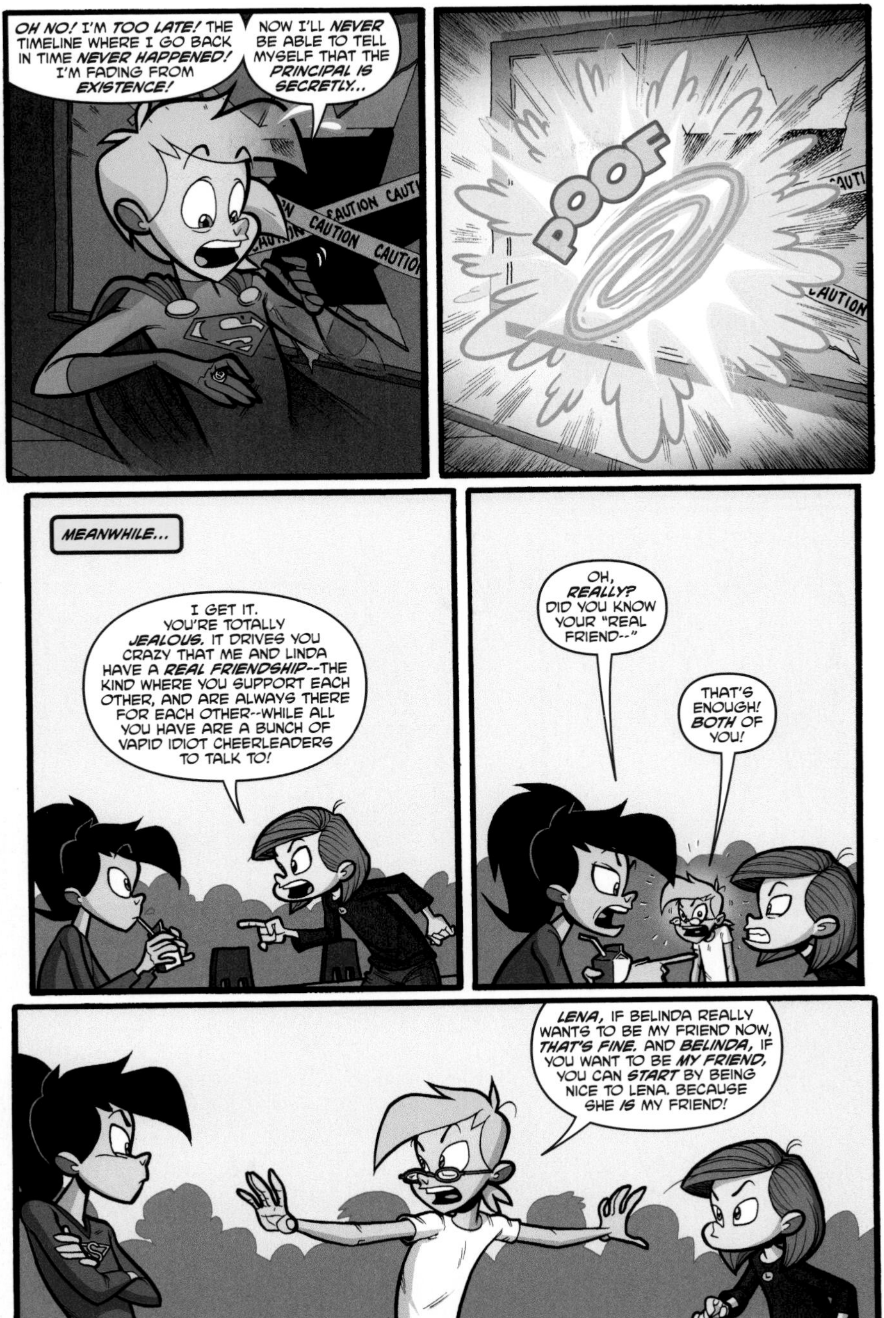

OH NO! I'M TOO LATE! THE TIMELINE WHERE I GO BACK IN TIME NEVER HAPPENED! I'M FADING FROM EXISTENCE!
NOW I'LL NEVER BE ABLE TO TELL MYSELF THAT THE PRINCIPAL IS SECRETLY...
CAUTION CAUTION
CAUTION
CAUTION
POOF
CAUTION
CAUTION
MEANWHILE...
I GET IT. YOU'RE TOTALLY JEALOUS. IT DRIVES YOU CRAZY THAT ME AND LINDA HAVE A REAL FRIENDSHIP--THE KIND WHERE YOU SUPPORT EACH OTHER, AND ARE ALWAYS THERE FOR EACH OTHER--WHILE ALL YOU HAVE ARE A BUNCH OF VAPID IDIOT CHEERLEADERS TO TALK TO!
OH, REALLY? DID YOU KNOW YOUR "REAL FRIEND--"
THAT'S ENOUGH! BOTH OF YOU!
LENA, IF BELINDA REALLY WANTS TO BE MY FRIEND NOW, THAT'S FINE. AND BELINDA, IF YOU WANT TO BE MY FRIEND, YOU CAN START BY BEING NICE TO LENA. BECAUSE SHE IS MY FRIEND!

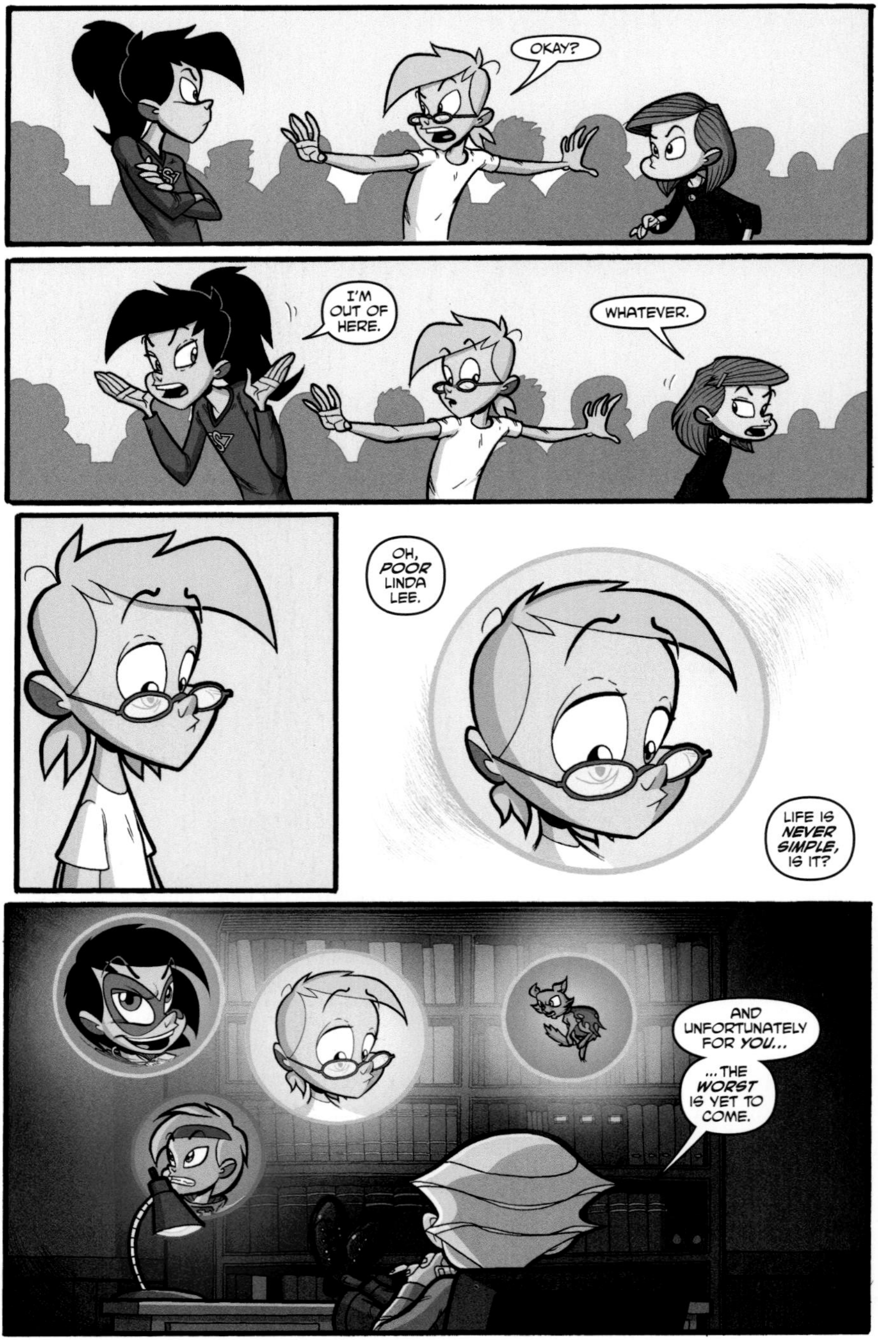
OKAY?
I'M OUT OF HERE.
WHATEVER.
OH, POOR LINDA LEE.
LIFE IS NEVER SIMPLE, IS IT?
AND UNFORTUNATELY FOR YOU...
...THE WORST IS YET TO COME.

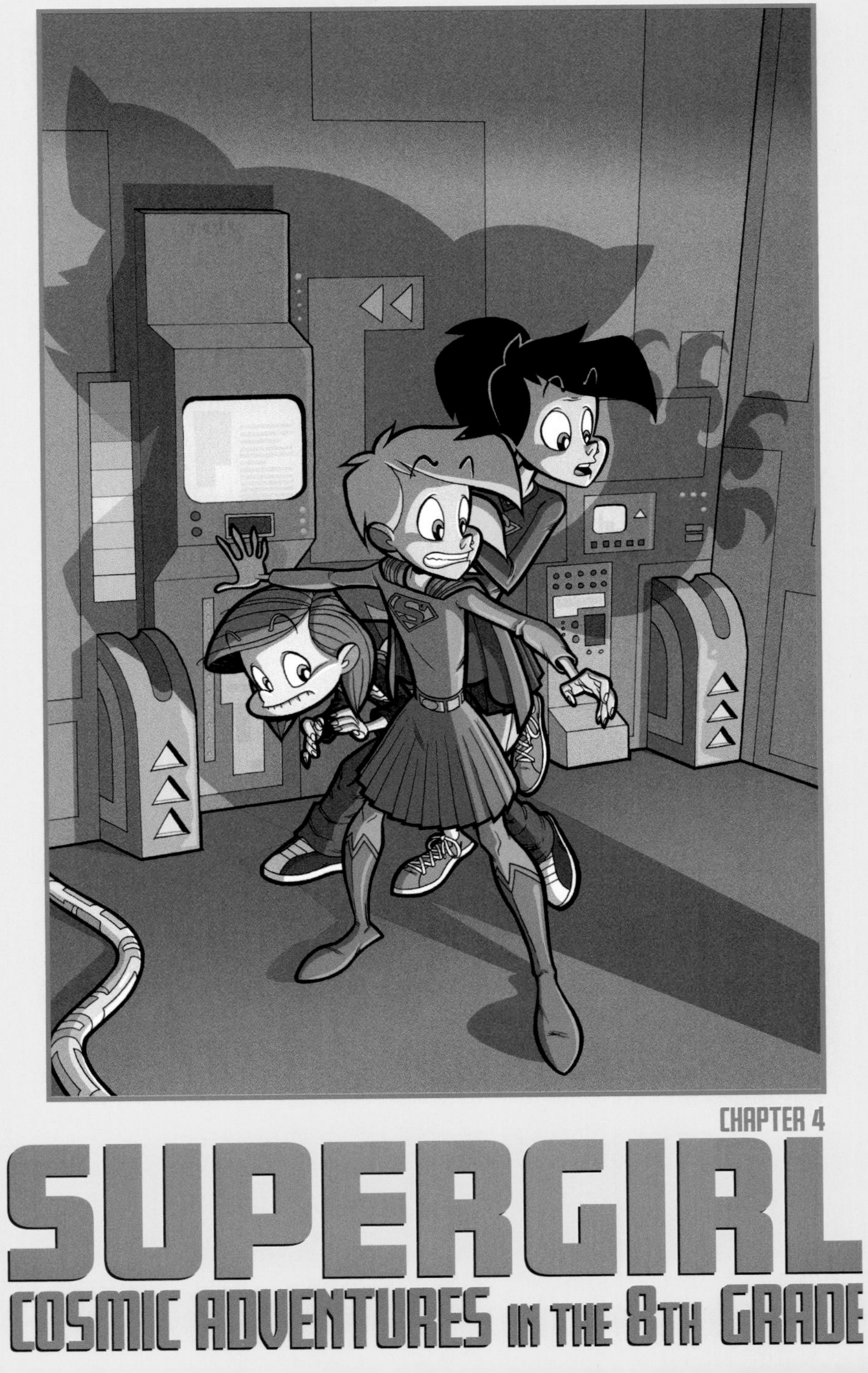

CHAPTER 4

SUPERGIRL

COSMIC ADVENTURES IN THE 8TH GRADE

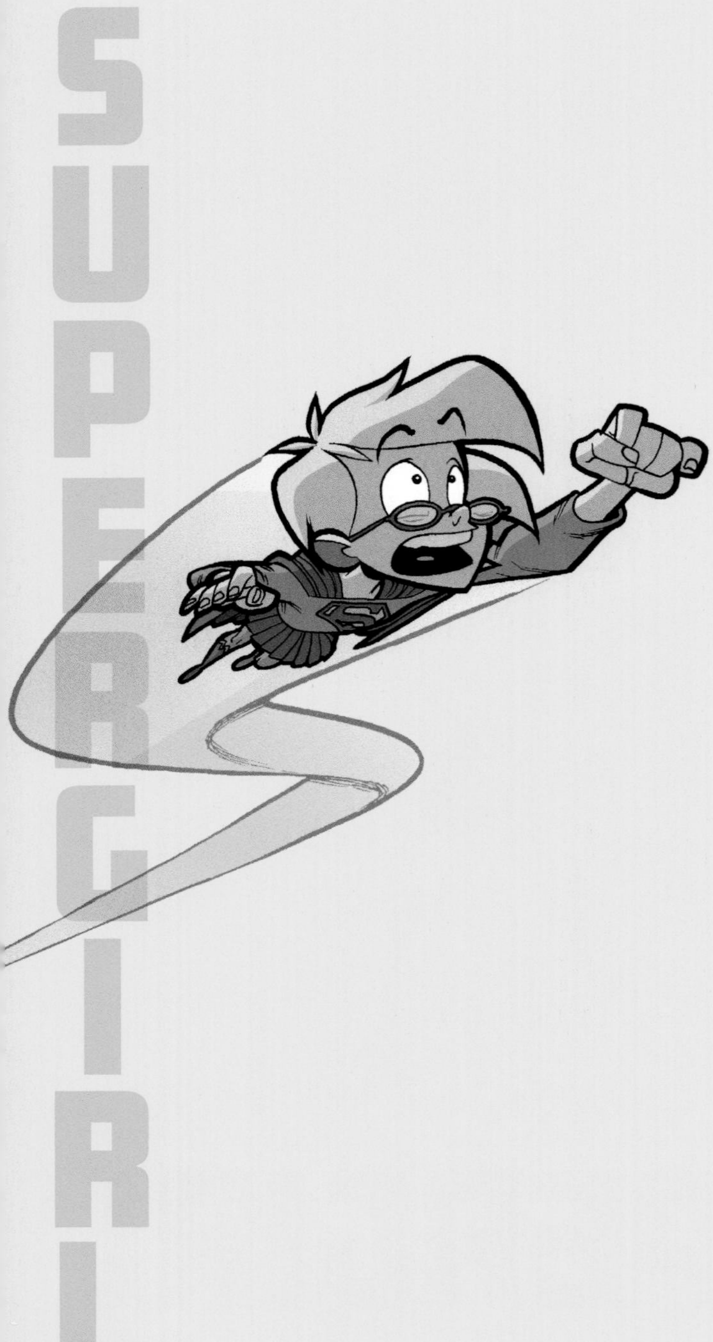
SUPERGIRL

PART 1: "SECRET ENTITY!"

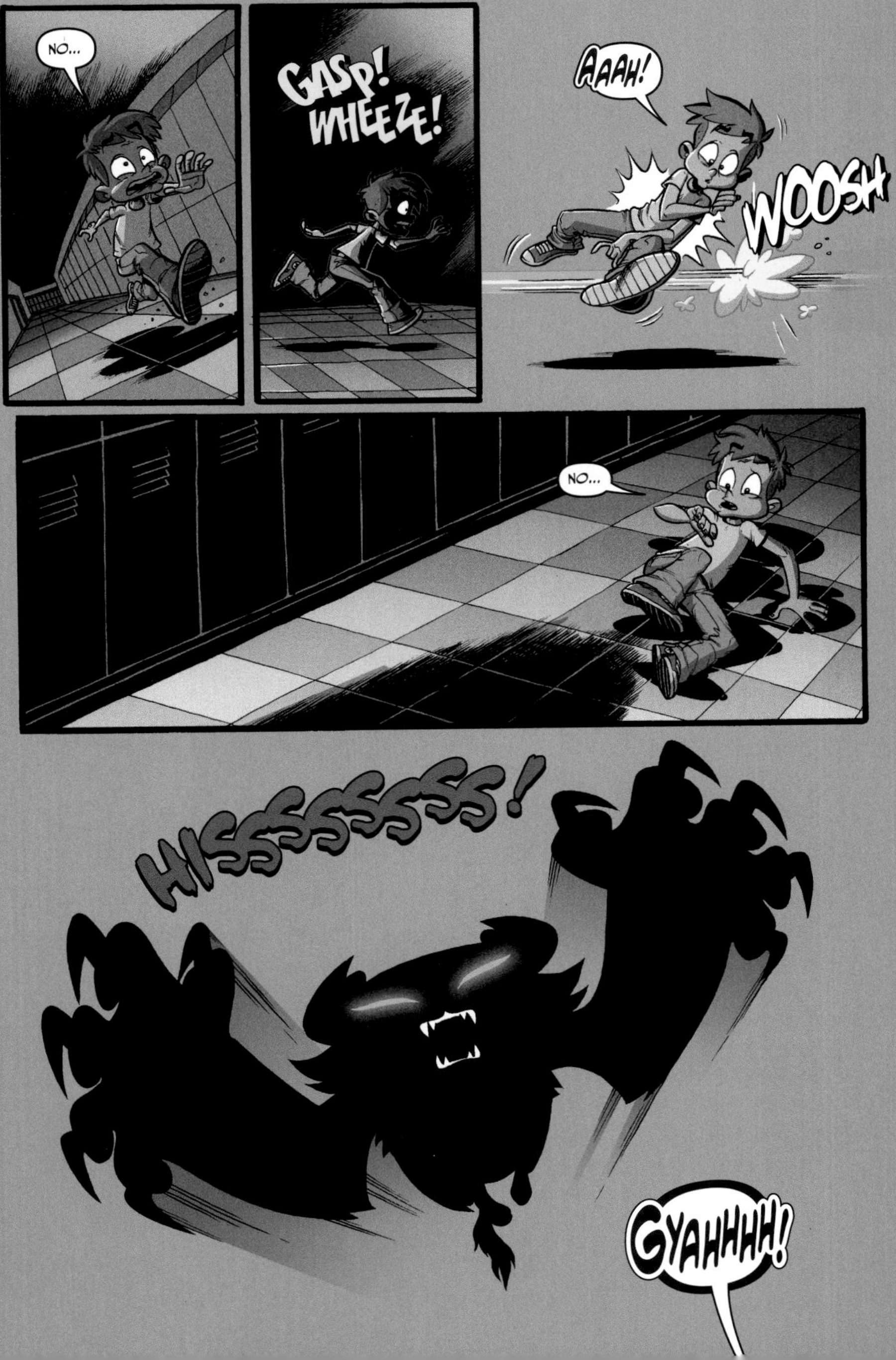
NO...
GASP! WHEEZE!
AAAH!
WOOSH
NO...
HISSSSSSSS!
GYAHHHH!

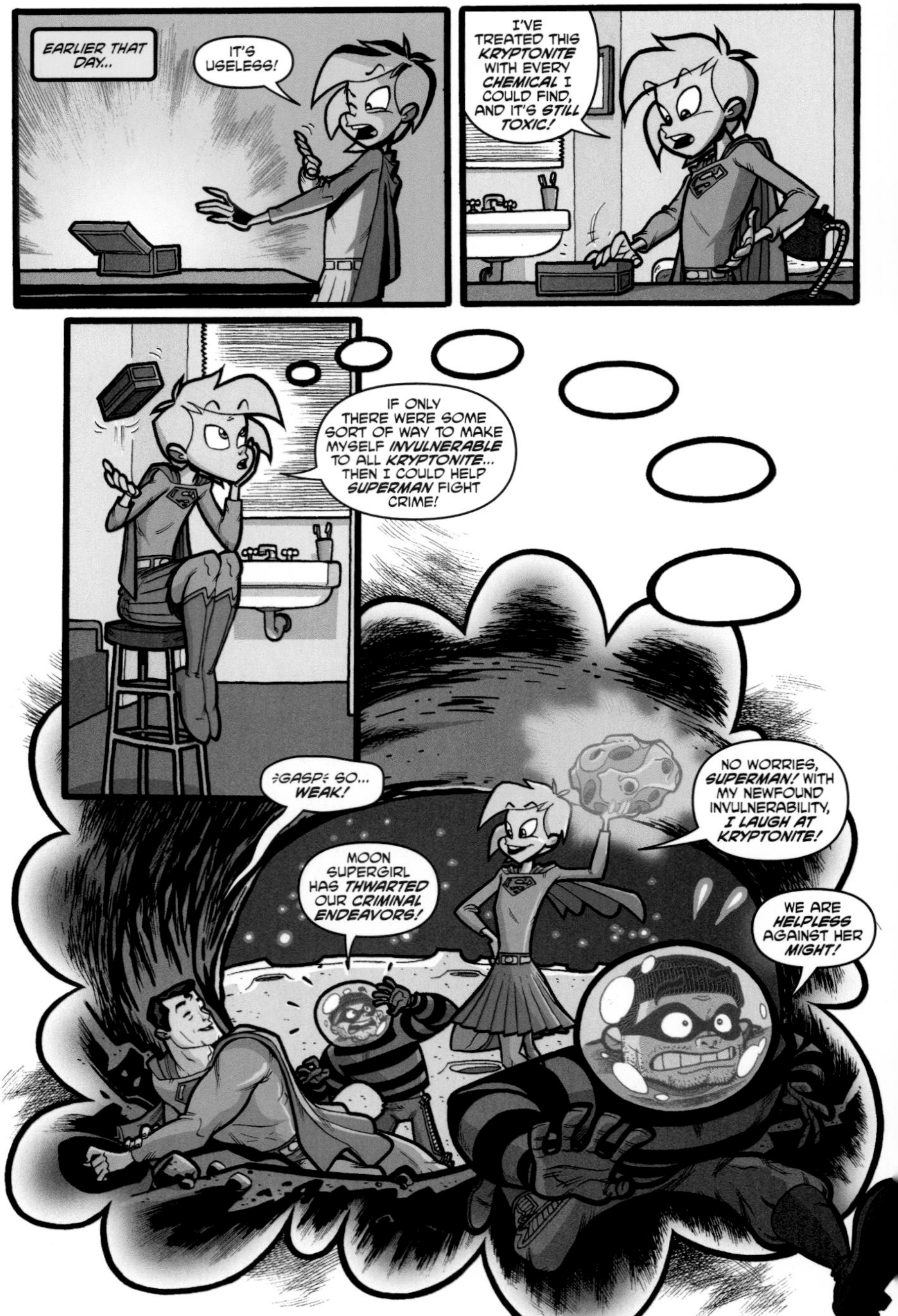
EARLIER THAT DAY...
IT'S USELESS!
I'VE TREATED THIS KRYPTONITE WITH EVERY CHEMICAL I COULD FIND, AND IT'S STILL TOXIC!
IF ONLY THERE WERE SOME SORT OF WAY TO MAKE MYSELF INVULNERABLE TO ALL KRYPTONITE... THEN I COULD HELP SUPERMAN FIGHT CRIME!
GASP SO... WEAK!
NO WORRIES, SUPERMAN! WITH MY NEWFOUND INVULNERABILITY, I LAUGH AT KRYPTONITE!
MOON SUPERGIRL HAS THWARTED OUR CRIMINAL ENDEAVORS!
WE ARE HELPLESS AGAINST HER MIGHT!

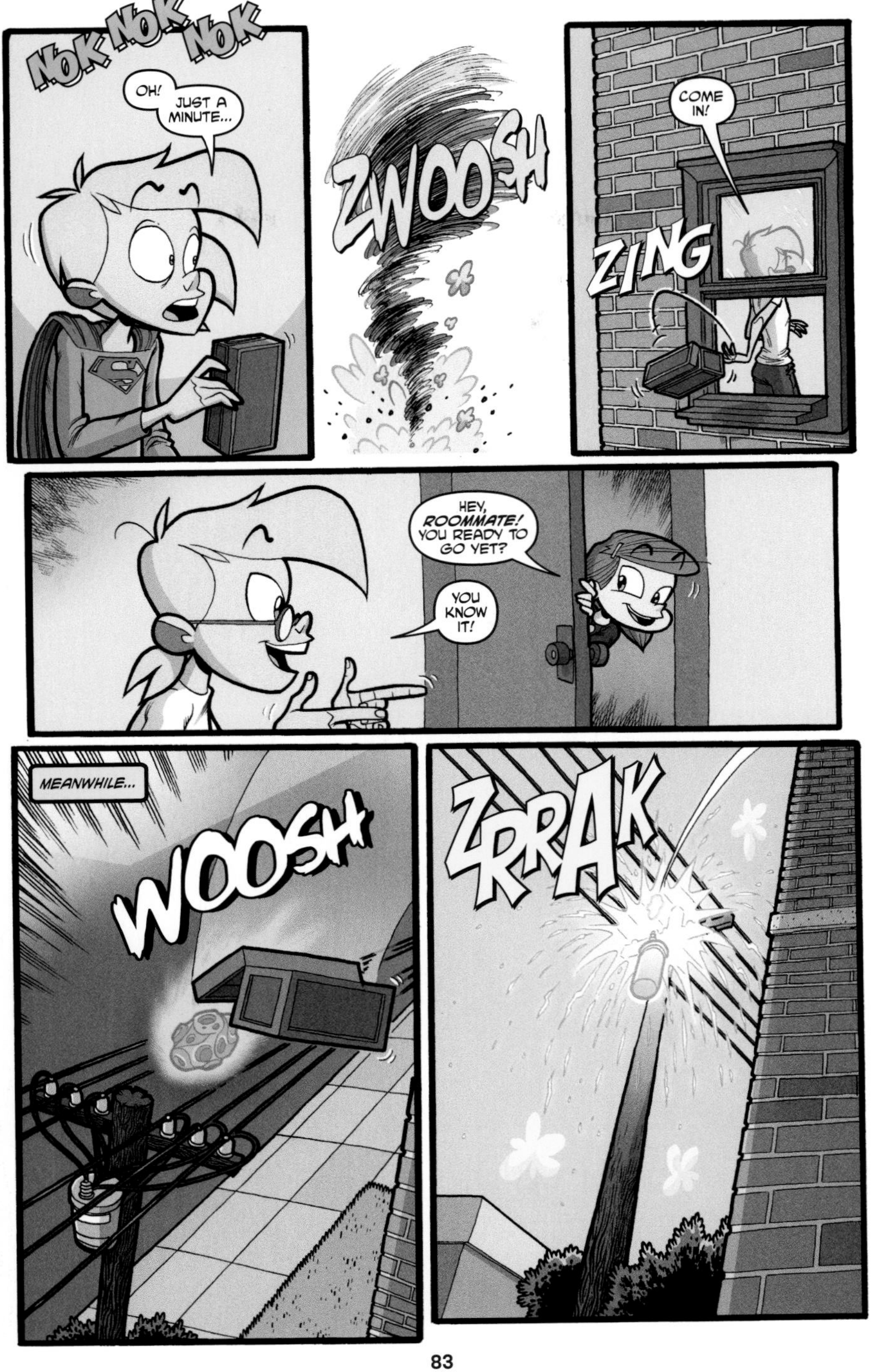
NOK NOK NOK
OH!
JUST A MINUTE...
ZWOOSH
COME IN!
ZING
HEY, ROOMMATE! YOU READY TO GO YET?
YOU KNOW IT!
MEANWHILE...
WOOSH
ZRRAK

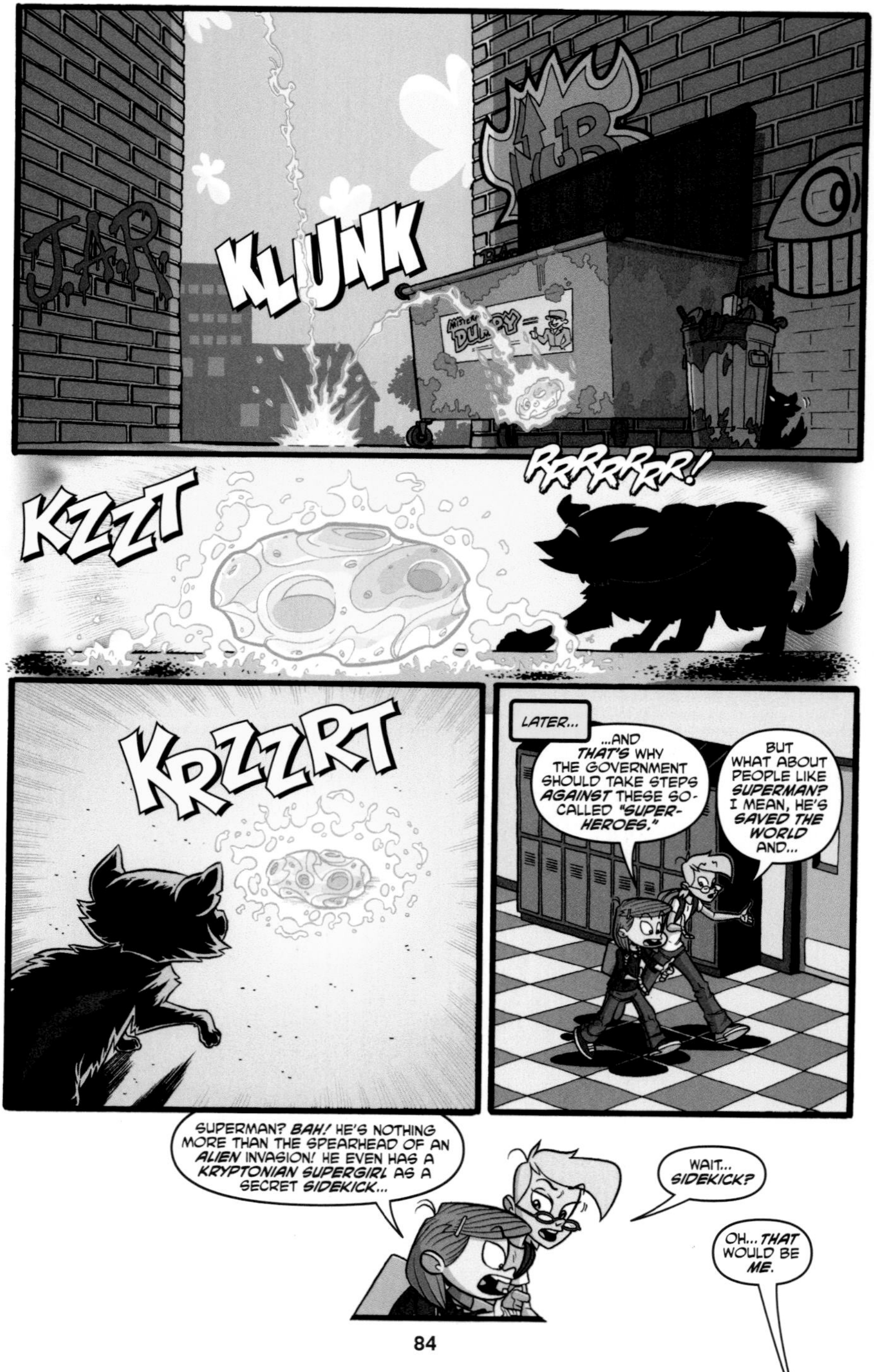

J.A.R.
KLUNK
MISTER DUMPY
KZZZT
RRRRRRRR!
KRZZZRT
LATER...
...AND THAT'S WHY THE GOVERNMENT SHOULD TAKE STEPS AGAINST THESE SO-CALLED "SUPER-HEROES."
BUT WHAT ABOUT PEOPLE LIKE SUPERMAN? I MEAN, HE'S SAVED THE WORLD AND...
SUPERMAN? BAH! HE'S NOTHING MORE THAN THE SPEARHEAD OF AN ALIEN INVASION! HE EVEN HAS A KRYPTONIAN SUPERGIRL AS A SECRET SIDEKICK...
WAIT... SIDEKICK?
OH... THAT WOULD BE ME.

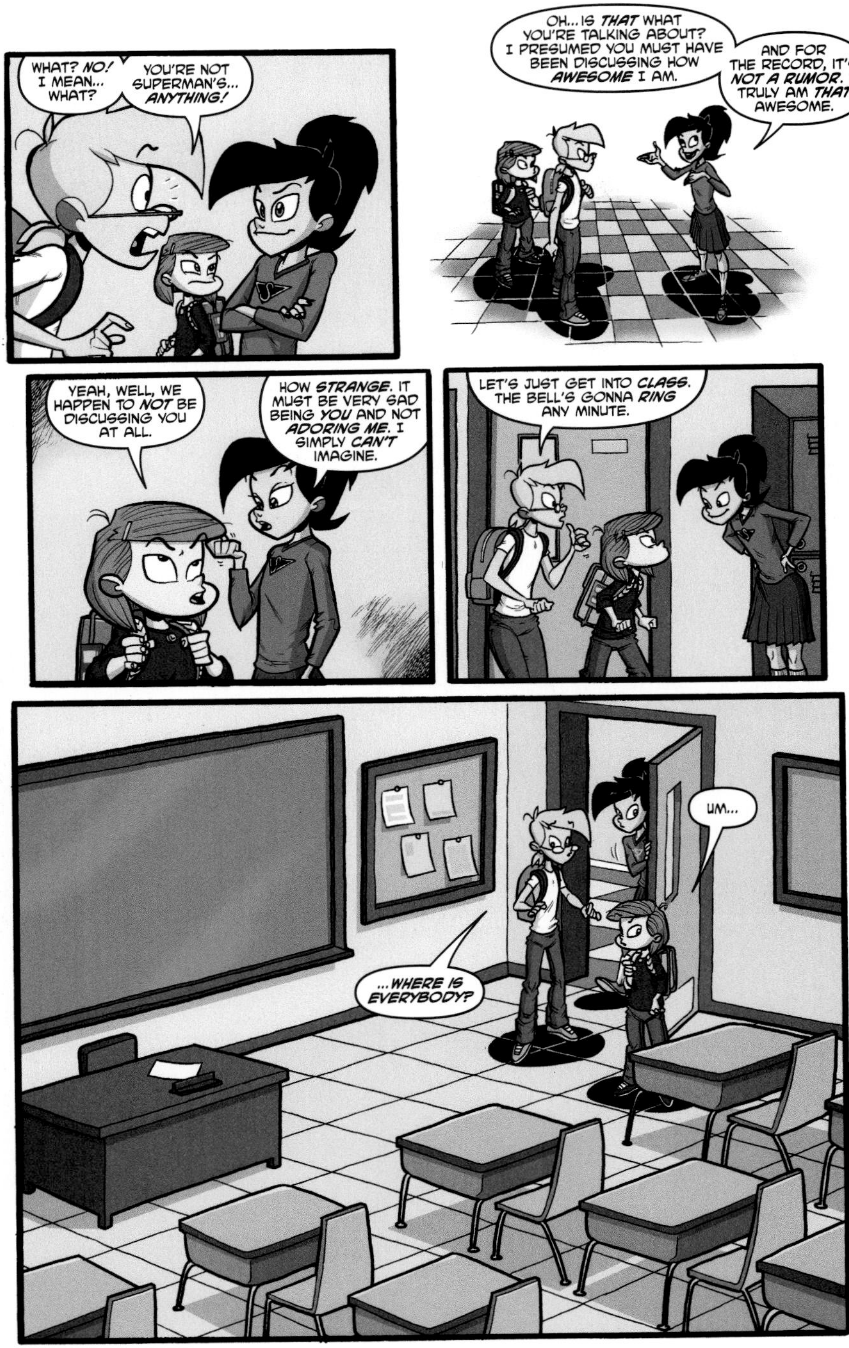
WHAT? NO! I MEAN... WHAT?
YOU'RE NOT SUPERMAN'S... ANYTHING!
OH... IS THAT WHAT YOU'RE TALKING ABOUT? I PRESUMED YOU MUST HAVE BEEN DISCUSSING HOW AWESOME I AM.
AND FOR THE RECORD, IT'S NOT A RUMOR. I TRULY AM THAT AWESOME.
YEAH, WELL, WE HAPPEN TO NOT BE DISCUSSING YOU AT ALL.
HOW STRANGE. IT MUST BE VERY SAD BEING YOU AND NOT ADORING ME. I SIMPLY CAN'T IMAGINE.
LET'S JUST GET INTO CLASS. THE BELL'S GONNA RING ANY MINUTE.
UM...
...WHERE IS EVERYBODY?

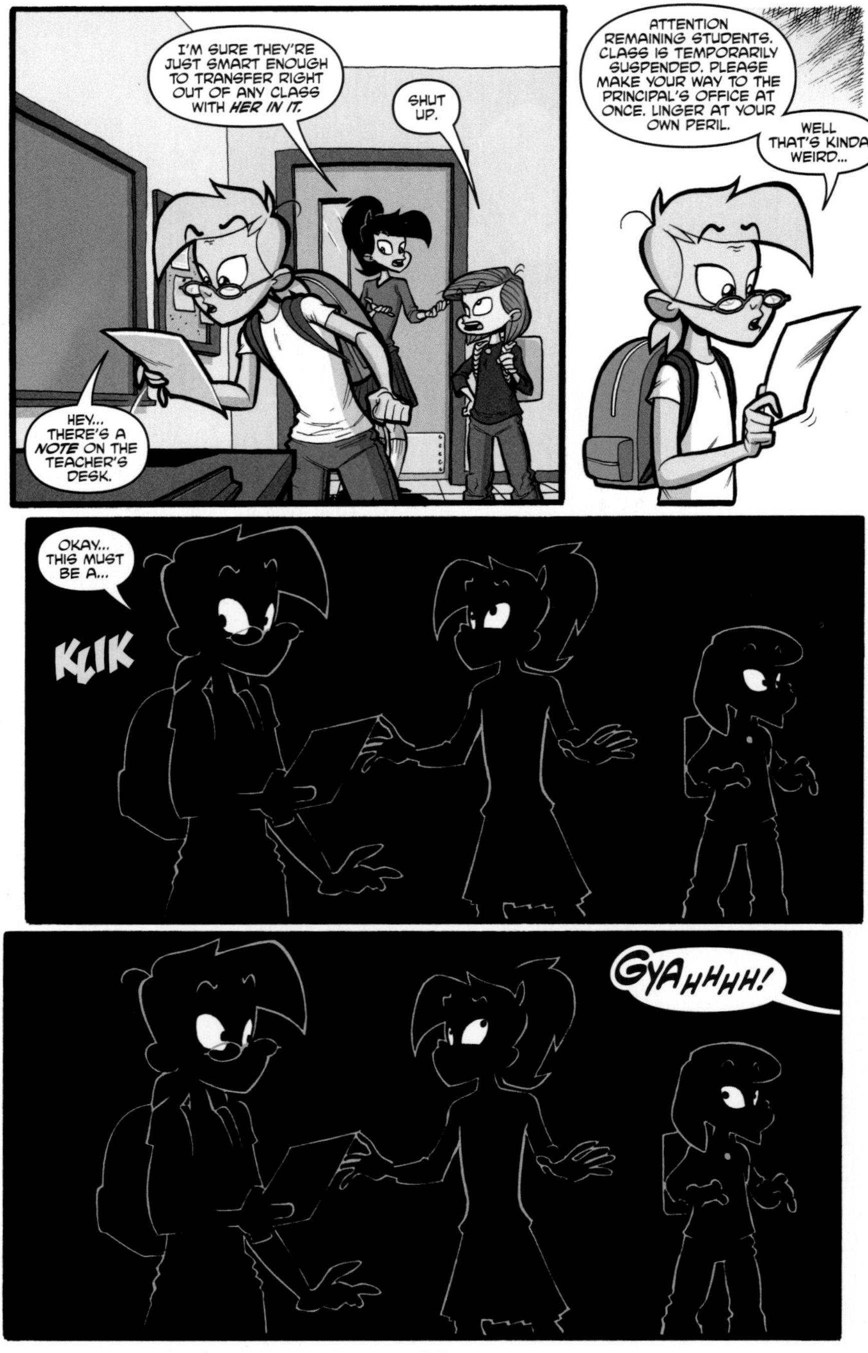
I'M SURE THEY'RE JUST SMART ENOUGH TO TRANSFER RIGHT OUT OF ANY CLASS WITH *HER IN IT.*
SHUT UP.
HEY... THERE'S A *NOTE* ON THE TEACHER'S DESK.
ATTENTION REMAINING STUDENTS. CLASS IS TEMPORARILY SUSPENDED. PLEASE MAKE YOUR WAY TO THE PRINCIPAL'S OFFICE AT ONCE. LINGER AT YOUR OWN PERIL.
WELL THAT'S KINDA WEIRD...
OKAY... THIS MUST BE A...
KLIK
GYAHHHH!

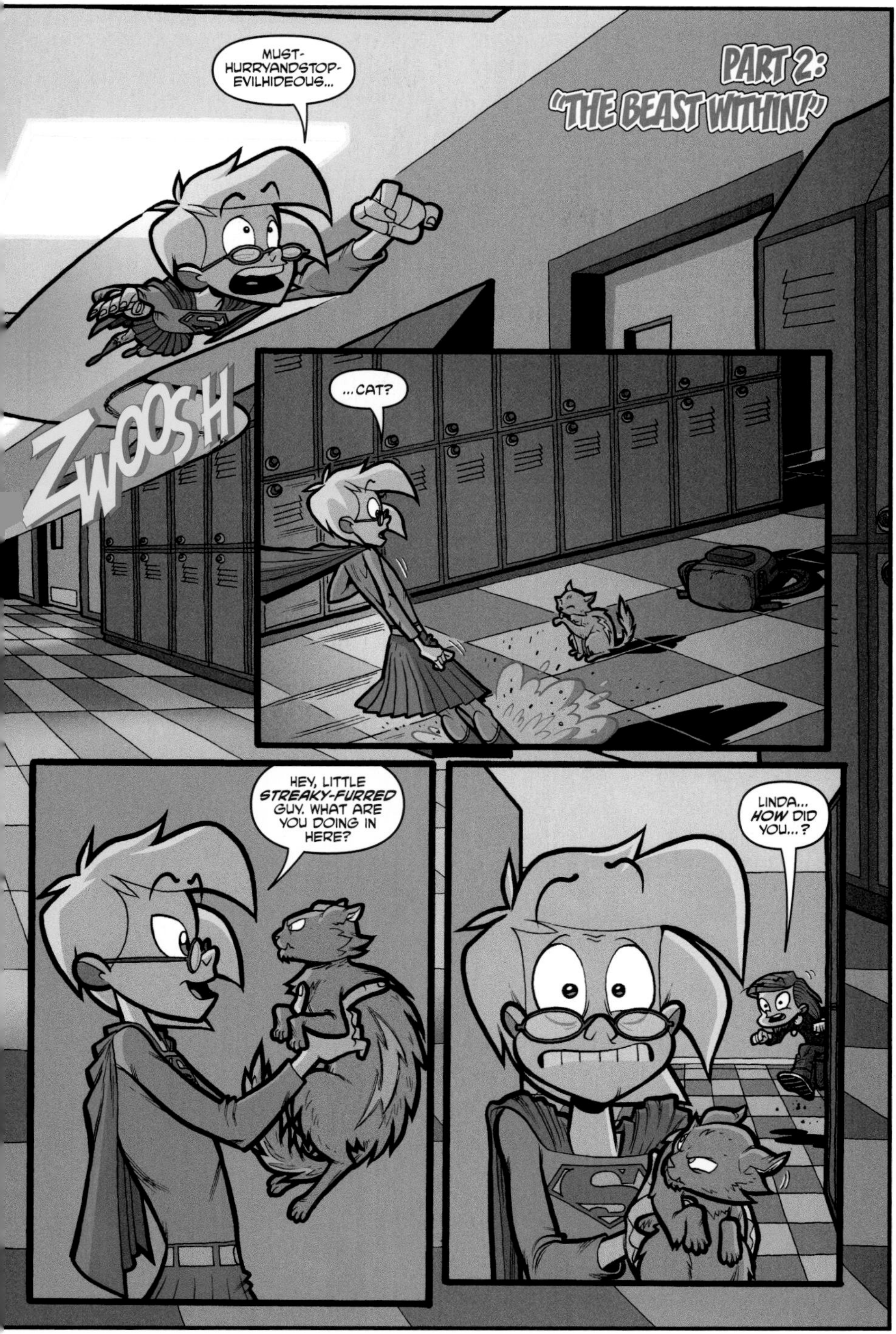

MUST-HURRYANDSTOP-EVILHIDEOUS...
PART 2:
"THE BEAST WITHIN!"
ZWOOSH
...CAT?
HEY, LITTLE STREAKY-FURRED GUY. WHAT ARE YOU DOING IN HERE?
LINDA... HOW DID YOU...?

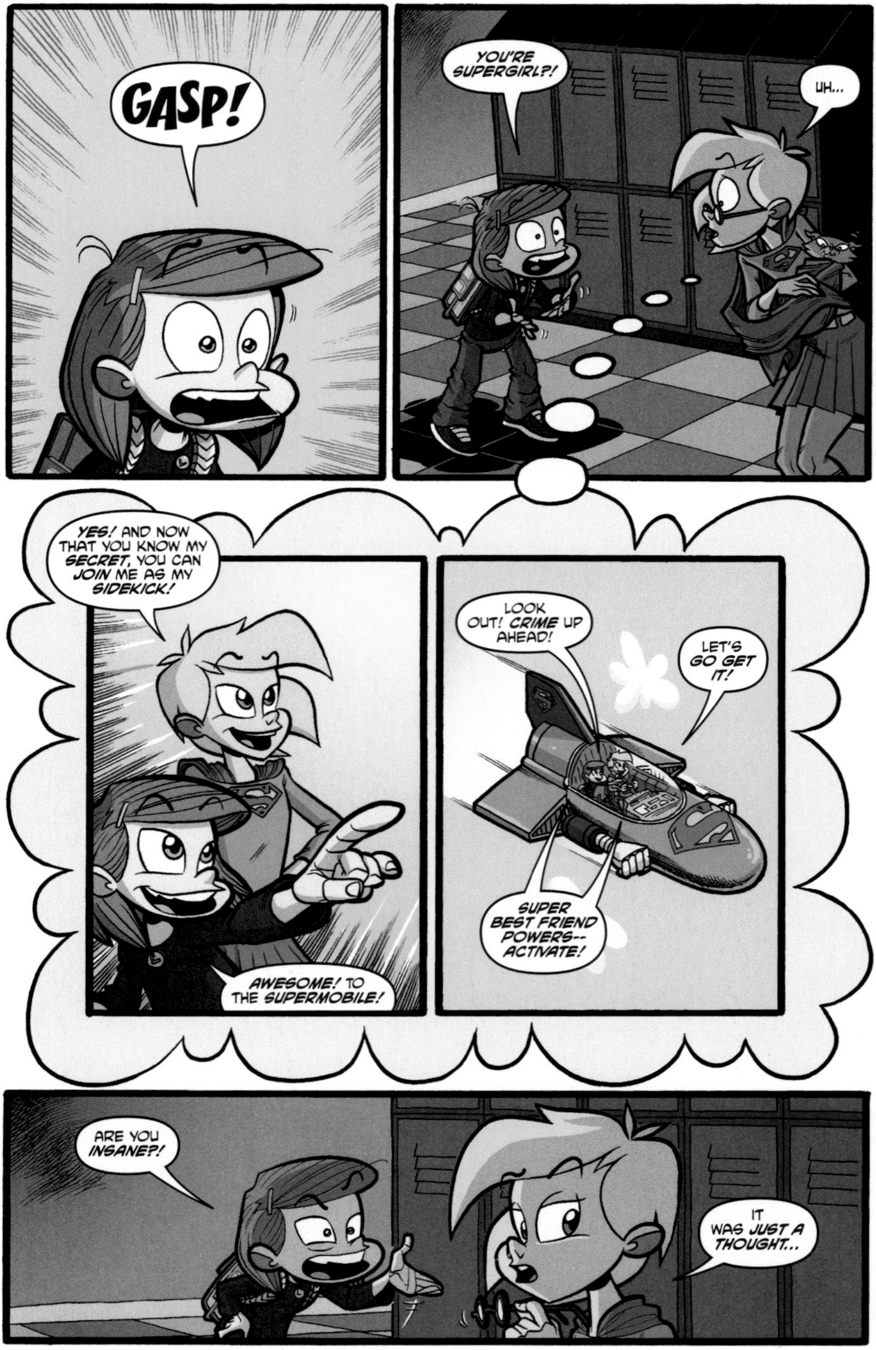
GASP!
YOU'RE SUPERGIRL?!
UH...
YES! AND NOW THAT YOU KNOW MY SECRET, YOU CAN JOIN ME AS MY SIDEKICK!
AWESOME! TO THE SUPERMOBILE!
LOOK OUT! CRIME UP AHEAD!
LET'S GO GET IT!
SUPER BEST FRIEND POWERS-- ACTIVATE!
ARE YOU INSANE?!
IT WAS JUST A THOUGHT...

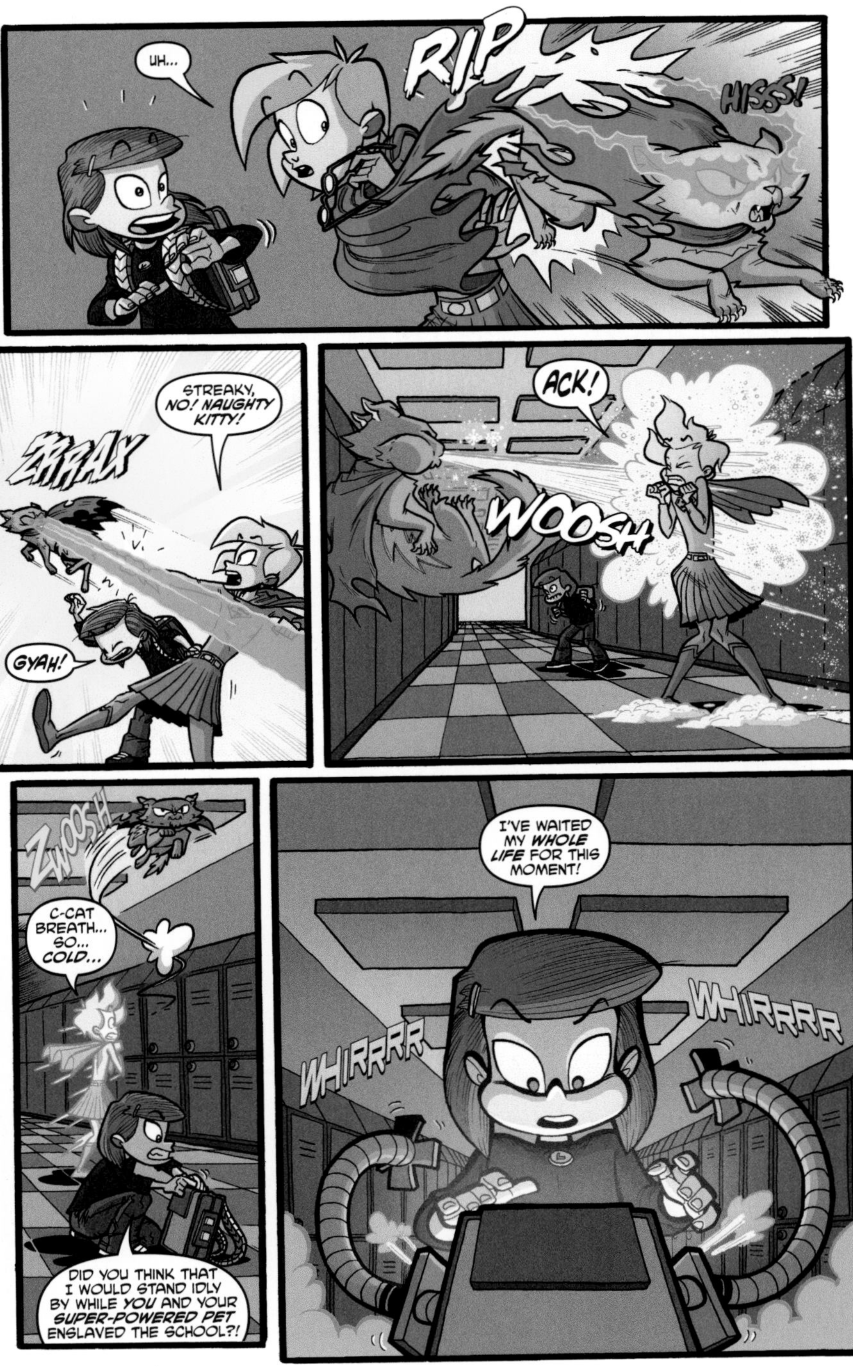
UH...
RIP
HISSS!
STREAKY, NO! NAUGHTY KITTY!
ZRRAX
GYAH!
ACK!
WOOSH
ZWOOSH
C-CAT BREATH... SO... COLD...
DID YOU THINK THAT I WOULD STAND IDLY BY WHILE YOU AND YOUR SUPER-POWERED PET ENSLAVED THE SCHOOL?!
I'VE WAITED MY WHOLE LIFE FOR THIS MOMENT!
WHIRRRR
WHIRRRR

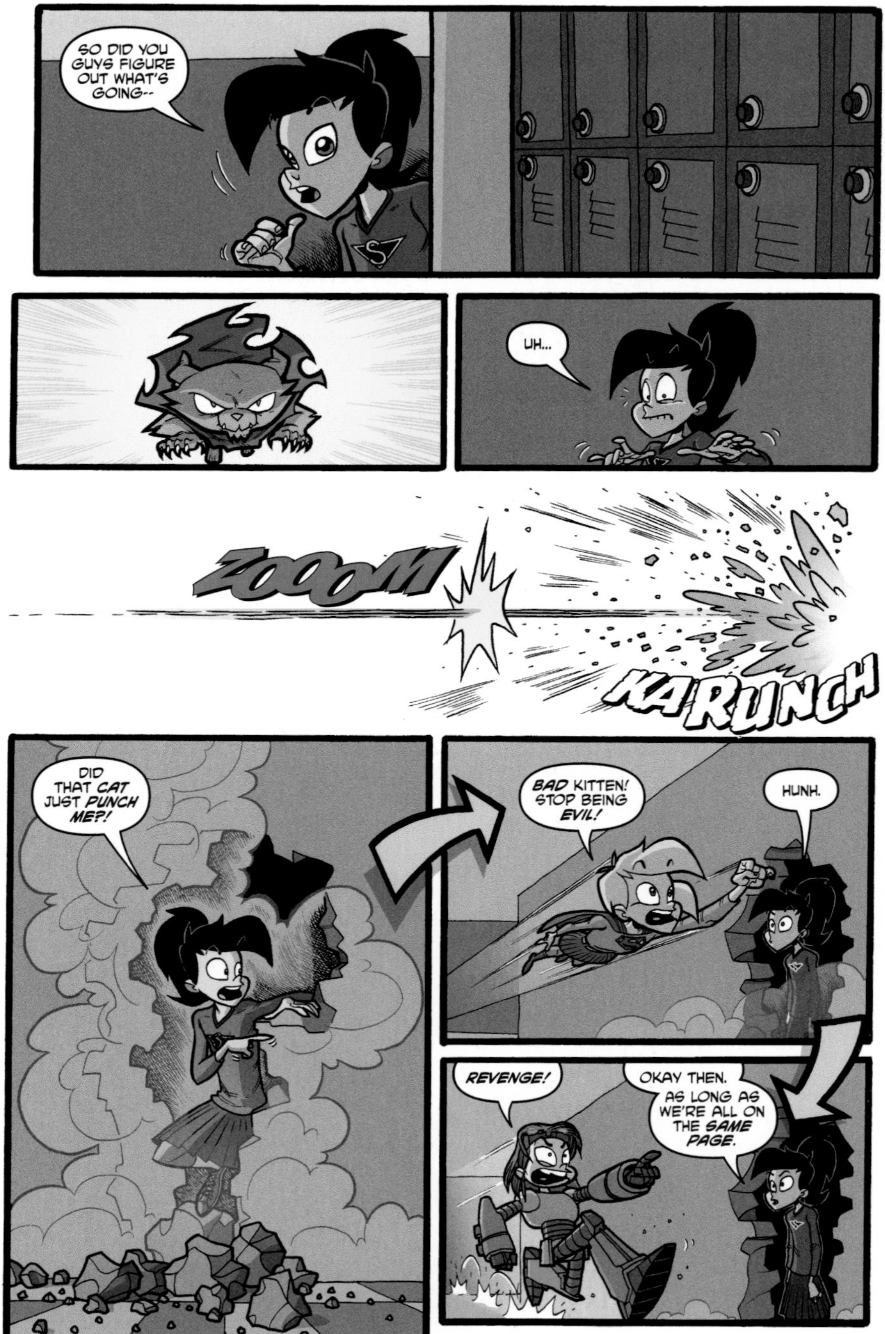
SO DID YOU GUYS FIGURE OUT WHAT'S GOING--
UH...
ZOOOOM
KA-RUNCH
DID THAT CAT JUST PUNCH ME?!
BAD KITTEN! STOP BEING EVIL!
HUNH.
REVENGE!
OKAY THEN. AS LONG AS WE'RE ALL ON THE SAME PAGE.

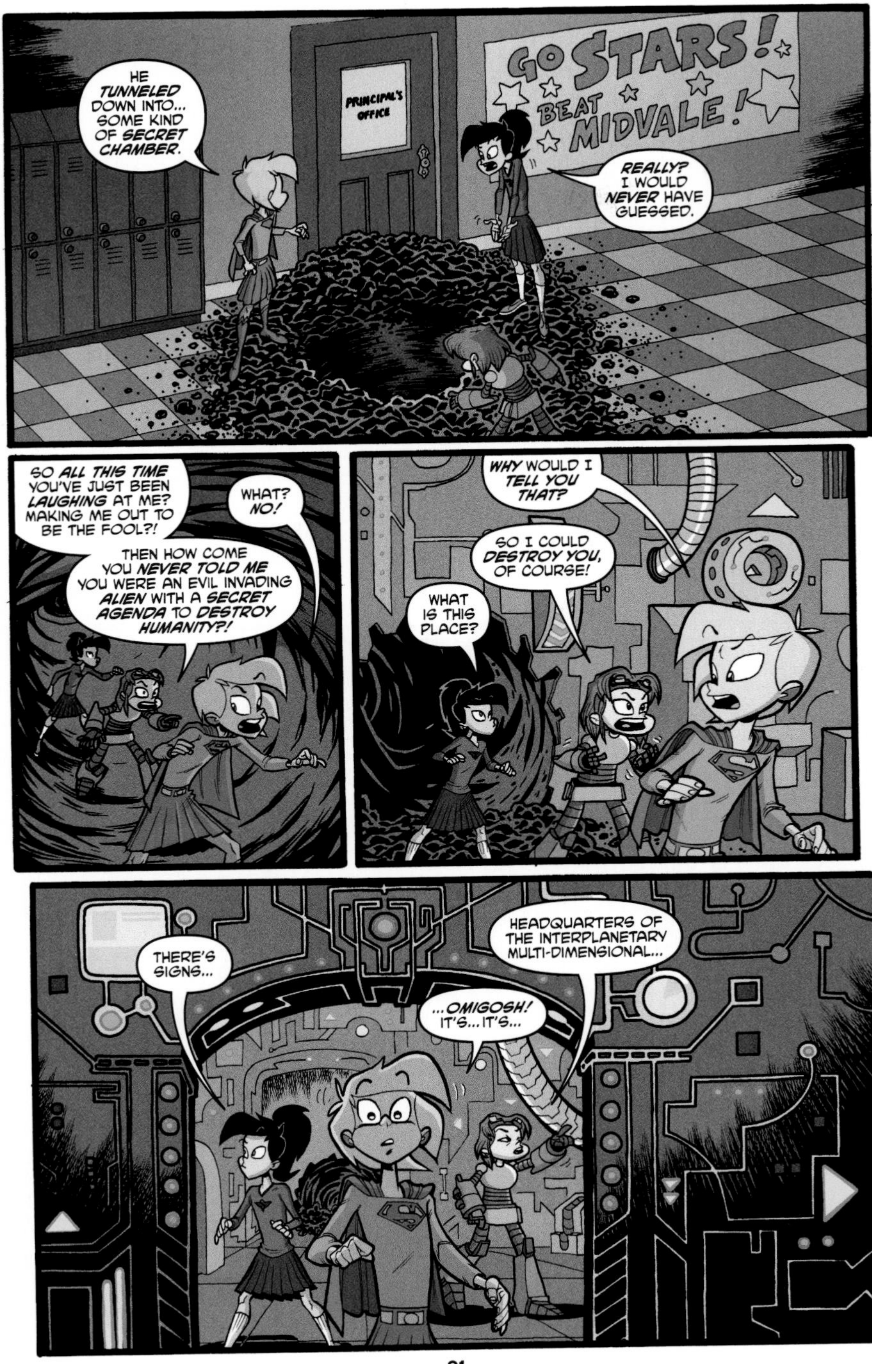
GO STARS! BEAT MIDVALE!
PRINCIPAL'S OFFICE
HE TUNNELED DOWN INTO... SOME KIND OF SECRET CHAMBER.
REALLY? I WOULD NEVER HAVE GUESSED.
SO ALL THIS TIME YOU'VE JUST BEEN LAUGHING AT ME? MAKING ME OUT TO BE THE FOOL?!
WHAT? NO!
THEN HOW COME YOU NEVER TOLD ME YOU WERE AN EVIL INVADING ALIEN WITH A SECRET AGENDA TO DESTROY HUMANITY?!
WHY WOULD I TELL YOU THAT?
SO I COULD DESTROY YOU, OF COURSE!
WHAT IS THIS PLACE?
THERE'S SIGNS...
HEADQUARTERS OF THE INTERPLANETARY MULTI-DIMENSIONAL...
...OMIGOSH! IT'S... IT'S...

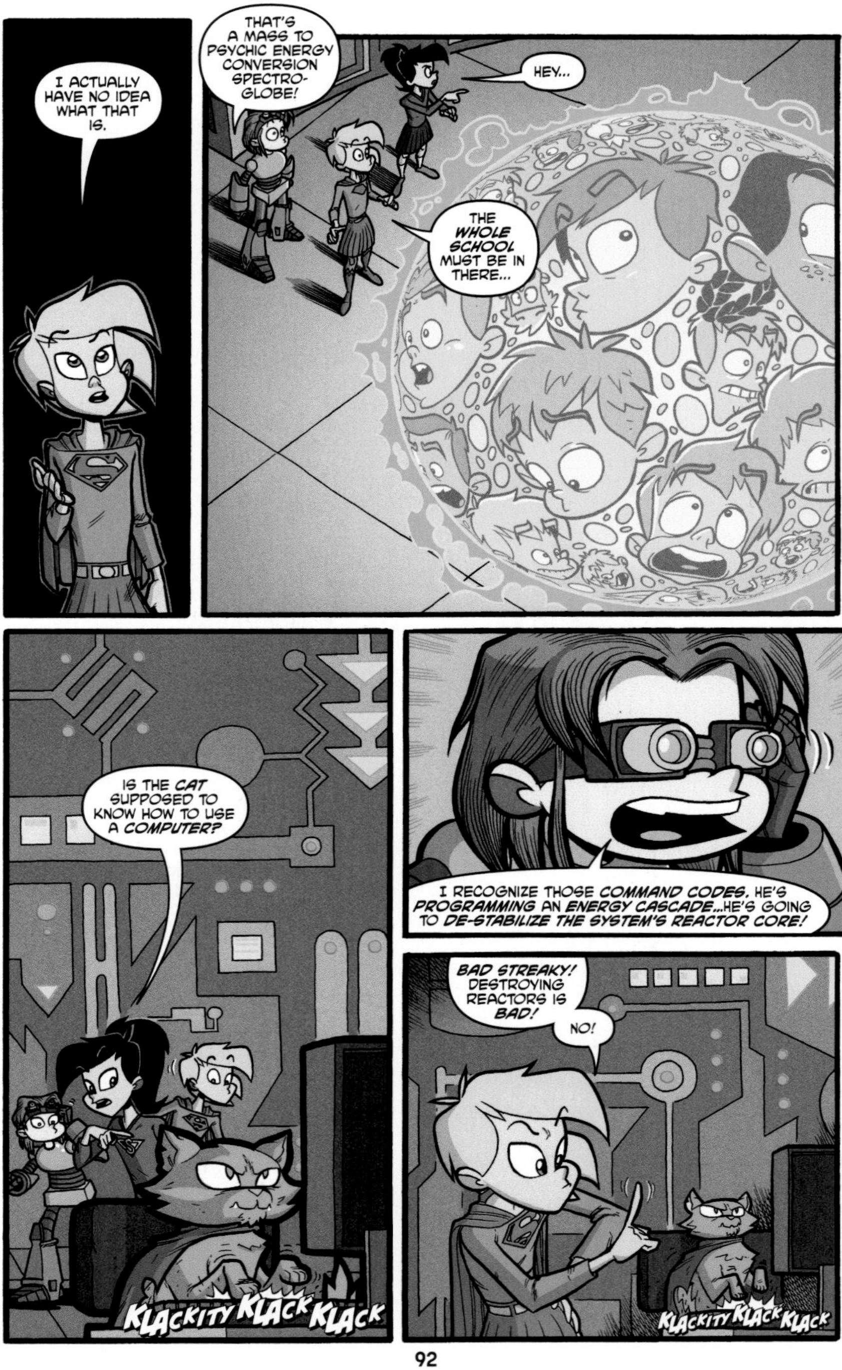
I ACTUALLY HAVE NO IDEA WHAT THAT IS.
THAT'S A MASS TO PSYCHIC ENERGY CONVERSION SPECTRO-GLOBE!
HEY...
THE *WHOLE SCHOOL* MUST BE IN THERE...
IS THE *CAT* SUPPOSED TO KNOW HOW TO USE A *COMPUTER?*
KLACKITY KLACK KLACK
I RECOGNIZE THOSE *COMMAND CODES.* HE'S *PROGRAMMING* AN *ENERGY CASCADE*...HE'S GOING TO *DE-STABILIZE THE SYSTEM'S REACTOR CORE!*
BAD STREAKY! DESTROYING REACTORS IS *BAD!*
NO!
KLACKITY KLACK KLACK

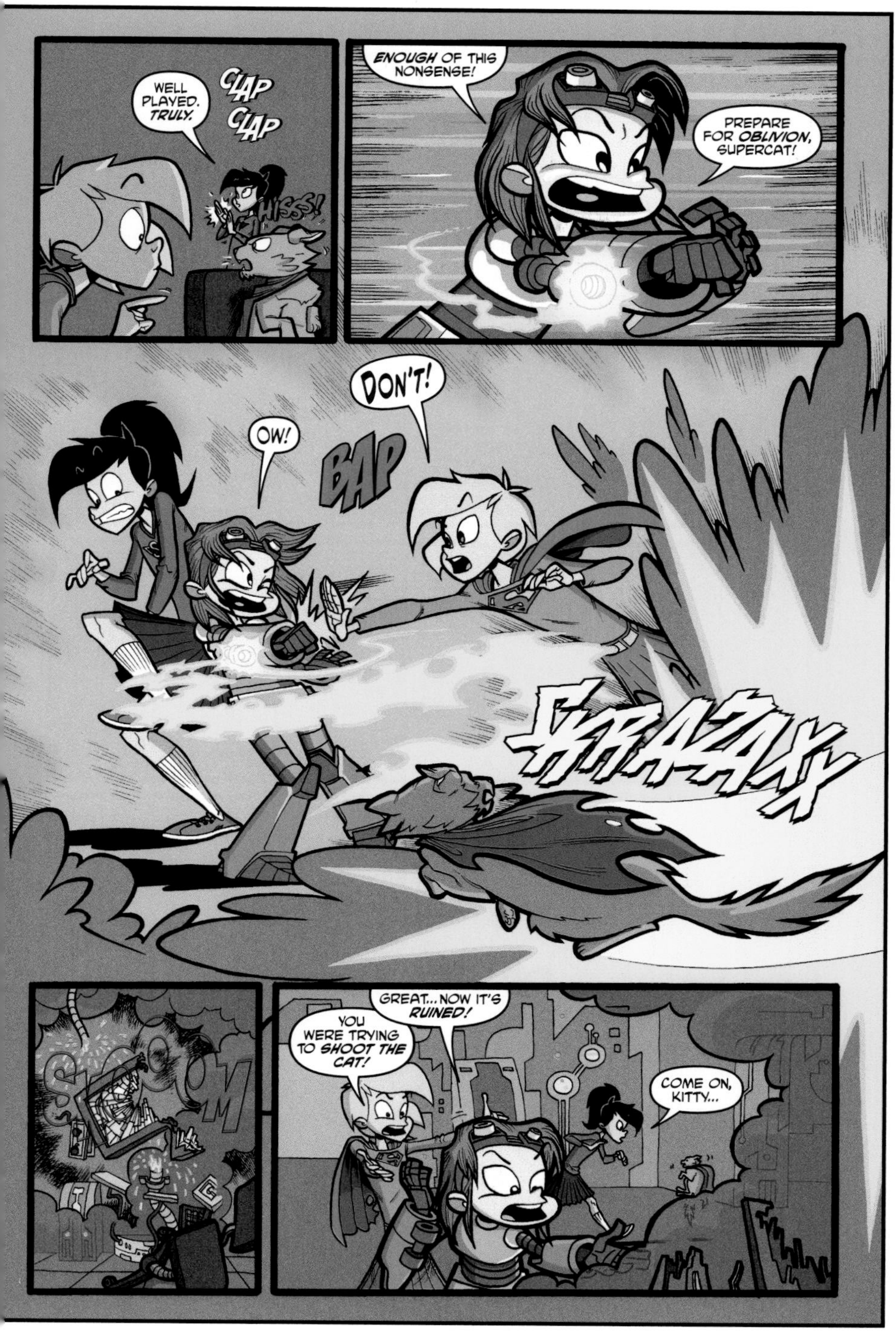
WELL PLAYED. TRULY.
CLAP CLAP
HISS!
ENOUGH OF THIS NONSENSE!
PREPARE FOR OBLIVION, SUPERCAT!
OW!
BAP
DON'T!
SKRAZAX
GREAT... NOW IT'S RUINED!
YOU WERE TRYING TO SHOOT THE CAT!
COME ON, KITTY...

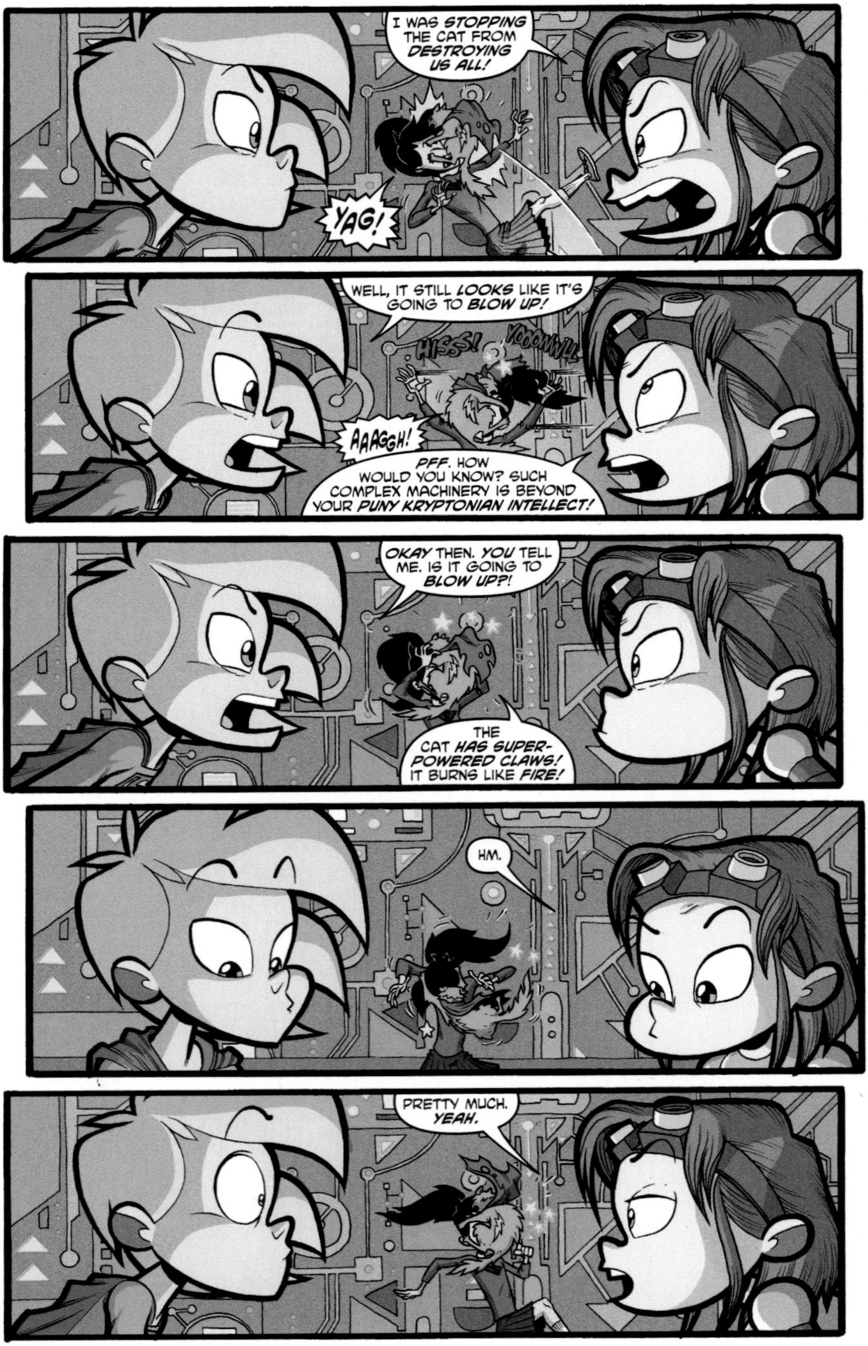
I WAS STOPPING THE CAT FROM DESTROYING US ALL!
YAG!
WELL, IT STILL LOOKS LIKE IT'S GOING TO BLOW UP!
HISSS!
YOOOWWLL
AAAGGH!
PFF. HOW WOULD YOU KNOW? SUCH COMPLEX MACHINERY IS BEYOND YOUR PUNY KRYPTONIAN INTELLECT!
OKAY THEN. YOU TELL ME. IS IT GOING TO BLOW UP?!
THE CAT HAS SUPER-POWERED CLAWS! IT BURNS LIKE FIRE!
HM.
PRETTY MUCH. YEAH.

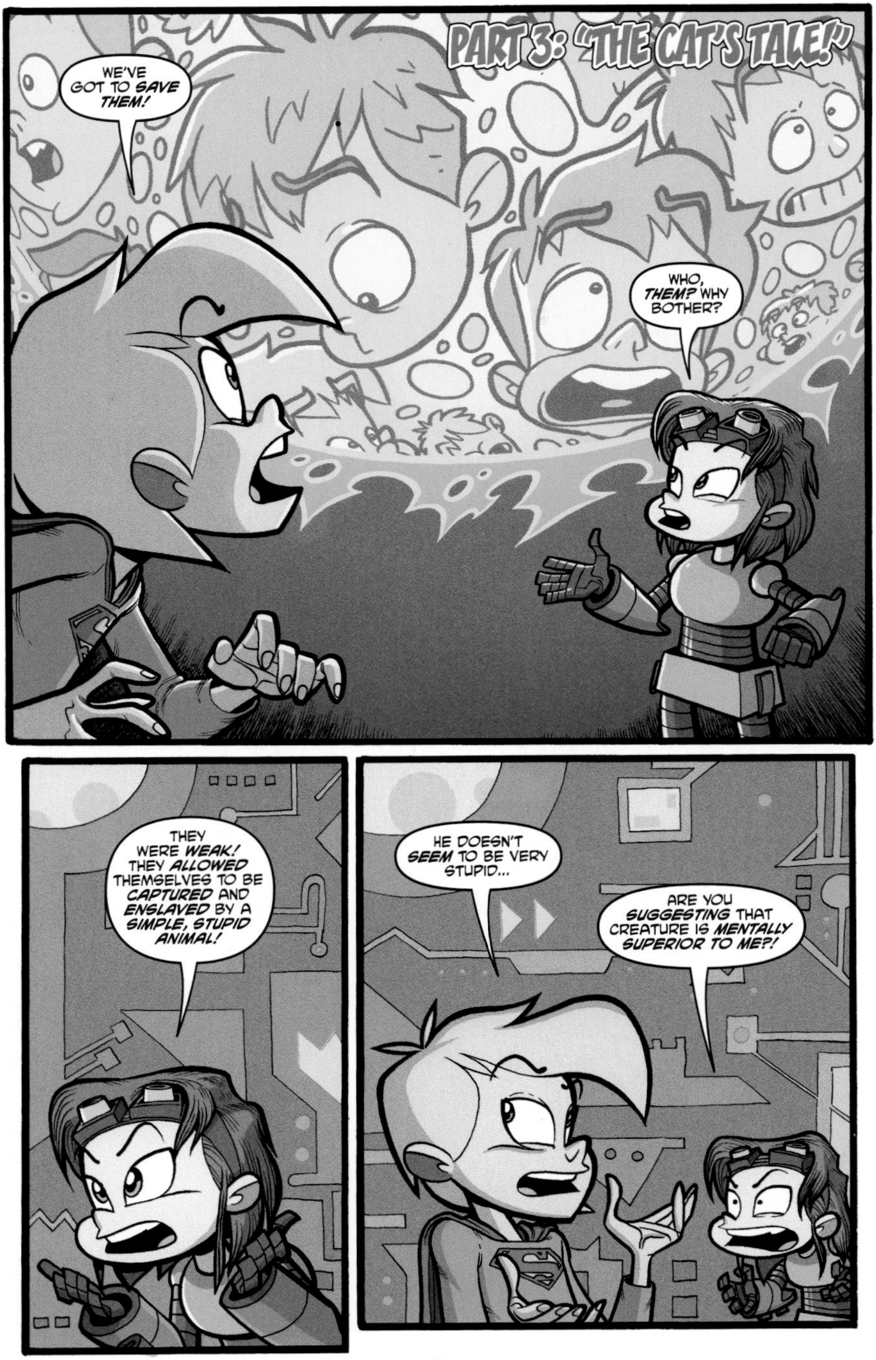
PART 3: "THE CAT'S TALE!"
WE'VE GOT TO SAVE THEM!
WHO, THEM? WHY BOTHER?
THEY WERE WEAK! THEY ALLOWED THEMSELVES TO BE CAPTURED AND ENSLAVED BY A SIMPLE, STUPID ANIMAL!
HE DOESN'T SEEM TO BE VERY STUPID...
ARE YOU SUGGESTING THAT CREATURE IS MENTALLY SUPERIOR TO ME?!

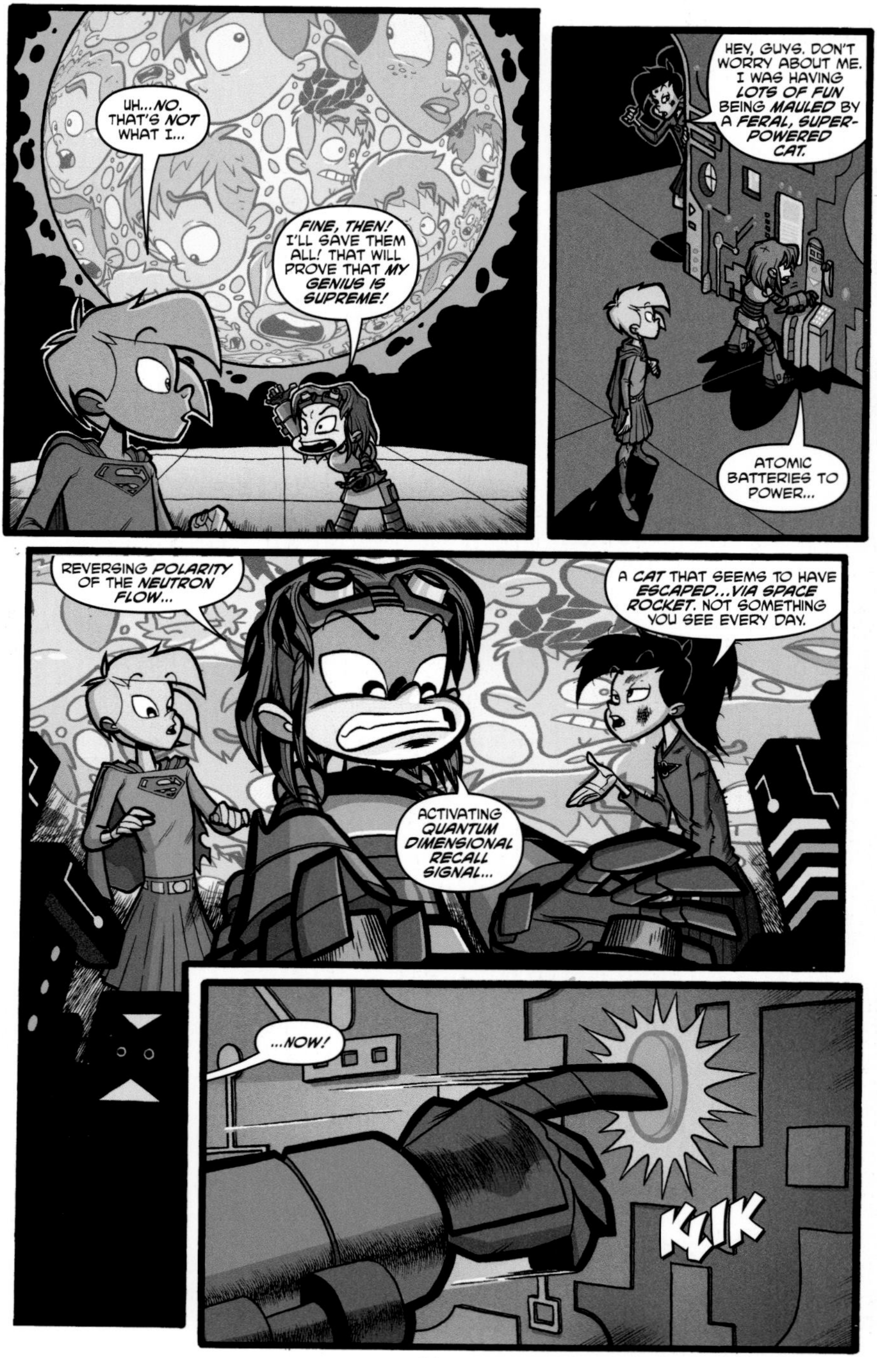
UH...NO. THAT'S NOT WHAT I...
FINE, THEN! I'LL SAVE THEM ALL! THAT WILL PROVE THAT MY GENIUS IS SUPREME!
HEY, GUYS. DON'T WORRY ABOUT ME. I WAS HAVING LOTS OF FUN BEING MAULED BY A FERAL, SUPER-POWERED CAT.
ATOMIC BATTERIES TO POWER...
REVERSING POLARITY OF THE NEUTRON FLOW...
A CAT THAT SEEMS TO HAVE ESCAPED...VIA SPACE ROCKET. NOT SOMETHING YOU SEE EVERY DAY.
ACTIVATING QUANTUM DIMENSIONAL RECALL SIGNAL...
...NOW!
KLIK

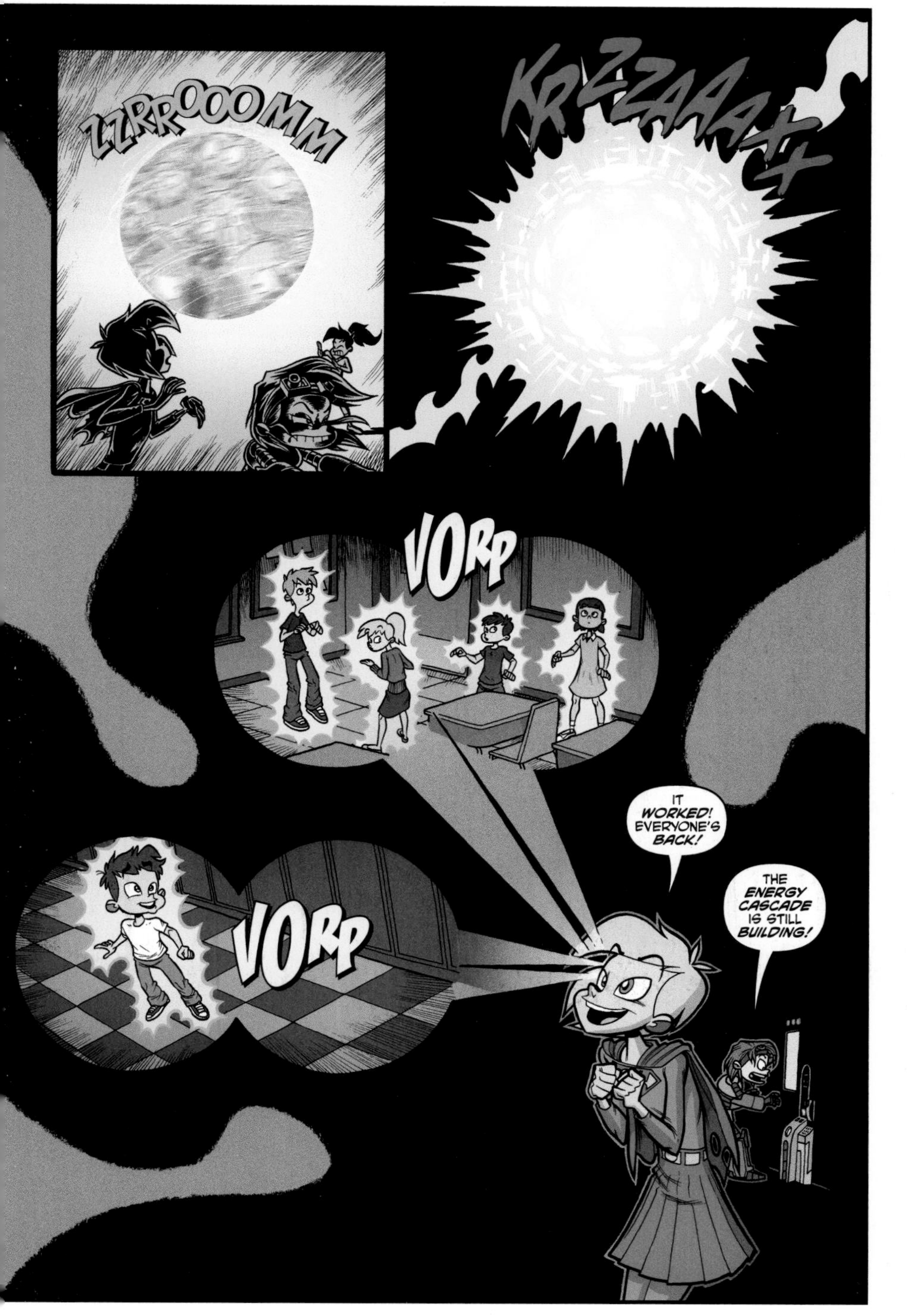
ZZRROOOMM
KRZZAAAAH
VORP
VORP
IT WORKED! EVERYONE'S BACK!
THE ENERGY CASCADE IS STILL BUILDING!

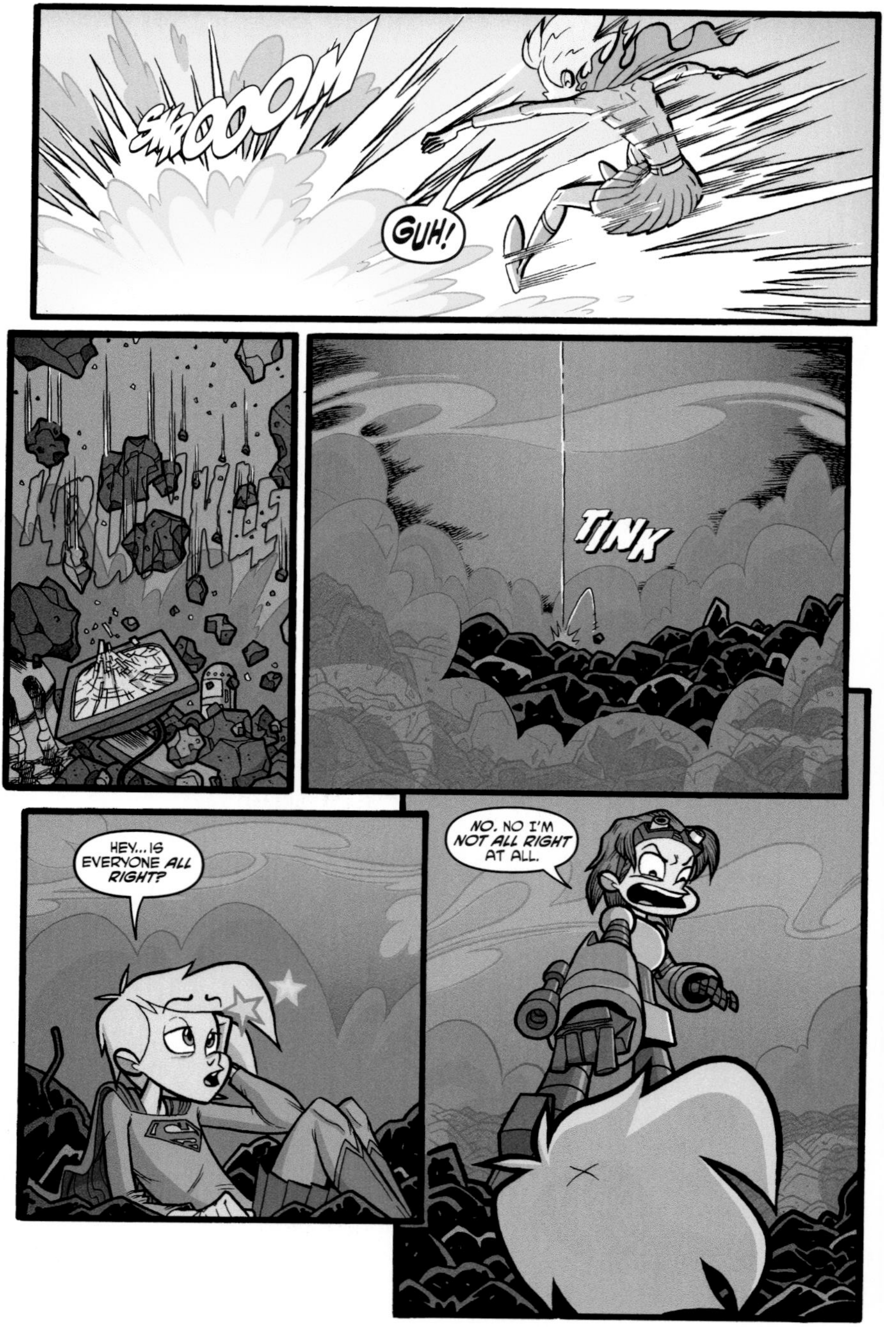
GUH!
TINK
HEY... IS EVERYONE *ALL RIGHT?*
NO. NO I'M *NOT ALL RIGHT* AT ALL.

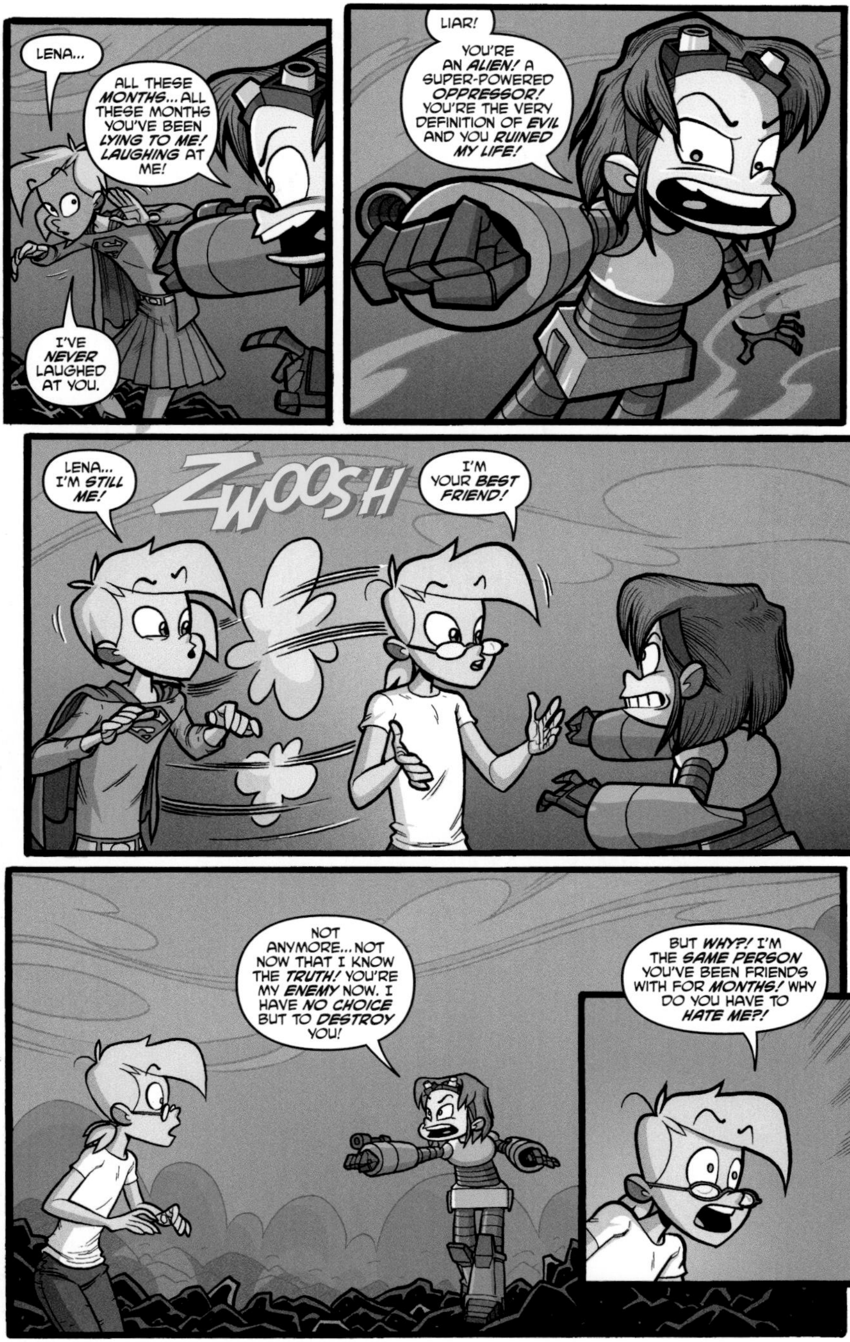

LENA...
ALL THESE MONTHS... ALL THESE MONTHS YOU'VE BEEN LYING TO ME! LAUGHING AT ME!
I'VE NEVER LAUGHED AT YOU.
LIAR!
YOU'RE AN ALIEN! A SUPER-POWERED OPPRESSOR! YOU'RE THE VERY DEFINITION OF EVIL AND YOU RUINED MY LIFE!
LENA... I'M STILL ME!
ZWOOSH
I'M YOUR BEST FRIEND!
NOT ANYMORE... NOT NOW THAT I KNOW THE TRUTH! YOU'RE MY ENEMY NOW. I HAVE NO CHOICE BUT TO DESTROY YOU!
BUT WHY?! I'M THE SAME PERSON YOU'VE BEEN FRIENDS WITH FOR MONTHS! WHY DO YOU HAVE TO HATE ME?!

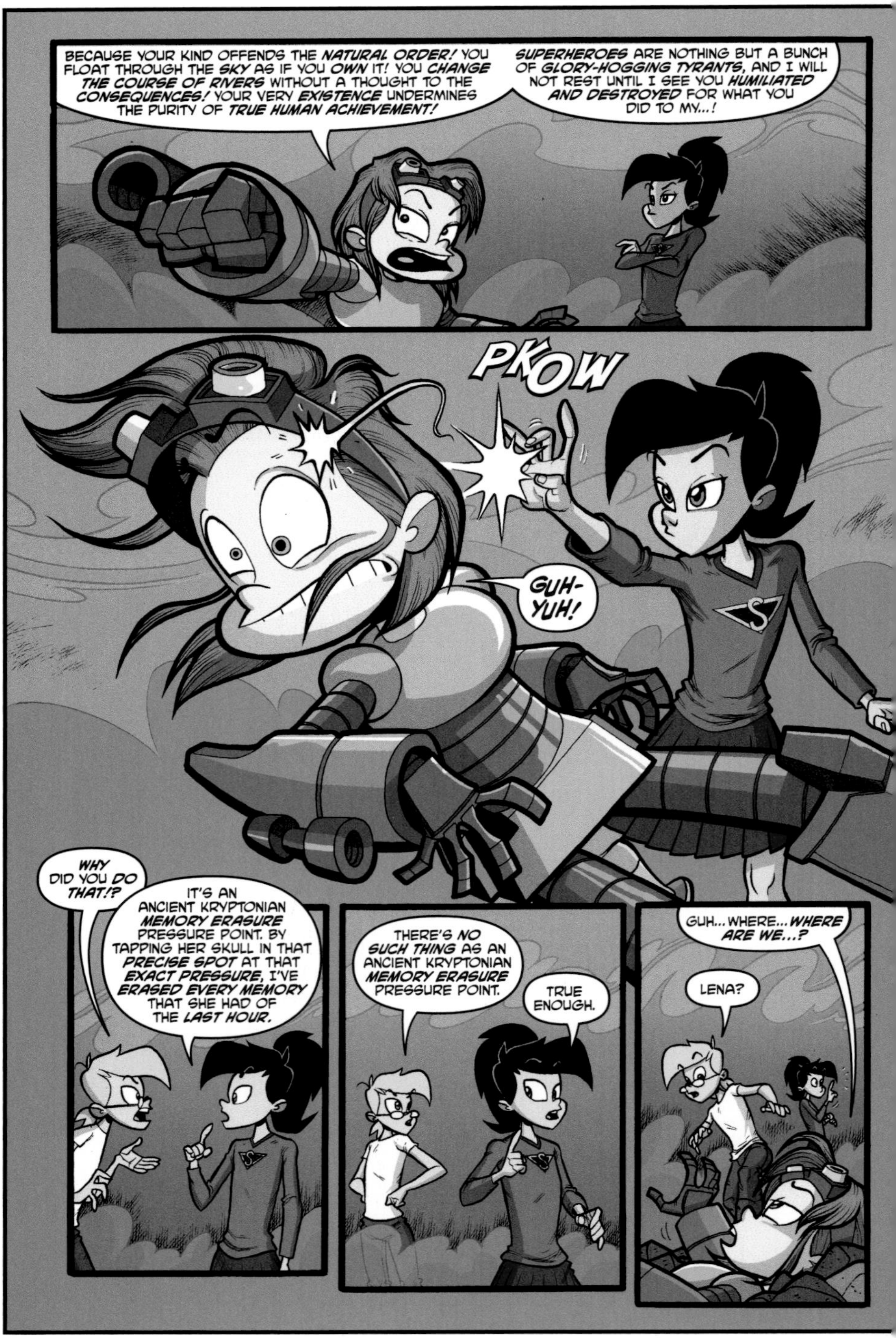
BECAUSE YOUR KIND OFFENDS THE NATURAL ORDER! YOU FLOAT THROUGH THE SKY AS IF YOU OWN IT! YOU CHANGE THE COURSE OF RIVERS WITHOUT A THOUGHT TO THE CONSEQUENCES! YOUR VERY EXISTENCE UNDERMINES THE PURITY OF TRUE HUMAN ACHIEVEMENT!
SUPERHEROES ARE NOTHING BUT A BUNCH OF GLORY-HOGGING TYRANTS, AND I WILL NOT REST UNTIL I SEE YOU HUMILIATED AND DESTROYED FOR WHAT YOU DID TO MY...!
PKOW
GUH-YUH!
WHY DID YOU DO THAT!?
IT'S AN ANCIENT KRYPTONIAN MEMORY ERASURE PRESSURE POINT. BY TAPPING HER SKULL IN THAT PRECISE SPOT AT THAT EXACT PRESSURE, I'VE ERASED EVERY MEMORY THAT SHE HAD OF THE LAST HOUR.
THERE'S NO SUCH THING AS AN ANCIENT KRYPTONIAN MEMORY ERASURE PRESSURE POINT.
TRUE ENOUGH.
GUH... WHERE... WHERE ARE WE...?
LENA?

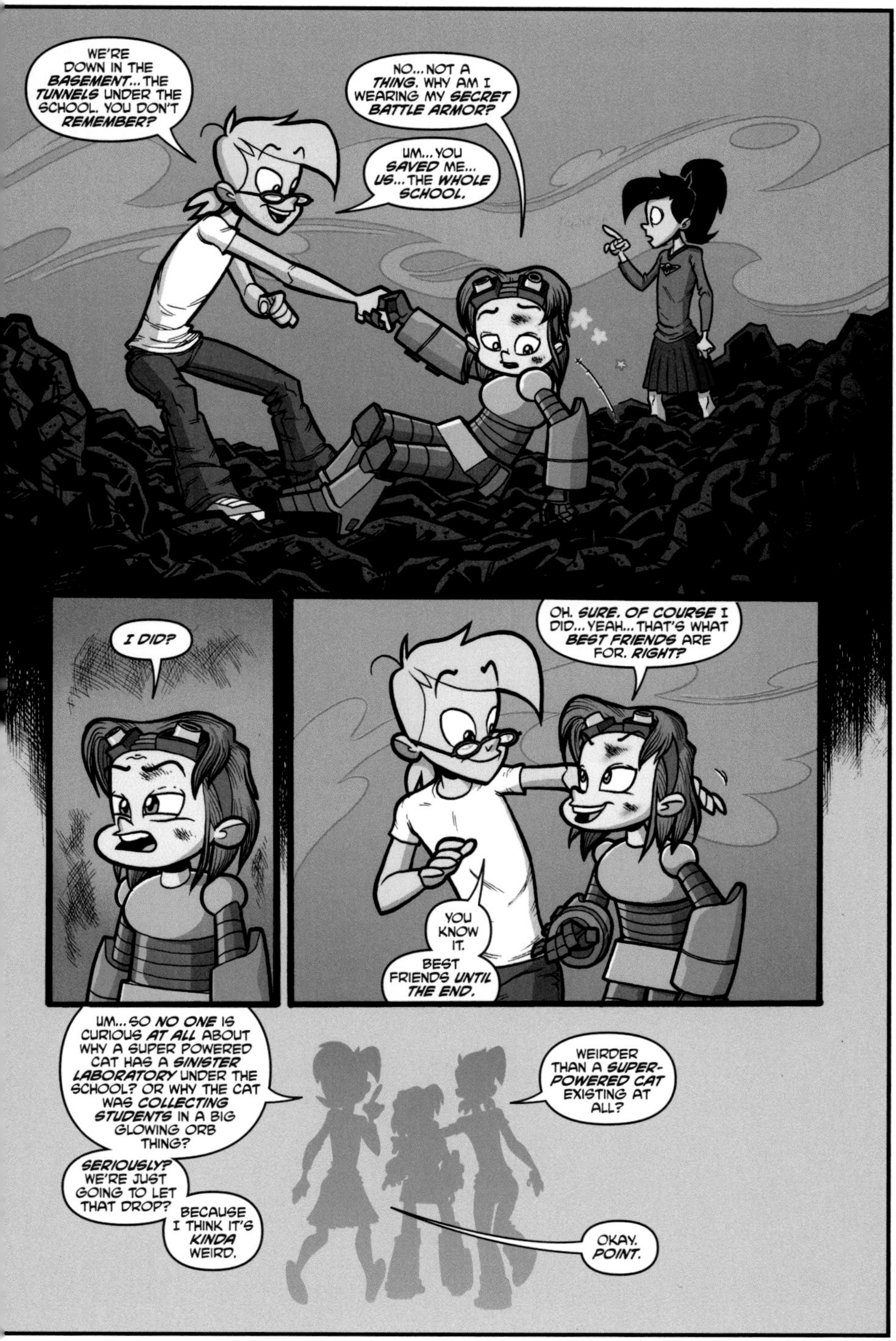
WE'RE DOWN IN THE BASEMENT... THE TUNNELS UNDER THE SCHOOL. YOU DON'T REMEMBER?
NO... NOT A THING. WHY AM I WEARING MY SECRET BATTLE ARMOR?
UM... YOU SAVED ME... US... THE WHOLE SCHOOL.
I DID?
OH. SURE. OF COURSE I DID... YEAH... THAT'S WHAT BEST FRIENDS ARE FOR. RIGHT?
YOU KNOW IT.
BEST FRIENDS UNTIL THE END.
UM... SO NO ONE IS CURIOUS AT ALL ABOUT WHY A SUPER POWERED CAT HAS A SINISTER LABORATORY UNDER THE SCHOOL? OR WHY THE CAT WAS COLLECTING STUDENTS IN A BIG GLOWING ORB THING?
SERIOUSLY? WE'RE JUST GOING TO LET THAT DROP?
BECAUSE I THINK IT'S KINDA WEIRD.
WEIRDER THAN A SUPER-POWERED CAT EXISTING AT ALL?
OKAY. POINT.

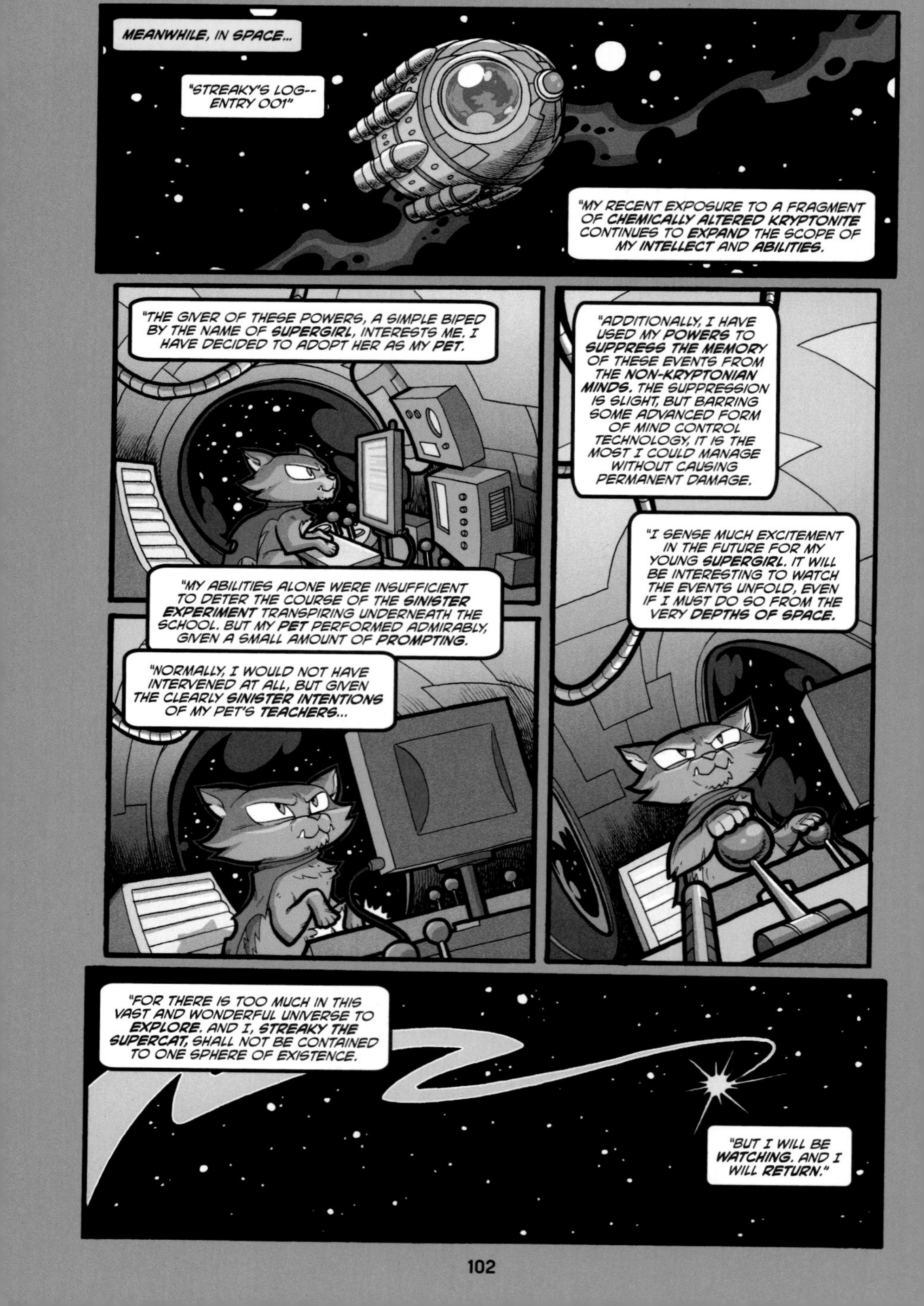
MEANWHILE, IN SPACE...
"STREAKY'S LOG-- ENTRY 001"
"MY RECENT EXPOSURE TO A FRAGMENT OF CHEMICALLY ALTERED KRYPTONITE CONTINUES TO EXPAND THE SCOPE OF MY INTELLECT AND ABILITIES.
"THE GIVER OF THESE POWERS, A SIMPLE BIPED BY THE NAME OF SUPERGIRL, INTERESTS ME. I HAVE DECIDED TO ADOPT HER AS MY PET.
"MY ABILITIES ALONE WERE INSUFFICIENT TO DETER THE COURSE OF THE SINISTER EXPERIMENT TRANSPIRING UNDERNEATH THE SCHOOL. BUT MY PET PERFORMED ADMIRABLY, GIVEN A SMALL AMOUNT OF PROMPTING.
"NORMALLY, I WOULD NOT HAVE INTERVENED AT ALL, BUT GIVEN THE CLEARLY SINISTER INTENTIONS OF MY PET'S TEACHERS...
"ADDITIONALLY, I HAVE USED MY POWERS TO SUPPRESS THE MEMORY OF THESE EVENTS FROM THE NON-KRYPTONIAN MINDS. THE SUPPRESSION IS SLIGHT, BUT BARRING SOME ADVANCED FORM OF MIND CONTROL TECHNOLOGY, IT IS THE MOST I COULD MANAGE WITHOUT CAUSING PERMANENT DAMAGE.
"I SENSE MUCH EXCITEMENT IN THE FUTURE FOR MY YOUNG SUPERGIRL. IT WILL BE INTERESTING TO WATCH THE EVENTS UNFOLD, EVEN IF I MUST DO SO FROM THE VERY DEPTHS OF SPACE.
"FOR THERE IS TOO MUCH IN THIS VAST AND WONDERFUL UNIVERSE TO EXPLORE. AND I, STREAKY THE SUPERCAT, SHALL NOT BE CONTAINED TO ONE SPHERE OF EXISTENCE.
"BUT I WILL BE WATCHING. AND I WILL RETURN."

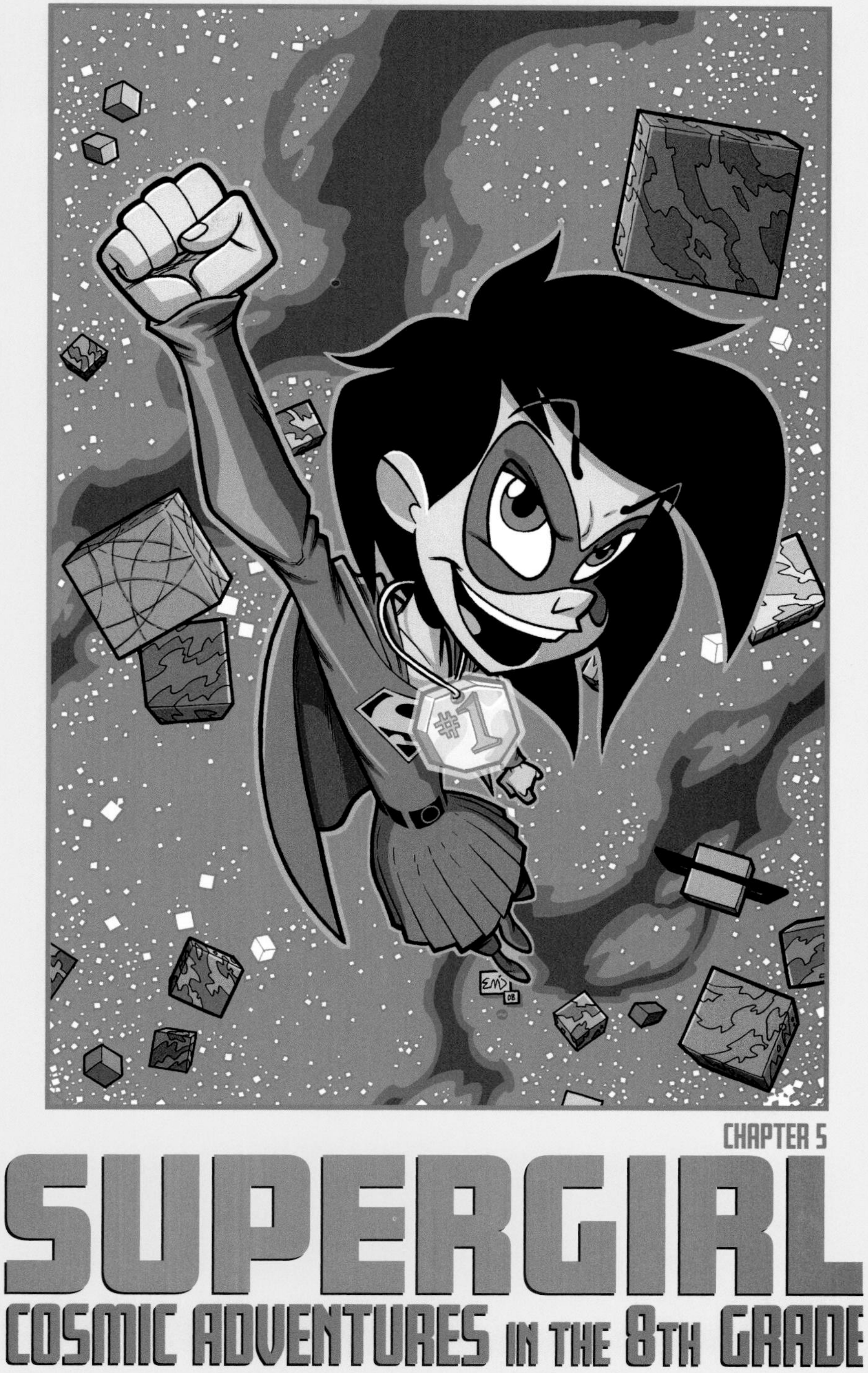
#1

CHAPTER 5

SUPERGIRL
COSMIC ADVENTURES IN THE 8TH GRADE

SUPERGIRL

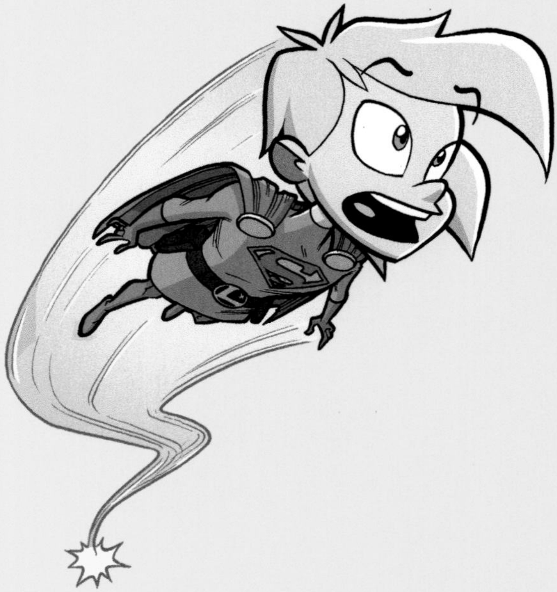

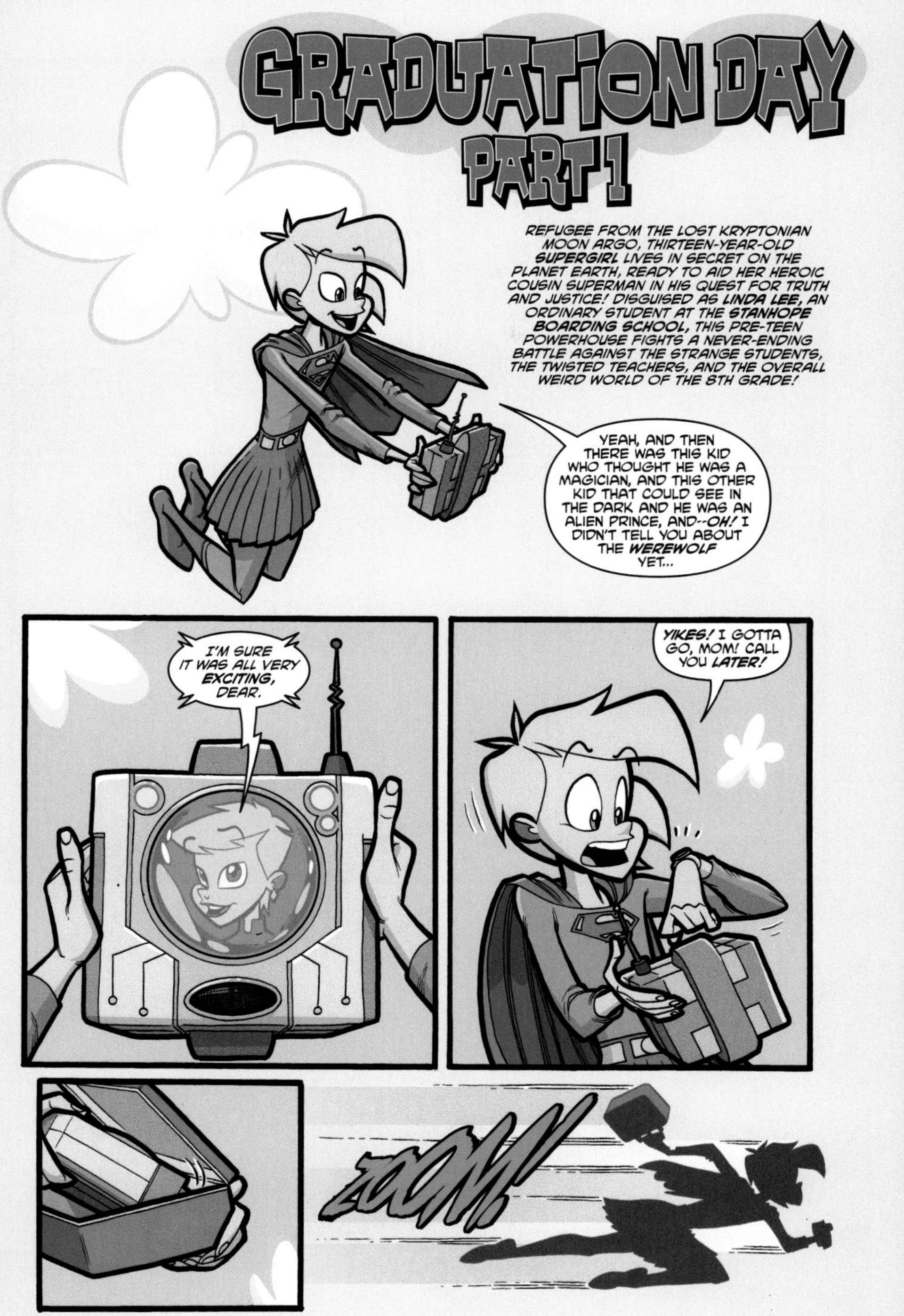

GRADUATION DAY PART 1
REFUGEE FROM THE LOST KRYPTONIAN MOON ARGO, THIRTEEN-YEAR-OLD SUPERGIRL LIVES IN SECRET ON THE PLANET EARTH, READY TO AID HER HEROIC COUSIN SUPERMAN IN HIS QUEST FOR TRUTH AND JUSTICE! DISGUISED AS LINDA LEE, AN ORDINARY STUDENT AT THE STANHOPE BOARDING SCHOOL, THIS PRE-TEEN POWERHOUSE FIGHTS A NEVER-ENDING BATTLE AGAINST THE STRANGE STUDENTS, THE TWISTED TEACHERS, AND THE OVERALL WEIRD WORLD OF THE 8TH GRADE!
YEAH, AND THEN THERE WAS THIS KID WHO THOUGHT HE WAS A MAGICIAN, AND THIS OTHER KID THAT COULD SEE IN THE DARK AND HE WAS AN ALIEN PRINCE, AND--OH! I DIDN'T TELL YOU ABOUT THE WEREWOLF YET...
I'M SURE IT WAS ALL VERY EXCITING, DEAR.
YIKES! I GOTTA GO, MOM! CALL YOU LATER!
ZOOM!

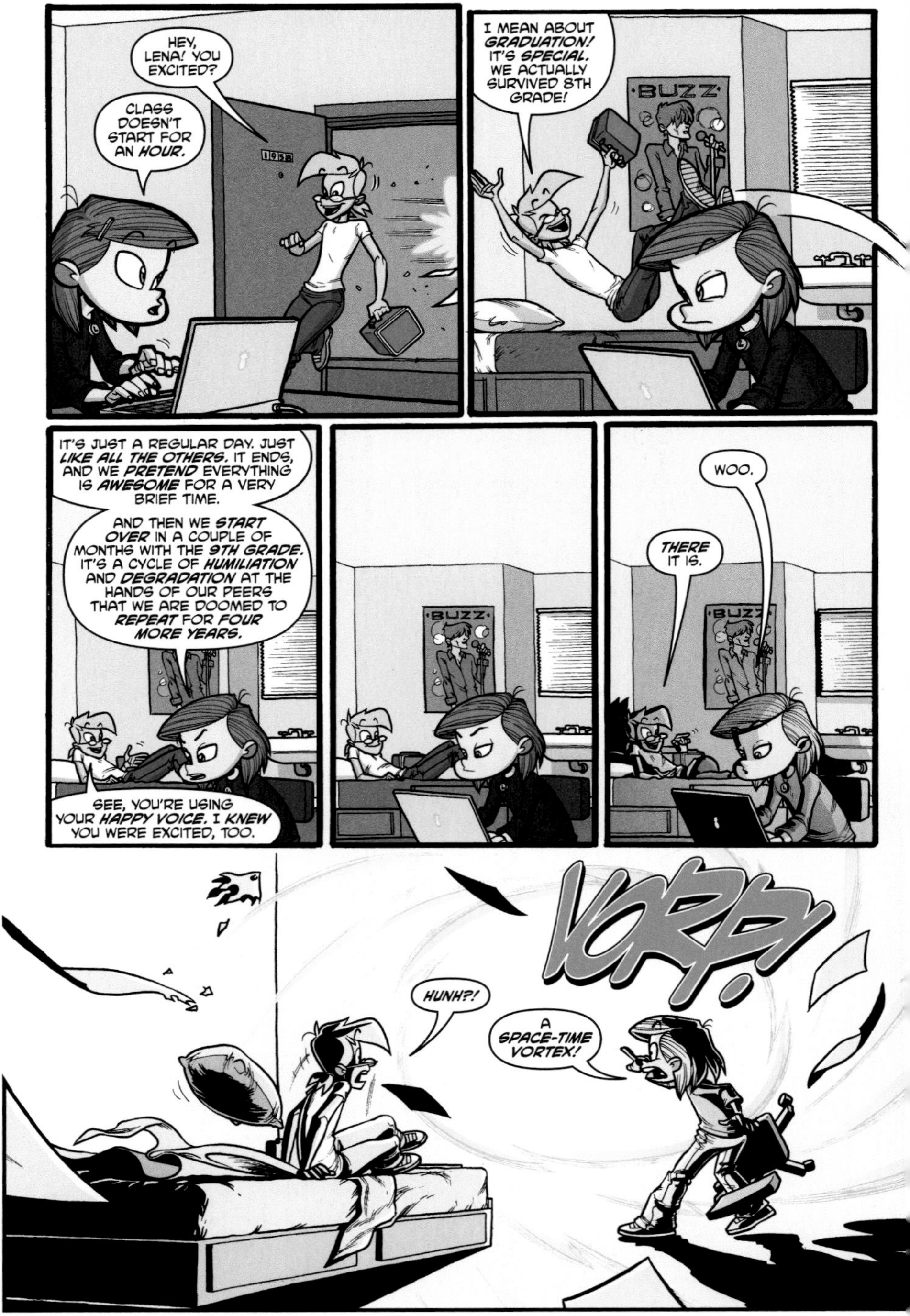
HEY, LENA! YOU EXCITED?
CLASS DOESN'T START FOR AN *HOUR.*
I MEAN ABOUT *GRADUATION!* IT'S *SPECIAL.* WE ACTUALLY SURVIVED 8TH GRADE!
BUZZ
IT'S JUST A REGULAR DAY. JUST *LIKE ALL THE OTHERS.* IT ENDS, AND WE *PRETEND* EVERYTHING IS *AWESOME* FOR A VERY BRIEF TIME.
AND THEN WE *START OVER* IN A COUPLE OF MONTHS WITH THE *9TH GRADE.* IT'S A CYCLE OF *HUMILIATION* AND *DEGRADATION* AT THE HANDS OF OUR PEERS THAT WE ARE DOOMED TO *REPEAT* FOR *FOUR MORE YEARS.*
SEE, YOU'RE USING YOUR *HAPPY VOICE. I KNEW* YOU WERE EXCITED, TOO.
WOO.
THERE IT IS.
VORP!
HUNH?!
A *SPACE-TIME VORTEX!*

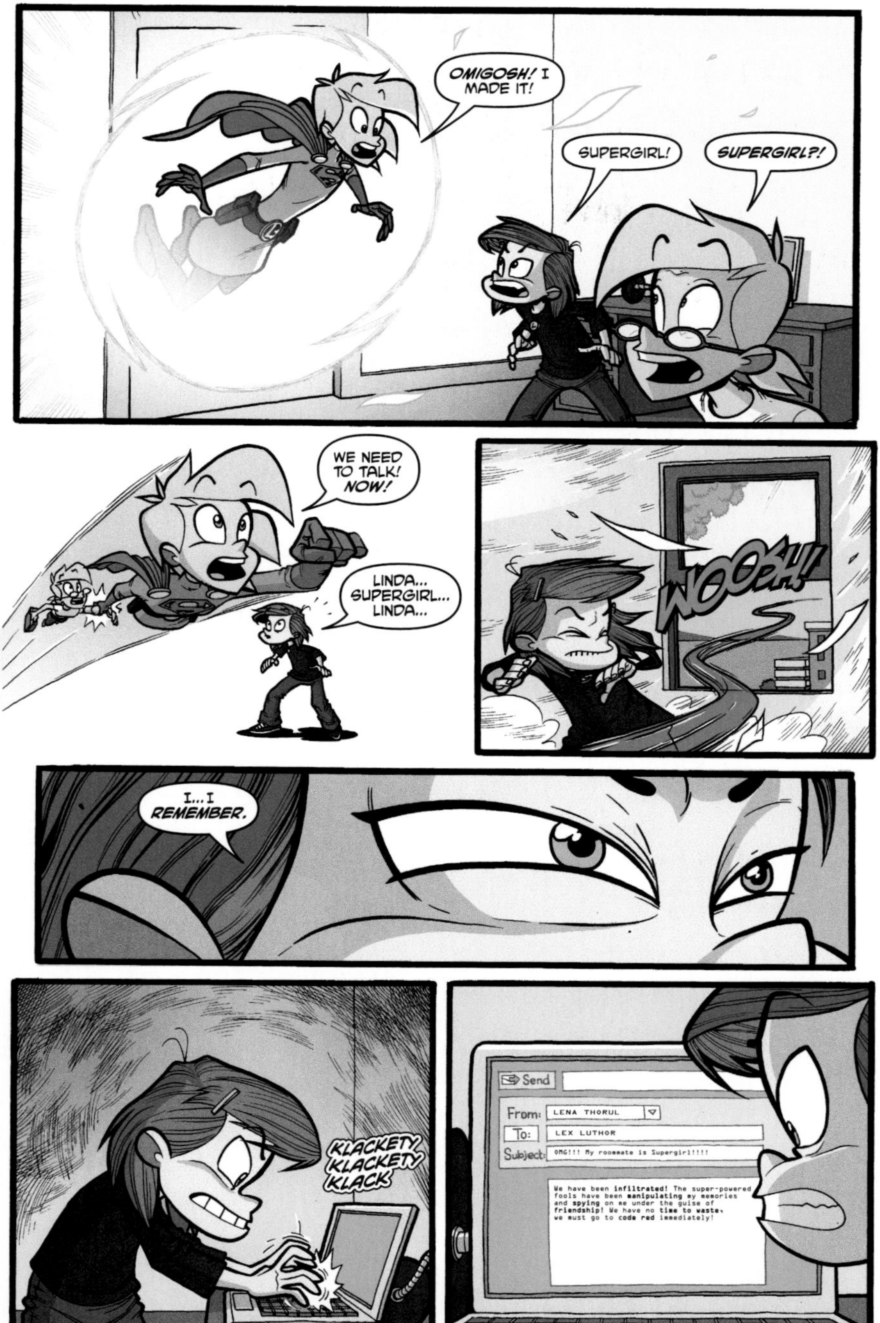
OMIGOSH! I MADE IT!
SUPERGIRL!
SUPERGIRL?!
WE NEED TO TALK! NOW!
LINDA... SUPERGIRL... LINDA...
WOOSH!
I...I REMEMBER.
KLACKETY KLACKETY KLACK
Send
From: LENA THORUL
To: LEX LUTHOR
Subject: OMG!!! My roommate is Supergirl!!!!
We have been infiltrated! The super-powered fools have been manipulating my memories and spying on me under the guise of friendship! We have no time to waste, we must go to code red immediately!

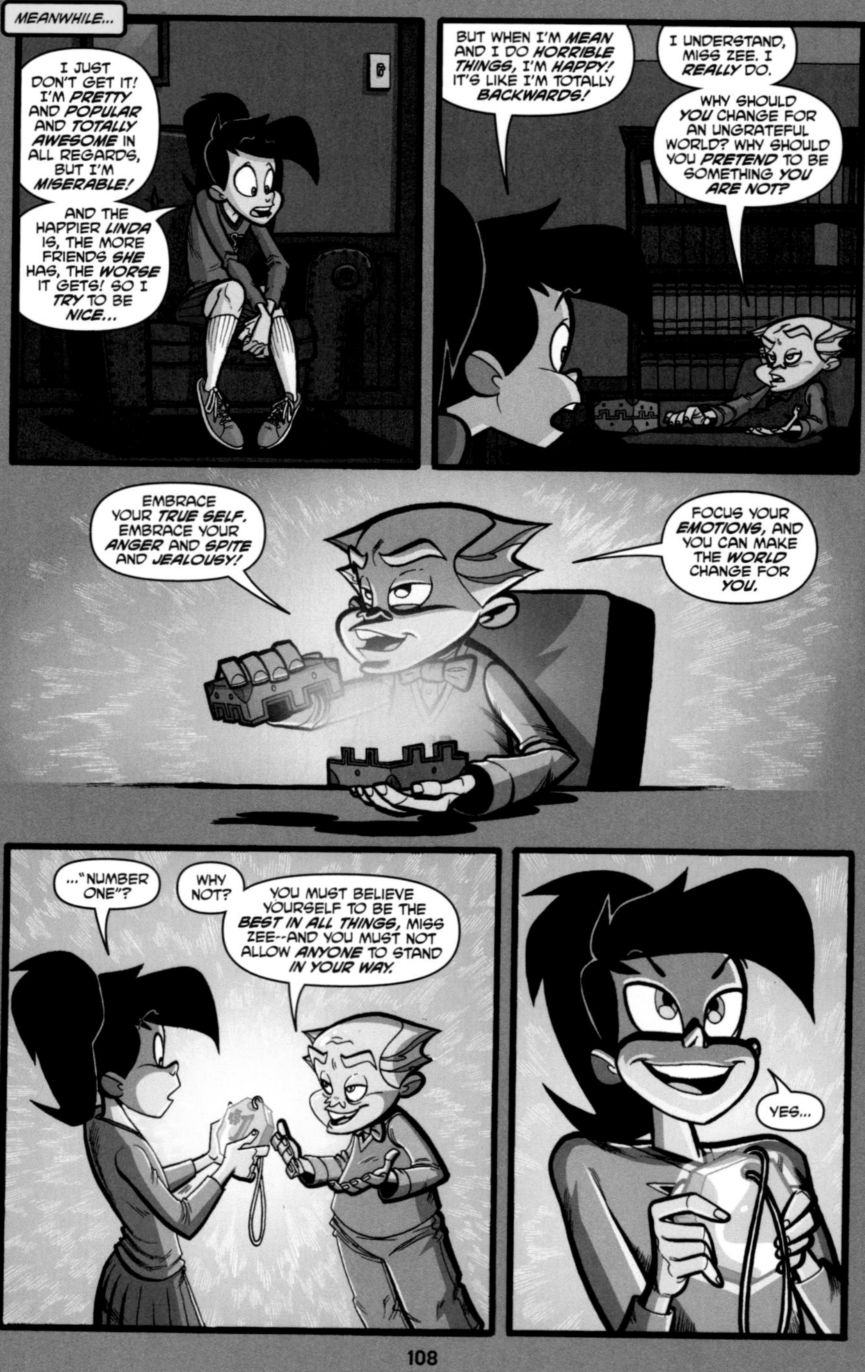

MEANWHILE...
I JUST DON'T GET IT! I'M PRETTY AND POPULAR AND TOTALLY AWESOME IN ALL REGARDS, BUT I'M MISERABLE!
AND THE HAPPIER LINDA IS, THE MORE FRIENDS SHE HAS, THE WORSE IT GETS! SO I TRY TO BE NICE...
BUT WHEN I'M MEAN AND I DO HORRIBLE THINGS, I'M HAPPY! IT'S LIKE I'M TOTALLY BACKWARDS!
I UNDERSTAND, MISS ZEE. I REALLY DO.
WHY SHOULD YOU CHANGE FOR AN UNGRATEFUL WORLD? WHY SHOULD YOU PRETEND TO BE SOMETHING YOU ARE NOT?
EMBRACE YOUR TRUE SELF. EMBRACE YOUR ANGER AND SPITE AND JEALOUSY!
FOCUS YOUR EMOTIONS, AND YOU CAN MAKE THE WORLD CHANGE FOR YOU.
..."NUMBER ONE"?
WHY NOT?
YOU MUST BELIEVE YOURSELF TO BE THE BEST IN ALL THINGS, MISS ZEE--AND YOU MUST NOT ALLOW ANYONE TO STAND IN YOUR WAY.
YES...

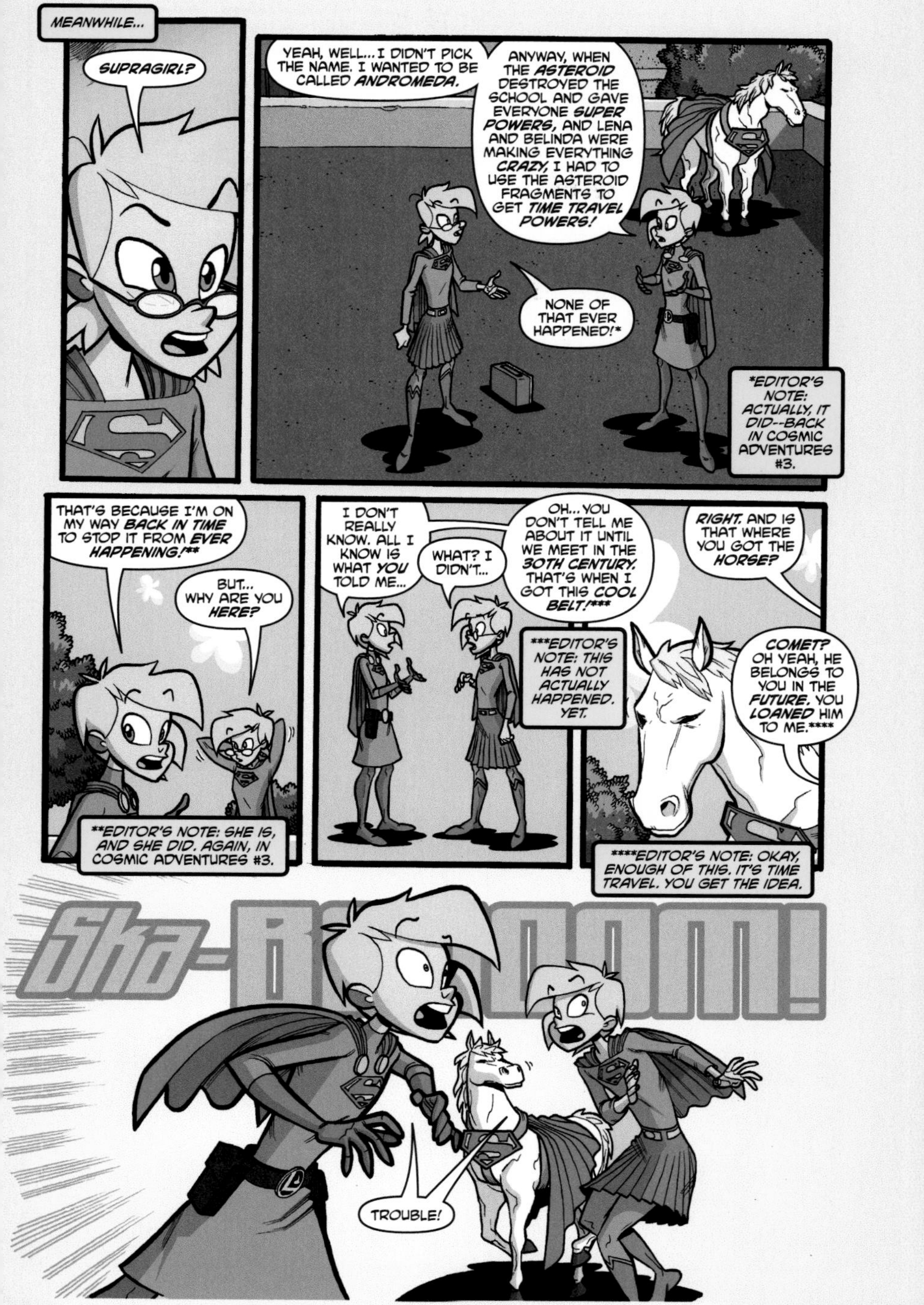
MEANWHILE...
SUPRAGIRL?
YEAH, WELL... I DIDN'T PICK THE NAME. I WANTED TO BE CALLED ANDROMEDA.
ANYWAY, WHEN THE ASTEROID DESTROYED THE SCHOOL AND GAVE EVERYONE SUPER POWERS, AND LENA AND BELINDA WERE MAKING EVERYTHING CRAZY, I HAD TO USE THE ASTEROID FRAGMENTS TO GET TIME TRAVEL POWERS!
NONE OF THAT EVER HAPPENED!*
*EDITOR'S NOTE: ACTUALLY, IT DID--BACK IN COSMIC ADVENTURES #3.
THAT'S BECAUSE I'M ON MY WAY BACK IN TIME TO STOP IT FROM EVER HAPPENING!**
BUT... WHY ARE YOU HERE?
**EDITOR'S NOTE: SHE IS, AND SHE DID. AGAIN, IN COSMIC ADVENTURES #3.
I DON'T REALLY KNOW. ALL I KNOW IS WHAT YOU TOLD ME...
WHAT? I DIDN'T...
OH... YOU DON'T TELL ME ABOUT IT UNTIL WE MEET IN THE 30TH CENTURY. THAT'S WHEN I GOT THIS COOL BELT!***
***EDITOR'S NOTE: THIS HAS NOT ACTUALLY HAPPENED. YET.
RIGHT. AND IS THAT WHERE YOU GOT THE HORSE?
COMET? OH YEAH, HE BELONGS TO YOU IN THE FUTURE. YOU LOANED HIM TO ME.****
****EDITOR'S NOTE: OKAY, ENOUGH OF THIS. IT'S TIME TRAVEL. YOU GET THE IDEA.
SHA-BOOOM!
TROUBLE!

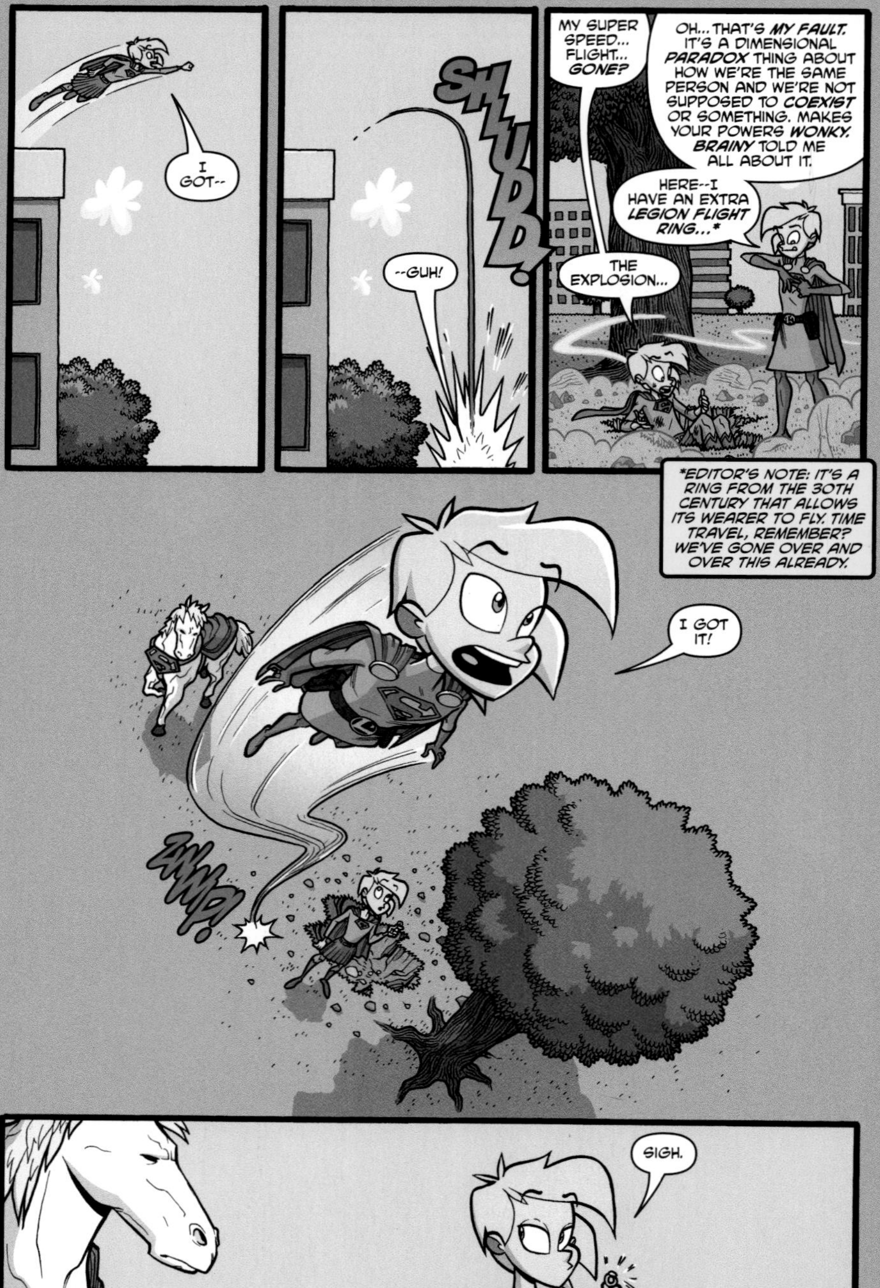

I GOT--
SHLUDD!
--GUH!
MY SUPER SPEED... FLIGHT... GONE?
THE EXPLOSION...
OH...THAT'S MY FAULT. IT'S A DIMENSIONAL PARADOX THING ABOUT HOW WE'RE THE SAME PERSON AND WE'RE NOT SUPPOSED TO COEXIST OR SOMETHING. MAKES YOUR POWERS WONKY. BRAINY TOLD ME ALL ABOUT IT.
HERE--I HAVE AN EXTRA LEGION FLIGHT RING...*
*EDITOR'S NOTE: IT'S A RING FROM THE 30TH CENTURY THAT ALLOWS ITS WEARER TO FLY. TIME TRAVEL, REMEMBER? WE'VE GONE OVER AND OVER THIS ALREADY.
I GOT IT!
ZWAMP!
SIGH.

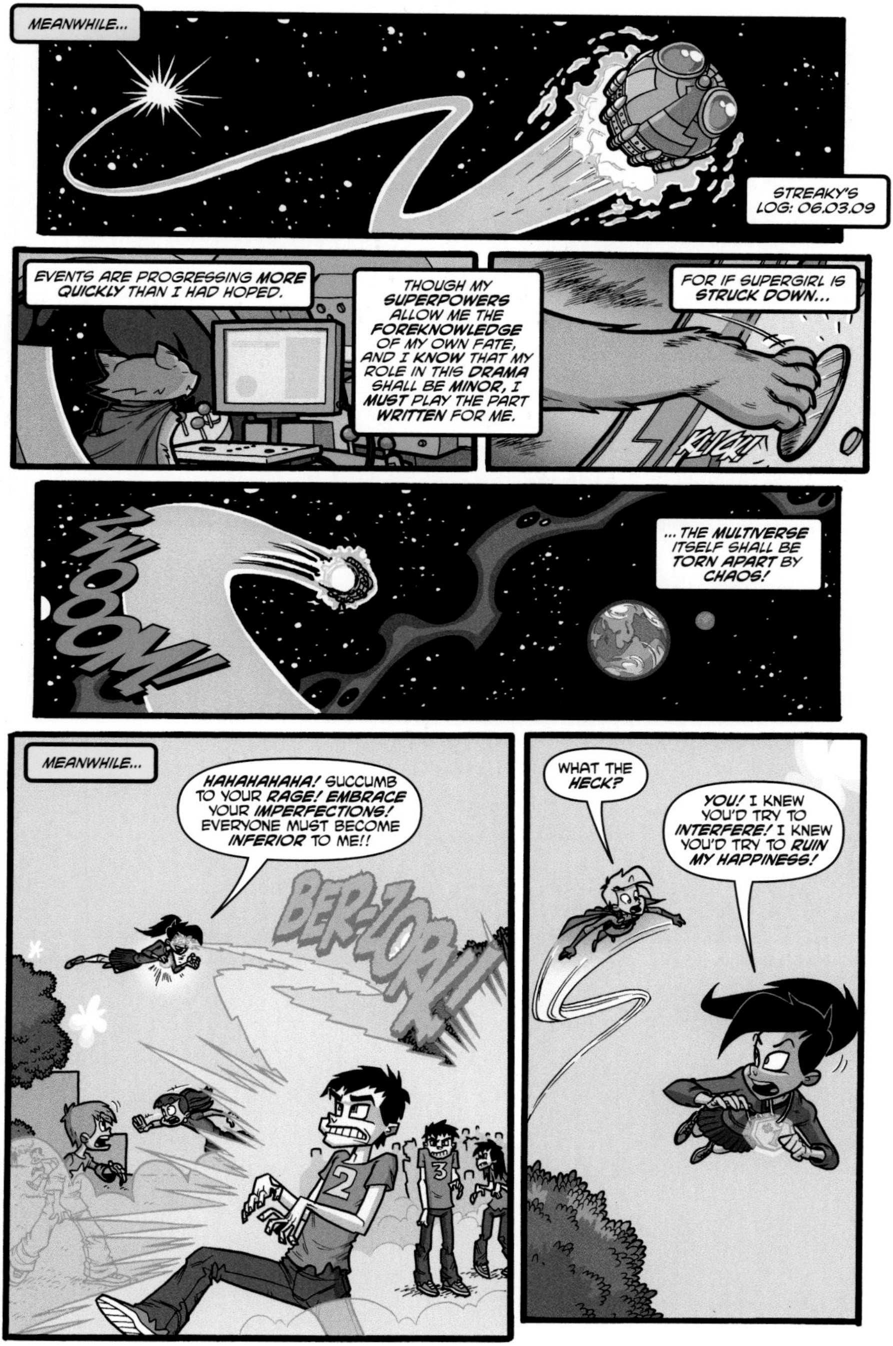
MEANWHILE...
STREAKY'S LOG: 06.03.09
EVENTS ARE PROGRESSING MORE QUICKLY THAN I HAD HOPED.
THOUGH MY SUPERPOWERS ALLOW ME THE FOREKNOWLEDGE OF MY OWN FATE, AND I KNOW THAT MY ROLE IN THIS DRAMA SHALL BE MINOR, I MUST PLAY THE PART WRITTEN FOR ME.
FOR IF SUPERGIRL IS STRUCK DOWN...
KLICK!
ZWOOOOM!
...THE MULTIVERSE ITSELF SHALL BE TORN APART BY CHAOS!
MEANWHILE...
HAHAHAHAHA! SUCCUMB TO YOUR RAGE! EMBRACE YOUR IMPERFECTIONS! EVERYONE MUST BECOME INFERIOR TO ME!!
BER-ZORK!!
WHAT THE HECK?
YOU! I KNEW YOU'D TRY TO INTERFERE! I KNEW YOU'D TRY TO RUIN MY HAPPINESS!

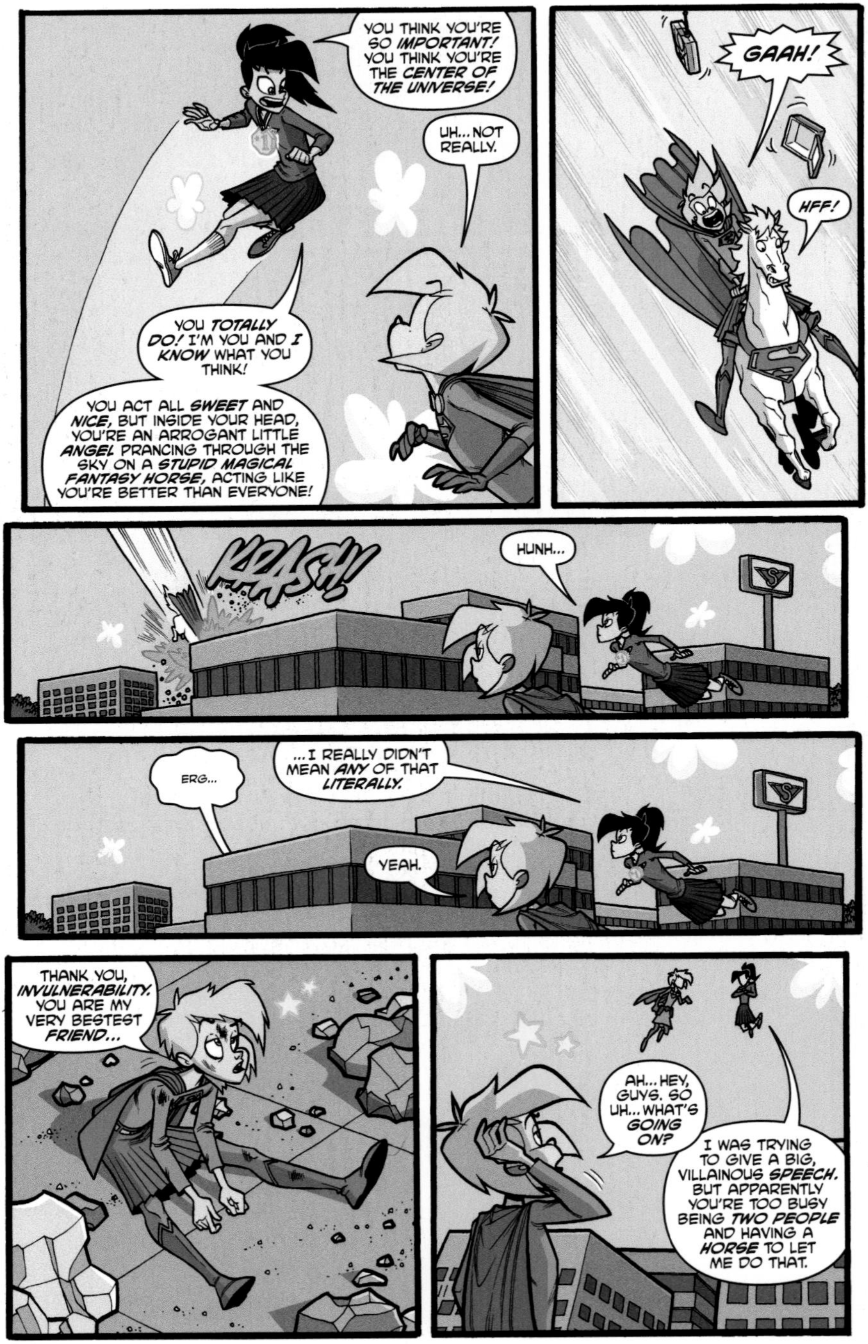

YOU THINK YOU'RE SO *IMPORTANT!* YOU THINK YOU'RE THE *CENTER OF THE UNIVERSE!*
UH... NOT REALLY.
YOU *TOTALLY DO!* I'M YOU AND *I KNOW* WHAT YOU THINK!
YOU ACT ALL *SWEET* AND *NICE*, BUT INSIDE YOUR HEAD, YOU'RE AN ARROGANT LITTLE *ANGEL* PRANCING THROUGH THE SKY ON A *STUPID MAGICAL FANTASY HORSE*, ACTING LIKE YOU'RE BETTER THAN EVERYONE!
GAAH!
HFF!
KRASH!
HUNH...
ERG...
...I REALLY DIDN'T MEAN *ANY* OF THAT *LITERALLY.*
YEAH.
THANK YOU, *INVULNERABILITY.* YOU ARE MY VERY BESTEST *FRIEND...*
AH... HEY, GUYS. SO UH... WHAT'S *GOING ON?*
I WAS TRYING TO GIVE A BIG, VILLAINOUS *SPEECH.* BUT APPARENTLY YOU'RE TOO BUSY BEING *TWO PEOPLE* AND HAVING A *HORSE* TO LET ME DO THAT.

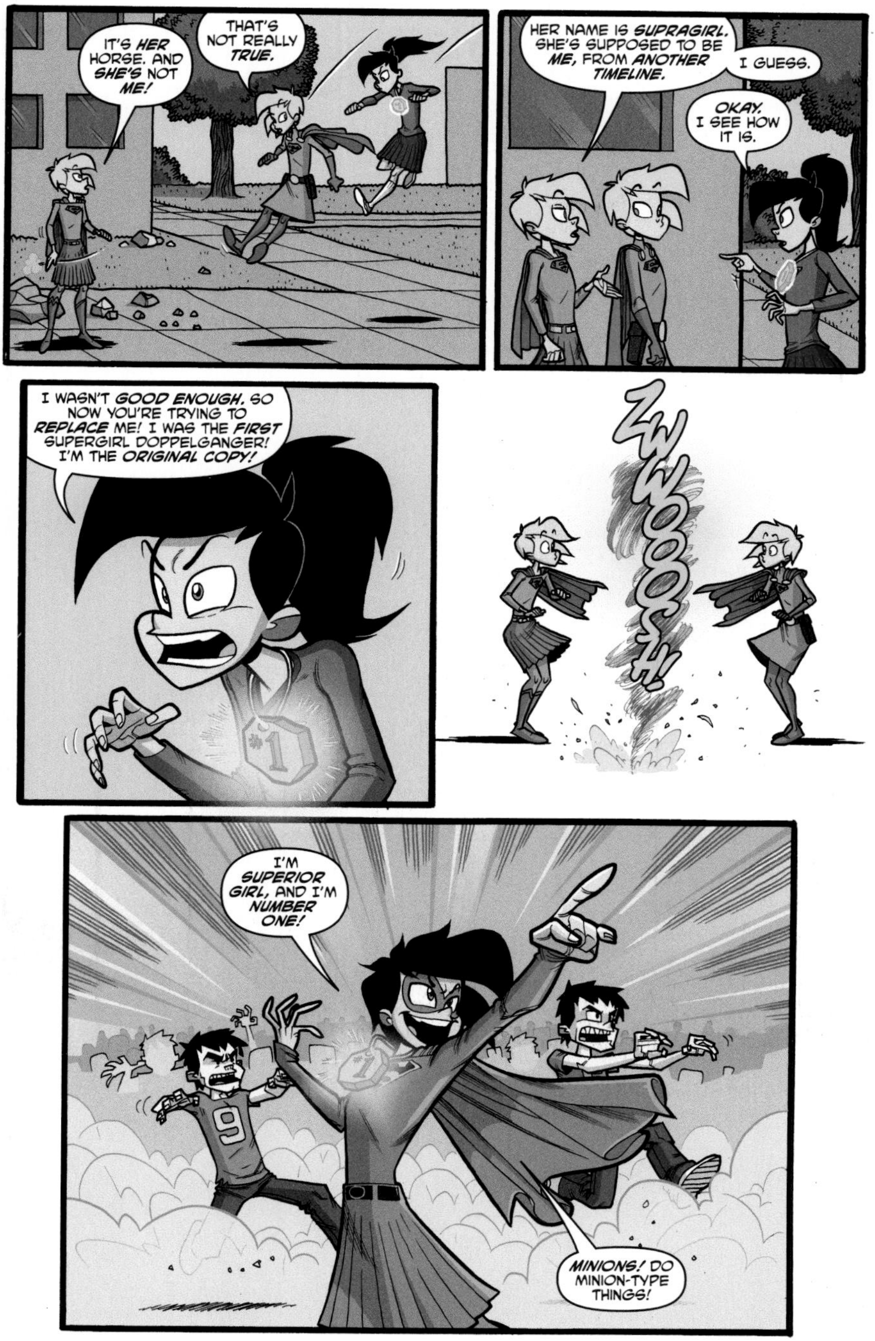
IT'S HER HORSE. AND SHE'S NOT ME!
THAT'S NOT REALLY TRUE.
HER NAME IS SUPRAGIRL. SHE'S SUPPOSED TO BE ME, FROM ANOTHER TIMELINE.
I GUESS.
OKAY. I SEE HOW IT IS.
I WASN'T GOOD ENOUGH. SO NOW YOU'RE TRYING TO REPLACE ME! I WAS THE FIRST SUPERGIRL DOPPELGANGER! I'M THE ORIGINAL COPY!
ZWWOOOOSH!
I'M SUPERIOR GIRL, AND I'M NUMBER ONE!
MINIONS! DO MINION-TYPE THINGS!

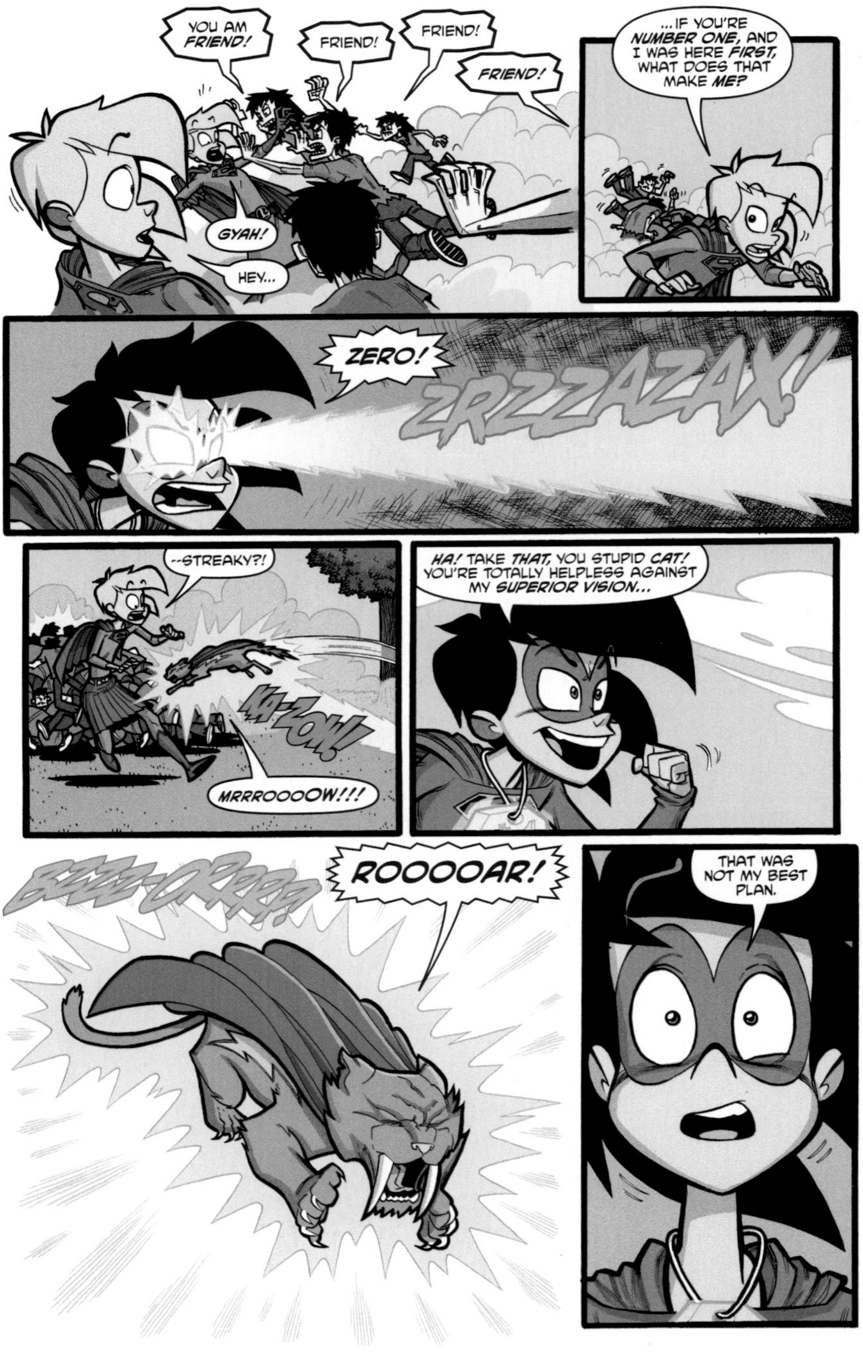
YOU AM FRIEND!
FRIEND!
FRIEND!
FRIEND!
GYAH!
HEY...
...IF YOU'RE NUMBER ONE, AND I WAS HERE FIRST, WHAT DOES THAT MAKE ME?
ZERO!
ZRZZZAZAX!
--STREAKY?!
KA-ZOW!
MRRROOOOW!!!
HA! TAKE THAT, YOU STUPID CAT! YOU'RE TOTALLY HELPLESS AGAINST MY SUPERIOR VISION...
ROOOOAR!
THAT WAS NOT MY BEST PLAN.

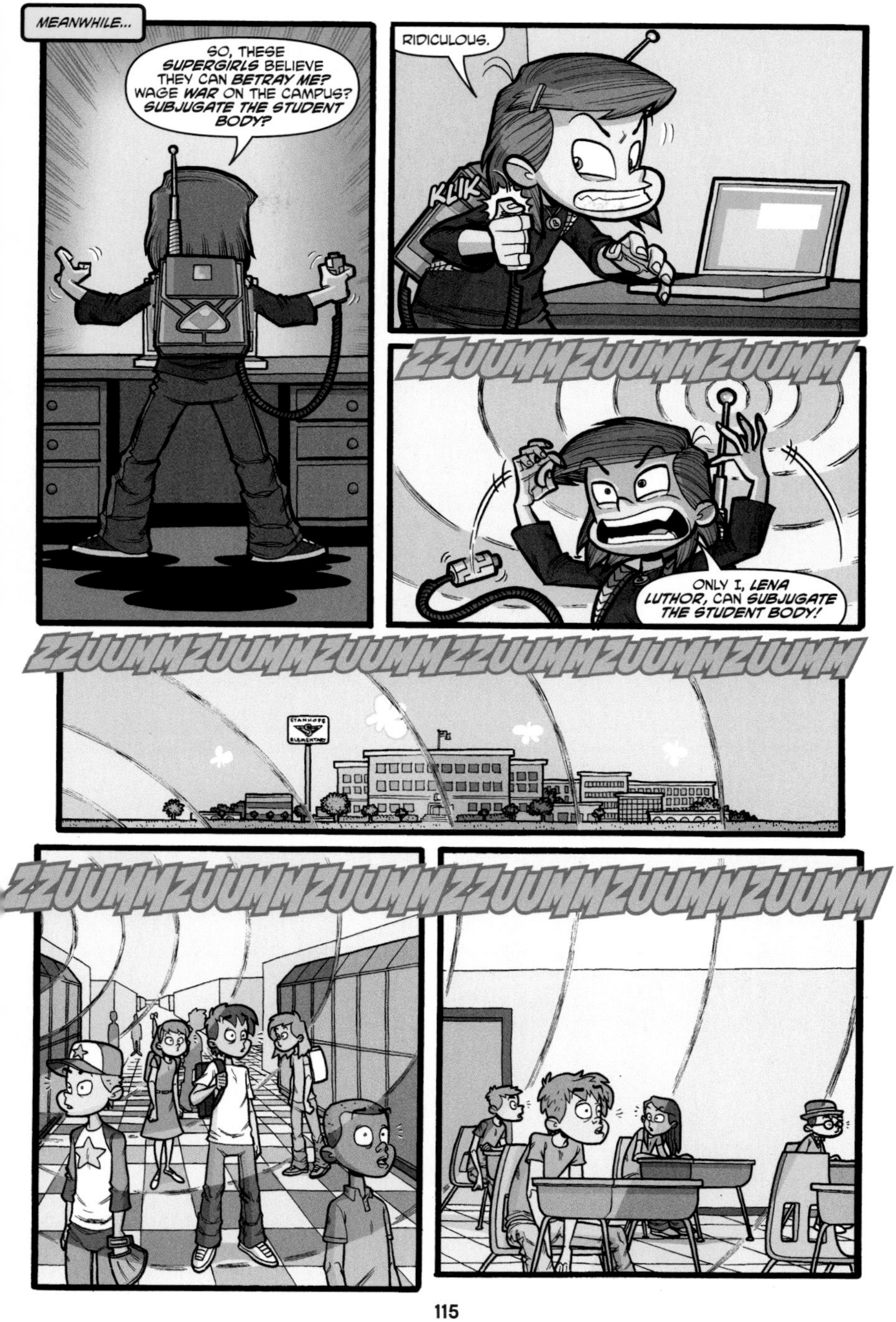
MEANWHILE...
SO, THESE SUPERGIRLS BELIEVE THEY CAN BETRAY ME? WAGE WAR ON THE CAMPUS? SUBJUGATE THE STUDENT BODY?
RIDICULOUS.
KLIK
ZZUUMMZUUMMZUUMM
ONLY I, LENA LUTHOR, CAN SUBJUGATE THE STUDENT BODY!
ZZUUMMZUUMMZUUMMZZUUMMZUUMMZUUMM
STANHOPE ELEMENTARY
ZZUUMMZUUMMZUUMMZZUUMMZUUMMZUUMM

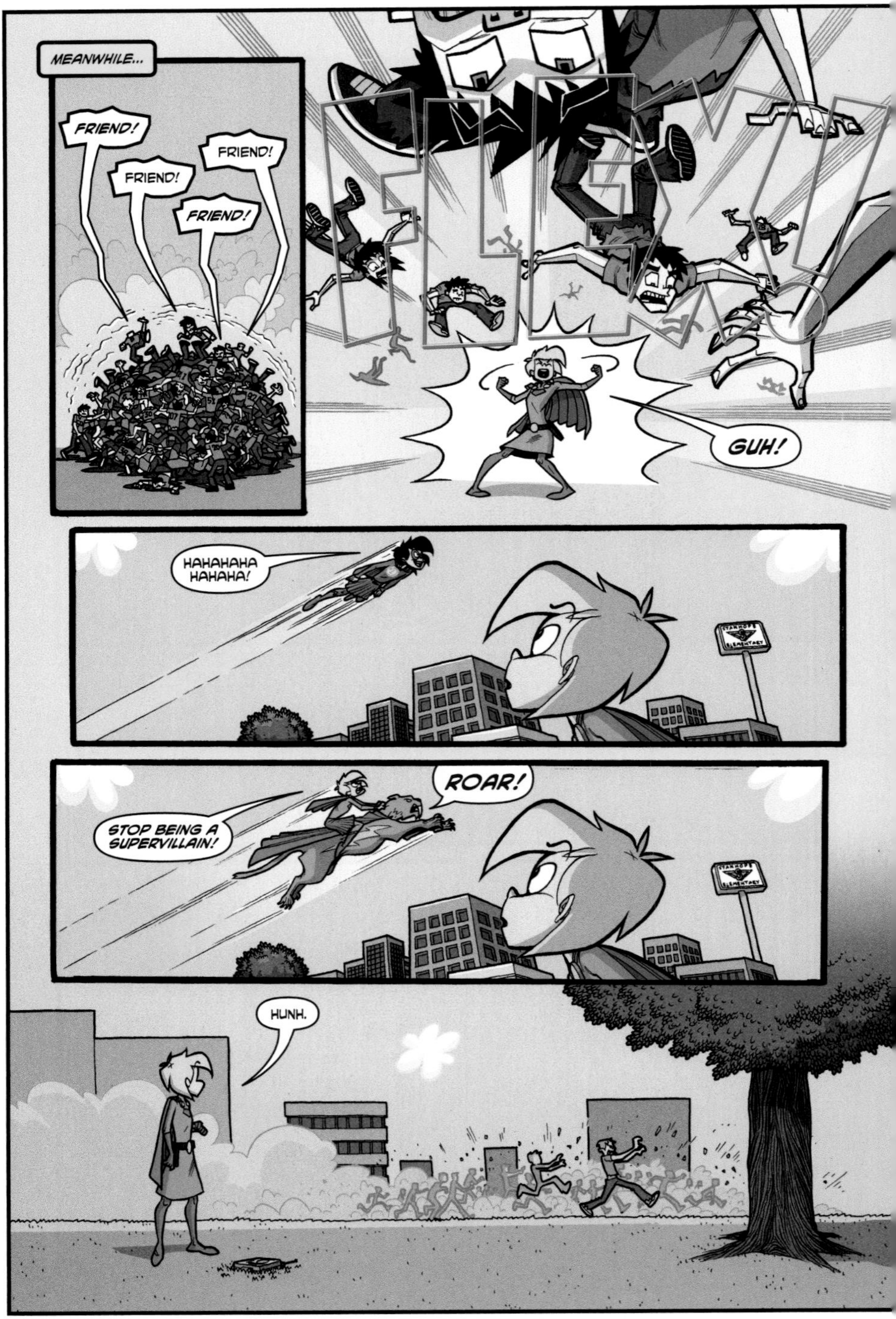
MEANWHILE...
FRIEND!
FRIEND!
FRIEND!
FRIEND!
GUH!
HAHAHAHA
HAHAHA!
STOP BEING A SUPERVILLAIN!
ROAR!
HUNH.

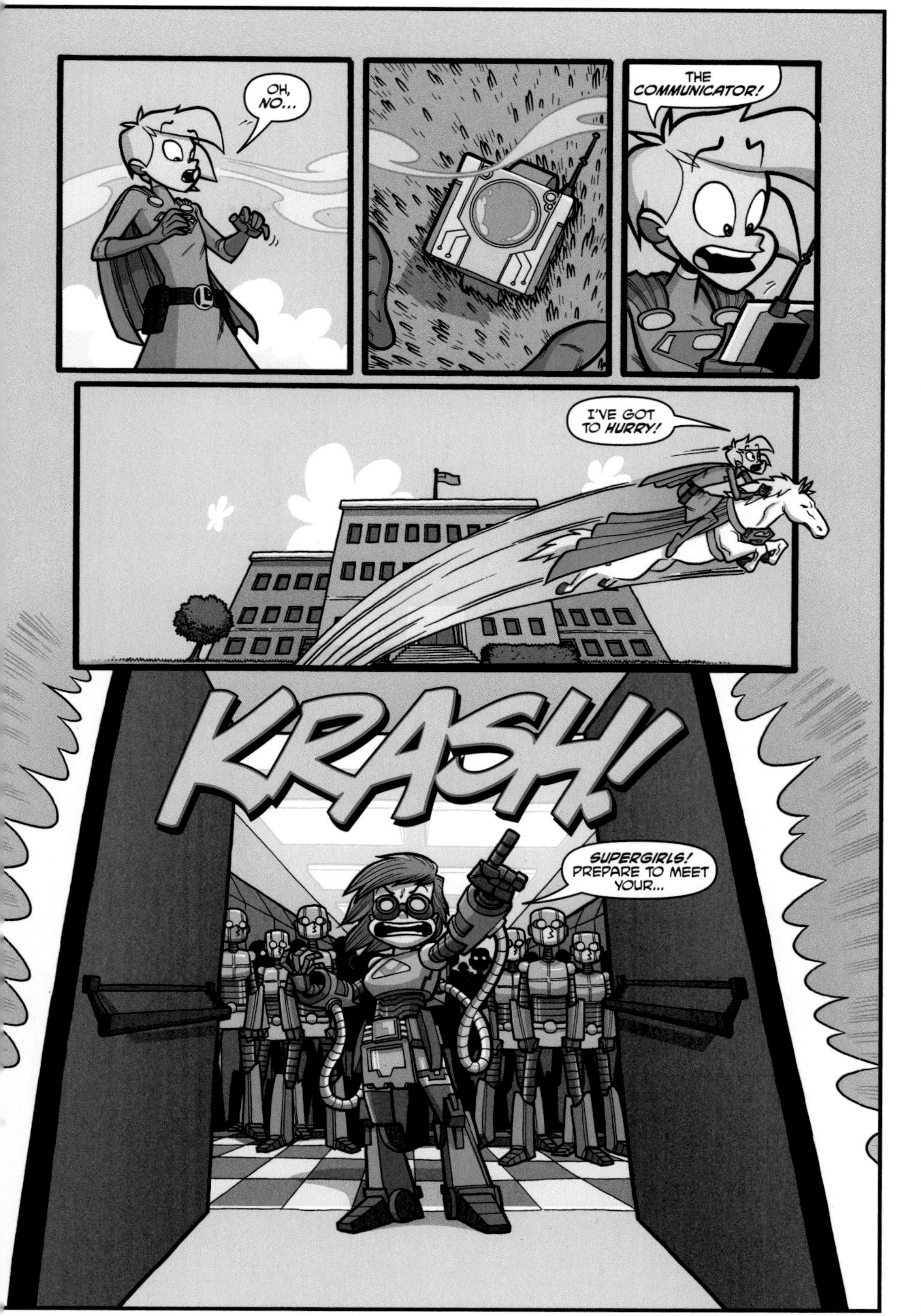
OH, NO...
THE COMMUNICATOR!
I'VE GOT TO HURRY!
KRASH!
SUPERGIRLS! PREPARE TO MEET YOUR...

OKAY. FINE. I'LL JUST GO STRAIGHT TO *STAGE TWO,* THEN. SEE IF I DON'T.

MEANWHILE...

ZZZZZRRRRRRMMMMMMMMM

ZZZZZRRRRRRMMMMMMMMMM

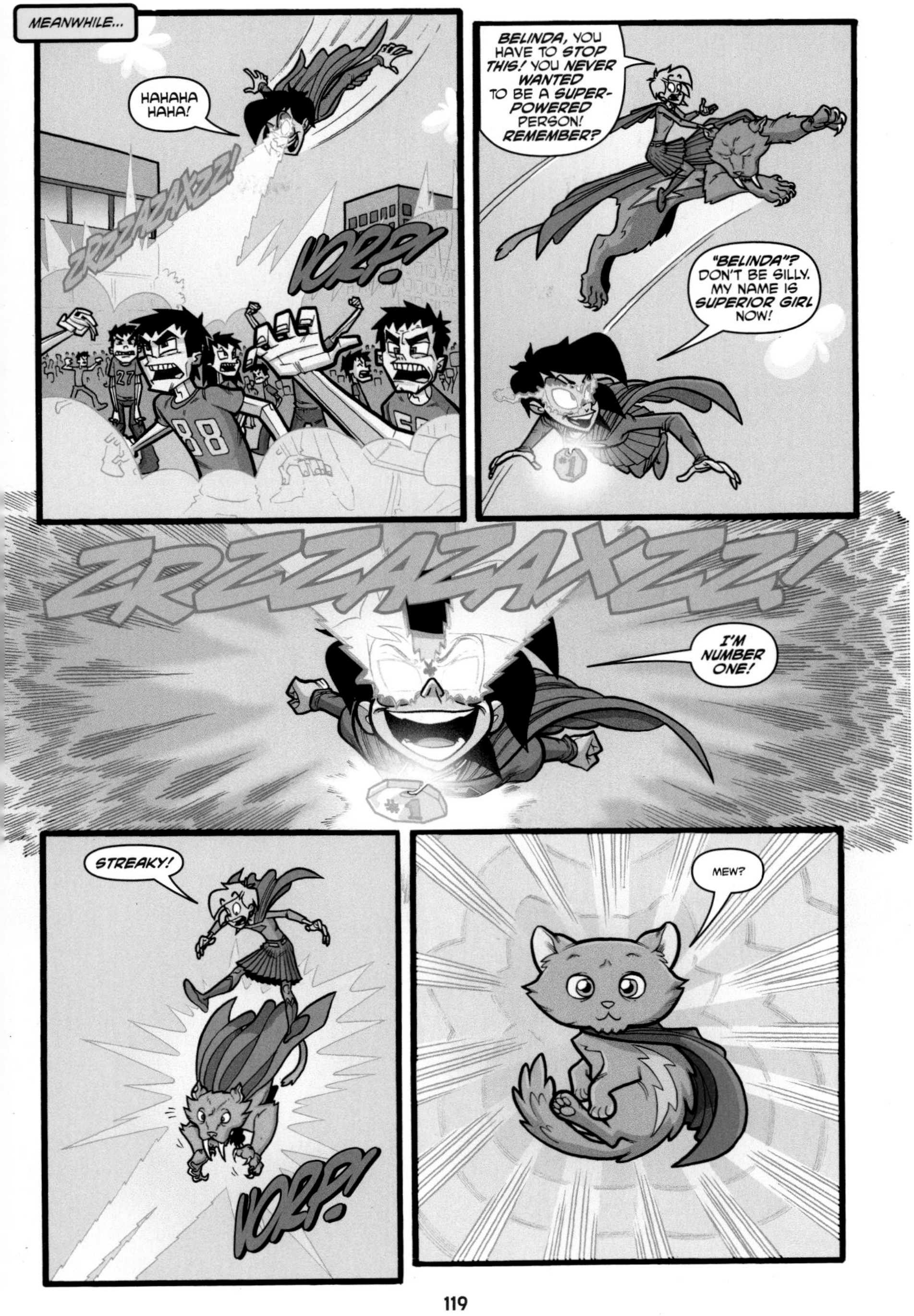
MEANWHILE...
HAHAHA HAHA!
ZRZZAZAXZZ!
VORP!
BELINDA, YOU HAVE TO STOP THIS! YOU NEVER WANTED TO BE A SUPER-POWERED PERSON! REMEMBER?
"BELINDA"? DON'T BE SILLY. MY NAME IS SUPERIOR GIRL NOW!
ZRZZAZAXZZ!
I'M NUMBER ONE!
STREAKY!
VORP!
MEW?

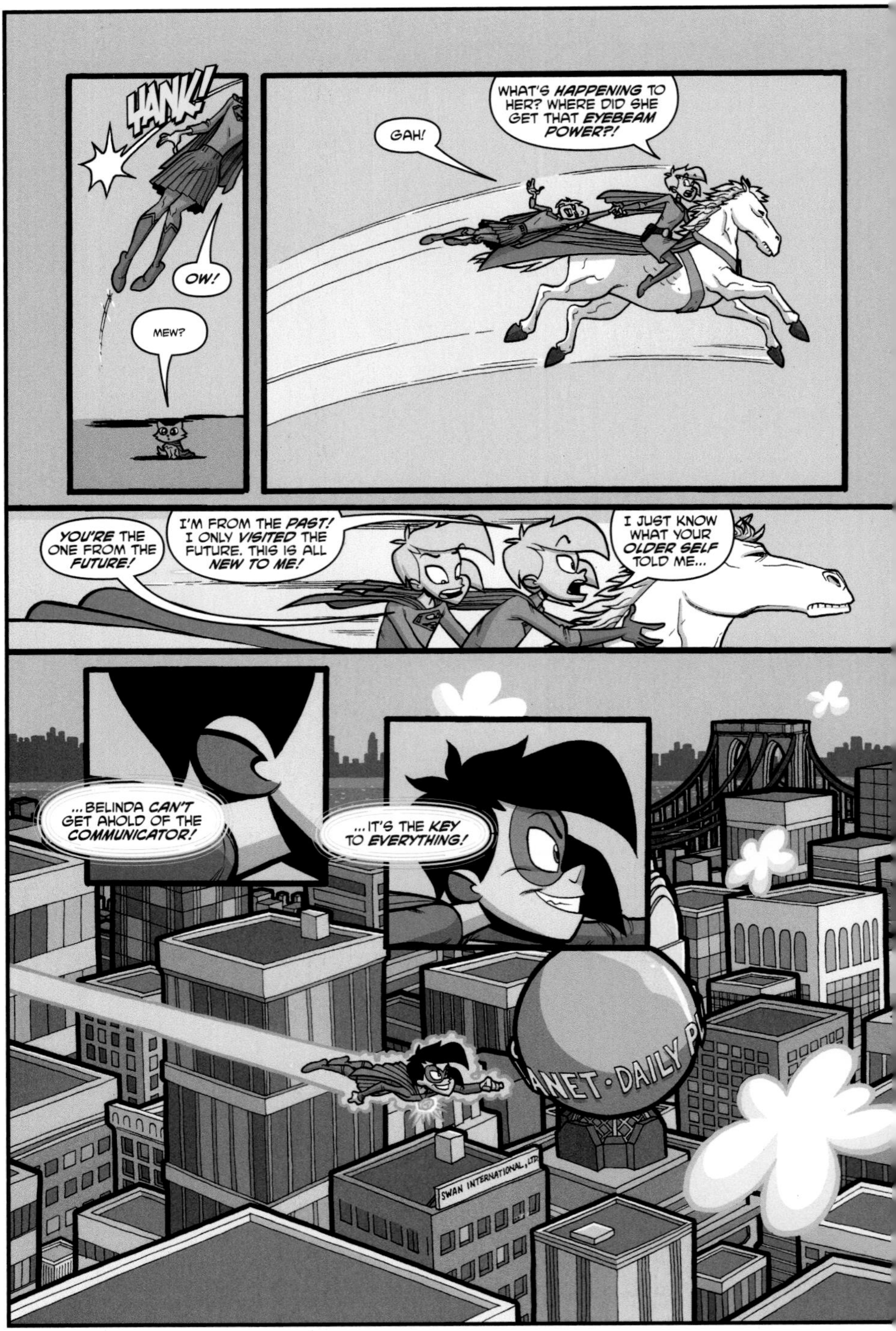
HANK!
OW!
MEW?
GAH!
WHAT'S HAPPENING TO HER? WHERE DID SHE GET THAT EYEBEAM POWER?!
YOU'RE THE ONE FROM THE FUTURE!
I'M FROM THE PAST! I ONLY VISITED THE FUTURE. THIS IS ALL NEW TO ME!
I JUST KNOW WHAT YOUR OLDER SELF TOLD ME...
...BELINDA CAN'T GET AHOLD OF THE COMMUNICATOR!
...IT'S THE KEY TO EVERYTHING!
SWAN INTERNATIONAL, LTD.

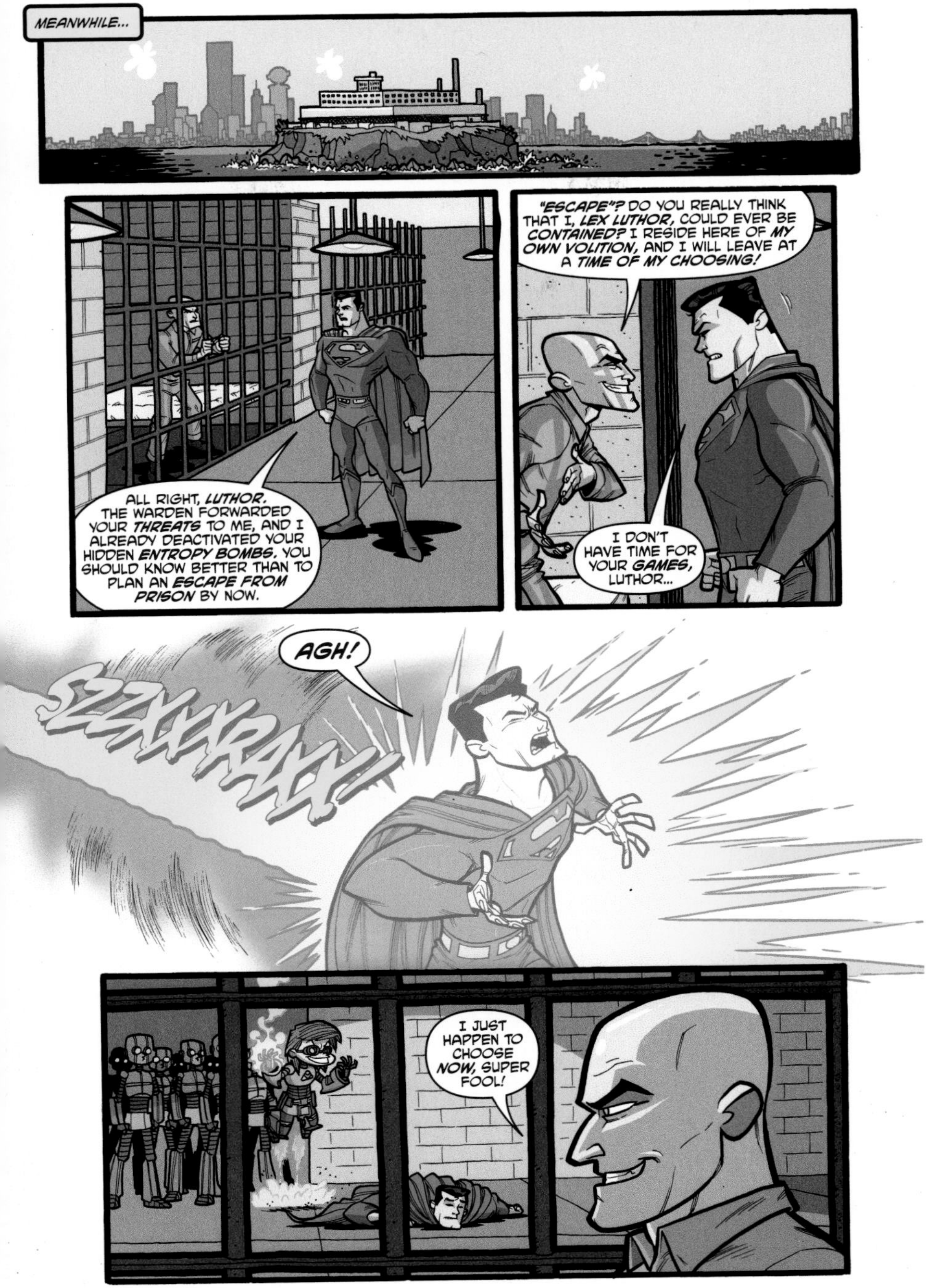
MEANWHILE...
ALL RIGHT, LUTHOR. THE WARDEN FORWARDED YOUR THREATS TO ME, AND I ALREADY DEACTIVATED YOUR HIDDEN ENTROPY BOMBS. YOU SHOULD KNOW BETTER THAN TO PLAN AN ESCAPE FROM PRISON BY NOW.
"ESCAPE"? DO YOU REALLY THINK THAT I, LEX LUTHOR, COULD EVER BE CONTAINED? I RESIDE HERE OF MY OWN VOLITION, AND I WILL LEAVE AT A TIME OF MY CHOOSING!
I DON'T HAVE TIME FOR YOUR GAMES, LUTHOR...
SZZKKRAKK!
AGH!
I JUST HAPPEN TO CHOOSE NOW, SUPER FOOL!

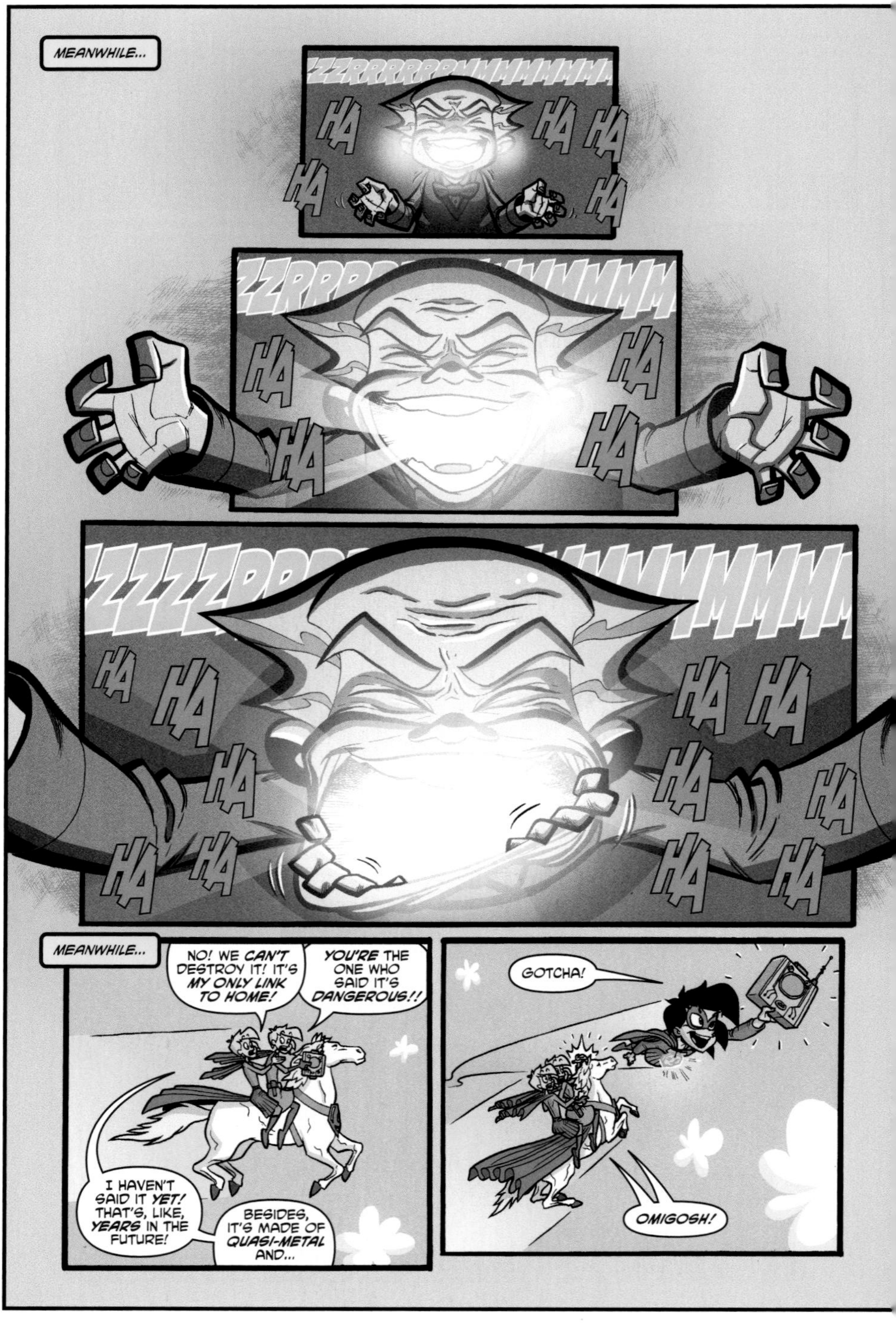

MEANWHILE...
ZZZRRRRRRMMMMMMM
HA HA HA HA HA
ZZRRRRRRMMMMMMM
HA HA HA HA
ZZZZZRRRRMMMMMMM
HA HA HA HA HA HA HA HA HA HA HA HA
MEANWHILE...
NO! WE CAN'T DESTROY IT! IT'S MY ONLY LINK TO HOME!
YOU'RE THE ONE WHO SAID IT'S DANGEROUS!!
I HAVEN'T SAID IT YET! THAT'S, LIKE, YEARS IN THE FUTURE!
BESIDES, IT'S MADE OF QUASI-METAL AND...
GOTCHA!
OMIGOSH!

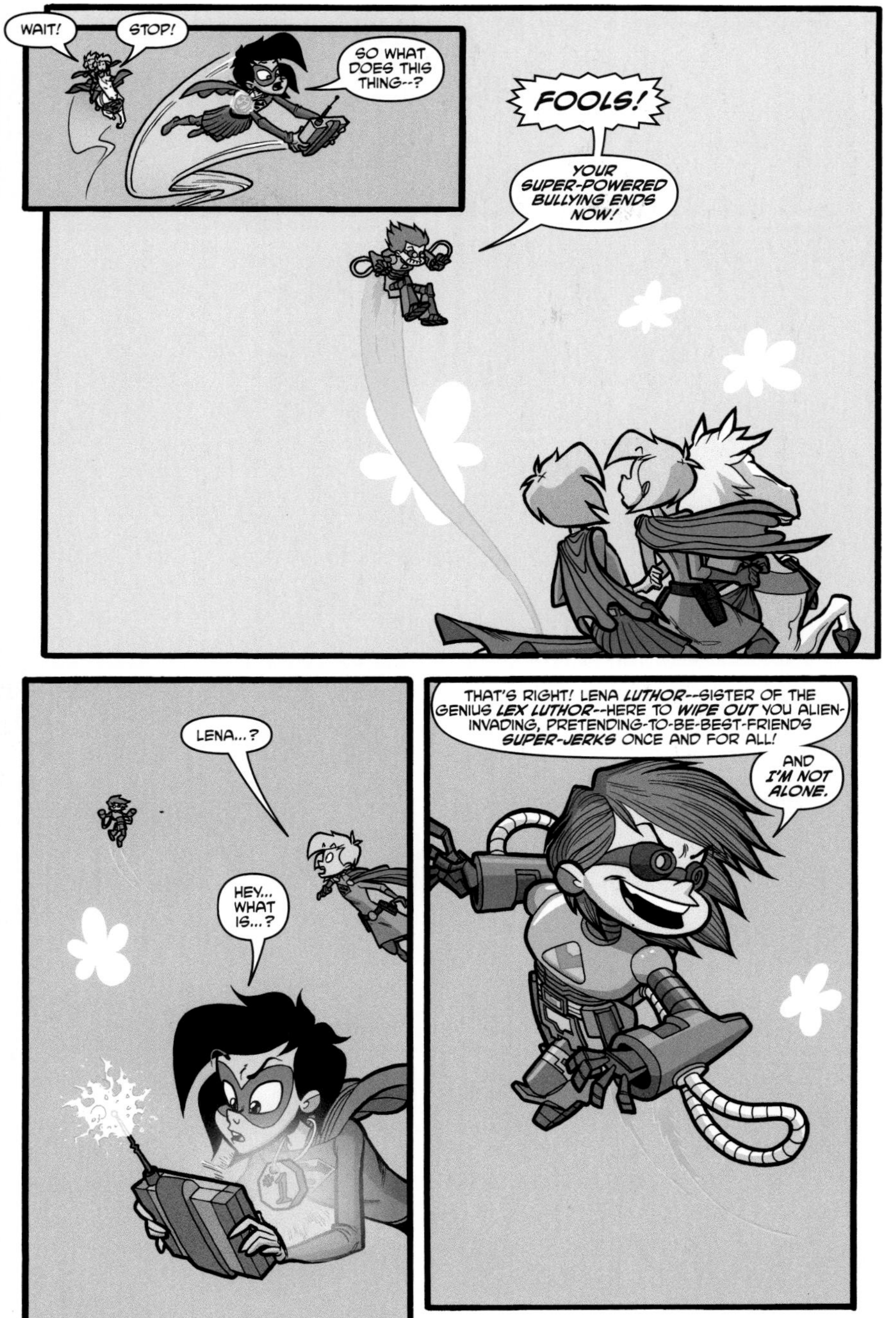
WAIT!
STOP!
SO WHAT DOES THIS THING--?
FOOLS!
YOUR SUPER-POWERED BULLYING ENDS NOW!
LENA...?
HEY... WHAT IS...?
THAT'S RIGHT! LENA LUTHOR--SISTER OF THE GENIUS LEX LUTHOR--HERE TO WIPE OUT YOU ALIEN-INVADING, PRETENDING-TO-BE-BEST-FRIENDS SUPER-JERKS ONCE AND FOR ALL!
AND I'M NOT ALONE.

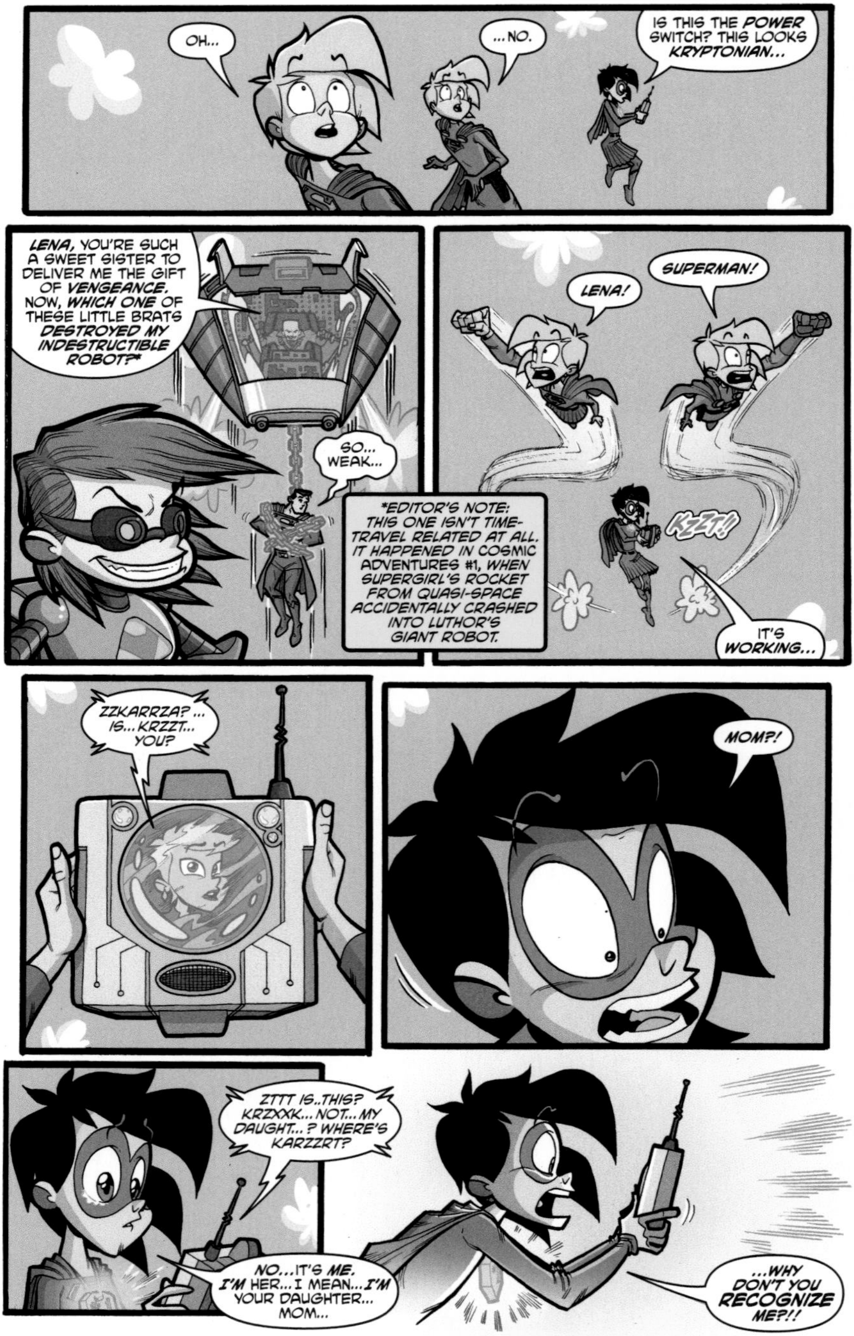
OH...
...NO.
IS THIS THE POWER SWITCH? THIS LOOKS KRYPTONIAN...
LENA, YOU'RE SUCH A SWEET SISTER TO DELIVER ME THE GIFT OF VENGEANCE. NOW, WHICH ONE OF THESE LITTLE BRATS DESTROYED MY INDESTRUCTIBLE ROBOT?*
SO... WEAK...
LENA!
SUPERMAN!
KZZT!!
*EDITOR'S NOTE: THIS ONE ISN'T TIME-TRAVEL RELATED AT ALL. IT HAPPENED IN COSMIC ADVENTURES #1, WHEN SUPERGIRL'S ROCKET FROM QUASI-SPACE ACCIDENTALLY CRASHED INTO LUTHOR'S GIANT ROBOT.
IT'S WORKING...
ZZKARRZA?... IS...KRZZT... YOU?
MOM?!
ZTTT IS..THIS? KRZXXK...NOT...MY DAUGHT...? WHERE'S KARZZRT?
NO...IT'S ME. I'M HER...I MEAN...I'M YOUR DAUGHTER... MOM...
...WHY DON'T YOU RECOGNIZE ME?!!

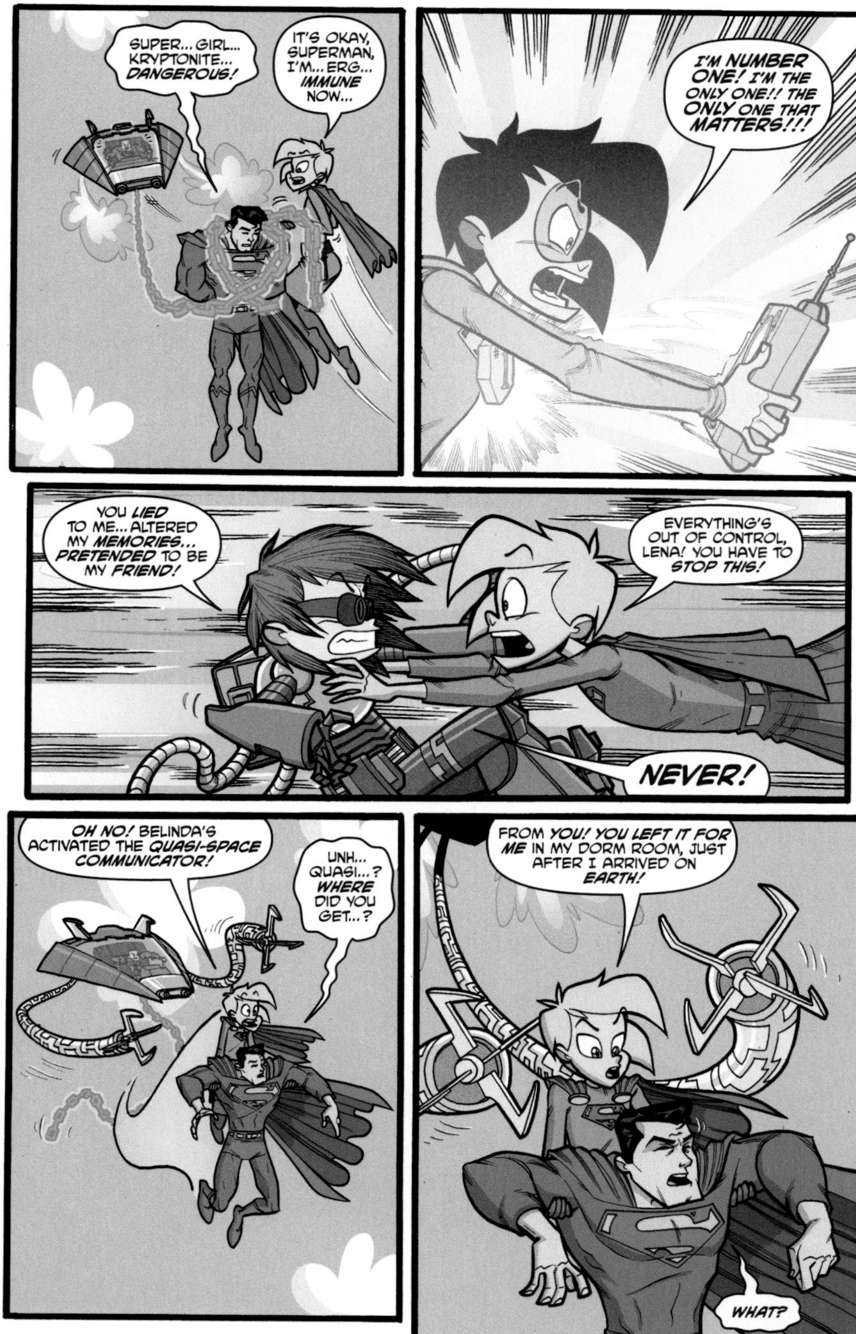
SUPER... GIRL... KRYPTONITE... DANGEROUS!
IT'S OKAY, SUPERMAN, I'M... ERG... IMMUNE NOW...
I'M NUMBER ONE! I'M THE ONLY ONE!! THE ONLY ONE THAT MATTERS!!!
YOU LIED TO ME... ALTERED MY MEMORIES... PRETENDED TO BE MY FRIEND!
EVERYTHING'S OUT OF CONTROL, LENA! YOU HAVE TO STOP THIS!
NEVER!
OH NO! BELINDA'S ACTIVATED THE QUASI-SPACE COMMUNICATOR!
UNH... QUASI...? WHERE DID YOU GET...?
FROM YOU! YOU LEFT IT FOR ME IN MY DORM ROOM, JUST AFTER I ARRIVED ON EARTH!
WHAT?

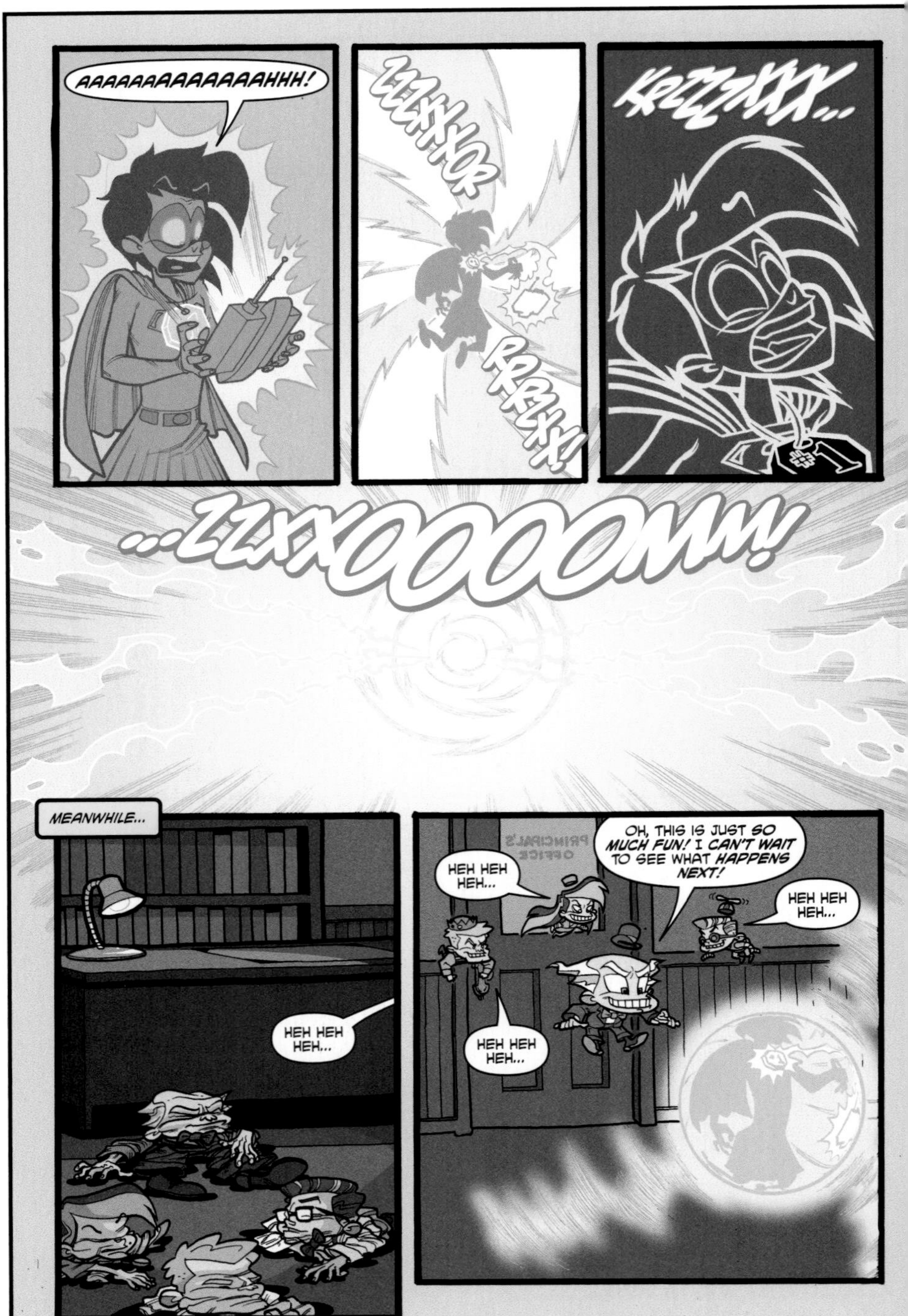
AAAAAAAAAAAAAAHHH!
ZZZXXXKOR
RRRKK!
KRZZZXXX...
...ZZXXOOOOOMM!
MEANWHILE...
HEH HEH HEH...
PRINCIPAL'S OFFICE
HEH HEH HEH...
OH, THIS IS JUST SO MUCH FUN! I CAN'T WAIT TO SEE WHAT HAPPENS NEXT!
HEH HEH HEH...
HEH HEH HEH...

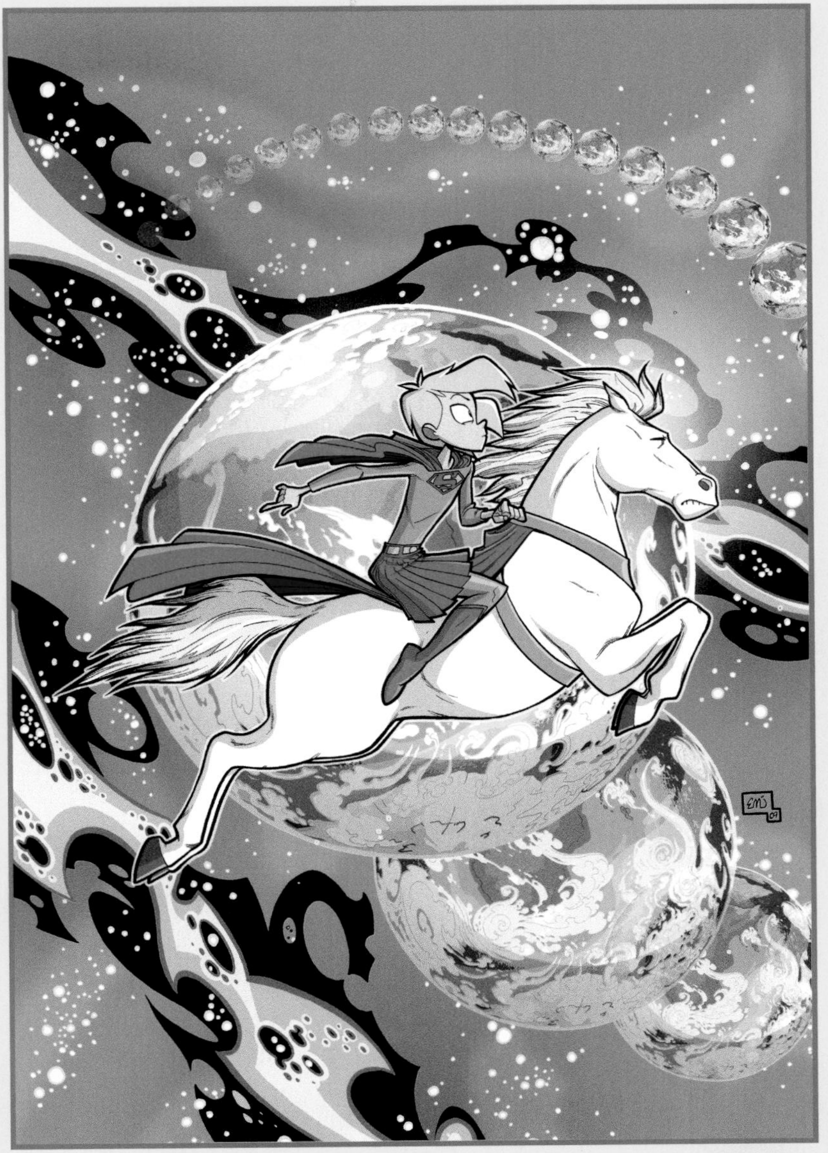

CHAPTER 6

SUPERGIRL

COSMIC ADVENTURES IN THE 8TH GRADE

SUPERGIRL

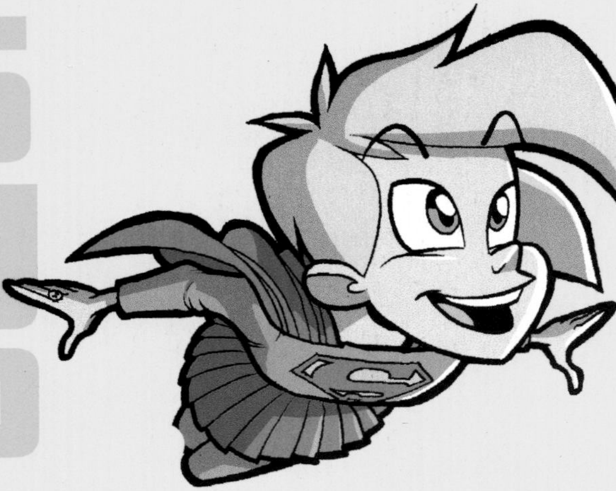

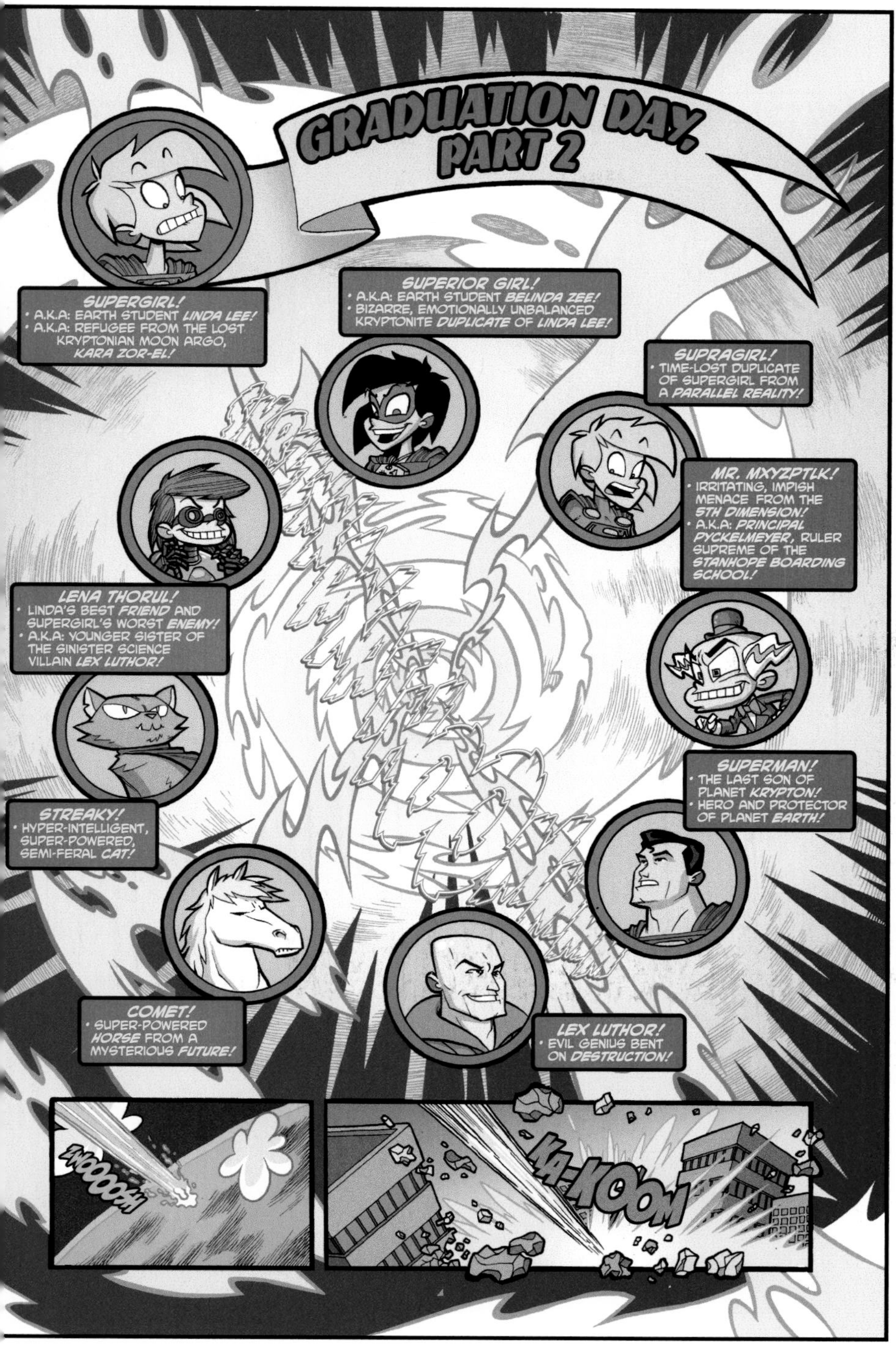
GRADUATION DAY, PART 2
SUPERGIRL!
• A.K.A: EARTH STUDENT LINDA LEE!
• A.K.A: REFUGEE FROM THE LOST KRYPTONIAN MOON ARGO, KARA ZOR-EL!
SUPERIOR GIRL!
• A.K.A: EARTH STUDENT BELINDA ZEE!
• BIZARRE, EMOTIONALLY UNBALANCED KRYPTONITE DUPLICATE OF LINDA LEE!
SUPRAGIRL!
• TIME-LOST DUPLICATE OF SUPERGIRL FROM A PARALLEL REALITY!
MR. MXYZPTLK!
• IRRITATING, IMPISH MENACE FROM THE 5TH DIMENSION!
• A.K.A: PRINCIPAL PYCKELMEYER, RULER SUPREME OF THE STANHOPE BOARDING SCHOOL!
LENA THORUL!
• LINDA'S BEST FRIEND AND SUPERGIRL'S WORST ENEMY!
• A.K.A: YOUNGER SISTER OF THE SINISTER SCIENCE VILLAIN LEX LUTHOR!
STREAKY!
• HYPER-INTELLIGENT, SUPER-POWERED, SEMI-FERAL CAT!
SUPERMAN!
• THE LAST SON OF PLANET KRYPTON!
• HERO AND PROTECTOR OF PLANET EARTH!
COMET!
• SUPER-POWERED HORSE FROM A MYSTERIOUS FUTURE!
LEX LUTHOR!
• EVIL GENIUS BENT ON DESTRUCTION!
ZWOOOOSH
KA-KOOOM

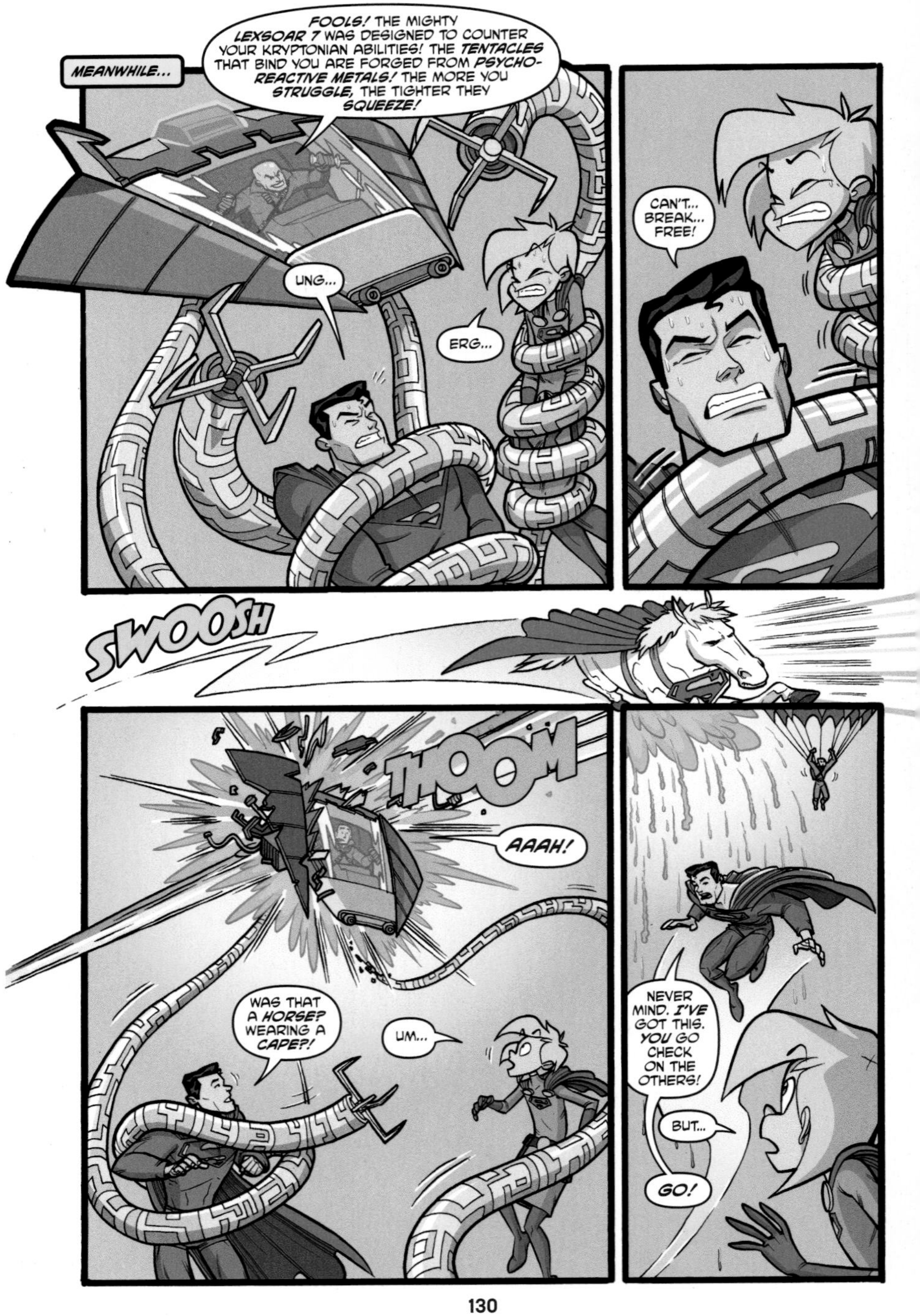
MEANWHILE...
FOOLS! THE MIGHTY LEXSOAR 7 WAS DESIGNED TO COUNTER YOUR KRYPTONIAN ABILITIES! THE TENTACLES THAT BIND YOU ARE FORGED FROM PSYCHO-REACTIVE METALS! THE MORE YOU STRUGGLE, THE TIGHTER THEY SQUEEZE!
UNG...
ERG...
CAN'T... BREAK... FREE!
SWOOSH
THOOOM
AAAH!
WAS THAT A HORSE? WEARING A CAPE?!
UM...
NEVER MIND. I'VE GOT THIS. YOU GO CHECK ON THE OTHERS!
BUT...
GO!

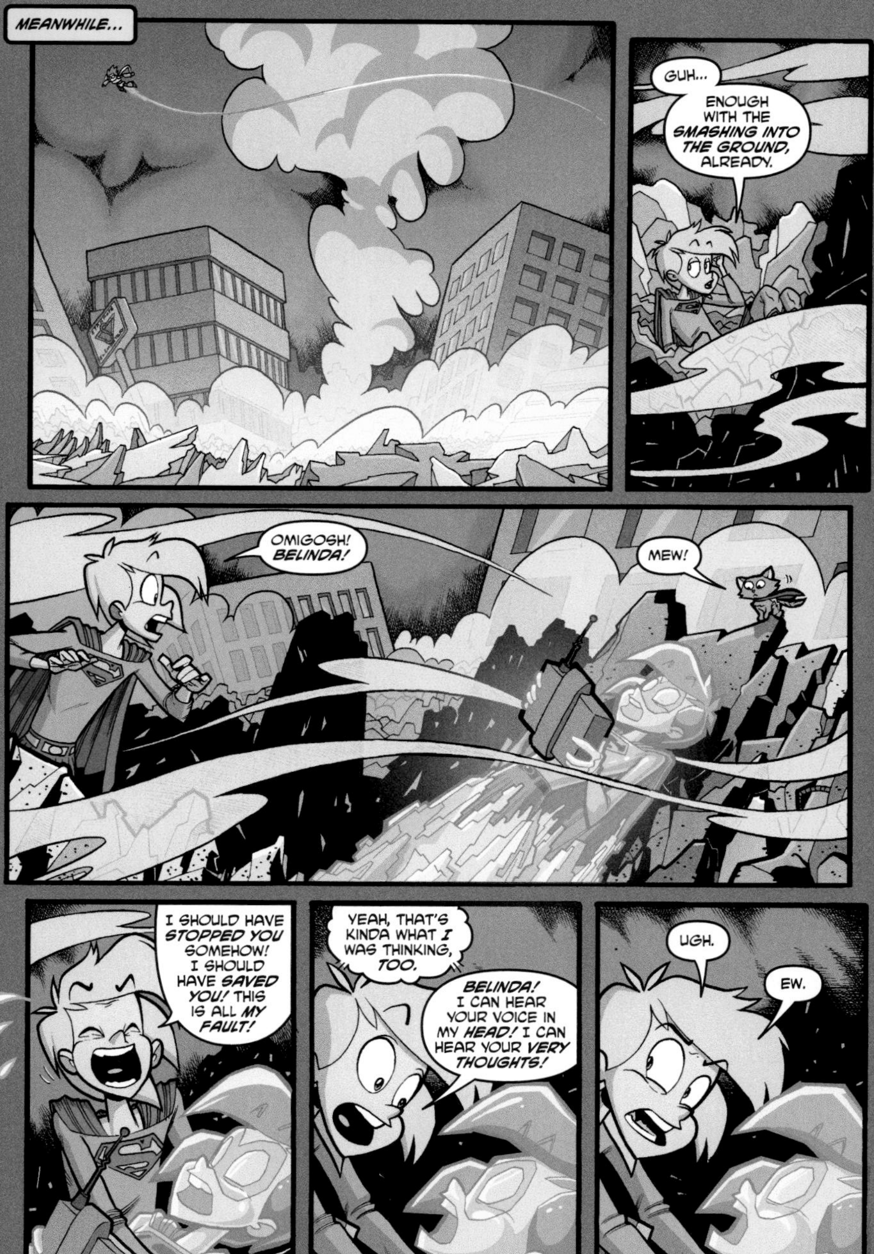
MEANWHILE...
GUH...
ENOUGH WITH THE SMASHING INTO THE GROUND, ALREADY.
OMIGOSH! BELINDA!
MEW!
I SHOULD HAVE STOPPED YOU SOMEHOW! I SHOULD HAVE SAVED YOU! THIS IS ALL MY FAULT!
YEAH, THAT'S KINDA WHAT I WAS THINKING, TOO.
BELINDA! I CAN HEAR YOUR VOICE IN MY HEAD! I CAN HEAR YOUR VERY THOUGHTS!
UGH.
EW.

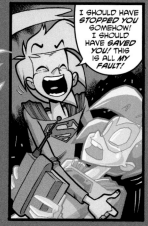

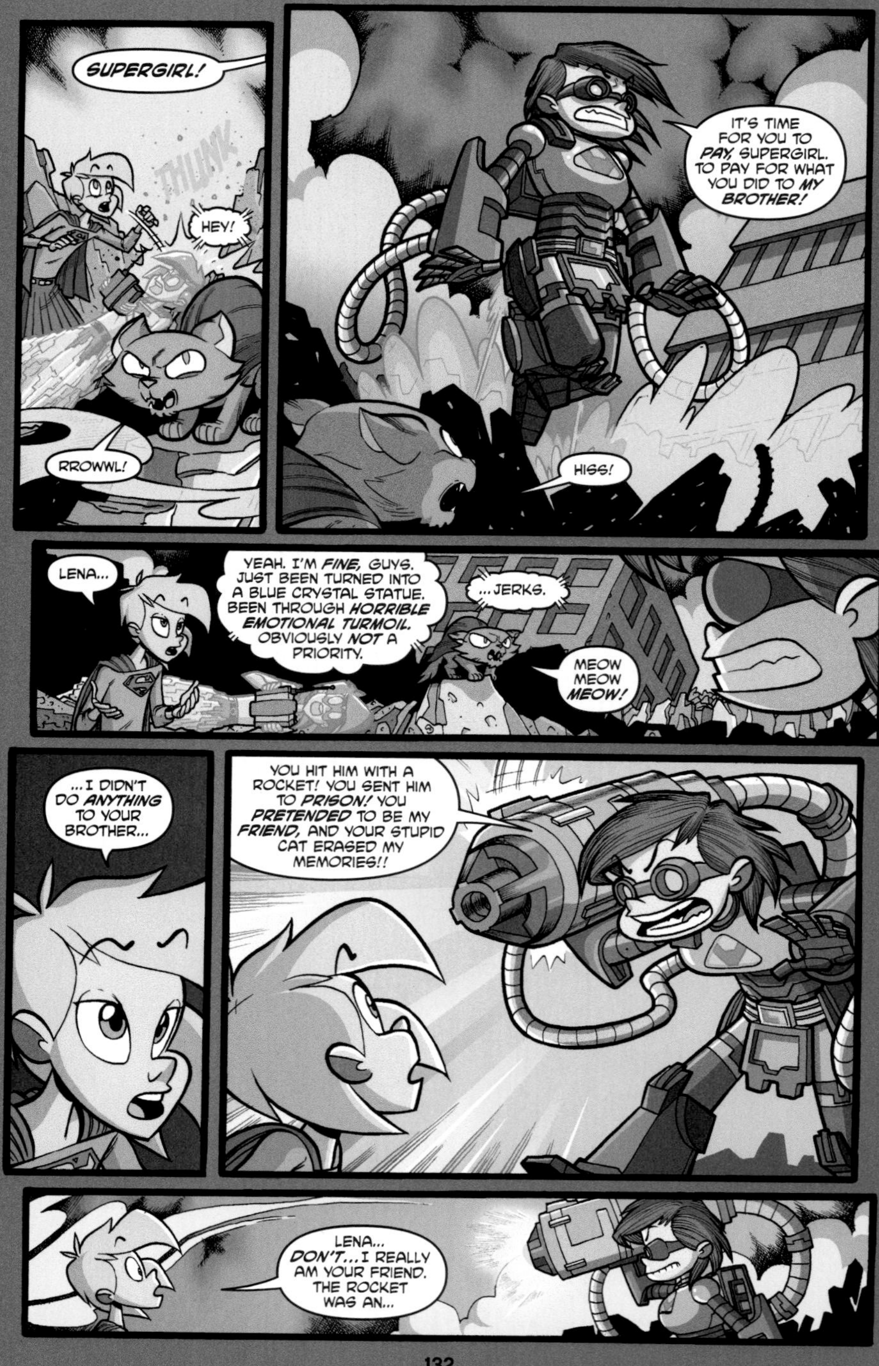

SUPERGIRL!
THUNK
HEY!
RROWWL!
IT'S TIME FOR YOU TO PAY, SUPERGIRL. TO PAY FOR WHAT YOU DID TO MY BROTHER!
HISS!
LENA...
YEAH. I'M FINE, GUYS. JUST BEEN TURNED INTO A BLUE CRYSTAL STATUE. BEEN THROUGH HORRIBLE EMOTIONAL TURMOIL. OBVIOUSLY NOT A PRIORITY.
...JERKS.
MEOW MEOW MEOW!
...I DIDN'T DO ANYTHING TO YOUR BROTHER...
YOU HIT HIM WITH A ROCKET! YOU SENT HIM TO PRISON! YOU PRETENDED TO BE MY FRIEND, AND YOUR STUPID CAT ERASED MY MEMORIES!!
LENA... DON'T... I REALLY AM YOUR FRIEND. THE ROCKET WAS AN...

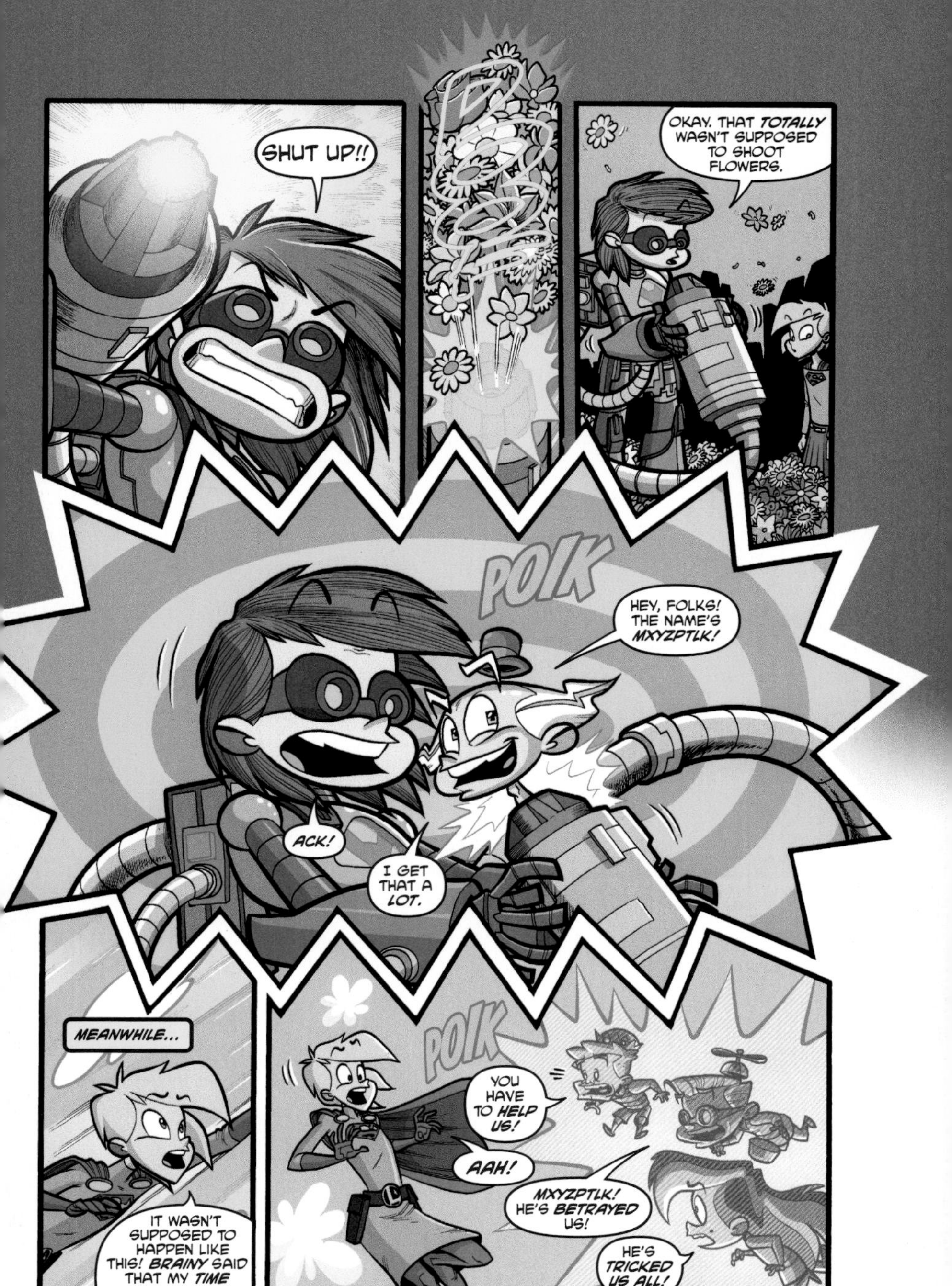
SHUT UP!!
OKAY. THAT TOTALLY WASN'T SUPPOSED TO SHOOT FLOWERS.
POIK
HEY, FOLKS! THE NAME'S MXYZPTLK!
ACK!
I GET THAT A LOT.
MEANWHILE...
IT WASN'T SUPPOSED TO HAPPEN LIKE THIS! BRAINY SAID THAT MY TIME POWERS WOULD...
POIK
YOU HAVE TO HELP US!
AAH!
MXYZPTLK! HE'S BETRAYED US!
HE'S TRICKED US ALL!

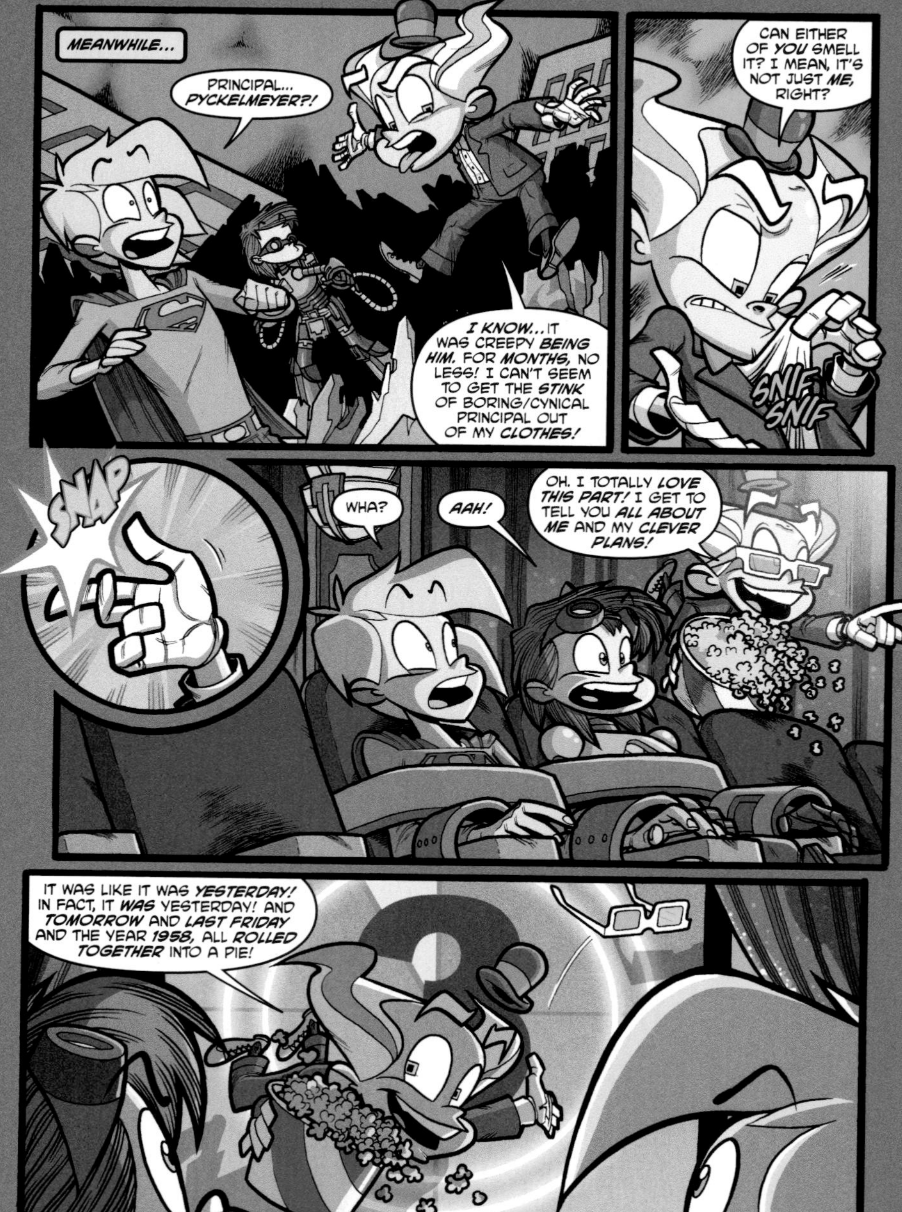
MEANWHILE...
PRINCIPAL... PYCKELMEYER?!
I KNOW... IT WAS CREEPY BEING HIM. FOR MONTHS, NO LESS! I CAN'T SEEM TO GET THE STINK OF BORING/CYNICAL PRINCIPAL OUT OF MY CLOTHES!
CAN EITHER OF YOU SMELL IT? I MEAN, IT'S NOT JUST ME, RIGHT?
SNIF SNIF
SNAP
WHA?
AAH!
OH. I TOTALLY LOVE THIS PART! I GET TO TELL YOU ALL ABOUT ME AND MY CLEVER PLANS!
IT WAS LIKE IT WAS YESTERDAY! IN FACT, IT WAS YESTERDAY! AND TOMORROW AND LAST FRIDAY AND THE YEAR 1958, ALL ROLLED TOGETHER INTO A PIE!
STOP TALKING NONSENSE!

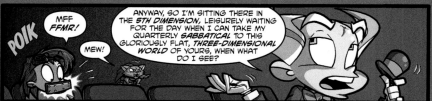

POIK

MFF *FFMR!*

MEW!

ANYWAY, SO I'M SITTING THERE IN THE *5TH DIMENSION,* LEISURELY WAITING FOR THE DAY WHEN I CAN TAKE MY QUARTERLY *SABBATICAL* TO THIS GLORIOUSLY FLAT, *THREE-DIMENSIONAL WORLD* OF YOURS, WHEN WHAT DO I SEE?

SUCH *SADNESS!* SUCH *ANGUISH* AND *TURMOIL!* IT BROKE MY FIVE-DIMENSIONAL HEART.

SO I WORKED A LITTLE *MXYZPTLK-BRAND MIRACLE* AND.... *WOOGH!* KARA ZOR-EL GETS A FREE *ONE-WAY TRIP* TO *EARTH!*

YOU...TOOK ME FROM MY *PARENTS?* MY *HOME?!*

LET'S JUST SAY *I HELPED THINGS ALONG.* MAYBE GAVE YOU A TINY *MENTAL PROMPTING* TO HIDE IN THE *ROCKET?* GUIDED IT RIGHT SMACK DAB INTO THE *MIDDLE* OF BIG OL' *METROPOLIS?*

SLAMMED IT STRAIGHT INTO *LEX LUTHOR'S* STUPID *GIANT ROBOT?*

MAYBE?

MFF!

HECK, I *MIGHT* HAVE EVEN GONE *BACK IN TIME* AND *DESTROYED* ALL OF KRYPTON JUST TO GET *YOU* WHERE *I WANTED YOU.*

WHO KNOWS?!

135

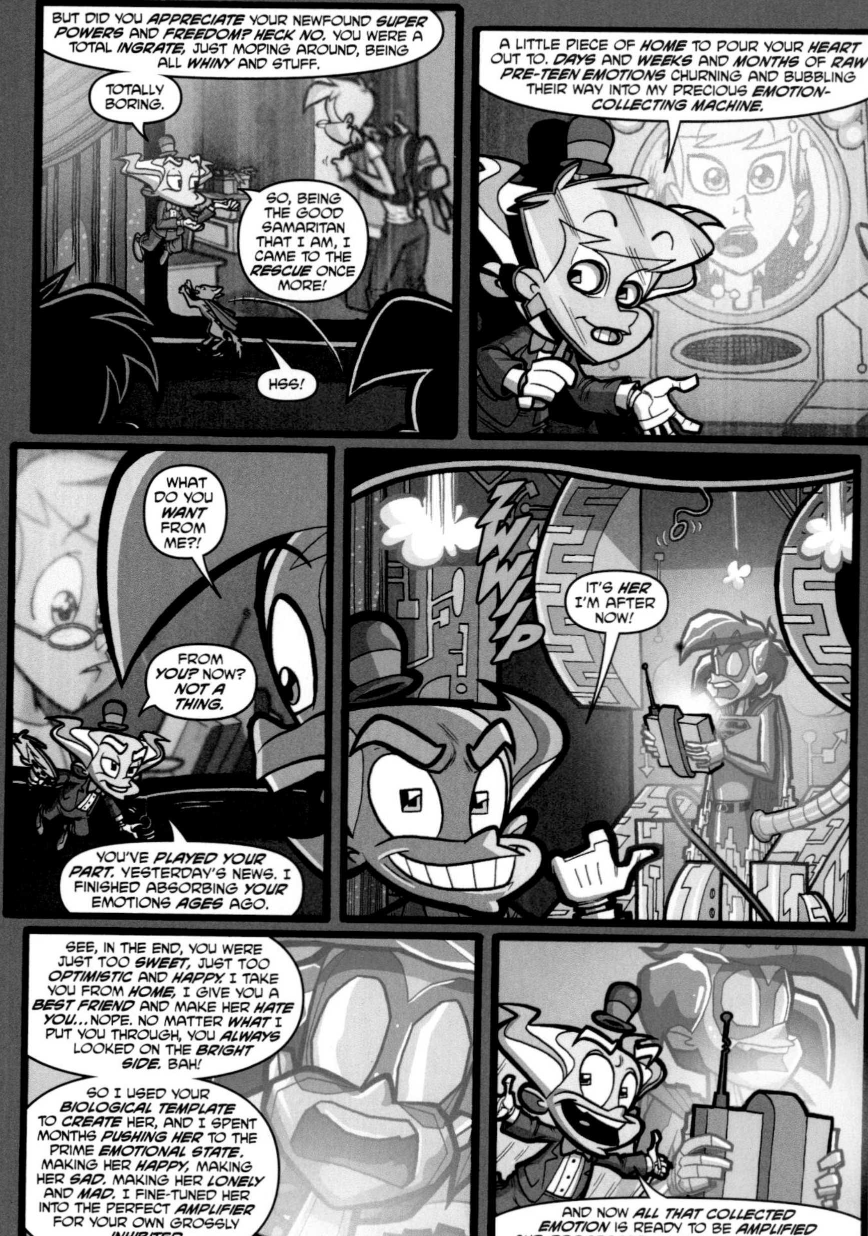
BUT DID YOU APPRECIATE YOUR NEWFOUND SUPER POWERS AND FREEDOM? HECK NO. YOU WERE A TOTAL INGRATE, JUST MOPING AROUND, BEING ALL WHINY AND STUFF.
TOTALLY BORING.
SO, BEING THE GOOD SAMARITAN THAT I AM, I CAME TO THE RESCUE ONCE MORE!
HSS!
A LITTLE PIECE OF HOME TO POUR YOUR HEART OUT TO. DAYS AND WEEKS AND MONTHS OF RAW PRE-TEEN EMOTIONS CHURNING AND BUBBLING THEIR WAY INTO MY PRECIOUS EMOTION-COLLECTING MACHINE.
WHAT DO YOU WANT FROM ME?!
FROM YOU? NOW? NOT A THING.
YOU'VE PLAYED YOUR PART. YESTERDAY'S NEWS. I FINISHED ABSORBING YOUR EMOTIONS AGES AGO.
ZWWIP
IT'S HER I'M AFTER NOW!
SEE, IN THE END, YOU WERE JUST TOO SWEET, JUST TOO OPTIMISTIC AND HAPPY. I TAKE YOU FROM HOME, I GIVE YOU A BEST FRIEND AND MAKE HER HATE YOU... NOPE. NO MATTER WHAT I PUT YOU THROUGH, YOU ALWAYS LOOKED ON THE BRIGHT SIDE. BAH!
SO I USED YOUR BIOLOGICAL TEMPLATE TO CREATE HER, AND I SPENT MONTHS PUSHING HER TO THE PRIME EMOTIONAL STATE. MAKING HER HAPPY, MAKING HER SAD. MAKING HER LONELY AND MAD. I FINE-TUNED HER INTO THE PERFECT AMPLIFIER FOR YOUR OWN GROSSLY INHIBITED EMOTIONS!
AND NOW ALL THAT COLLECTED EMOTION IS READY TO BE AMPLIFIED AND PROCESSED THROUGH A MACHINE BUILT TO REPLICATE YOUR KRYPTONIAN BIOLOGY AND MY 5TH-DIMENSIONAL AWESOMENESS. SO YOU SEE, IT'S NOT JUST ANY OLD MACHINE...

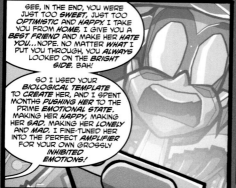

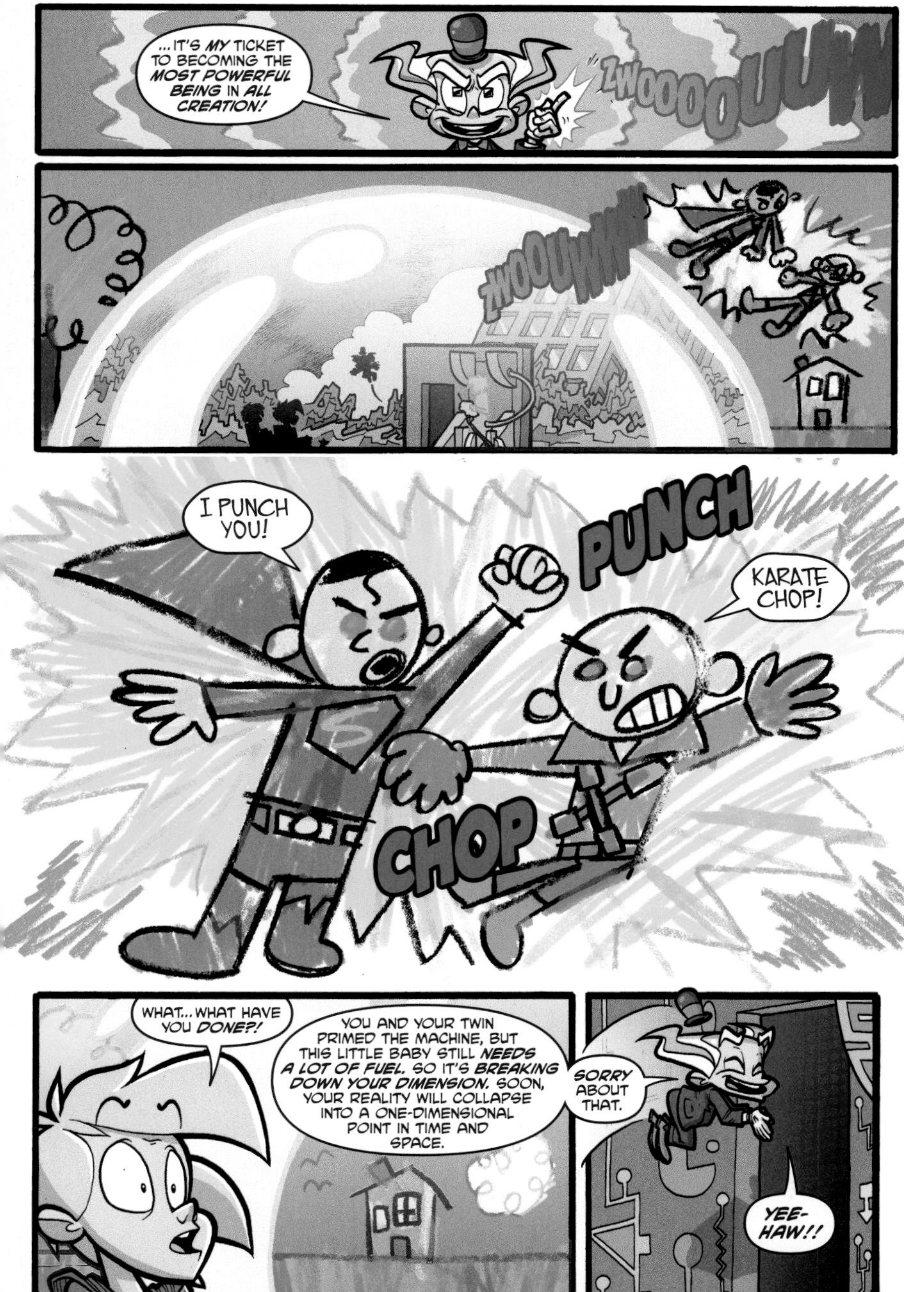
...IT'S *MY* TICKET TO BECOMING THE *MOST POWERFUL BEING* IN *ALL CREATION!*
ZWOOOOOUUUWW
ZWOOUWWW
I PUNCH YOU!
PUNCH
KARATE CHOP!
CHOP
WHAT...WHAT HAVE YOU *DONE?!*
YOU AND YOUR TWIN PRIMED THE MACHINE, BUT THIS LITTLE BABY STILL *NEEDS A LOT OF FUEL.* SO IT'S *BREAKING DOWN YOUR DIMENSION.* SOON, YOUR REALITY WILL COLLAPSE INTO A ONE-DIMENSIONAL POINT IN TIME AND SPACE.
SORRY ABOUT THAT.
YEE-HAW!!

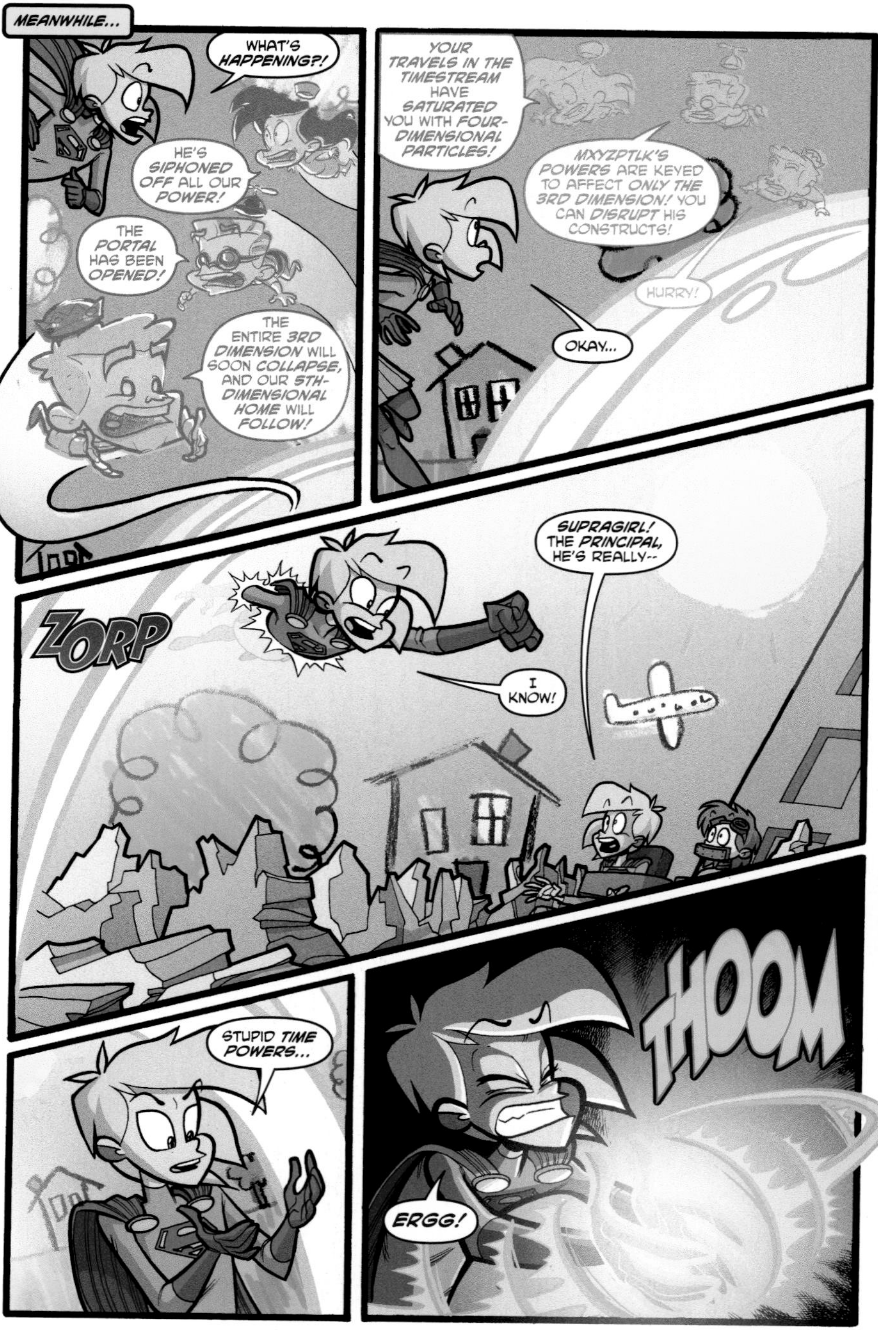

MEANWHILE...
WHAT'S HAPPENING?!
HE'S SIPHONED OFF ALL OUR POWER!
THE PORTAL HAS BEEN OPENED!
THE ENTIRE 3RD DIMENSION WILL SOON COLLAPSE, AND OUR 5TH-DIMENSIONAL HOME WILL FOLLOW!
YOUR TRAVELS IN THE TIMESTREAM HAVE SATURATED YOU WITH FOUR-DIMENSIONAL PARTICLES!
MXYZPTLK'S POWERS ARE KEYED TO AFFECT ONLY THE 3RD DIMENSION! YOU CAN DISRUPT HIS CONSTRUCTS!
HURRY!
OKAY...
SUPRAGIRL! THE PRINCIPAL, HE'S REALLY--
ZORP
I KNOW!
STUPID TIME POWERS...
THOOM
ERGG!

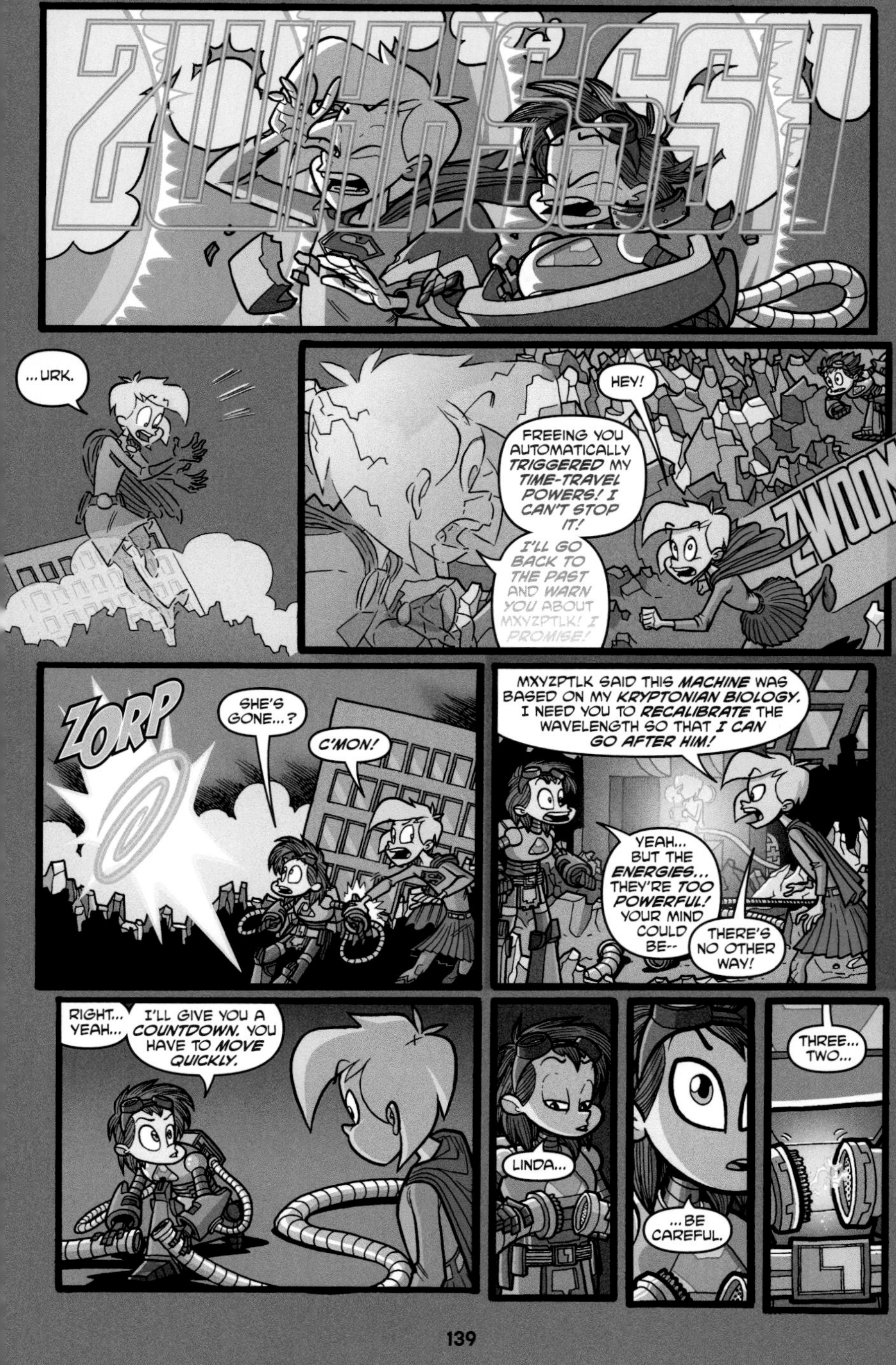
ZHHHKSSSSH!
...URK.
HEY!
FREEING YOU AUTOMATICALLY TRIGGERED MY TIME-TRAVEL POWERS! I CAN'T STOP IT!
I'LL GO BACK TO THE PAST AND WARN YOU ABOUT MXYZPTLK! I PROMISE!
ZWOOM
ZORP
SHE'S GONE...?
C'MON!
MXYZPTLK SAID THIS MACHINE WAS BASED ON MY KRYPTONIAN BIOLOGY. I NEED YOU TO RECALIBRATE THE WAVELENGTH SO THAT I CAN GO AFTER HIM!
YEAH... BUT THE ENERGIES... THEY'RE TOO POWERFUL! YOUR MIND COULD BE--
THERE'S NO OTHER WAY!
RIGHT... YEAH...
I'LL GIVE YOU A COUNTDOWN. YOU HAVE TO MOVE QUICKLY.
LINDA...
...BE CAREFUL.
THREE... TWO...

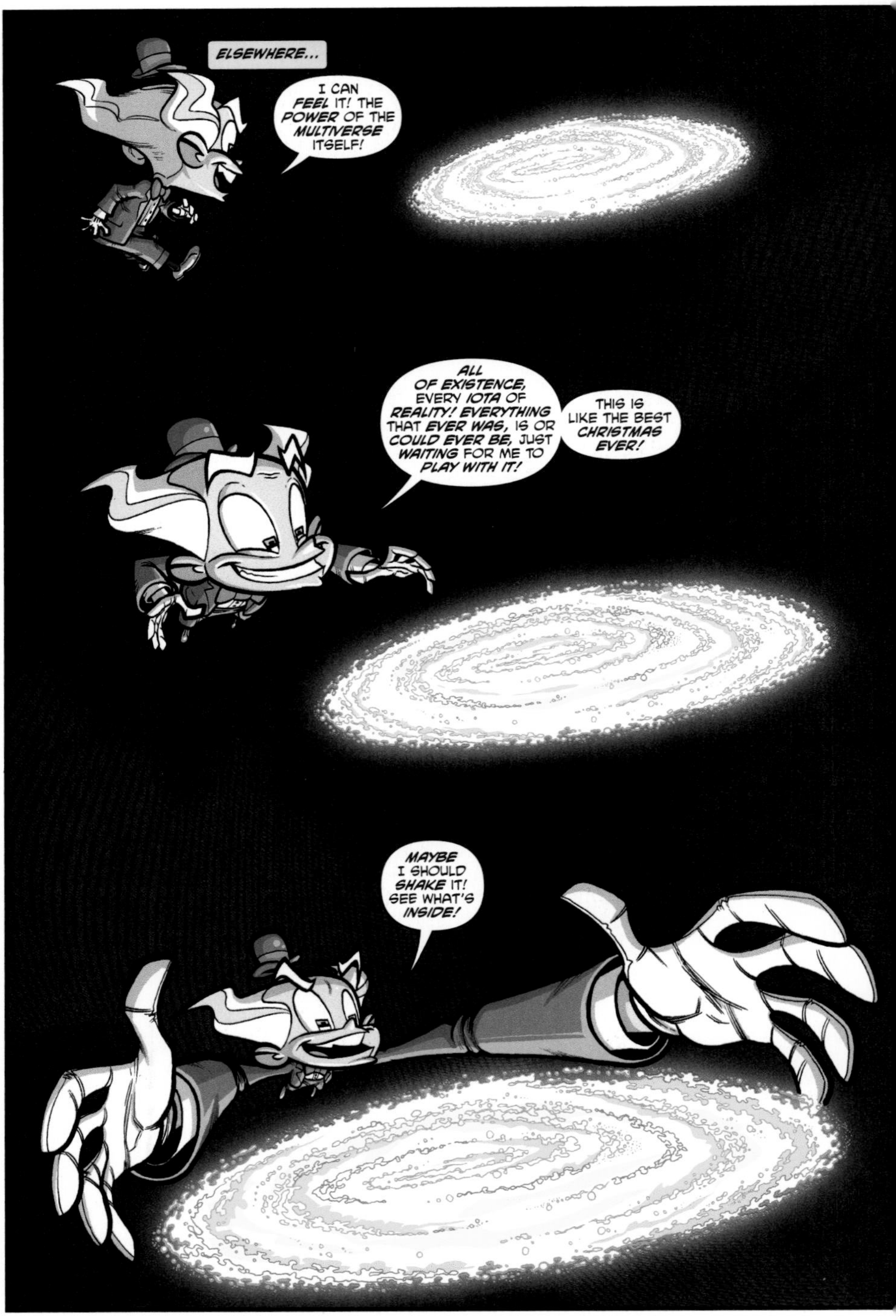
ELSEWHERE...
I CAN FEEL IT! THE POWER OF THE MULTIVERSE ITSELF!
ALL OF EXISTENCE, EVERY IOTA OF REALITY! EVERYTHING THAT EVER WAS, IS OR COULD EVER BE, JUST WAITING FOR ME TO PLAY WITH IT!
THIS IS LIKE THE BEST CHRISTMAS EVER!
MAYBE I SHOULD SHAKE IT! SEE WHAT'S INSIDE!

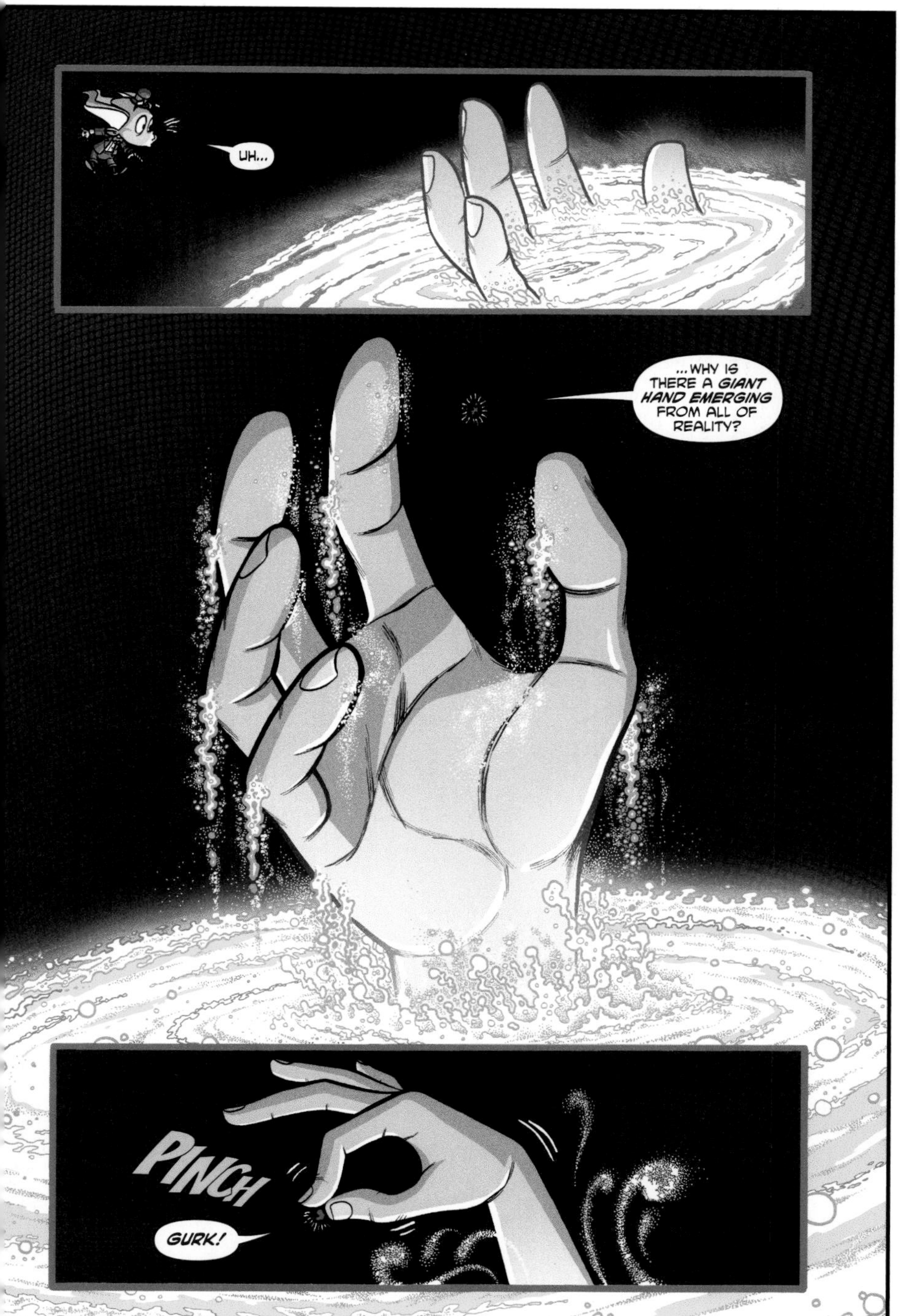
UH...
...WHY IS THERE A GIANT HAND EMERGING FROM ALL OF REALITY?
PINCH
GURK!

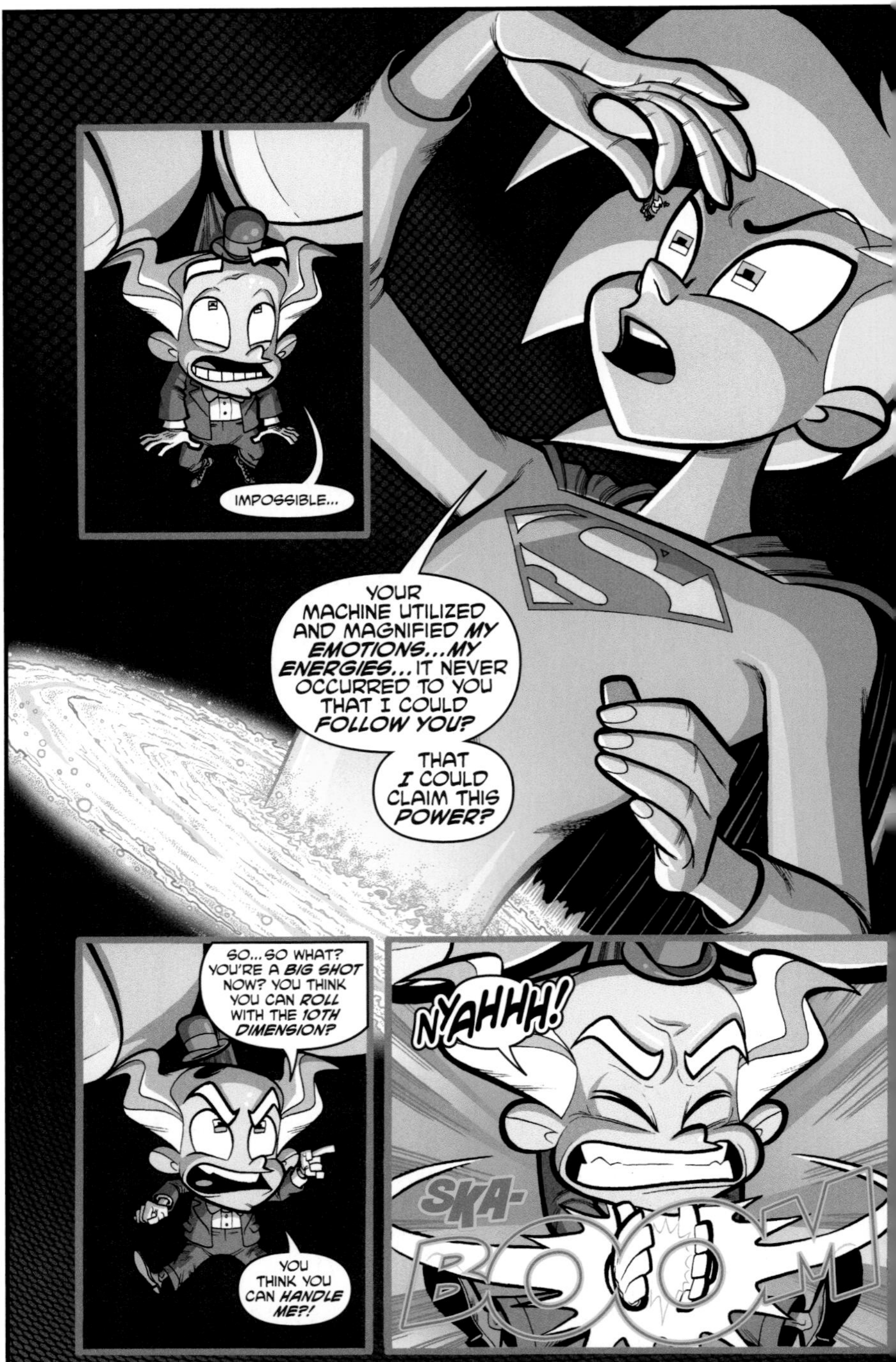

IMPOSSIBLE...
YOUR MACHINE UTILIZED AND MAGNIFIED MY EMOTIONS...MY ENERGIES... IT NEVER OCCURRED TO YOU THAT I COULD FOLLOW YOU?
THAT I COULD CLAIM THIS POWER?
SO... SO WHAT? YOU'RE A BIG SHOT NOW? YOU THINK YOU CAN ROLL WITH THE 10TH DIMENSION?
YOU THINK YOU CAN HANDLE ME?!
NYAHHH!
SKA-
BOOOM

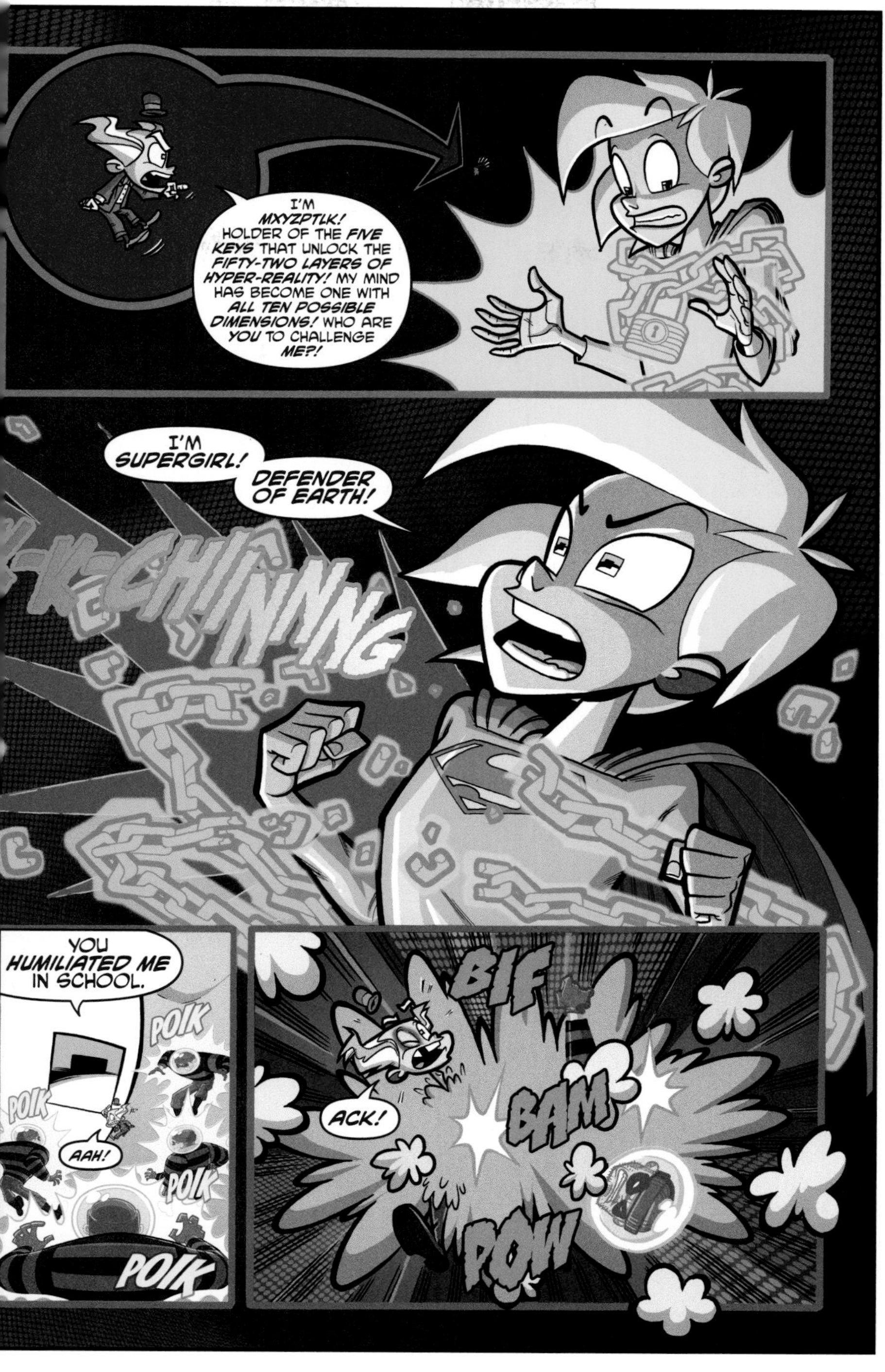
I'M MXYZPTLK! HOLDER OF THE FIVE KEYS THAT UNLOCK THE FIFTY-TWO LAYERS OF HYPER-REALITY! MY MIND HAS BECOME ONE WITH ALL TEN POSSIBLE DIMENSIONS! WHO ARE YOU TO CHALLENGE ME?!
I'M SUPERGIRL!
DEFENDER OF EARTH!
K-CHINNNG
YOU HUMILIATED ME IN SCHOOL.
POIK
POIK
AAH!
POIK
POIK
BIF
ACK!
BAM
POW

YOU ATTACKED MY FRIENDS!
POIK
HSSS
HEY... HEY, C'MON NOW...
YOU TOOK ME FROM MY FAMILY!!
KRAKA-THOOOOM
I HAVE ALL THE POWER YOU EVER DREAMED OF!
MY KRYPTONIAN CELLS ARE SUPERCHARGED WITH THE LIGHT OF A MILLION BILLION SUNS!
AND I'M NOT GOING TO LET YOU DESTROY THE 3RD DIMENSION!
KLT... KLTPZYXM...?

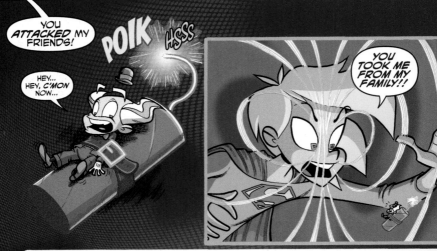

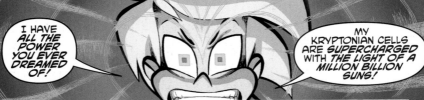

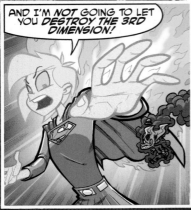

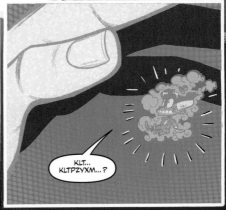

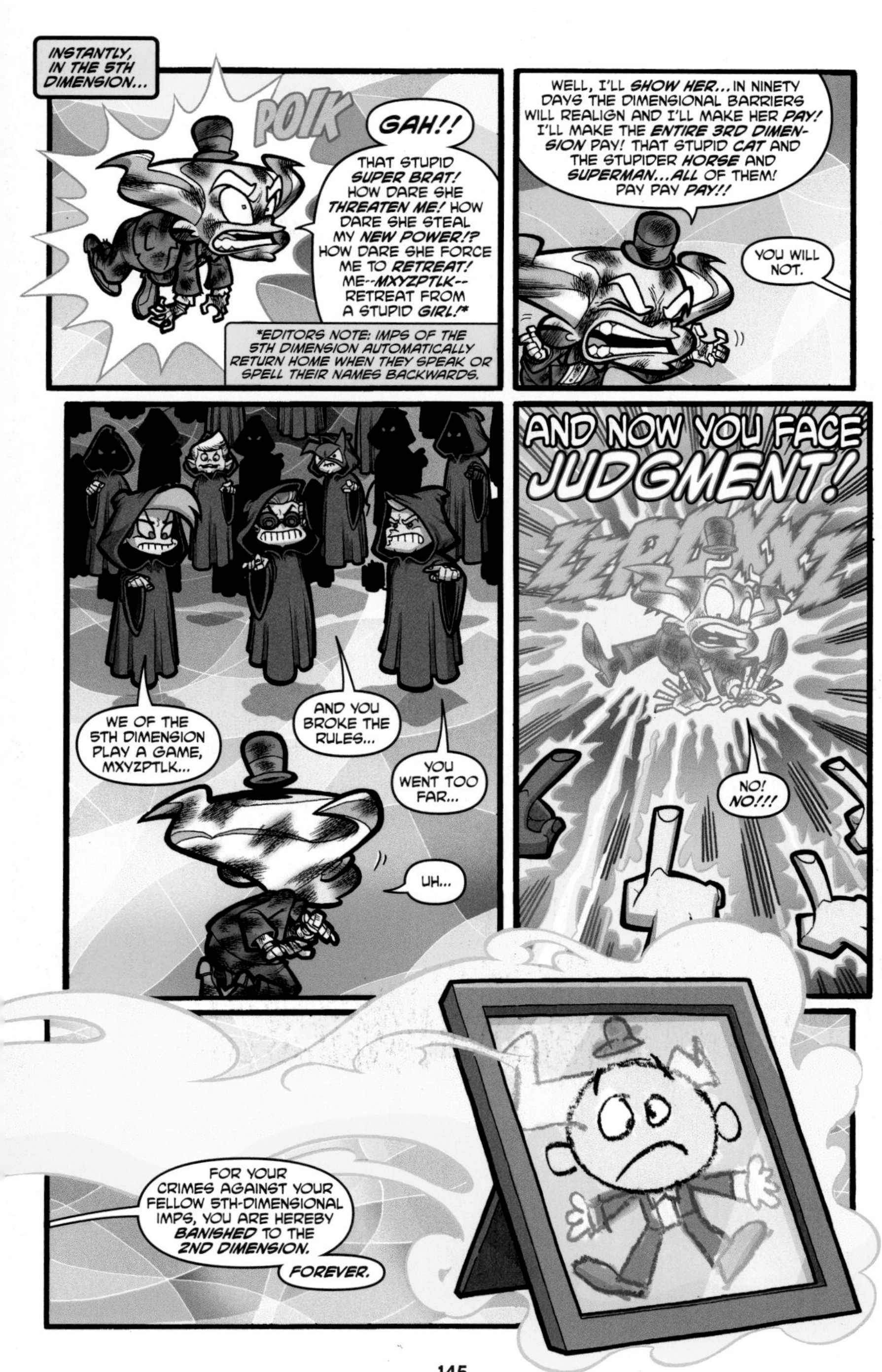
INSTANTLY, IN THE 5TH DIMENSION...
POIK
GAH!!
THAT STUPID SUPER BRAT! HOW DARE SHE THREATEN ME! HOW DARE SHE STEAL MY NEW POWER!? HOW DARE SHE FORCE ME TO RETREAT! ME--MXYZPTLK--RETREAT FROM A STUPID GIRL!*
*EDITORS NOTE: IMPS OF THE 5TH DIMENSION AUTOMATICALLY RETURN HOME WHEN THEY SPEAK OR SPELL THEIR NAMES BACKWARDS.
WELL, I'LL SHOW HER... IN NINETY DAYS THE DIMENSIONAL BARRIERS WILL REALIGN AND I'LL MAKE HER PAY! I'LL MAKE THE ENTIRE 3RD DIMENSION PAY! THAT STUPID CAT AND THE STUPIDER HORSE AND SUPERMAN...ALL OF THEM! PAY PAY PAY!!
YOU WILL NOT.
WE OF THE 5TH DIMENSION PLAY A GAME, MXYZPTLK...
AND YOU BROKE THE RULES...
YOU WENT TOO FAR...
UH...
AND NOW YOU FACE JUDGMENT!
ZZROKKZ
NO! NO!!!
FOR YOUR CRIMES AGAINST YOUR FELLOW 5TH-DIMENSIONAL IMPS, YOU ARE HEREBY BANISHED TO THE 2ND DIMENSION.
FOREVER.

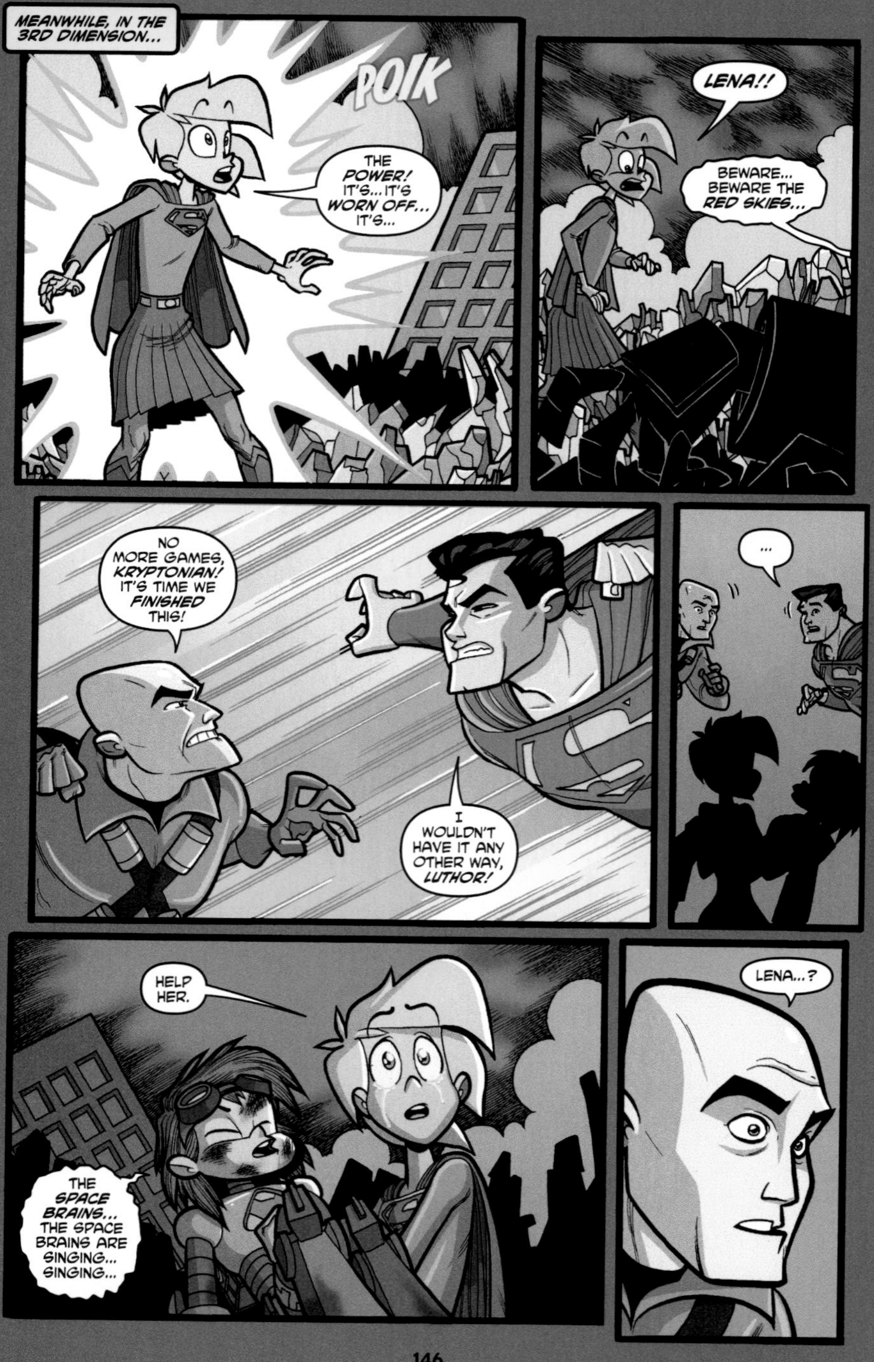

MEANWHILE, IN THE 3RD DIMENSION...
POIK
THE POWER! IT'S... IT'S WORN OFF... IT'S...
LENA!!
BEWARE... BEWARE THE RED SKIES...
NO MORE GAMES, KRYPTONIAN! IT'S TIME WE FINISHED THIS!
I WOULDN'T HAVE IT ANY OTHER WAY, LUTHOR!
...
HELP HER.
THE SPACE BRAINS... THE SPACE BRAINS ARE SINGING... SINGING...
LENA...?

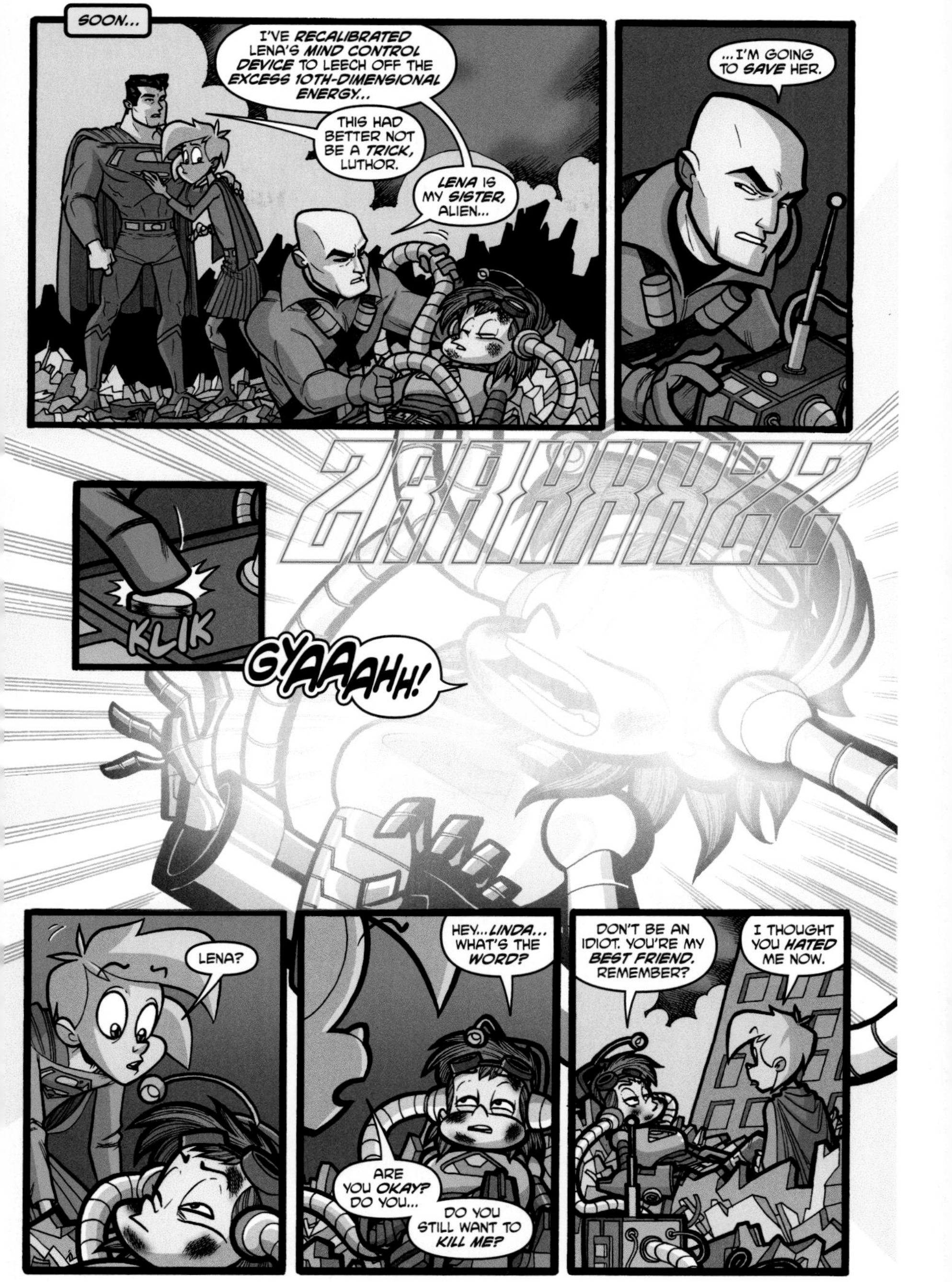
SOON...
I'VE RECALIBRATED LENA'S MIND CONTROL DEVICE TO LEECH OFF THE EXCESS 10TH-DIMENSIONAL ENERGY...
THIS HAD BETTER NOT BE A TRICK, LUTHOR.
LENA IS MY SISTER, ALIEN...
...I'M GOING TO SAVE HER.
ZRRRRRZZ
KLIK
GYAAAAHH!
LENA?
HEY...LINDA... WHAT'S THE WORD?
ARE YOU OKAY? DO YOU...
DO YOU STILL WANT TO KILL ME?
DON'T BE AN IDIOT. YOU'RE MY BEST FRIEND. REMEMBER?
I THOUGHT YOU HATED ME NOW.

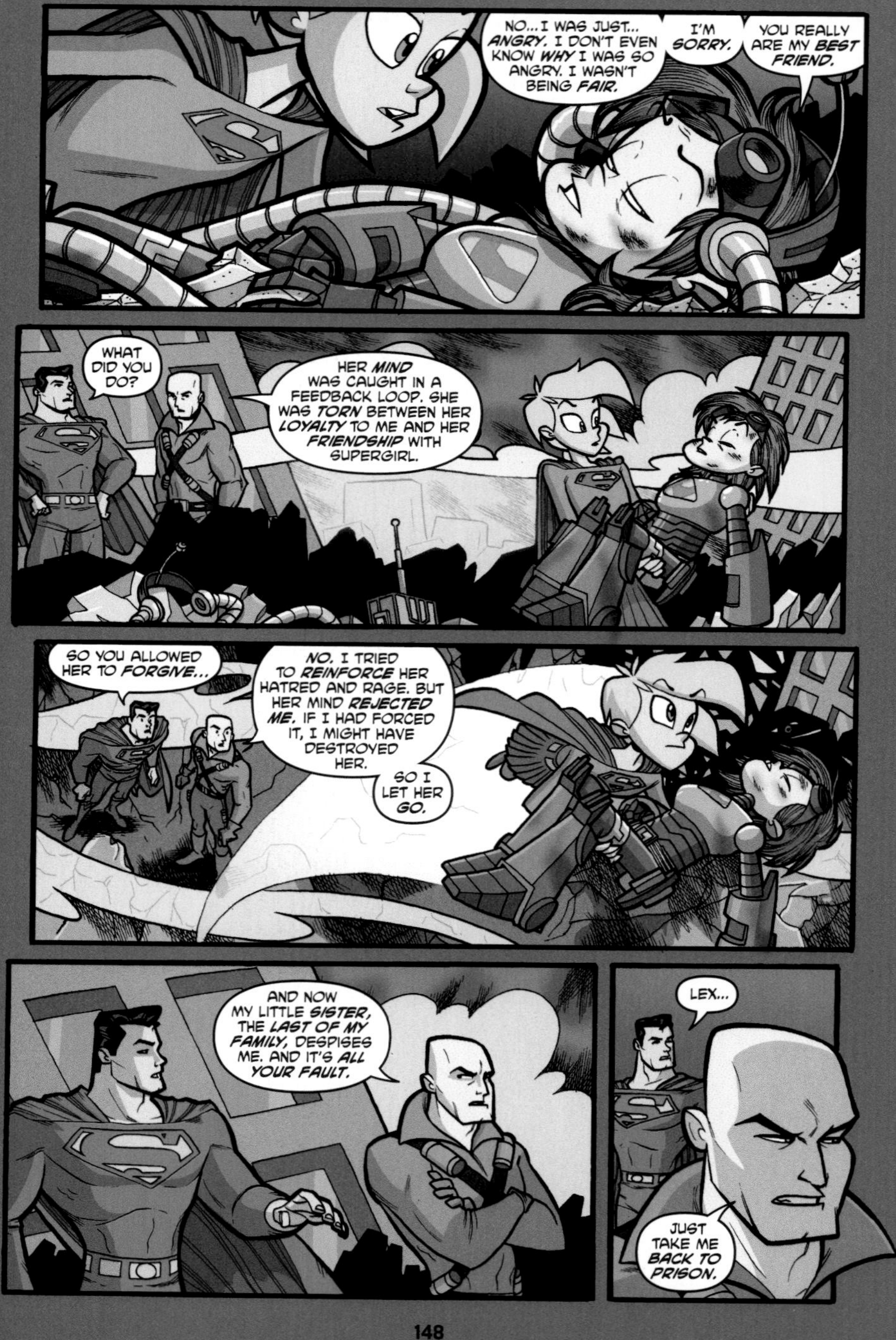
NO... I WAS JUST... ANGRY. I DON'T EVEN KNOW WHY I WAS SO ANGRY. I WASN'T BEING FAIR.
I'M SORRY.
YOU REALLY ARE MY BEST FRIEND.
WHAT DID YOU DO?
HER MIND WAS CAUGHT IN A FEEDBACK LOOP. SHE WAS TORN BETWEEN HER LOYALTY TO ME AND HER FRIENDSHIP WITH SUPERGIRL.
SO YOU ALLOWED HER TO FORGIVE...
NO. I TRIED TO REINFORCE HER HATRED AND RAGE. BUT HER MIND REJECTED ME. IF I HAD FORCED IT, I MIGHT HAVE DESTROYED HER.
SO I LET HER GO.
AND NOW MY LITTLE SISTER, THE LAST OF MY FAMILY, DESPISES ME. AND IT'S ALL YOUR FAULT.
LEX...
JUST TAKE ME BACK TO PRISON.

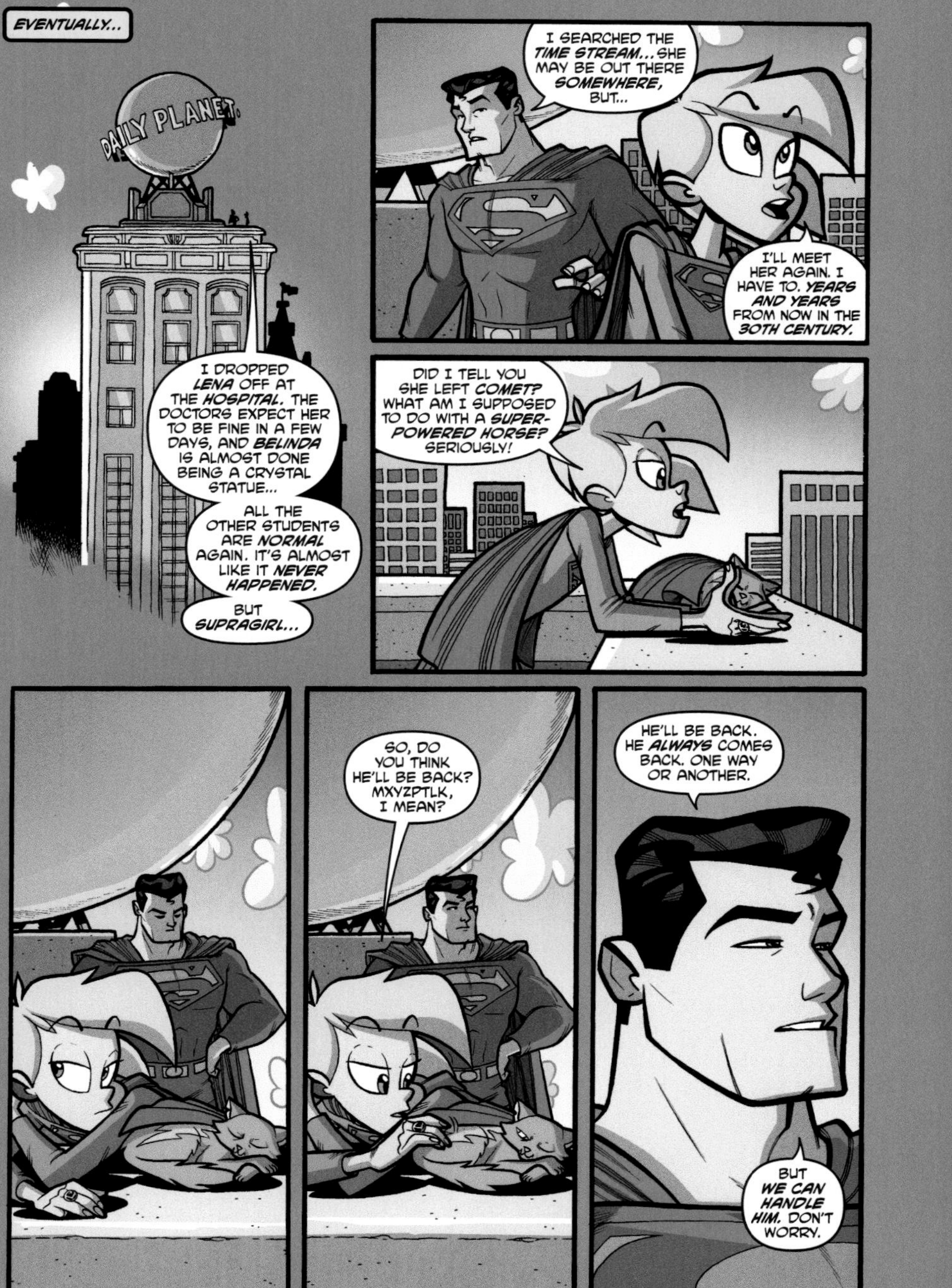
EVENTUALLY...
DAILY PLANET
I DROPPED LENA OFF AT THE HOSPITAL. THE DOCTORS EXPECT HER TO BE FINE IN A FEW DAYS, AND BELINDA IS ALMOST DONE BEING A CRYSTAL STATUE...
ALL THE OTHER STUDENTS ARE NORMAL AGAIN. IT'S ALMOST LIKE IT NEVER HAPPENED.
BUT SUPRAGIRL...
I SEARCHED THE TIME STREAM... SHE MAY BE OUT THERE SOMEWHERE, BUT...
I'LL MEET HER AGAIN. I HAVE TO. YEARS AND YEARS FROM NOW IN THE 30TH CENTURY.
DID I TELL YOU SHE LEFT COMET? WHAT AM I SUPPOSED TO DO WITH A SUPER-POWERED HORSE? SERIOUSLY!
SO, DO YOU THINK HE'LL BE BACK? MXYZPTLK, I MEAN?
HE'LL BE BACK. HE ALWAYS COMES BACK. ONE WAY OR ANOTHER.
BUT WE CAN HANDLE HIM. DON'T WORRY.

OH! I ALMOST FORGOT... I HAVE *SOMETHING* FOR YOU.

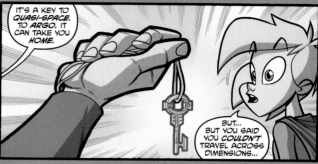

IT'S A KEY TO *QUASI-SPACE*. TO *ARGO*. IT CAN TAKE YOU *HOME*.

BUT... BUT YOU SAID YOU *COULDN'T* TRAVEL ACROSS DIMENSIONS...

I CAN'T. BUT *YOU* CAN. IT JUST TOOK ME A WHILE TO FIGURE OUT HOW TO *HELP YOU ALONG.*

OF COURSE, *YOU* COULD HAVE TAKEN YOURSELF HOME WHEN YOU WERE FIGHTING MXYZPTLK. YOU HAD THE POWER *THEN.*

I WAS KINDA *DISTRACTED...*

THIS WILL *REALLY* TAKE ME *HOME?*

ANYTIME YOU WANT.

WELL... MAYBE *LATER,* THEN...

RIGHT NOW *WE HAVE A PLANET TO PROTECT.*

DAILY PLANET

The End!

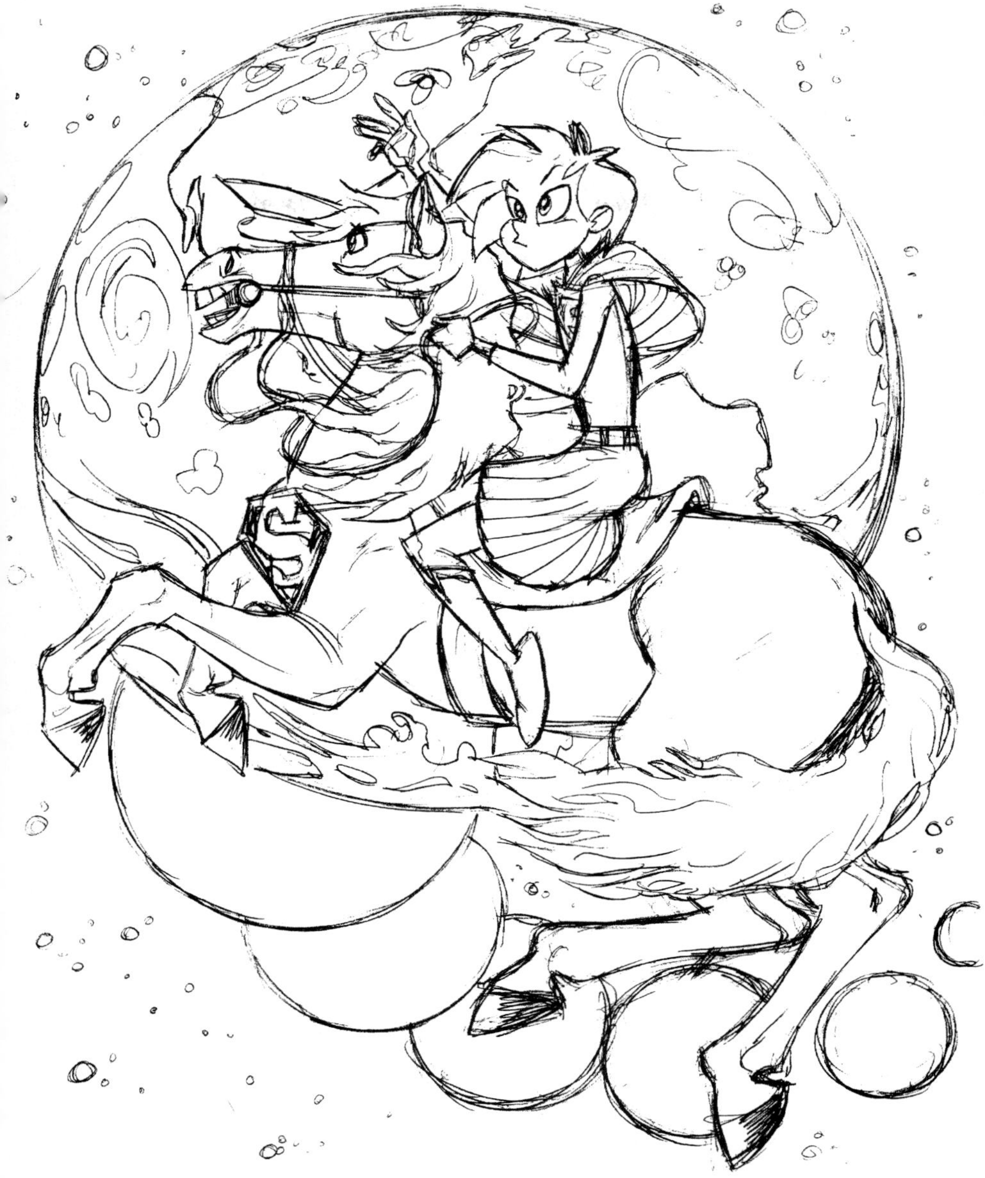

This is an early version of the cover to issue #6. It was the final issue, and we wanted a cover where Supergirl basically rode off into the sunset.

We debated whether to use this design. This scene never takes place in the book, but it does capture the essence of the series and the character as we imagined her.

It was, and still is, a good note to end on.

Picking the right look for Supergirl was not an easy choice. Should she be young? Old? Shy? Outgoing?

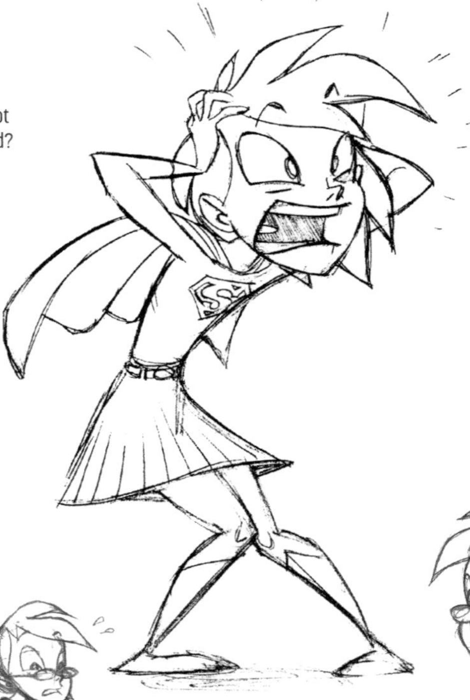

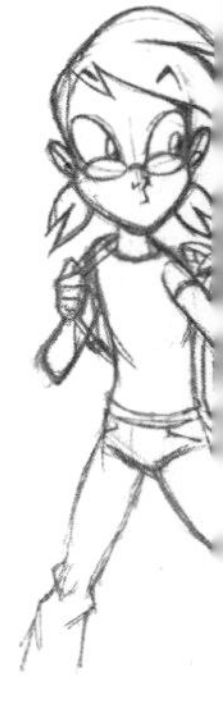

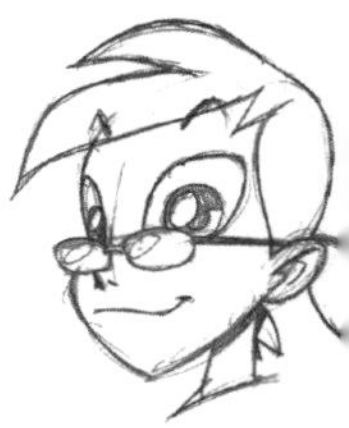

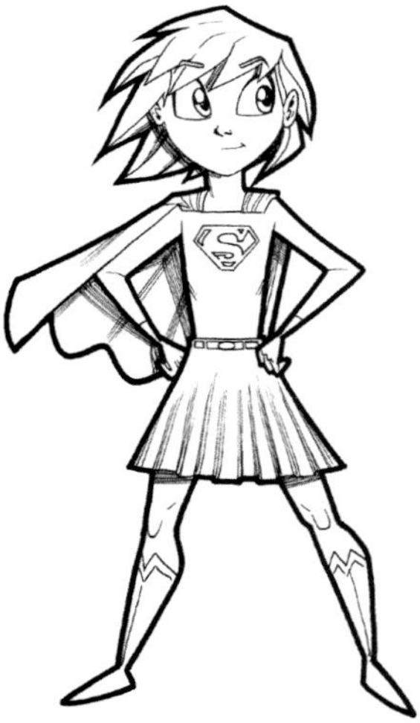

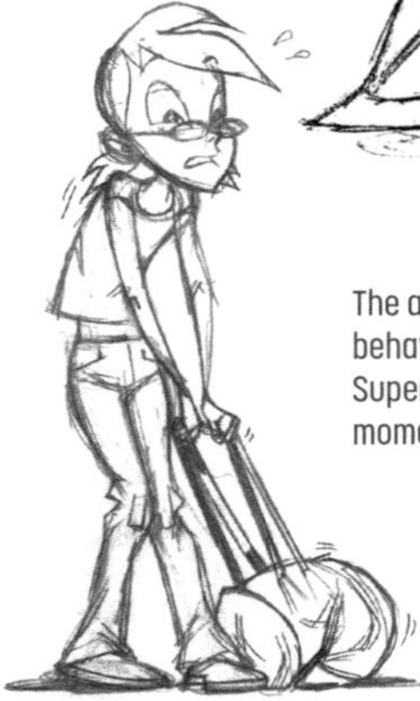

The art in a comic can help dictate the way a character behaves. When the design was finalized, we knew how our Supergirl should act. Awkward and uncomfortable one moment, graceful and heroic the next.

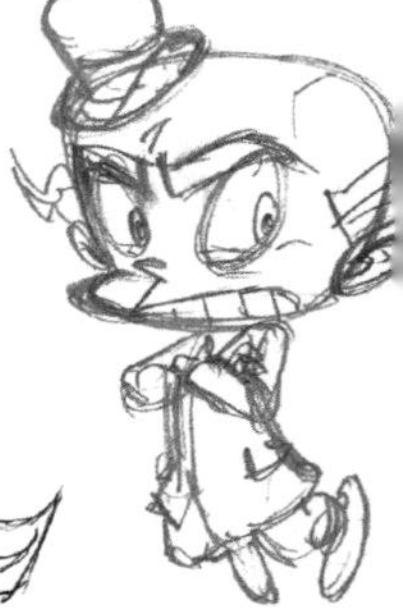

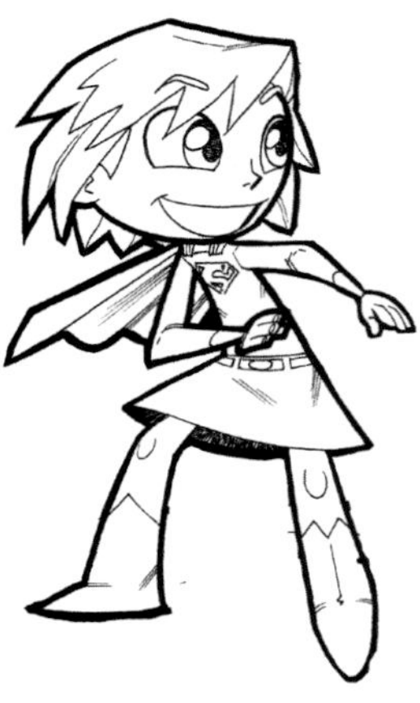

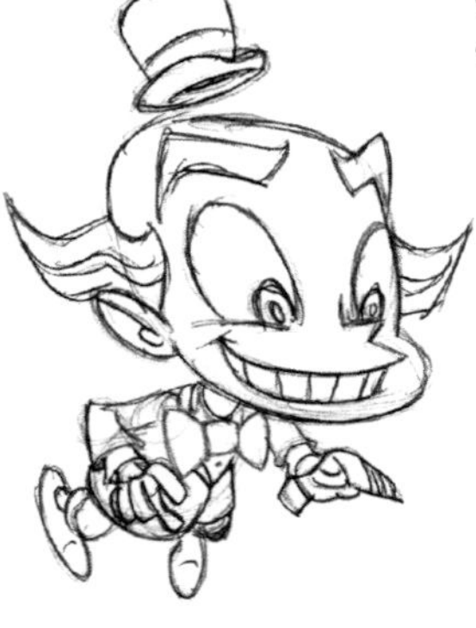

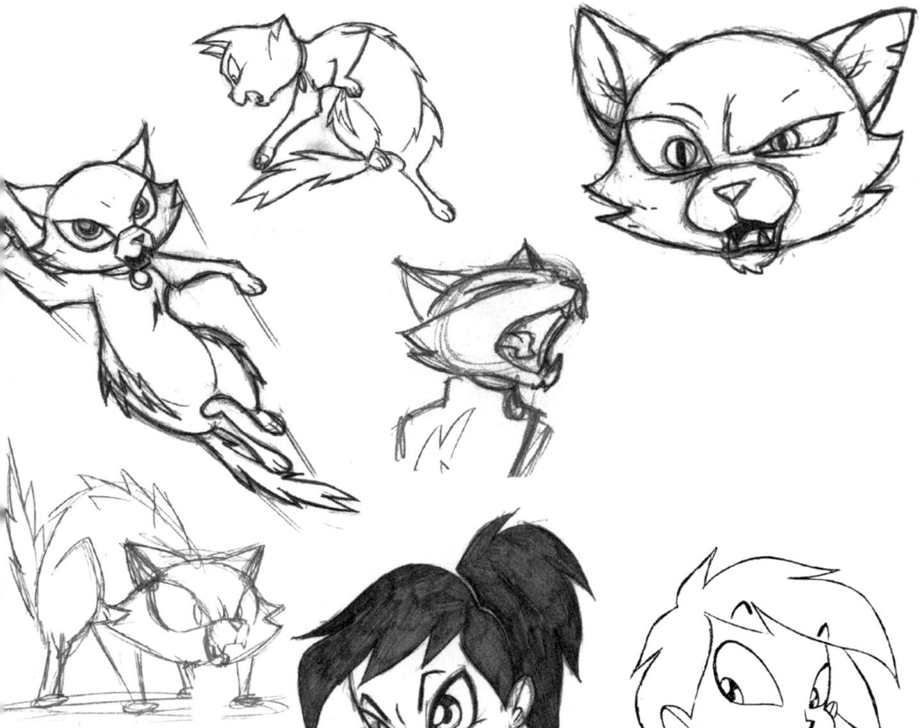

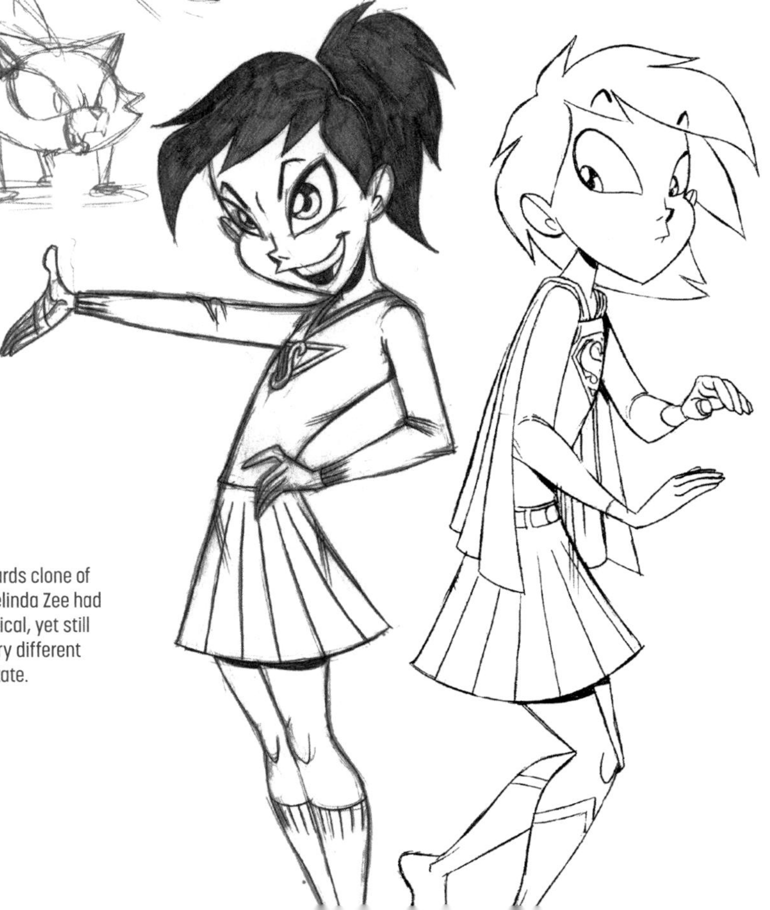

As a backwards clone of Supergirl, Belinda Zee had to look identical, yet still display a very different emotional state.

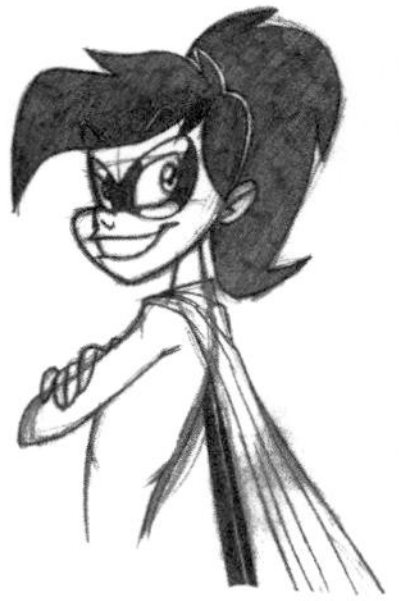

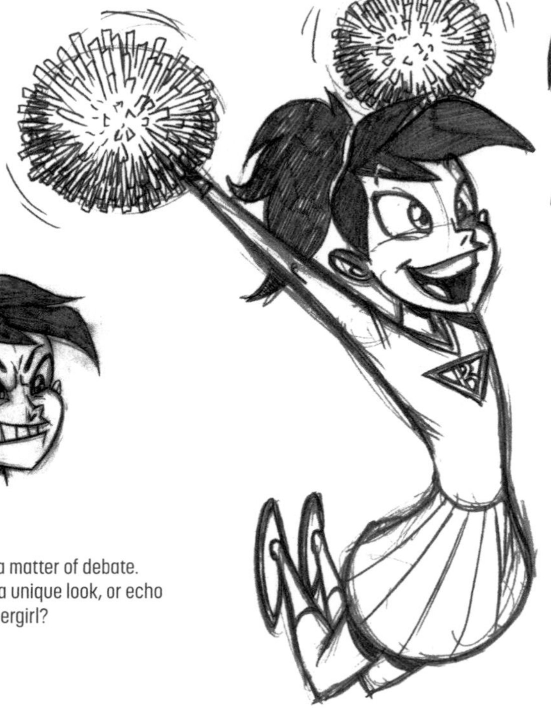

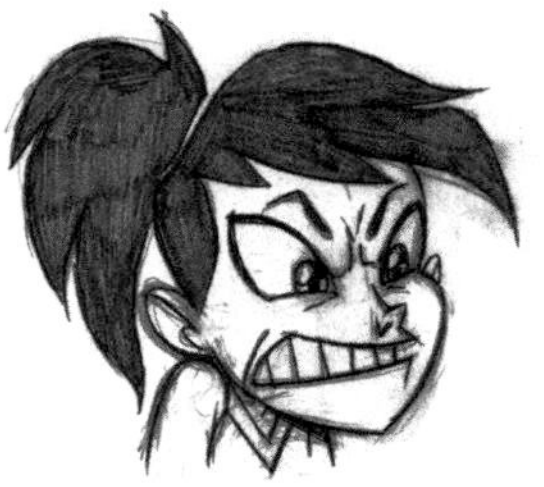

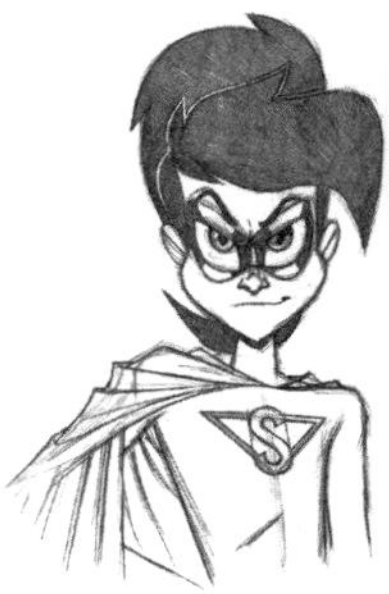

Superiorgirl was a matter of debate. Should she have a unique look, or echo the design of Supergirl?

Lena was one of the most fun to write and draw. A nice combination of sweet and sinister.

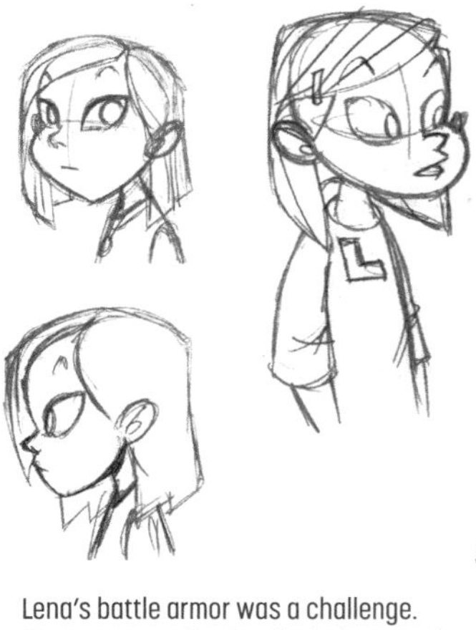

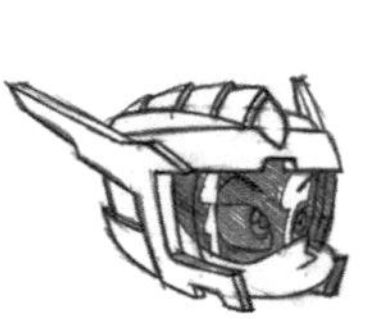

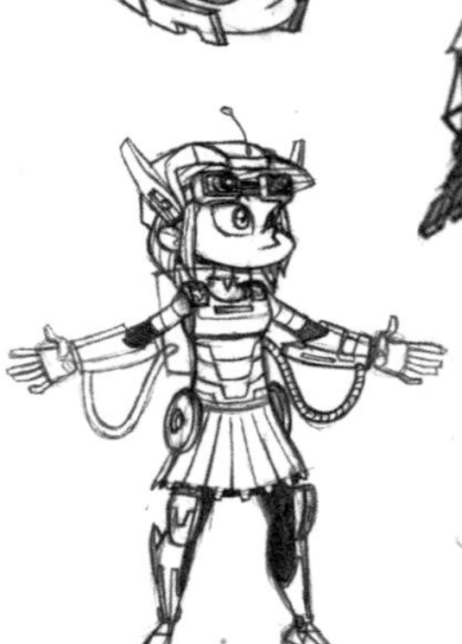

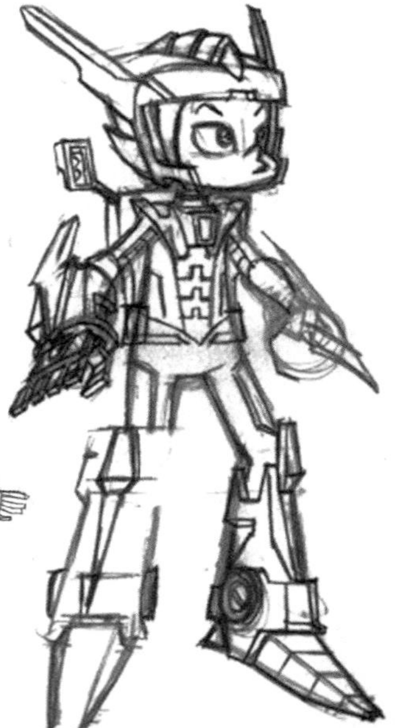

Lena's battle armor was a challenge. Here are a couple of early designs. In the end, we decided to stick with the classic Luthor armor.

New York Times bestselling authors Shannon Hale and Dean Hale team up with artist Victoria Ying to introduce a princess who really just needs a friend.

Turn the page for a sample from Wonder Woman's earliest adventure!

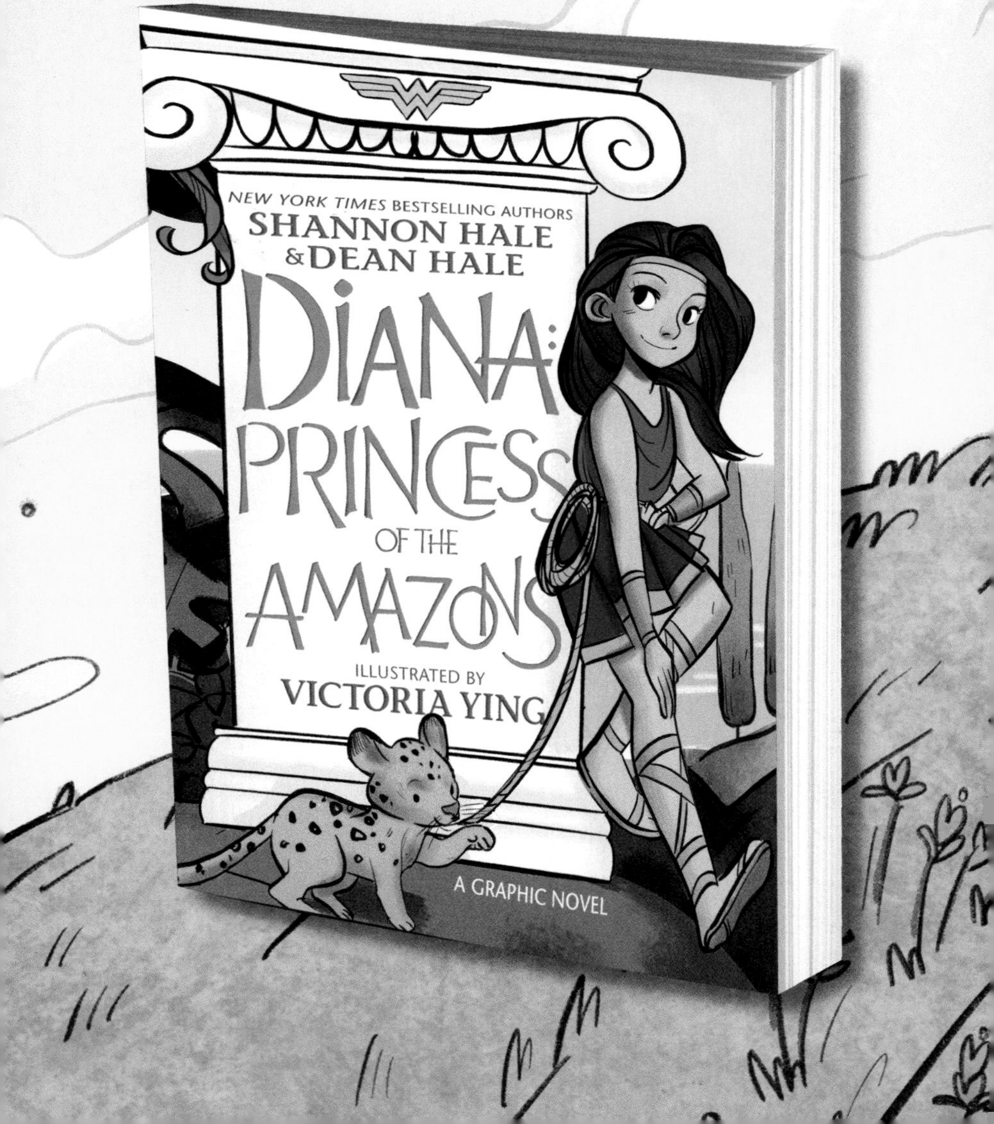
NEW YORK TIMES BESTSELLING AUTHORS
SHANNON HALE
& DEAN HALE
DIANA:
PRINCESS
OF THE
AMAZONS
ILLUSTRATED BY
VICTORIA YING
A GRAPHIC NOVEL

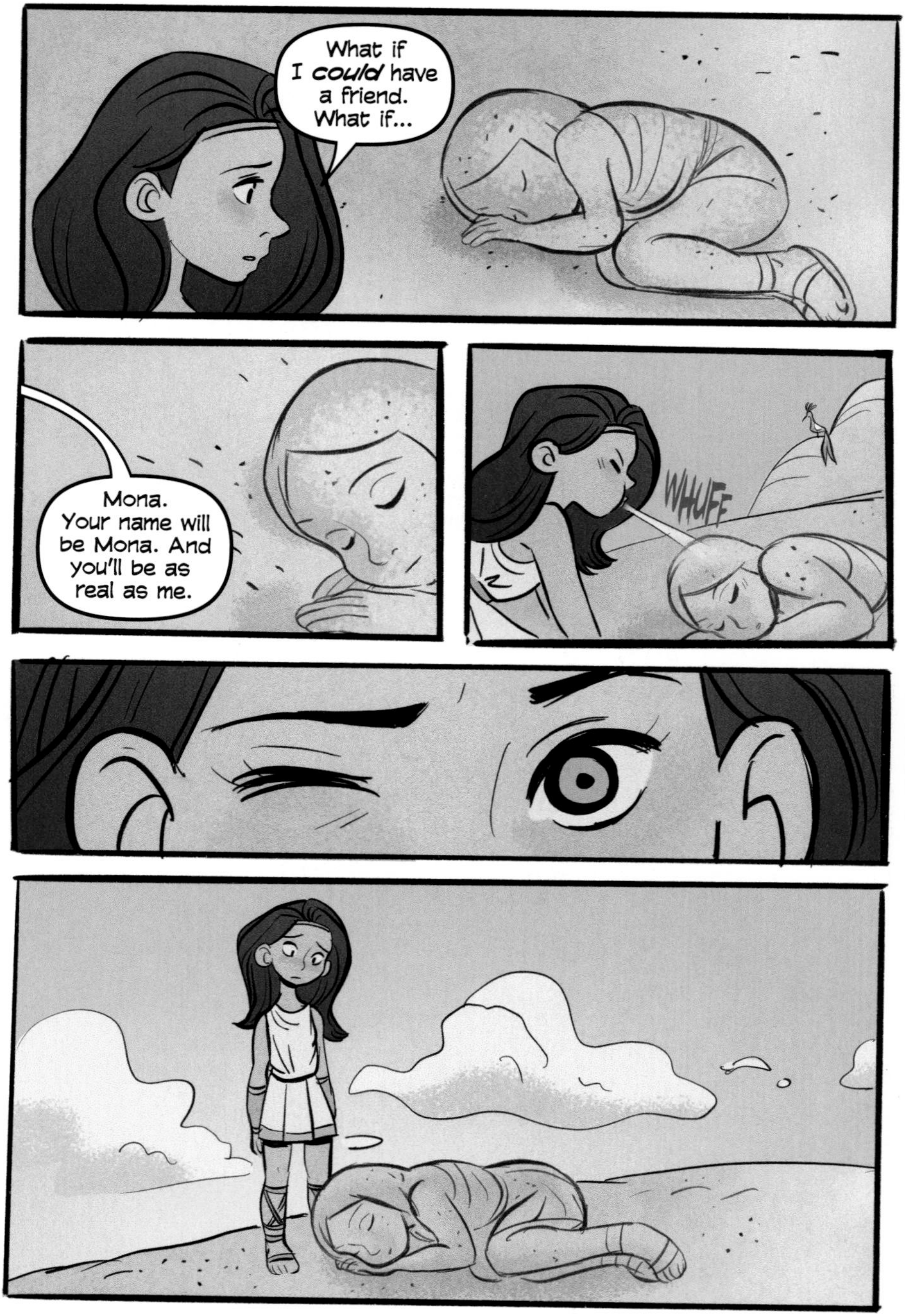
What if I *could* have a friend. What if...
Mona. Your name will be Mona. And you'll be as real as me.
WHUFF

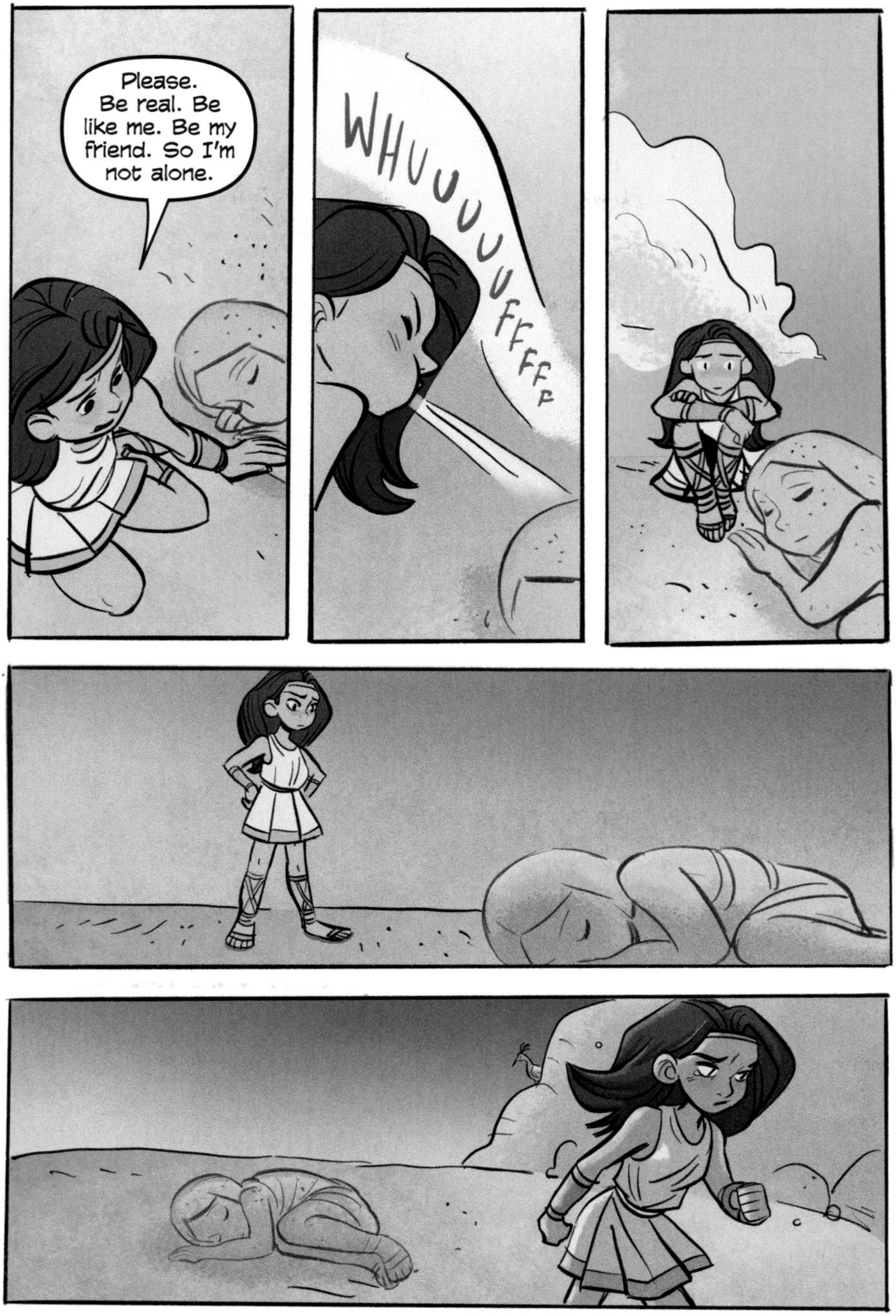
Please. Be real. Be like me. Be my friend. So I'm not alone.
WHUUUUUUFFFFF

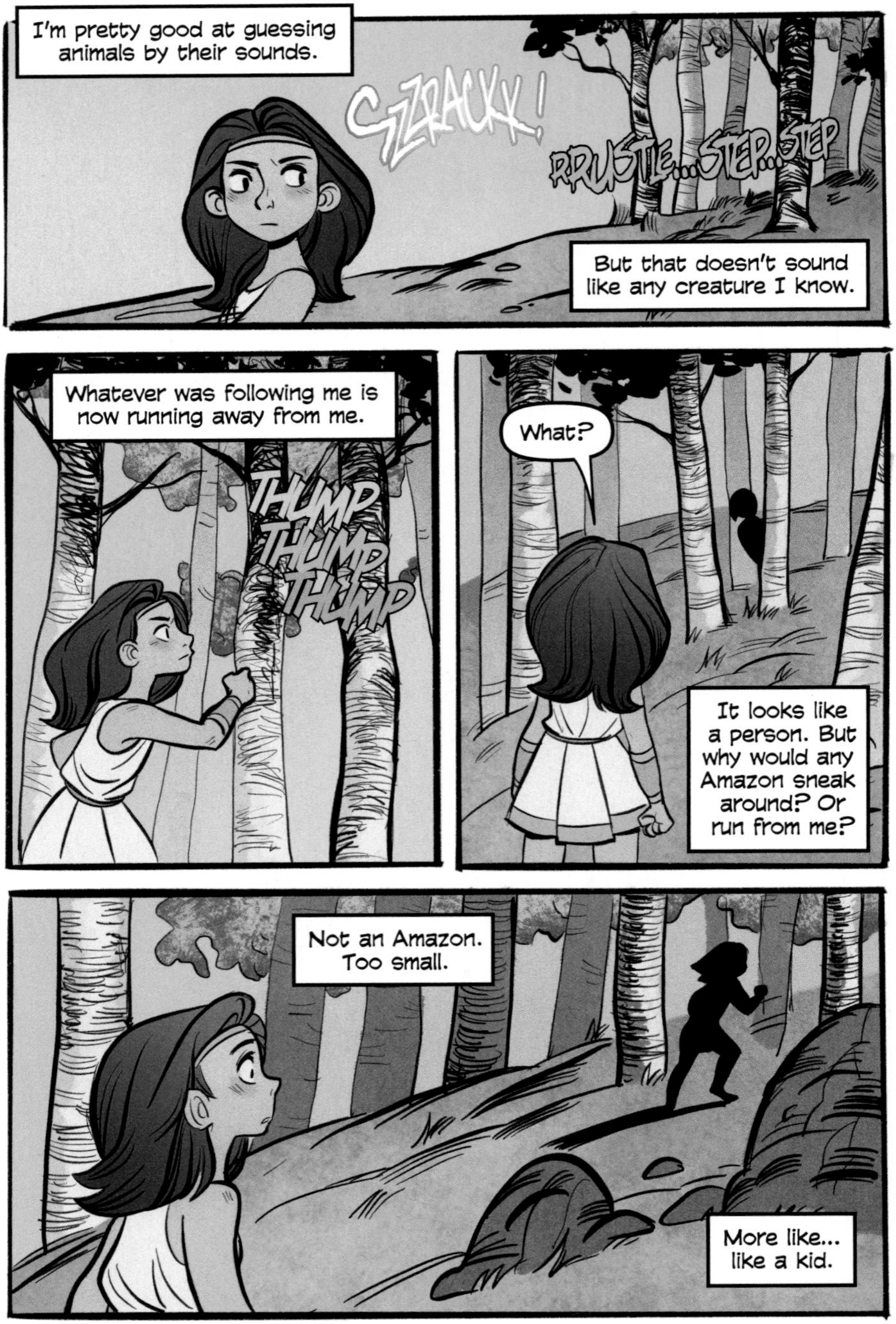
I'm pretty good at guessing animals by their sounds.
CZZRACKK!
RRUSTLE...STEP...STEP
But that doesn't sound like any creature I know.
Whatever was following me is now running away from me.
THUMP THUMP THUMP
What?
It looks like a person. But why would any Amazon sneak around? Or run from me?
Not an Amazon. Too small.
More like... like a kid.

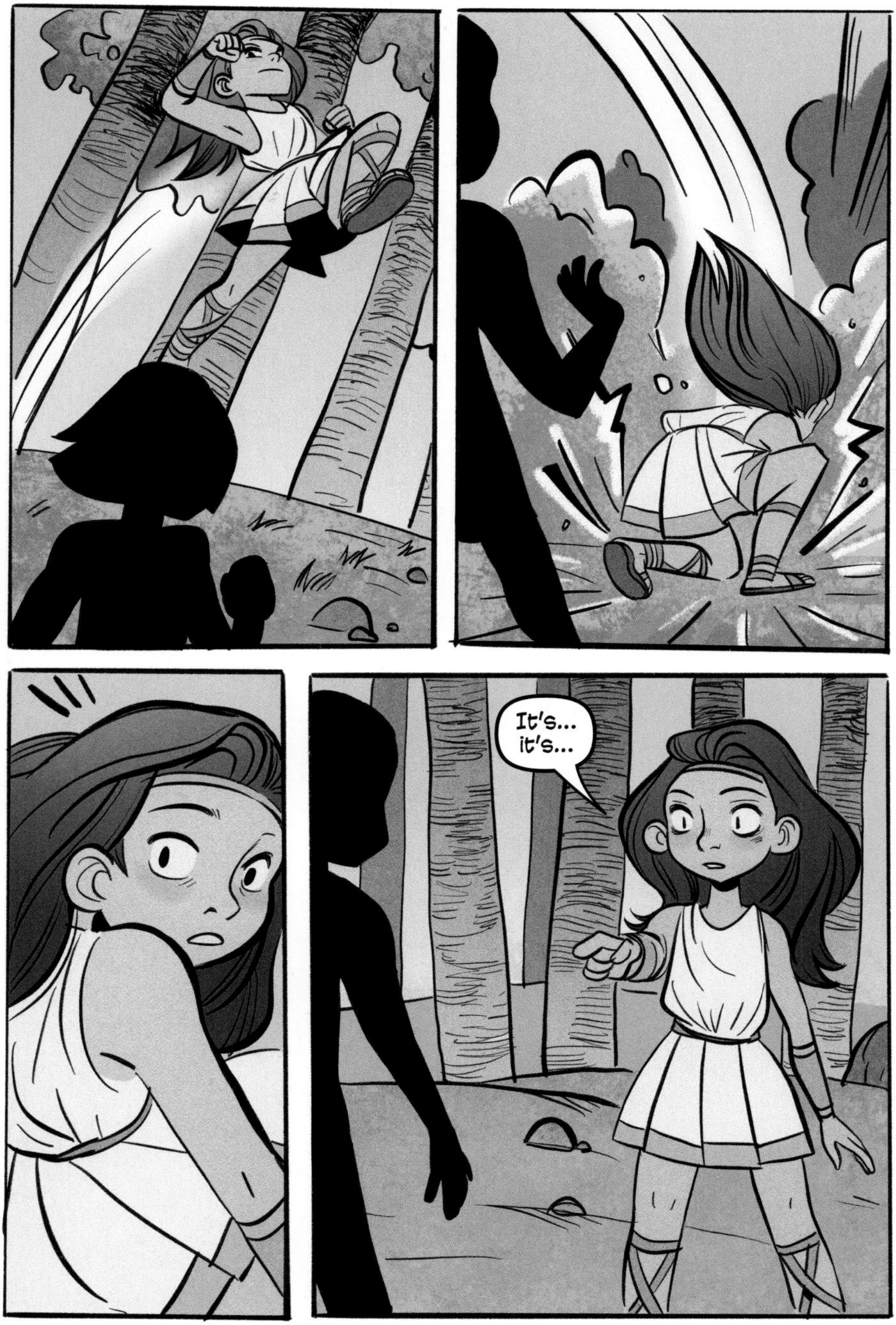
It's... it's...

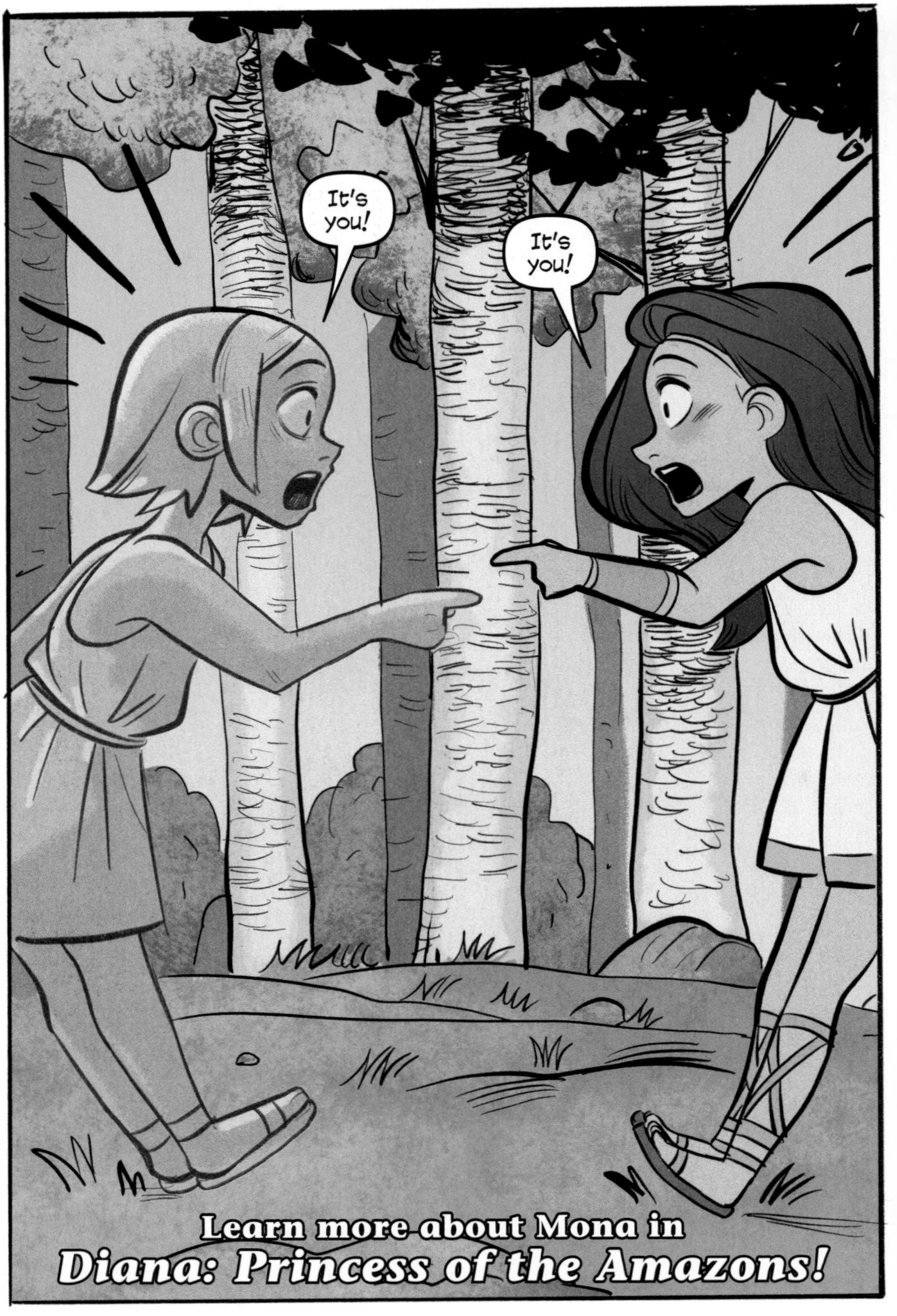
It's you!
It's you!
Learn more about Mona in
Diana: Princess of the Amazons!